# RESEARCH ON FOREIGN STUDENTS AND INTERNATIONAL STUDY

## An Overview and Bibliography

*by*
*Philip G. Altbach,*
*David H. Kelly, and*
*Y. G-M. Lulat*

PRAEGER SPECIAL STUDIES • PRAEGER SCIENTIFIC

New York • Philadelphia • Eastbourne, UK
Toronto • Hong Kong • Tokyo • Sydney

R
016.37
A 465r

**Library of Congress Cataloging in Publication Data**

Altbach, Philip G.

Research on foreign students and international
study. An Overview and Bibliography

(The Praeger special studies series in comparative
education)
"Published in cooperation with the Comparative Education Center, State University of New York, Buffalo."
1. Educational exchanges—Bibliography. 2. Foreign
study—Bibliography. 3. Students, Foreign—Bibliography.
I. Kelly, David H. II. Lulat, Y. G-M. III. State University of New York at Buffalo. Comparative Education
Center. IV. Title. V. Series.
Z5814.E23A44 1985    [LB2375] 016.37019'6    85-3372
ISBN 0-03-071922-4 (alk. paper)

Published in 1985 by Praeger Publishers
CBS Educational and Professional Publishing, a Division of CBS Inc.
521 Fifth Avenue, New York, NY 10175 USA

© 1985 by Praeger Publishers

56789 052 987654321

Printed in the United States of America on acid-free paper

---

## INTERNATIONAL OFFICES

Orders from outside the United States should be sent to the appropriate address listed below. Orders
from areas not listed below should be placed through CBS International Publishing, 383 Madison Ave.
New York, NY 10175 USA

### Australia, New Zealand
Holt Saunders, Pty, Ltd., 9 Waltham St., Artarmon, N.S.W. 2064, Sydney, Australia

### Canada
Holt, Rinehart & Winston of Canada, 55 Horner Ave., Toronto, Ontario, Canada M8Z 4X6

### Europe, the Middle East, & Africa
Holt Saunders, Ltd., 1 St. Anne's Road, Eastbourne, East Sussex, England BN21 3UN

### Japan
Holt Saunders, Ltd., Ichibancho Central Building, 22-1 Ichibancho, 3rd Floor, Chiyodaku, Tokyo, Japan

### Hong Kong, Southeast Asia
Holt Saunders Asia, Ltd., 10 Fl, Intercontinental Plaza, 94 Granville Road, Tsim Sha Tsui East,
Kowloon, Hong Kong

Manuscript submissions should be sent to the Editorial Director, Praeger Publishers, 521 Fifth
Avenue, New York, NY 10175 USA

Published and Distributed by the
Praeger Publishers Division
(ISBN Prefix 0-275)
of Greenwood Press, Inc.,
Westport, Connecticut

# ACKNOWLEDGMENTS

This volume was made possible by a grant from the Exxon Education Foundation and additional financial support from the National Association for Foreign Student Affairs (NAFSA) and the Institute of International Education. This research was part of the ongoing program of the Comparative Education Center, State University of New York at Buffalo. We are indebted to these agencies for their support, without which this project could not have been completed. The project's advisory group provided useful suggestions. Thus, we are indebted to Dr. Barbara Burn of the University of Massachusetts at Amherst, Dr. Elinor Barber of the IIE, John Reichard of NAFSA, Dr. Joseph Williams and Professor Stephen Dunnett of SUNY/Buffalo. The Comparative Education Center's graduate assistants were responsible for much of the basic data collection, and we are indebted to Jose Misael Agudelo, Brian K. Anderson, Nana Henne, Cherif Sadki, Jan Sadlak, and Nanzhao Zhou for their efforts; in addition, Alan Smith of the European Institute of Education and Social Policy. Manfred Stassen of the Deutscher Akademischer Austauschdienst, George Tillman of the Canadian Bureau of International Education and Robert Mashburn of NAFSA provided information and logistical support. J. Cordaro assisted with the introductory essay.

This research effort has produced several other publications as well as this volume. A special issue of the Comparative Education Review focusing on foreign students was published in May 1984. This issue includes a bibliography by Y. G.-M. Lulat, which includes some of the items in this book. Two smaller bibliographies were produced for the National Association for Foreign Student Affairs. These focused on "International Development and the Foreign Student" and on "Public and Academic Policies and Foreign Students." Both of these bibliographies are available from NAFSA.

We hope to continue our bibliographical efforts and to serve the community of scholars, policy makers, and professionals with an interest in foreign students and international education.

Philip G. Altbach

David H. Kelly

Y. G.-M. Lulat

# INTRODUCTION

This volume is divided into two parts. The first section includes an essay which provides an overview of the research on foreign students and which focuses attention on the key issues relating to this topic. The essay serves as a context for the bibliography which follows. The bulk of this book is a selected and partly annotated bibliography which includes 2,811 listings. The bibliography is divided by topic. We selected the most valuable and recent items for annotation and in our annotations tried to provide a basic understanding of the item as well as to indicate the key findings of the reference. Of course, in a paragraph, it is impossible to indicate more than a preliminary summary.

The bibliography is selective in that we have chosen items deemed to be relevant to a broad understanding of foreign students. We have included books, doctoral dissertations and theses, articles in journals and magazines and, to a lesser extent, reports and government documents. We have not included unpublished material because such items are usually difficult or impossible to obtain. Our rule of thumb was to include material that can be obtained in a good library or on a readily available data base. Within each subject category we have listed materials alphabetically with books (and theses) first, then articles and finally reportage (short items of relevance to foreign students from key periodical publications).

The bibliography is international in scope, and indeed is the first effort to provide an international perspective on foreign students. We have included references in English, French, Spanish, German, and Russian. The large bulk of the material is in English, reflecting both the nature of the literature and the availability of materials to the compilers. English dominates the literature on foreign students—the key publications are in English and the largest number of the world's foreign students are studying in English-speaking countries—the United States, Britain, Canada, and Australia particularly. Additional significant numbers study in the Philippines and in India, both of which use English as a key medium of instruction in higher education.

This bibliography tries to fill a gap in the literature and, in a sense, helps to define a growing field of study and analysis. Its focus is on material published in the past few decades, although we have included a few items which were published prior to 1965 which are of particular interest. This volume follows the pioneering effort of Seth Spaulding and Michael Flack in their The World's Students in the United States: A Review and Evaluation of Research on Foreign Students, published in 1976. Our book has a different focus in that we are concerned with presenting as comprehensive an overview as possible of the field, while Spaulding and Flack were largely interested in providing an analysis of the research. Nevertheless, their conceptualization of the field as well as some of their research provide an important base for our work. We hope that the two studies are complementary and that the serious researcher will wish to consult both volumes.

The organization and conception of this bibliography is straight-forward. We hope to serve those concerned with foreign students and international study by providing as comprehensive a bibliography as possible. We are convinced that those concerned with policy as well as academic officers concerned with foreign student affairs will find this volume useful. We are particularly interested that policy makers in Third World nations, the major "senders" of foreign students, be aware of the currents in the literature and the key research available. Thus, this bibliography has as its major goal the provision of a resource and data base for considering foreign student issues. As foreign students and international study have become major issues in higher education, necessitating adjustments in academic programs and costing considerable sums, the issue has become a topic of considerable debate. It is hoped that this bibliography will provide a useful resource base to help inform these debates.

# CONTENTS

*The Praeger Special Studies*
*Series in Comparative Education*

*General Editor:* **Philip G. Altbach**

Published in Cooperation with the
Comparative Education Center,
State University of New York, Buffalo

STUDYING TEACHING AND LEARNING: Trends in Soviet
and American Research
*Robert Tabachnick, Thomas S. Popkewitz, Beatrice Beach Szekely*

INTERNATIONAL BIBLIOGRAPHY OF
COMPARATIVE EDUCATION
*Philip G. Altbach, Gail P. Kelly, David H. Kelly*

SYSTEMS OF HIGHER EDUCATION IN TWELVE
COUNTRIES: A Comparative View
*Nell P. Eurich*

ADULT EDUCATION AND TRAINING IN
INDUSTRIALIZED COUNTRIES
*Richard E. Peterson, John S. Helmick, John R. Valley,
Sally Shake Gaff, Robert A. Feldmesser, H. Dean Nielsen*

WOMEN'S EDUCATION IN DEVELOPING COUNTRIES:
Opportunities and Outcomes
*Audrey Chapman Smock*

THE SCIENCE PROFESSION IN THE THIRD WORLD:
Studies from India and Kenya
*Thomas Owen Eisemon*

NONFORMAL EDUCATION AND NATIONAL
DEVELOPMENT: A Critical Assessment of Policy,
Research, and Practice
*John Charles Bock, George John Papagiannis*

EDUCATION IN THE ARAB WORLD
*Byron G. Massialas, Samir Ahmed Jarrar*

BETTER SCHOOLS: International Lessons for Reform
*John Simmons*

EDUCATION AND SOCIAL CHANGE IN THE PEOPLE'S
REPUBLIC OF CHINA
*John N. Hawkins*

EDUCATION AND INTERGROUP RELATIONS:
An International Perspective
*John N. Hawkins and Thomas J. La Belle*

RESEARCH ON FOREIGN STUDENTS AND
INTERNATIONAL STUDY: An Overview and
Bibliography
*Philip G. Altbach, David H. Kelly, and Y. G-M. Lulat*

# INTERNATIONAL STUDENTS IN COMPARATIVE PERSPECTIVE: TOWARD A POLITICAL ECONOMY OF INTERNATIONAL STUDY
## Philip G. Altbach and Y. G-M. Lulat

Introduction

International (foreign) students are a growth "industry" in higher education. It has been estimated that in the United States alone more than $2.5 billion is devoted to the education of students from other countries each year. More than 336,000 international students are studying in American colleges and universities, constituting about 3% of the total enrollment in postsecondary education. International students are even more important in graduate education, constituting about 15% of the total, and in some fields such as engineering and computer science, foreign students comprise about half of the total enrollment. Other countries (such as Canada, France, the United Kingdom, and the Soviet Union) also have large numbers of international students. (see Table 1)

While the "sending" nations (home countries) are often ignored in discussions concerning international students, the issues are important in these nations as well. In fact, in a number of Third World countries, their total internal university student population is less than the external student population. (Examples include Malaysia, Hong Kong, Saudi Arabia, most of the Arabian Gulf nations and several others.) A few of the smaller nations, such as Cyprus, have virtually no postsecondary educational institutions and rely on foreign institutions for their training needs. While there are no firm statistics, it can be estimated that there are more than one million students worldwide studying outside their native countries.

This essay has two primary purposes: to provide a balanced discussion of major themes, and to present an overview of the literature as a whole--with a view toward suggesting gaps in the literature that need to be filled, as well as avenues of further research in a relatively new area that we have termed "the Political Economy of International Study."

TABLE 1

International Student Flows: Major Indicators

(a) The Top 20 of the World's Leading Hosts of International Students (1980/81)

(b) The Top 20 of the World's Leading Senders of International Students (1980/81)

| Country | Total Number of students | Country of origin | Total number of students |
|---|---|---|---|
| U.S.A. | 325 628 | Iran | 65 521 |
| France | 114 181 | Malaysia | 35 693 |
| U.S.S.R.* | 62 942 | Greece | 31 509 |
| Germany, Federal | | China | 30 127 |
| Republic | 61 841 | Nigeria | 26 863 |
| United Kingdom | 56 003 | Morocco | 20 876 |
| Canada | 32 303 | Hong Kong | 20 625 |
| Italy | 27 784 | U.S.A. | 19 843 |
| Lebanon | 26 343 | Japan | 18 066 |
| Egypt | 21 751 | Venezuela | 17 755 |
| Australia | 17 694 | Canada | 17 714 |
| Switzerland | 15 515 | Jordan | 17 030 |
| Austria | 12 885 | Germany, Federal Republic | 16 983 |
| Belgium | 12 875 | Palestine(refugees) | 15 414 |
| India* | 11 761 | Lebanon | 15 117 |
| Spain | 10 997 | India | 15 238 |
| Holy See | 9 104 | Turkey | 14 606 |
| Argentina** | 8 649 | Saudi Arabia | 14 298 |
| Greece*** | 8 304 | Italy | 13 848 |
| Philippines | 7 901 | Syria | 13 701 |

Source: Unesco Statistical Yearbook, 1983.

*1978          **1976          ***1979

## 1. Foreign Study in Historical Perspective

While current interest in issues relating to international study may give the impression that the phenomenon is of recent origin, this is not so. International study has a very long historical tradition going back to the very beginning of universities as institutions of higher learning. An important study, and probably the only one of its kind that extensively documents the historical origins of international study is Brickman's (1975) Two Millenia of International Relations in Education. Other studies of relevance here include Dedijer (1968) and Hess (1982: 1-25). Indeed, universities throughout much of history have been truly international institutions, enrolling students from many nations as an integral part of their policies and practices. In fact, it was only with the rise of the modern nation-state in Europe that universities began to teach in the national language rather than the international language, Latin.

Although the Western higher education model is now dominant throughout the world, this was not always the case, and non-Western academic systems were also international in scope. The Islamic university, still exemplified by Al-Azhar in Cairo, sees itself as an international institution, serving Islamic civilization rather than any one country. (Dodge, 1961) Al-Azhar uses Arabic as the medium of instruction--the international language of Islamic culture. The traditional Hindu and Buddhist universities, such as the Universities of Taxila and Nalanda in India, (which are among the earliest known universities, going as far back as 600 B.C.) also were international in scope and welcomed both teachers and students from other countries. (see Altekar, 1948; Nurullah and Naik, 1956) These institutions used international languages--Sanskrit or Pali--as the medium for teaching; and thus, students from many countries that used these languages could attend the universities. These institutions were largely religious in orientation, but secular subjects were often taught as well. It should be remembered that the great Islamic libraries of Egypt and Spain kept much of Western culture alive during the Dark Ages (see, for example, Parsons, 1952). When Western scholars again came into contact with this knowledge through the Islamic universities the Renaissance, in part, got its start. Thus, continuing international contacts in higher education have proved quite important to the preservation and transmission of knowledge--and at some periods of history, Western scholars were dependent on academic institutions and traditions in other parts of the world for knowledge.

The medieval universities in Europe (such as the Universities of Bolognan, Cordova, Florence, Louvain, Paris, and Salerno) were, of course, the forerunners of contemporary institutions, and these institutions were basically international in nature. (see Haskins, 1966; also Cobban, 1975; Rashdall, 1936) The language of instruction was, for a time, the international language of the period, Latin. The very organization of the student bodies was into "nations" that represented the various nationality groups studying at the university. The faculty, too, was generally international in nature. In Italy, the medieval universities themselves often moved from town to town in search of more congenial surroundings. Thus, the core of the medieval university was international. Foreign students were the norm, not the exception. This tradition of openness to foreign currents and individuals has been a powerful force in higher education ever since the medieval period. Later, as European nationalism grew and universities came under the domination of local princes and later of the nation-states, gradually shifting the medium of instruction from Latin to the various national languages, some of the previous internationalism was lost; but access to universities remained open to students from various countries. The concept of the "wandering student" was a strong one, and sometimes these sojourns included studying in another country. The metropolitan nations of Europe--France, and later Germany and to some extent, Austria--provided a powerful magnet for students from other countries. For certain periods, universities in Poland, the Netherlands, and Sweden also attracted many foreign students.

In the nineteenth century, when the United States was building its academic system and graduate education was being established, young scholars typically studied in Europe, especially in Germany, during the latter part of the century, in order to ensure an academic career in the United States. At this period, American higher education was, in a sense, an intellectual colony of Europe. (Veysey, 1965) The flow of foreign students was almost completely from America to Europe. The United States did not emerge as a major center of foreign study for international students until after World War II, when American higher education expanded rapidly and dramatically improved its quality.

Turning to the modern period, once again one perceives a long historical tradition in the migration of students--especially Third World students going to the West. During the colonial era, students from the colonies often studied in the metropole to prepare themselves for the colonial civil service or for positions in emerging trade and industrial enterprises. While the numbers were small, these individuals were often very influential in intellectual development, in nationalist and revolutionary movements, and eventually in the politics of the emerging nations after World War II. The French, who were slow to establish academic institutions in their colonies, brought many students from Indochina (including Ho Chi Minh) and from their dependencies in Africa to France to study. The British (especially in India), who were quicker to found colleges and universities and encouraged local educational initiatives, brought fewer students to England, but many did study there, including Jawaharlal Nehru and many others. Sukarno, the founder of the Indonesian nation, studied in the Netherlands when his country was under colonial rule, and many of the concepts of Indonesian nationalism were forged in the universities of Holland by colonial students.

It is possible to see discernible patterns in the transnational migration of students over a long period of time. Indeed, historical trends buttress the general concept that students migrate from the peripheries to the centers and that foreign study is very much part of an international knowledge system. None of the problems that are evident at present--the brain drain, adjustment issues, the relevance of the curriculum, language issues--are entirely new.

In the medieval period, students were sometimes so sufficiently unpopular that the entire university was forced to move from place to place. Issues relating to the cosmopolitanism of the international academic community versus local populations created disputes. Thus, for example, King Henry III of England in an address to the townspeople of the city of Cambridge, warned them, stating: "...unless you conduct yourselves with more restraint and moderation towards them (international students)... they will be driven by your exactions to leave your town and, abandoning their studies, leave the country, which we by no means desire." (Quoted in Williams, 1982, pp. 10-11) The medieval universities, in comparison to their modern counterparts, were considerably more international in terms of not only the curricula, but student and staff composition as well.

While the flow of students across borders has deep historical precedents, it has to be noted that the characteristics of the present flow of international students differ from that of previous times in a number of respects, such as: the magnitude of numbers involved is much greater today than was the case in the past, the students of the past were often scholars in their own right, and the staff of the institutions were very heterogeneous in terms of national origins. Perhaps the most important distinction, however, between the present and the past is that today, the general pattern of international student flow is close to unilinear, that is, it is skewed in the direction of a largely south to north movement (from less industrialized to more industrialized nations).

## 2. International Student Flow Patterns

The numbers of students traversing the globe is considerable. Table 2 indicates some of the contemporary flows of students. Despite variations in these flows, some general patterns can be discerned. The following chart provides an overview of the basic international flow of students.

TABLE 2

Regional Destinations of International Students from the Top
10 of the Industrialized Market Economies with the
Largest Numbers of International Students
Abroad (1980/81)

| Home Countries | Total Number of Students Abroad | Regions of Destination | | |
| --- | --- | --- | --- | --- |
| | | Industrialized Market Economies | Planned Economies | Third World Countries |
| Greece | 31 509 | 30 282 | 748 | 479 |
| U.S.A. | 19 843 | 19 071 | 339 | 433 |
| Japan | 18 066 | 17 498 | 381 | 187 |
| Canada | 17 714 | 17 594 | 82 | 38 |
| Germany, Federal Republic | 16 983 | 16 765 | 120 | 98 |
| United Kingdom | 15 776 | 14 669 | 73 | 1 034 |
| Italy | 13 848 | 13 014 | 90 | 744 |
| France | 11 159 | 10 312 | 82 | 765 |
| Spain | 7 035 | 6 080 | 10 | 945 |
| The Netherlands | 5 178 | 5 145 | 14 | 19 |

Source: Based on data from the Unesco Statistical Yearbook, 1983

---

## Chart 1

### Flow Patterns of International Students

| | | |
|---|---|---|
| Third World students | to | Industrialized Market-economy nations |
| Third World students | to | Socialist nations |
| Third World students | to | other Third World nations |
| Industrialized Market-economy students | to | other Industrialized Market-economy nations |
| Industrialized Market-economy students | to | Third World nations |
| Socialist nation students | to | other Socialist nations |
| Socialist nation students | to | Industrialized Market-economy nations |
| Industrialized Market-economy students | to | Socialist nations |

---

The magnitude and direction of the flows has over the years remained fairly stable though slight variations do occur. This section discusses the nature of some of these flows and some of the reasons for them.

While the major international flow of students (as mentioned earlier) is from the Third World to the industrialized market economy nations, an important flow of students is among the industrialized market-economy nations themselves. (see Table 2) Here, motivations for study abroad differ from that of Third World students and the length of study is generally shorter. Relatively few stay to complete their entire degree program abroad. More typical of the industrialized nations is the American pattern of "study abroad" programs which typically provide undergraduate students with a year's experience overseas, usually in Western Europe. (Brown, 1983) It is significant that only about 5% of Americans participating in such programs study in Third World nations. About 30,000 American college students participate in study-abroad programs. This period of overseas study is generally counted as part of the American undergraduate degree. An exception to this generalization is in the field of medical education, where many Americans, generally those unable to gain admission to United States based medical education, study abroad for their entire medical training.

In Western Europe, the Council of Europe, the European Economic Community (Common Market), CRE (the organization of European higher education administrators), and other groups have supported a variety of student exchanges. The Common Market, for example, guarantees that students from member states of the Community pay fees equivalent to domestic students and provides relatively open access to the universities of the community. Under these circumstances of relative freedom, it is surprising that only a very small percentage of European students choose to study abroad. Thus, while there is movement across European borders for academic exchange and study, the total numbers involved are modest. Very often, European students perceive that a foreign degree will put them at a disadvantage in terms of professional advancement in their own countries and with the exception of students in language and perhaps international affairs, higher education tends to be fairly insular. (Roeloffs, 1982)

There is also considerable mobility among students in the Eastern European Socialist nations. Arrangements exist among the COMECON nations to exchange students, but it seems that the largest flow is from nations such as the German Democratic Republic, Cuba, Czechoslovakia, and Bulgaria to the Soviet Union, with relatively few Russian students studying abroad.

There is a good deal of mobility from one Third World nation to another, although this is a phenomenon not widely researched. (see Table 3) India and the Philippines host large numbers of foreign students. The Indian government provides scholarships for study in India for students in the South Asian region and also from Africa. Many students from Southeast Asia and less frequently from other regions gravitate to India, in part because costs are very much lower than in most other parts of the world and in part because admission in many fields is easier. To some degree the curricula are more attuned to conditions in the Third World. The Philippines, with its large educational system functioning in English and with many private universities, also attracts many international students, mostly from Southeast Asia. Mexico and Argentina serve as foci for Latin American students because of their well developed academic systems and Egypt has been a traditional center for students from the Middle East. Lebanon, with its English and French medium universities, until recently also served as a destination for many Middle Eastern students (see Smith, Woesler de, Panafieu, and Jarousse, 1981).

## TABLE 3

### The Top 10 of the Third World Nations Hosting the Largest Numbers of International Students, and a Breakdown of the Students by

World Regions of Origin (1980/81)*

| Host-Country | Total Number of International Students | Africa Asia South America | Europe | U.S.S.R. | North America | Oceania | Other: Not Specified |
|---|---|---|---|---|---|---|---|
| Lebanon | 26,343 | 14,308 | 255 | - | 216 | - | 11,564 |
| Egypt | 21,751 | 21,618 | 110 | 1 | 22 | - | - |
| Saudi Arabia | 14,298 | 12,987 | 28 | 58 | 38 | - | - |
| India** | 11,671 | 11,145 | 211 | 8 | 97 | 210 | - |
| Argentina*** | 8,649 | 6,327 | 2,005 | 15 | 301 | 1 | - |
| Philippines | 7,901 | 6,105 | 830 | - | 966 | - | - |
| Turkey | 6,378 | 5,571 | 449 | - | 9 | 1 | 348 |
| Kuwait | 3,153 | 2,701 | 6 | - | 4 | - | 442 |
| Senegal | 3,065 | 2,732 | 318 | - | 15 | - | - |
| Ivory Coast | 2,314 | 1,988 | 293 | - | 19 | 2 | 12 |

Source: Based on data from the Unesco Statistical Yearbook, 1983.

* Note that source did not allow disaggregation of data along the same regional lines as those determined for Table 2

** 1978

***1976

The internal host country flow pattern (or "intranational pattern") is also very important in understanding overall flows. International students are not distributed randomly in an academic system. They tend to concentrate in particular institutions, fields of study and departments. For example, engineering is the choice of 25% and business and management studies of another 16% of the foreign students studying in the United States. More than one-third of all foreign students (35.9%) are graduate students (Boyan, 1981). In engineering and management studies, foreign students constitute about half of the total enrollment at the graduate level in many universities. The five leading states in foreign student enrollments (California, New York, Texas, Florida, and Massachusetts) had 41% of all such students in the United States. Foreign students tend to congregate in the larger colleges and universities. Particular nationality groups often choose particular institutions, due to informal contacts and for other reasons. This nonrandom internal flow pattern of international students is found in other nations as well.

We have, in general terms, described some of the key elements of the international flow of students. There are many reasons that account for these flows or may induce changes. (see Chart 2) Despite minor variations, however, the stability in the general flow since World War II is clear and is related to the overall trend of students to go from the peripheries (by and large the Third World) to the centers (mainly the industrialized market-economy nations that use the major international languages--English and French). In our following section concerning dependency and international students, many of the factors related to this major theme are discussed. It is possible, in broader terms, to point to some of the basic elements that produce flows of students and which affect changes, usually within the broader framework of the movement from the periphery to the center of the world economic system.

Flows of students are affected by policy changes in the host countries. In general, economic problems in the industrialized market-economy nations in the 1970s stimulated a reevaluation of policies regarding the education of international students and in some countries--several of the American states, Australia, Britain, and German Federal Republic--made moves to reduce the flow or significantly increase fees. (For a synoptic account of these changes on selected countries see appendix F in Williams, 1982.) Political factors in the host countries can also have an impact on student flows. In the postwar period, foreign policy considerations induced many industrialized nations to welcome larger numbers of international students and even to provide scholarship assistance in the post-war years. Host country policies concerning particular countries may also affect flows--the American government has been less sympathetic toward granting visas to students from Iran since the revolution in that country. Educational and cultural factors can also affect flows. In the United States, for example, a commitment to "internationalizing" the curriculum in higher education has made many universities more conscious of their role as international institutions. In Western Europe, efforts have been made to make intra-European mobility easier.

## Chart 2

Variables Affecting the Magnitude
and Direction of Major Flow Patterns

Host Country Variables | Home Country Variables

1. Economic difficulties leading to restrictions on international students through measures such as higher tuition fees, e,g., United Kingdom, Australia.

1. Economic difficulties leading to reduction in available state funds as well as available foreign exchange, e.g., Nigeria, Venezuela.

2. Population changes leading to increase in available student places, e.g., some states in the U.S.

2. Economic boom leading to expansion of demand for trained personnel and hence an increase in numbers of students going abroad, e.g.,oil producing nations before the oil glut on the world market.

3. Changes in foreign policy leading to completion of bilateral agreements, e.g., between China and the U.S. or Ethiopia and the USSR.

3. Economic policy changes leading to emphasis in areas with a dearth in requisite person power and training facilities, and hence necessitating that students go abroad, e.g., China.

4. Reemphasis of political commitments leading to increase on inflow of international students from a given politically volatile region, e.g., the inflow of students from Afghanistan.

4. Political changes (such as revolution) leading to changes in foreign policy and hence change inflow direction, e.g., Nicaragua.

5. Education policy changes leading to emphasis on international area and language studies and hence a greater commitment to study abroad programs, e.g., the United States.

5. Educational changes such as completion of appropriate training facilities--hence leading to reduction in numbers of students abroad, e.g., India.

Policy changes in the home (sending) nations also affect student flows. Economic factors are a key element. The changes in oil prices have affected flows of students from such nations as Venezuela and Nigeria, which have had to curtail both their scholarship programs dramatically and limit the availability of foreign exchange for their students studying abroad. Political changes can drastically affect flows. A well-known example is Iran, where the overthrow of the Shah caused major alterations in student numbers and induced many Iranian students abroad not to return. Political changes in countries such as South Vietnam, Angola, Ethiopia, Nicaragua, Somalia, and others have also determined the direction of student flows as well as the numbers of students going abroad. International educational changes also impact on student flows overseas. At one time, India was a major "exporter" of students, but with the growth and development of Indian higher education, fewer Indian students now study abroad.

## 3. Motivations for Study Abroad

Research indicates that there are a myriad of push and pull factors involved in foreign study. (See Glaser and Habers, 1978; Rao, 1979; see also Chart 3) Individual students and their families have their own interests and concerns, and governments in the industrialized nations also have priorities. Therefore, in many instances, there is more than one motivation involved; for example, American authorities are interested in "internationalizing" American higher education, providing assistance to students from the Third World, and expanding American influence abroad. (Jenkins, 1983) It is useful to consider some of these motivations as a means of understanding some of the important implications of foreign study.

It seems likely that a majority of the world's international students provide their own financial support and are not sponsored by any agency or government. Some eventually are able to obtain support from a university or other agency, while many rely on personal or family resources for their entire sojourn. Thus, the decision to undertake foreign study is largely an individual one. Individual decisions are made for many reasons. Some international students see their studies as a preliminary to emigration, and statistics on the "brain drain" from countries such as Taiwan, South Korean, and several others support this idea. (see Myers, 1972; as well as Glaser, 1978; and Rao, 1979) Obtaining visas for study overseas is relatively easy and such students hope that the study sojourn can be turned into permanent residency. Such hopes are often realized, though this is now becoming increasingly difficult.

Probably the largest number of international students—particularly those from Third World nations—wish to improve their professional opportunities at home by studying abroad. In many cases, they obtain training in technological or other fields which are not available at home. In others, the prestige value of a foreign degree is a major motivation. Both the skills obtained abroad and the benefits of having studied abroad are highly valued. In most Third World countries, such

## Chart 3

Key Variables Affecting the Personal Decision to Study Abroad
by Third World Students

| Key Variables Pertaining to Home-Country (Push Factors) | Key Variables Pertaining to Host-Country (Pull Factors) |
|---|---|
| 1. Availability of scholarships for study abroad. | 1. Availability of scholarships to international students. |
| 2. Poor quality educational facilities. | 2. Good quality education. |
| 3. Lack of research facilities. | 3. Availability of advanced research facilities. |
| 4. Lack of appropriate educational facilities. | 4. Availability of appropriate educational facilities with likely offer of admission. |
| 5. Failure to gain admission to local institution(s). | 5. Presence of relatives willing to provide financial assistance |
| 6. Enhanced value (in the market place) of a foreign degree. | 6. Congenial political situation. |
| 7. Discrimination against minorities. | 7. Congenial socio-economic and political environment to migrate to. |
| 8. Politically uncongenial situation. | 8. Opportunity for general international life experience. |

foreign qualifications are quite useful on the job market and usually yield higher salaries and better prospects for promotions.

Students who are unable to obtain admission to academic institutions at home often choose to come abroad for their education. In some countries, local academic systems are very small and highly selective and large numbers of qualified individuals cannot obtain entry to local institutions. In other cases, policies regarding entrance favor specific groups in the population and some racial or ethnic groups find themselves excluded. The vicissitudes of privately funded international students are often considerable. In some instances, changes in home country policies, economic crises, or personal circumstances make support from home difficult or impossible and students are left without funds. When students come abroad for study for political reasons, they sometimes find it difficult to return home leading to considerable problems for themselves and the host country.

Despite tightened immigration policies and other restrictions, privately funded students remain a large and important portion of the total population. The motivations of privately funded students differ and they tend to study where they can obtain admission and where the cost of education suits their ability to pay. In recent years, India and the Philippines have become relatively popular among foreign students because of the relatively inexpensive education offered.

The motivations of Third World governments in providing opportunities for study abroad are relatively clear. In most instances, they cannot provide sufficient educational opportunities at home. As secondary education expanded, increasing numbers of middle-class young people demanded access to higher education and local academic systems were unable to absorb their increased numbers. Governments began to provide scholarships for study abroad to meet this demand. In other cases, needed academic specializations--from nuclear physics to management studies, were not available at home and thus funding was provided for overseas to these and other fields. Countries such as Saudi Arabia, Kuwait, Venezuela, and Malaysia have spent very large sums of money on overseas study programs although there have been significant cutbacks recently because of difficult economic circumstances in these countries. There has also been some rethinking of priorities as a result of problems with some of the returning students. Questions concerning the relevance to local needs of some kinds of foreign training have been raised, and there have been some difficulties in graduate readjustment. From the point of view of Third World governments, foreign study programs are a way of reducing pressure on indigenous academic resources--although the costs are quite high--as well as a means of quickly providing needed expertise without making permanent investment in local academic institutions.

The motivations of the host countries are even more complex and combine altruistic, pragmatic, and foreign policy factors. American debates have also stressed the value of foreign students on campus in "internationalizing" the American higher education system. Western governments have wished to maintain their influence overseas and see foreign study opportunities as a means of doing this. (Coombs, 1964) The

United States, which has no colonial heritage (with the exception of the Philippines and Puerto Rico) to draw on, has tried for 30 years to build links with Third World nations and with universities. The Fulbright program has a new "International Linkages" component which is attempting to foster such connections. French policy has sought to continue relationships with France's former colonies and to foster the French language overseas. In the Third World, policies have also contributed to the maintenance of ties. Malaysia has traditionally sent its government-funded students to England and altered this policy only when the British government dramatically raised fees for foreign students. Thus, official policies and informal relationships tend to maintain contacts. In the case of the United States, the development of scholarship programs, institutional development efforts and other policies over a 30-year period have built up some linkages as well. (For analyses of several American efforts see Coleman, 1984; Hanson, 1968; and Mazrui, 1975).

The motivations for study abroad among students from the industrialized nations differ significantly from those from the Third World. These students typically do not obtain a foreign academic degree but rather go abroad for linguistic training, cultural enrichment, or learning and often for the experience of living in another environment. Many academic institutions in North America and Western Europe provide academic credit for foreign study and in some fields, such as foreign languages, overseas study is an important part of the curriculum. The value of a foreign academic degree in most industrialized countries is less than a domestic qualification, so the impetus for obtaining such degrees is limited. The most extreme case is probably Japan, where foreign degrees are in some fields and in some universities, not recognized. In Western Europe, the European Community has made it easier and less costly to study in its member states. There has been no comprehensive study of the motivations of students from the industrialized nations who study abroad, but it seems clear that the impetus is more personal and cultural than it is professional or economic.

Motivations are quite difficult to discern and push and pull factors vary considerably. The equation for students from the Third World is quite different than for those from industrialized nations. Politics, economics, and prestige as well as desire for knowledge enter into the motivating forces for international study. Recently, in a number of host nations (such as Australia, Canada, and Britain) foreign policy aims and altruistic goals regarding international study have come into conflict with economic and political pressures to restrict educational opportunities for Third World students (see, for example, Williams, 1982; Fraser, 1984). The result has usually been an ambivalent response by the government concerned: a reemphasis of commitment to provide educational opportunities for international students at the rhetorical level and at the practical level the reestablishment of legal and economic restrictions.

## 4. The Economics of Foreign Study

This section considers some of the major policy issues relating to the economics of international study. Later, we discuss in detail some of the most important components of research on this topic. There is probably no more complex topic, nor one more highly debated at present, than the relative costs and benefits of foreign study. Much of the literature recently has focused on the costs to the host countries of international students. (see Blaug, 1981; Jenkins, 1983; Sims and Stelcner, 1981; Winkler, 1981) This literature has been stimulated by debates in the host-nations concerning international students, with policy makers often arguing that large numbers of international students are costly and that they add a new and sometimes difficult element to the educational equation. It is argued that the education of international students is subsidized by general tax revenues, since in almost all countries higher education is subsidized by the state or in some cases provided virtually without cost to the individual. Britain, Canada, and Australia have raised questions about whether they can afford these subsidies. Several states in the United States have also questioned the wisdom of large enrollments of foreign students.

In federal systems such as the United States, Canada, and Australia the situation is particularly complex, since the national government may have policies which reflect broader national concerns while the bulk of funding comes from the governments of the states or provinces, whose policy makers may have little interest in national affairs and are mainly concerned with serving the needs of local residents and protecting their immediate fiscal interests. In the United States, private universities generally charge tuition fees that reflect the cost of education and public institutions have traditionally charged more to students from other states (and countries) while providing subsidies to all students by charging fees that are less than the cost of education. There has been increasing pressure in some states to raise out-of-state tuition rates even higher as a revenue-creating measure. A few states have discussed quotas on foreign students. There has been increasing concern over the large proportion of foreign students in graduate fields such as engineering, computer science, and management, which are in any case relatively high-cost fields. The Western European nations have also been concerned about the costs of educating foreign students. A few, such as the German Federal Republic, have placed restrictions on the enrollment of foreign students in certain fields of study. Others have been debating how to deal with rising costs of postsecondary education. The European nations are somewhat limited in their options by the agreements they have in the context of the European Community. The point of this discussion is to point out that there is a growing concern in the industrial nations concerning the costs of educating large numbers of foreign students.

The economic costs for the home countries are, if anything, even less well understood than those of the host-nations. And for a number of Third World nations, the cost of sending students abroad for education is very high. The costs can be calculated in many ways. The expenditure in foreign exchange, a rare commodity in many Third World nations, includes funds spent by families and individuals as well as by government agencies and the private sector. Some nations, such as India, restrict the amount of foreign exchange that can be taken out of the country for foreign study (as well as for other purposes) and for many fields in which India has self-sufficiency in higher education, students are not permitted to matriculate abroad unless they have scholarships from external sources. Other countries permit virtually anyone to study abroad as long as the student is able to obtain admission to a foreign school. It is therefore very difficult to calculate the costs to individuals for study abroad--but without question the amount is very substantial.

The direct economic costs to public agencies in the Third World is quite large in a number of countries. Malaysia, Saudi Arabia, Kuwait, Venezuela, Colombia, among others, have central agencies responsible for providing funding and guidance for their students studying abroad. Sometimes the infrastructures of these agencies are impressive and include not only placement and counseling assistance but also guidance on curricular questions and the choice of institutions, job assistance on return and, of course, disbursement of funds while studying. There is also some monitoring of academic progress while abroad. These agencies have very large budgets and sometimes sponsor thousands of students abroad. They have full-time staff abroad to assist their students. Even such small countries as Singapore and Kuwait maintain full-time overseas offices for their overseas students. The costs of scholarships and stipends are substantial as are the overhead costs. The cost of educating a student overseas is generally higher than that of a domestic education, but the equation becomes complex if the very high infrastructural costs of universities, particularly in the sciences and medicine, are added.

Most countries build universities as a matter of national independence and do not wish to rely on foreign training for their students. Nevertheless, in many fields and specializations, foreign training remains a necessity where domestic facilities do not exist or cannot provide the needed numbers of graduates. There are also severe pressures from the educated middle classes to have access to higher education and this is also a motivation for public expenditures for foreign study.

Funding for international students comes from many sources in the industrialized nations. Direct financial assistance in the form of scholarships are provided by many agencies--foreign assistance bodies, philanthropic foundations, academic institutions, professional societies, and even industrial firms. According to the Institute of International Education, fewer than 15% of the foreign students studying in the United States in 1983 were directly financed by American sources, with the largest part (8.9%) of funding costs coming directly from colleges and universities as scholarships and assistantships. (Institute of International Education, 1983, p. 42)

It is also possible to argue, from the perspective of home- or host-countries, of budget managers or foreign policy analysts, of world-conscious humanitarians, or narrow-minded legislators, about the relative economic costs and benefits of international study. Further, it is often possible to determine the outcome of economic analysis on this topic by manipulating the variables. In a later section, we suggest some of the key factors that must be considered in any analysis of the detailed economics of foreign study. But it is clear that while economic analysis can add to a debate, it cannot be the determining factor. The issues are quite complicated and necessarily extend beyond what is measurable by economic analysis. It has been argued that the presence of international students and faculty enrich the academic life and the ambience of a university. It is impossible to measure this enrichment. International graduate students in some fields provide needed research and teaching assistance at low cost. (Bailey, Pialorsi, and Zukowski-Faust, 1984) The foreign policy interests of some countries are enhanced by providing education to international students. It is hoped that long-term trade and other relationships will be cemented by the experience of international study. And that altruistic and noneconomic goals of mutual understanding and cooperation may be involved as well. Thus, while it is theoretically possible to measure some of the direct and indirect costs of international students, economically measurable costs and benefits are only part of the equation.

## 5. International Study as Educational Dependence

An important element to understand in any consideration of international study is that it takes place in a context of global economic, technological, and political inequality. The context of inequality is particularly dramatic precisely where the largest flows of students takes place--between the Third World nations and the industrialized market economy countries. Discussion of the inequalities between nations has been rare in debates concerning international study and it is our conviction that in order to understand the political economy of international study, it is necessary to comprehend these factors. It has been stated earlier that it is possible to see the historical and contemporary international flows of students from centers of knowledge and power to peripheries. Third World nations look to the industrialized nations as models of how to modernize. The norms and values learned during overseas study as well as technological knowledge are brought home. International study, as a phenomenon, is therefore a relationship of considerable inequality. (Weiler, 1984) While there is increasing concern that foreign study implies the transformation of the Third World according to the models and policies of the industrialized nations (see Fuenzalida, 1981), most discussions of foreign study are couched in terms of exchanges, mutual understanding, cooperation, and related issues. Few observers have discussed foreign study from the perspective of global inequalities and the continuing domination of the industrialized nations over the Third World. Yet, it is important to consider foreign study in its broader international context--and that context is one of global inequality that foreign study, in some ways hopefully helps to alleviate by bringing skills to the Third World while in other ways it helps to perpetuate existing dependent relationships by linking Third World academic systems to those of the metropoles.

It is not the purpose of this discussion to claim that all foreign study is necessarily detrimental to the Third World but rather to point out the paradoxical character of foreign study from the perspective of the Third World—the principal generator of international student flows. International study for Third World nations must represent a mixed blessing. (Altbach, 1981; and Altbach, 1983; see also Glimm and Kuper, 1980 and Stauffer, 1979) Thus, as international students from the Third World participate in a flow from the periphery to the center, they learn the values as well as the skills of the major metropolitan universities and academic systems. They must not only be proficient in the language of the metropole but if they are to succeed in meeting their academic goals they have to internalize the methodological and often the substantive concerns of the academic systems in which they study. They naturally return home, in many cases, and seek to replicate the institutions and practices that they learn in the industrialized nations. (Bochner, 1979) Some who have written about foreign study have pointed out that this informal and often invisible bond to the industrialized nation is one of the positive outlines of a liberal international student policy and that it ought to be pursued by the industrialized nations. (Wallace, 1981)

Thus there are many kinds of expertise that are learned as a result of foreign study. In addition to scientific and technological knowledge, international students also obtain what might be called the "cultural capital" (Bourdieu and Passeron, 1977) that permits them to function in technological societies. The term "cultural" has been applied in an American context to indicate that young middle-class children learn from family and school a particular set of behavioral skills and attitudes that permit them to flourish in the mainstream of American society. The same concept can be applied internationally to that minority (the elite) in the Third World that becomes proficient in the language, technologies, and orientations of the industrialized nations. These skills not only permit this group to hold the reins of power but also develops a particular life style which is more attuned to the West than to realities in many Third World nations. (For further discussion of these and related issues, see Sauvant and Mennis, 1980; and Gagnino, 1980) Therefore, international students not only learn Western technical skills but they also learn the cultural styles, metropolitan languages and orientations of the West. They learn to use Western consumer products and tend to try to import these when they return home. The problems of readjustment to the local environment are related to these factors—it has been a common complaint of foreign graduates that they are unable to work effectively in their native countries, that scientific facilities are not up to an international standard, and that working conditions are inadequate. (Gama and Pedersen, 1977)

Foreign students become acclimated to working in an international language—usually English or French—and often find it difficult to use an indigenous language for scientific work at home. Language issues are a very important part of the international student experience but in this context it is not so much the problem of adequate knowledge of the language of instruction at the beginning of the sojourn (a much researched topic, see Kaplan, 1984) but rather the ties to the foreign language and its culture that are forged during the sojourn. On the one hand, graduates are acclimated to using an international language in research, teaching, and for intellectual discourse generally. They make use of the major international journals—largely published in English or

French--and they tend to focus their scholarship on the concerns of these journals and of the international scientific community. They are, in many ways, socialized in part through language into the scientific ethos of the West. The use of a foreign language provides a link with the most current developments in a field of knowledge. In many disciplines, scientific terms do not exist in the indigenous languages and appropriate textbooks have not been published, and access to an international language is necessary.

There are also potentially negative consequences of working in an international language. The scholar is sometimes cut off from discourse in the local language and very frequently does not help to develop a scientific life in that language. There is a complete reliance on the international language. Those with foreign qualifications are sometimes unwilling to shift their work into an indigenous language or to assist in preparing textbooks or learning materials. The continued use of the metropolitan language has implications beyond the use of a foreign language itself.

The question of indigenization is a complex one which is only partly related to foreign study. Language is part of the equation--Third World nations have tried with varying degrees of success to utilize indigenous languages for instruction and research. (Gopinathan, 1984) Many have found that it has been necessary to retain a metropolitan language, usually the language of colonialism, for a variety of political, academic, and other reasons. A few countries--Malaysia and Indonesia among them, have made the shift from a colonial to an indigenous language for education. Others, such as China, Thailand, and the Latin American nations, did not face this problem. There are also other aspects of indigenization that relate to foreign study. The research foci and other examples used in the industrialized nations are often brought back by those who have studied overseas along with textbooks, laboratory equipment, and ideas about the curriculum. There are many reasons for the expansion of American ideas about university organization and the curriculum in the Third World. One of them is the fact that many returning scholars have brought back their experiences and have tried to implement them at home. (Hawkins, 1984) While foreign study may be valuable in many respects, it does not assist in the building of indigenous models of higher education or the growth of original curricula aimed at local problems.

There is a natural tendency to look toward the international centers of knowledge for research guidelines and methodologies and for innovations in most scientific fields. (Kumar, 1979) It has been pointed out that the major internationally circulated journals are published in the Western nations and that these tend to dominate their fields. Most scientific discoveries take place in the West. Even without foreign-returned graduates, these trends would be a powerful force, but individuals who have studied in the West have been particularly good conduits for the continuing involvement with Western models and ideas. After all, these individuals were trained to respect and use these ideas. In short, the links forged during the foreign sojourn often last into the professional careers of those who have undergone this often powerful experience.

In many Third World countries, foreign study very often adds a measure of prestige and perhaps power to an individual. In Africa, the term "been to" signifies that an individual has studied overseas and it traditionally has been a measure of considerable achievement. Foreign training permits an individual in many situations to have more ready access to positions of authority, leadership, and power than someone who has not had foreign training. It is implicitly assumed that the "best and the brightest" are sent overseas and that the quality of foreign training has been high--a powerful combination. While there has been no careful research that has correlated foreign study with rapid advancement, in the educational system, government or in industry and commerce, there are indications that foreign training does provide certain advantages.

The location of foreign study may also make a difference, not only in one's outlook and attitudes but also in professional opportunities. The methodological and sometimes the ideological approach to fields of study differs from one country to another and this will make a difference in outlook and orientation. A student who had obtained an academic degree in the Soviet Union in economics will probably have a quite different approach to the field than one who had studied in the United States. Even academic systems which resemble each other more closely, such as the British and the American, exhibit considerable variations. An academic degree from a particular country may create intellectual loyalties to that country. Certainly, there will be a tendency to look back on the overseas experience when thinking of textbooks, the purchase of imported equipment or perhaps the hiring of expatriate advisers. As more students have studied in the United States, there has been a trend toward looking toward American models of higher education for reform efforts in the Third World.

The locale of foreign study also creates important linguistic affinities and links. Students who have studied in Francophone nations naturally have their orientation to French-language journals, universities, and expertise. Those who have studied in Anglophone institutions have similar loyalties. Indeed, there are generally closer links between, for example, universities in Anglophone Africa and those in Britain, Canada or the United States than between Anglophone and Francophone universities within Africa. Politics can also play a role. When revolution came to Ethiopia, for example, American-trained academics and policy makers were in many instances killed by the new pro-Soviet revolutionary government. This is an extreme example, but politics can play a role in determining the preferred locale of foreign study or the influence of graduates of particular countries. At present, the graduates of Soviet-bloc universities are regarded with some suspicion in many Third World nations; this has created some problems since large numbers of graduates are being produced in Eastern Europe.

Links between industrialized and Third World nations are key determinants of the nature of international student flows and of continuing intellectual and academic relationships between those two countries. Most important, of course, are the continuing links between France and Britain and their former colonial possessions. Traditionally, students from the colonies tended to go to their metropole. Linguistic factors, perceptions of educational quality, and prestige, links between examination systems, an "old boy" network, and official policies of governments all contribute to this situation. In many instances, there has been an official recognition of these traditional links through acceptance of secondary school examinations, etc. Current British debates concerning foreign student fees and numbers have included discussions of the traditional role of Britain as educator of large numbers of students from such countries as Cyprus (which has no university of its own), Hong Kong, and Malaysia.

The experiences of international students from the Third World and their roles on returning to their home countries reinforce links to the metropole, its culture, language, academic styles, and values. There are, of course, many international students who return home only to reject Western values. The government of Malaysia, for example, is concerned about the fundamentalist Islamic values that many of its students adopt while overseas, perhaps as a reaction to the secularism of the West. Further, the technical skills learned abroad are of great importance for development. Thus, it is not inevitable that foreign study will build dependence on the industrialized nations. But there is evidence that in many ways foreign study does make for close ties and reinforces traditional patterns of inequality.

## 6. The International Education Infrastructure:  An Emerging Profession

There is a growing community of professional educators and support personnel who deal with issues concerning international students and broader questions of international education policy and practice. This emerging profession is best developed in the United States, where it is represented by organizations such as the National Association for Foreign Student Affairs (NAFSA) and the American Association of Collegiate Registrars and Admissions Officers (AACRAO). Backman describes the scope of international education activities of many American colleges and universities. Year-abroad programs for undergraduates, services for visiting scholars and faculty, foreign student admissions personnel, advisers for international students, campus-wide administrators for international programs and other staffs are some of the functions now common in many institutions. These activities are fairly new in American higher education and the emergence of professional staff to deal with the many aspects of international education is also recent. In general, there are no specific training programs for international education staff members, although some hold advanced degrees is such fields as higher education administration, comparative and international education, student personnel, and related areas.

International education responsibilities in the larger institutions are becoming incresingly differentiated. Foreign student admissions is a good example. In many universities, specialized staff now deal with this task and increasingly specialized knowledge is required. The nuances of overseas credentials, the problems of visas, and other matters require specialized knowledge. Communications networks, through NAFSA and AACRAO as well as other agencies are developing. Specialized publications, such as AACRAO's "World Education Series" have developed to provide guidance to those responsible for foreign student admissions. The Institute of International Education also provides statistical information and other publications that are helpful to this emerging community. NAFSA's newsletter, circulated to more than 5,000 professionals in the field, contains information relevant to the international education community. Organizations such as the American Council on Education have taken an interest in international education as well.

Universities and colleges are still struggling with appropriate definitions, functions and responsibilities for the newly emerging profession dealing with international education. And in a period of fiscal constraint, it is always a problem to ensure that sufficient personnel are assigned to these functions. There is, nevertheless, a growing recognition that the developing international role of academic institutions inevitably means that competent professional staff are needed to ensure the effective administration of these programs. The United States, with its large administrative cadres in higher education, has moved most quickly to recognize the need for professionals in international education. Other countries have also developed professional expertise. In Canada, the Canadian Bureau for International Education is quite active in developing data, issuing reports, and representing the international education community. Similar groups exist in Britain, West Germany, and Japan. Australia has been very much concerned with international education issues.

Professionalism in dealing with international education is inevitable in higher education. The various and growing functions involved require such expertise and long-term professional commitment. Few have thus far thought about the implications of a growing group of professionals in the field. It is inevitable that these functions be met but it is not as yet clear how the emerging profession will fit into academic systems or what its role or status will be.

## 7. A Review of Past Research on International Students

We have tried to consider some of the important issues relating to international students. Now we turn to a more detailed discussion of our review of the research relating to international students undertaken over the past two and a half decades. Naturally, our consideration can only touch the surface of a varied literature. We have attempted to organize this analysis according to some of the major themes of the literature. Some of these themes overlap with topics we discussed earlier. Others do not. Our aim is to provide an overview of the literature and then to present some suggestions for future research.

The literature concerning international students is by now extensive, but it is of relatively recent origin for the most part. American researchers are responsible for the bulk of the literature to date—our guess is that perhaps 70% of the research uses North American data and is by scholars in North America. This fact will naturally affect the topics and orientations of the research, since the concerns and methodological orientations of North American researchers will be largely reflected in the literature. Further, issues of student adjustment, cross-cultural relations and similar topics seem to dominate the literature. There is relatively little directly concerning policy, economics, or politics of foreign study. The topic of international study has, with a few exceptions, not attracted much attention from social scientists although as issues have become more complex and as funding from external agencies has become available, there has been a growth of interest from a wider community of scholars. One of the problems is that there is at present no research community--the organizations, such as the National Association for Foreign Student Affairs, in the field have been largely concerned with concrete issues rather than with research. Related fields such as comparative education have not been directly concerned with issues of international study.

In reviewing the extensive research on international students to date, one is immediately struck by three distinct characteristics of this research: a great proportion of it (as mentioned earlier) is based on American data; and much of this U.S. research is lopsided in the direction of exploring either the cross-cultural consequences of studying abroad or the conditions and means necessary to help international students adapt and succeed in an alien institutional and cultural environment. At the same time the research is characterized by a great deal of haphazard diversity in terms of topics covered, findings, and conclusions. It is not uncommon for two or more studies on the same topic to emerge with radically different conclusions and recommendations (throwing the prospective policy maker into a quandary). Given this character of the research what follows is not a synopsis of all the findings in the research but a summary of recurrent themes supported by usually more than one study, albeit based usually on a different population sample.

### 7a. The U-Curve Hypothesis

Taking the cross-cultural studies first--there does not seem to be much empirical support for the celebrated "U-curve" hypothesis first advanced by Sverre Lysgaard following his study of the 1953 Norwegian Fulbright grantees in 1953, and which states: "Adjustment as a process over time seems to follow a U-shaped curve: adjustment is felt to be easy and successful to begin with; then follows a "crisis" in which one feels less well adjusted, somewhat lonely and unhappy; finally one begins to feel better adjusted again, becoming more integrated into the foreign community." (Lysgaard, 1955; see also Gullahorn and Gullahorn, 1963) Thus, one of the few truly international studies (Klineberg and Hull, 1979) designed to study the cross-cultural problems that international students face while abroad, and the strategies used to cope with these problems, concluded that their data presented almost no support for the hypotheses. They found that the frequency of occurrence of the key variables (personal depression; loneliness; homesickness, and so on) pertaining to the hypotheses had no relationship to the duration of the foreign sojourn.

## 7b. Cross-cultural Contact

If Lysgaard's hypothesis has turned out to be questionable, his formulation of it at least has not been without benefit--he alerted researchers to the fact that international study was potentially fraught with stress for those who undertook it. That is stress arising from sojourn in an alien cultural setting and taking such forms as loneliness, personal depression, various psychosomatic illnesses, etc. (see Boer, 1981, Horner and Vandersluis, et al., 1981) Research shows that the principal cause is what may be referred to as the cross-cultural isolation factor. International students almost everywhere complain about this factor. For, unless an international student is able to establish frequent, (or as desired) easy and harmonious interrelationships with the natives of the host-country it is almost absolutely predictable that his/her sojourn will be one of considerable dissatisfaction. For, next to academic success, positive contact with natives of the host-country ranks at the very top of international student needs. Thus, as Hull (1978) found in his U.S. study of this issue, those international students who reported frequent positive cross-cultural contact with Americans (via such practices as joint academic work, visits, outings, discussions, participation in artistic/social/communal activities, and so on) were the ones most likely to report "less loneliness and homesickness, more favorable attitudes about their experience in general, less desire to return home, less discrimination, and basically fewer negative reactions of experiences during their sojourn in the United States." This finding is corroborated by a similar finding for international students studying in other countries such as Brazil, Canada, France, India, Iran, Japan, and Kenya. (see Klineberg and Hull, 1979)

Among the variables that stand out in determining positive cross-cultural contact, research indicates the following three to be very important: language proficiency; previous travel experience; absence of discrimination and cultural background. Adequate facility with the language of the host-country and institution is, to state the obvious, not only an important determinant of academic success but also success in breaking down cross-cultural isolation.

Klineberg and Hull, (1979) found that those international students who had had travel experience away from their home countries for at least a month tended to be better adapted at establishing positive contact. Language proficiency and previous travel experience in itself is of little use if the response from the host natives is one of hostility. And therefore insofar as discrimination against people of other races, religion, etc. exists in a given country, positive cross-cultural contact for international students in that country is to that extent curtailed. It is interesting to note on this point that the Klineberg/Hull study found that those international students most likely to report the existence of discrimination were to be found in France, followed by the United States, and then the United Kingdom, and finally Canada. However, when it came to experiencing personal discrimination, international students studying in Japan were the largest number of respondents to report such discrimination (44.4%) and then followed by those in Hong Kong (36.6%); France (35.8%); Kenya (34.5%); Canada (34.2%); U.S.

(30.6%); India (30.4%); Iran (22.2%); U.K. (22.0%); West Germany (17.9%) and Brazil (11.6%). A recent study involving international students from a number of East African countries found that North America scored the lowest followed by Western Europe, in terms of satisfaction rating for cultural and racial relations. The score for Eastern Europe was the highest. (Maliyamkono, et al., 1982). For an illuminating article on discrimination against international students in, Japan, see Michii (1981).

The fourth important factor in inhibiting or facilitating cross-cultural contact is the international student's own cultural background. Thus, for example, White and White (1981) report that the factor of cultural background was (they surmised) so significant that it even overrode the langauge proficiency factor when they tried to correlate it to social adjustment, in their comparative study of Indian and Chinese students. Thus they state: "...English language proficiency may be related to acculturation but this relationship appears to be neither strong nor consistent across groups of foreign students whose national origins differ." (p.65) (see also Dunnett, 1981)

An important dimension of research in the area of cross-cultural contact issues is the research aimed toward developing formal programs to enhance cross-cultural contact via educational activities. For example, programs would be developed to use international students and faculty as educational resources in the classroom on campus, as well as in schools off campus. (Relevant studies in this particular area include: Christensen and Thielen, 1983; Mestenhauser, 1981; Neff, 1981; Paige, 1978; Robinson and Hendel, 1981)

### 7c. Attitudes

While studies pertaining to stress dominate within the area of cross-cultural consequences of studying abroad, there are a significant number of studies that look at the attitudinal dimension. (see for example Bowman, 1978; Hasan, 1976; Hegazy, 1968; Hensley, 1979; Kelman, 1975; Kumagai, 1977) That is, studies that examine attitudes of international students toward the host country, as well as attitudinal change regarding self. With regard to the former, available evidence does not suggest any clear-cut pattern in the attitudes of international students, except that positive or negative attitudes toward the host country were principally a matter of satisfactory social and academic adjustment and to a much lesser extent national origin. Thus for instance, Hull found in his study that in general European and African students had negative attitudes toward the U.S. where as Asian students had much more positive attitudes. There does not seem to be much support for the "national status" hypothesis (which states that a student's attitude toward the host-country will be influenced by his perception of the status (superior/inferior) of his own country in relation to the host country). Certainly the Klineberg/Hull study found only limited evidence in support of the hypothesis to the extent that the data were able to address the matter. As for change in attitudes there does not seem to be any evidence to demonstrate a consistent change during the sojourn, though this certainly is not the case with attitudes pertaining to self.

Here there is strong evidence that those international students who are abroad for two years or more demonstrate a consistent change in their attitudes during their stay, albeit not necessarily of an overwhelming magnitude. Generally, it seems, change is in the direction of liberal (understood here to mean less rigid or more open-minded) attitudes with regard to such matters as religion, relations with the opposite sex, etc. for those international students in the West coming from Third World countries, but without alteration in basic or fundamental beliefs, which tend to remain stable. In the matter of personal and intellectual growth, however, there is most noticeable change. As evidence from research in the U.S. indicates: "...the sojourn and educational experience tends to engender a more sophisticated, differentiated, personalized and concretized knowledge and perception of the host society, its achievements and problems, its peoples and policies, and of its way of life as compared to 'knowledge' and images held before. The result is a soberer appraisal of some of its features, values and practices and of their relevance to one's own role, one's field of activity, and one's own country." (Flack, 1976)

A number of studies have looked at attitudes of international students toward those with whom, among the host natives, they share a common racial heritage. Two groups of international students studying in the U.S. quickly come to mind: European students and African students. Strangely, it appears that both groups of students display negative attitudes toward those Americans who on the surface bear the closest resemblance to them. Thus Europeans tend to have a negative attitude about the U.S., and similarly, research indicates that there is a general negative attitude on the part of Africans toward black Americans—explained in part by basic sociocultural differences, and in part by their perception of a supposed superiority complex shared by black Americans vis-a-vis the Africans, and in part by a tangible lessening of discrimination toward the Africans, once they were identified, by white Americans. (see Becker, 1973; Heath, 1970; Markham, 1967; Miller, 1967; Odenyo, 1970; Pierce, 1969; and Wakita, 1971)

Does the presence of international students have any impact on the attitudes of the host population? This question has unfortunately not received adequate attention in international student research. What little research there is indicates a nonconclusive finding. If however, one is to go by indirect evidence on the matter, then the conclusion to be reached is that the mere act of studying in a foreign country does not of itself assist in breaking down cultural barriers—in fact it may even reinforce these barriers. Thus, as a comparative study (by Miller, et al., 1971) on the ability of students from East Asia studying in the U.S., and the U.S. students in East Asia, to achieve "warm friendship and understanding" with host nationals found out, for both groups of international students, the only source of such friendship and understanding was themselves. Similarly, the Klineberg/Hull study (1979) reports that overall, with respect to all international students in all 11 countries of their study, they found "a tremendous amount of disappointment and even discouragement when respondents were seeking, were open to, or were expecting more social contact with local students and individuals than they found." (p. 178) (For other relevant studies on the impact of international students on the host population, see

Brickman, 1967; Cowser, 1978; Deutsch, 1970; Ebbers and Peterson, 1981; Marion and Thomas, 1980; Matross, 1982; and Neville, 1981)

The general conclusion, sadly, to be drawn from the overall research on the cross-cultural dimension of international study is that the potential for an enriching and positive cross-cultural experience for both hosts and guests, has yet to be realized. However, this is not to say that there are no nonacademic benefits of international study—at least from the perspective of the individual international student. On the contrary, evidence indicates a consistent finding that among the almost assured nonacademic benefits an international student can expect from his foreign sojourn are those to be found in the areas of intellectual development, personal development, independence, and self-confidence. (Brislin, 1981; see also Goodwin and Nacht, 1984)

At first glance, it may appear, when reviewing the research on international students, that studies on the cross-cultural consequences of studying abroad dominate the research. This, however, is not so. It is in the area of assisting international students in adjusting to, and succeeding in the alien academic environment that the majority of the studies on international students are to be found. And the topics that have been covered in this area range widely: admission, advising and counseling, language proficiency, academic achievement, curricular relevance, and so on. And here again, as pointed out earlier, the bulk of the research is dominated by U.S. data.

### 7d. Recruitment and Admission

Within the area of admissions there are two major concerns reflected in the literature: the absence of specific institutional policy regarding admission of international students and the problem of effective evaluation of international credentials. A number of studies lament the fact that almost no university in the U.S. has specific policies regarding such issues as optimum international student numbers; balance in fields of study they pursue, balance in their geographical origins; balance in gender division, and so on. This situation is perhaps not surprising considering that in many instances the top-level administrators responsible for institutional policy are far removed from those who deal directly with international students.

Admissions officers seem to be perpetually grappling with the problem of developing an effective system for evaluating credentials of international applicants—this of course is to be expected given the complex diversity of educational systems that are represented by the credentials of the international applicants. However, to assist admission officers with their onerous task, one of the major and active organizations in the field of international study in the U.S., the National Association for Foreign Student Affairs, has published a number of guides. Supplementing these guides are the World Education Series materials being produced by the American Association of Collegiate Registrars and Admissions Officers. As for research pertaining to this particular area, the following studies are relevant: Dixon, et al., 1976; Fisher and Dey, 1979; Patrick, 1983; and Turner, 1979.

One issue pertinent to the area of admissions that has recently come to the fore in the U.S. (and other countries such as U.K.) is the matter of recruitment of international students. Faced with declining enrollments, some institutions are aggressively venturing into the international student market, with the result that in some instances unsavory practices have come to light--such as making ability to pay the only criterion for granting admission to the prospective international applicant. To try to eliminate such practices, efforts are under way to come up with an ethical code of conduct that institutions may ascribe to--if they are not to lose to the government their highly prized prerogative of who, how and when to admit international student applicants. (See Berendzen, 1983; Fiske, 1981; Jenkins, 1980; Jenkins, 1983 (b); and William, 1984)

### 7e. Advising and Counseling

A fairly large number of studies have concerned themselves with the role and effectiveness of international student advisers. (See for example, Benson, 1968; Higbee, 1961; Miller, 1968; Pedersen, 1981; Putman, 1965; and Woolston, 1983) They often point out that while many U.S. institutions with significant international student populations find that they cannot do without international student advisers, they are not usually accorded the necessary top-level academic and administrative authority. With regard to academic authority their offices seem to have almost none whatsoever, with the result that not only is there lack of coordination between academic advisement and general advisement of the international student, but often there tends to be no provision at all of academic advisement services specifically geared toward the needs of the international student.

On the whole, the conclusion regarding the effectiveness of international student advisers is that when viewed from within the context of administrative and budgetary constraints, they seem to be performing their functions fairly well. (See for example Lockett, 1970) This general finding however, applies mainly to the four-year institutions. As for the two-year institutions, evidence suggests a bleak picture: often those appointed to the role of international student advisers are poorly qualified, and even those who may be qualified are severly hampered in effectively performing their functions by administratively imposed constraints.

Before turning to the area of counseling, one further observation that needs to be made about international student advising services is the important finding by Hull (1978) of the need for advisers to "reemphasize their functions as educators within the educational community as well as within the surrounding communities." (p.188) That is, they must develop resources and skills aimed at the creation and implementation of programs that can facilitate more meaningful cross-cultural contact with Americans (both on-campus and off-campus).

International students present special problems when it comes to provision of psychological counseling services for three major reasons: first, a very significant proportion of them report suffering from acute bouts of personal depression (one quarter of the sample in the Klineberg/Hull study); second, for cultural reasons, they are not generally prone to seek counseling help and hence, by the time they do so they are usually in very serious need of it; and third, the varied cultural backgound of the international students renders counseling that much more difficult for the counselor. To elaborate on the last point: it is quite clear that the values and assumptions that American counselors for example, will bring to the counseling situation will be very different from that of the international student. In general, for instance, it is known that many Third World students come from cultures that tend to see one's life circumstances as essentially determined by external factors (political, economic, etc) beyong one's control. On the other hand Americans generally believe that one's life circumstances are very much within the control of the individual. To take another example, many Third World students come from cultural background that do not in general allow nonrelatives and those who are not close friends, access to their personal problems. In contrast Americans believe that an individual's personal problems can be made the legitimate business of a stranger (a professional) with a view toward arriving at a joint solution. (For further details on these and other differences see Stewart, 1975; and Sue, 1978) Given these circumstances of international students, it is surprising that many institutions do not consider provision of counseling services a special need separate from the general advisement service provided by the international student office. (Among the studies relevant to this area see the following for further details: Akoff, et al., 1966; Alexander, et al., 1981; Higginbotham, 1979; Horner and Vandersluis, et al., 1981; Story, 1982; Yeh, 1972; and Zunin and Rubin, 1967)

7f. Language Proficiency

A number of studies have documented the pivotal character of proficiency in the medium of instruction of the host institution for adjustment and success in meeting academic goals. Thus studies indicate a high correlation between success in English-as-a-foreign-language tests (such as T.O.E.F.L. administered world-wide by the Education Testing Service in Princeton, New Jersey) and academic success. (See, for example, Heil and Aleamoni, 1974; Martin, 1971; Melendez-Craig, 1970; and Uehara, 1969) There are, however, almost no studies that go beyond this finding, such as attempting to evaluate the success rates of language remedial programs at various U.S. institutions, or determine the major factors encouraging or inhibiting rapid acquisition of proficiency among different international groups, and so on.

The importance of ascertaining proficiency in the language of instruction among international students is beginning to receive greater attention in countries that traditionally assumed such proficiency to be present among international applicants. A case in point is New Zealand, where the issue of a mandatory language proficiency test for all international applicants has been raised--albeit not without some controversy. The reason for this, of course, is the increasing diversity in the background of international students coming to these countries in comparison to those students who came in the past (who were usually from countries that used English as their official language).

## 7g. Academic Achievement

Beside the variable of language proficiency, research indicates a number of other variables of significance that come into play when determining achievement or academic success among international students. These variables include the student's academic background prior to enrollment in the foreign institution (and viewed longitudinally); source of financial support (scholarship/assistantship students, for self-evident reasons have been found to perform better than self-supported students); and national origin (again for self-evident reasons students from countries with educational systems similar to the American educational system seem to perform better academically then those from countries with dissimilar educational systems).

A number of studies that attempt to correlate variables such as age, sex, and marital status to academic achievement have found that these variables are of comparatively little significance, and attempts to correlate personal and social adjustment with academic achievement have run into the "chicken-and-egg" problem--which comes first? The frequently used academic aptitude tests in American institutions have been the subject of some studies, and the general finding surprisingly (considering the pervasive use of these tests) is that the tests seem to have little prognosticatory value, perhaps because of the factor of cultural bias creeping into the tests. (see Sharon, 1971; Sugimoto, 1966) Evidence suggests that departments would do better (in terms of evaluation of an international applicant's ability to succeed academically) by relying on two principal indicators: the applicant's prior academic track record and his/her performance on a language proficiency test.

An interesting question that has been raised but not yet properly addressed in the literature concerns success rates of international students in meeting academic goals. How many international students manage to get their degrees, certificates, etc. that they set out to obtain? Hull (1978) surmises (on the basis of a random investigation of U.S. universities) that nearly all international students do eventually obtain the credentials they set out to get. As for comparative studies on success rates among both international students and local students, there seem to be almost none of significance. However, what little evidence there is on this turns out to be conflicting, part suggesting that they do better than local students, and part suggesting they perform less well than local students. (see Rao, 1979, p. 75) Blaug (1981) notes that they found a general agreement among British university teaching staff that international students seemed to perform academically less well than native students; however, he goes on to say: "But all these statements were no more than several impressions: despite persistent probing by the research team, nobody produced hard facts about the differential performance rates of home and overseas students." (p. 64; see also Bie, 1976)

## 7h.  Curricula

Are the academic programs offered by U.S. institutions relevant to the needs of international students?  A few studies have tried to look at this issue--which is an important issue especially considering that the majority of international students (roughly 85%) do not remain in the U.S. upon completion of their studies.  The few studies that have looked at this issue indicate that, in general, U.S. curricula are not particularly suited to the needs of international students coming from Third World countries--especially with respect to the technical disciplines (engineering, agriculture, etc.) at the advanced levels. These studies also indicate that international student returnees find technical knowledge (gained from practical training experience where this has been possible to obtain following completion of studies) more useful than the theoretical knowledge obtained from their training.  There is also evidence to suggest that those students with set or predetermined career goals (usually sponsored students) tend to express dissatisfaction with their academic programs more often than those with less determined career goals.

It seems that generally, in this area of curricular relevance, research is still in its infancy, and hence much still needs to be done. (Relevant studies in this area include: Baron, 1979; Cooper, 1983; Harari, 1970; Moock, 1984; Myer, 1979; Ronkin, 1969; Stone, 1969; Susskind and Schell, 1968)

## 7i.  Needs

Numerous studies have looked at the nebulous issue of "international student needs"; (needs relating to such nonacademic matters as finance, housing, health, information, leisure, etc.).  Of particular relevance here is an extensive research study by Lee, et al., (1981) under the auspices of the National Association for Foreign Student Affairs on needs of international students from developing nations at U.S. colleges and universities.  Among their principal findings are the following: ranking high at the top of the list of needs of respondents were first, adequate finance; second, acquisition of credentials; third, acquisition of relevant specialized skills and knowledge; fourth, obtaining a job at home commensurate with one's training, and fifth, obtaining relevant practical training experience in the U.S. before returning home.  Ranking low at the bottom of the list of needs were first, need for information on obtaining one's customary food and food ingredients; second, need for information on English courses for international students; third, need for sharing housing with U.S. nationals; fourth, need for observing religious practices.  There were other needs that ranked even lower than these, such as the need to get used to U.S. food, or need for information on dating customs, etc.

The other findings of this thorough and extensive study include the following: scholarship/assistantship students were more satisfied with their overall sojourn than the self-supported students (this finding conflicts with that of Hull, 1978); there was emphasis among respondents on the need for relevant curricula, particularly by agricultural students; national origin was a determining factor in the identification and weighting of needs, (for example, they note: "One of the groups which perceived the least satisfaction in receiving equal acceptance by faculty and human respect by U.S. students was the group most likely to return home, i.e., African students." p. 32), those students who already had jobs waiting for them at home tend to be more satisfied with their overall experience than those who did not; and those whose roommates were local students tended to be more satisfied with their sojourn than those who did not have local roommates. This finding is supported by both the Hull (1978) study and the Klineberg and Hull (1979) study; however, the Klineberg and Hull study cautions that "the person with whom one shares a residence may not be the most important factor at the sojourn location in terms of the overall coping and adaptation processes...data would rather suggest, as already indicated, that access to local people (amount of contact and kinds of contact) is more important than sharing residence with a local student." (p. 187)

Besides these two major areas of international student research (the cross-cultural consequences of studying abroad; and the academic adjustment and success factors) there are two other areas of research that must be examined: one well represented in the literature and the other underrepresented. Beginning with the latter, there exists some research on international students who have returned home. The general thrust of this research has been essentially to poll returnees on their experiences and attitudes during their sojourn. Much of the information obtained from these studies generally corroborate the findings of studies on similar issues conducted among students still present in the host country. (see, for example, Galtung, 1965) There are almost no studies on such important matters as the overall impact of returnees on the development of their societies, etc. This and related issues will be raised again below.

### 7j. Brain Drain

The better represented research is on what is generally called "brain drain," that is, the voluntary nonreturn of Third World international students following completion of their studies, and hence constituting a "brain drain" on their home countries. It should be pointed out that the term "brain drain" is also used in the voluntary migration of skilled persons who are not necessarily students from their home countries to other nations. Note must also be made of the fact that the migration or nonreturn is voluntary and not as a result of political persecution, etc. where remaining or returning to the country may imply placing life and livelihood in jeopardy. Since the percentage of officially sponsored students coming under various bilateral agreements who don't return home is extremely small (around 2%, according to one study (Rao, 1979, p. xii), brain drain should generally be understood to refer to privately sponsored students. The factors that have been identified as prominent in the voluntary nonreturn of international students are as follows: Given that a preponderant number of self-sponsored Third World students tend to be minorities of one kind or another (racial, religious, etc.) seeking to achieve upward social mobility via higher education abroad, there is already a built-in self-selection bias among them toward a tendency to consider not returning home as a serious option (barring host-country legal restrictions). This is especially so in circumstances where the student's minority status may subject him/her to the possibility of experiencing the worst sides of nepotism and corruption in employment and promotion practices at home. (This is not to say, however, that self-sponsored students are usually from low-economic class background, in fact on the contrary. The very fact that they are self-sponsored points to the opposite.)

Besides the economic advantages to be gained from remaining in the host-country, there may also be a career advantage to be gained. Thus, for example, a very able Third World student with a deep commitment to pursue further research in his or her field may be tempted to remain in the host country because returning home may mean curtailing the research due to lack of appropriate logistical support (funds, equipment, peers, etc.) In fact, one international study concludes that a very large proportion of international students who have returned home end up being underemployed--that is, they are employed in jobs for which their training is not fully used. (Glaser and Habers, 1978) This of course also applies to highly talented artists, especially if their art is of the type that is almost unmarketable at home through lack of demand--e.g., a symphony director. The brain drain--especially when it pertains to international students--is considered a highly undesirable phenomenon from the perspective of both the home country and the host country, and in the case of international students, more so by the latter than the former. Hence, the measures that have been implemented or advocated to discourage international students from remaining after completion of their studies include: (a) tightening the legal restrictions in the host country that allow international students to remain (such as the proposed American Simpson/Mazzoli bill); (b) encouraging home countries to accord the same employment opportunities as those enjoyed by the sponsored students; (c) developing joint training agreements between host country institutions and home country institutions that would allow the training in international students (private and sponsored) according to the skill and knowledge requirements of the home country without necessarily involving major redefinitions of graduate curricula of host institutions. The benefit deriving from such an arrangement would be bilateral--the opportunity for international students to remain would be lessened because their training would be of greater relevance to the home country than to the host country; and the host institutions would be assured of a more steady, homogenous flow of students--one amenable to planning. It should be pointed out that while statistics on the number of international students constitute a smaller fraction than the total brain drain migrants, it is a problem that must be addressed--especially from the perspective of developing and implementing solutions, something that is distinctly lacking in this area of international student research.

7k. Evaluation of Exchange Programs

A significant amount of research on international study has been devoted, not surprisingly, to the area of program evaluation. Sponsoring agencies, such as the U.S. Agency for International Development have funded research projects to evaluate the effectiveness of some of their exchange programs. A good example is the massive study done by the American University's Development Education and Training Research Institute (DETRI) on behalf of the Office of International Training of the U.S. Agency for International Development (A.I.D.) of some 10,000 A.I.D. scholarship holders from approximately 75 countries over the period 1966 to 1972. (see Kimmel, Ockey, and Sander, 1972) The aim of this study was to determine the satisfaction ratings of the students with respect to their overall training and life experiences in the U.S. and general evaluation of the exchange programs via "exit interviews" as they left the U.S. for home after completion of studies. The conclusions of the study were, in general, in conformity with findings of other research on international student issues though there were some in conflict. For example, the study found little correlation between sojourn satisfaction and language proficiency problems, problems of access to orientation programs, and financial problems. Overall, the study concluded that roughly 50-70% of the students found their training and life experience in the U.S. highly or near highly satisfactory. (Other relevant studies pertaining to this area include: the A.I.D. Participant Evaluation Program evaluation studies (involving a survey of returned students in their home countries) published by A.I.D. in 1966, but separately under four regional headings: Far East, Latin America, North Africa, and Near East and South Asia; Crespi, 1978 International Research and Exchanges Board, 1980; Collin, 1979; Uhlig, Crotton, and Thompson, 1978)

## 8. Gaps in Past Research

These then are some of the major issues that have dominated research on international students over the last two decades. There have been other topics examined too, but on a smaller scale, such as alumni issues (Dolibois, 1976; Goodwin and Nacht, 1984; Rogers, 1983), health (physical and mental) (see for example Coelho, 1973; Cole, Allen, and Green, 1980; Klineberg, 1981), legal questions (Anthony, 1980; Bedrosian, 1983; Gray, 1982; Smith, 1981), disciplinary (or fields of study), specific issues (see Babiker, et al., 1980; Fouad and Jones, 1979; Rogers, 1971; Shaw, 1982). But with all these topics, the underlying theme has been to find ways and means of aiding international students in achieving their goals; that is, in making their sojourn both productive and pleasant. It is research that has been almost entirely conducted from the perspective of the international student to the exclusion of other perspectives: such as that of the department, or institution, or the host country, or even the home country.

It is necessary now to direct research attention toward these other perspectives--and especially in the direction of what may be called "the political economy of international study." This, of course, is not to say by any means that the research conducted hitherto has been misguided or irrelevant--in fact, this traditional, micro-level, student-oriented research has been very necessary during the growth of international student population flows, but the stage has now been reached where the present sizable population of international student flow demands the examination of other dimensions of it--that is, the dimensions at the macro-level. Before turning to what the research agenda aimed toward a political economy of international study may look like, it is necessary that mention be made of some of the major research gaps in the traditional literature that still remain to be filled.

## 8a.  International Student Impact

An area of considerable importance that to date has not received sufficient attention is that of the impact of international students on the academic life of their host institutions, as well as on the attitudes of the host population--both students and nonstudents. Taking the latter point first, of particular interest is the issue of change in attitudes (in a positive direction) and gain in knowledge about other cultures, peoples, etc. through interaction with international students. It may well be that the "internationalizing" influence that high-level administrators so often speak of when called upon to justify the presence of international students on their campuses is merely well-meaning rhetoric. That is, it is likely that only those within the campus and off-campus communities already inclined toward internationalizing their knowledge and life experience (usually a small minority) make the effort to know and interact with international students. The vast majority, on the other hand, prefer to remain aloof and uninvolved. Or it could be that the appropriate communication structures (constructed through creative programming) are simply lacking, and hence the potential for an internationalizing influence from the presence of international students goes unrealized.

Do international students have any impact on the academic life of the host institutions? This is an important question that must be asked in light of the fact that in a significant number of institutions in the U.S. (as well as nations such as France, Britain, and Canada), departments such as those for physical and engineering sciences are dominated by international students at the graduate level. The statistics for the U.S. in this regard for example, are sobering: whereas in 1960, international students claimed 33.5% of all Ph.Ds awarded in the engineering sciences in the U.S. (Business Higher Education Forum, 1982), by 1982 this figure had climbed to 51%. The magnitude of international graduate student participation in the engineering sciences, however, becomes even more dramatic when viewed from the perspective of individual departments. Taking the example of State University of New York at Buffalo, the percentage share of total departmental graduate enrollment claimed by international students is 61% for the Department of Mechanical Engineering.

Given the increased numbers of international graduate students, it is necessary that questions such as the following be raised and answered: What effects, if any, do international students have on the number of courses offered, the content of these courses, and the general curricula of these departments? What impact, if any, do international students have on the kinds of research that is undertaken and the quantity of research accomplished, by both faculty and students? To what extent do the departments rely on international students for teaching assistants, and how does this affect the quality of undergraduate teaching? Does the presence of international students encourage departments in developing international programs, consultancy agreements, training projects, etc.?; and does such encouragement come from alumni contacts?

At the same time, an important dimension of research in this area is the question of the general attitude of faculty toward international students regarding the students' competence, diligence, achievement; and the general presence of international students in the department. Preliminary investigations seem to suggest that the dramatic increases in graduate level enrollment of international students in departments such as those in engineering sciences have been accompanied by a general lowering of morale among faculty as they face nontraditional students with a nonfamiliar cultural and educational background. Thus, Goodwin and Nacht (1983) state that they found considerable animosity among faculty toward international students with frequent use of analogies to describe international students: "Wet noodles soaking up anything you pour over them"; and "bazaar merchants haggling over grades." If their preliminary findings represent a general situation prevalent in many other institutions throughout the U.S., then research needs to be done on the causes of such negative attitudes, their effect on international students and ways and means of ameliorating the situation.

## 8b. Institutional Policy

It could well be that there is a certain numerical threshold beyond which any increase in international student presence leads to disruption in the academic life of the department, precipitating a general breakdown in morale among faculty. If this is so then it is necessary to determine what that numerical threshold is. The point brings one to the whole question of institutional policy. Surprisingly many institutions lack a coherent institutional policy. Therefore, research is necessary to determine a general institutional policy on international students, a call that has been made by a number of others recently. (see, for example, American Council on Education, 1982; Australian government, 1984; Goodwin and Nacht, 1983; Carrigan, 1977; Williams, 1982; see also NAFSA, 1972 as an example of the kind of study that is needed in this area). Such an institutional policy would comprise, among others, statements on the following elements: Admission procedures and criteria. For example, must international students meet the same admission requirements as domestic students? Student Profile. How many international students should be admitted in a given department? How should the balance be struck in terms of geographical origin, gender, fields of study, and so on, among the international students that are admitted? Financial Aid. Should international students be allowed access to university scholarships and departmental scholarships; and if so, what should be the qualification criteria? Student services. What services specifically geared toward the international students must be provided by the university, and who should bear the cost of providing these services? (For example, should international students be charged a fee to pay for these services?) Housing. Does the university have an obligation to ensure that the housing needs of international students are met via specific campus and off-campus arrangements? Curricular and Program Relevance. Does the university have an obligation to the international student to make every arrangement possible (without disrupting its basic academic programs geared toward the domestic clientele) to provide international students access to courses/programs designed for their needs? (For example, a critical omission among graduate programs is the provision of public administration and management courses for international students. The need for such courses is considerable considering that an overwhelming majority of international students who return home end up in administrative and managerial positions that often demand sophisticated administrative and managerial skills permeated with originality and initiative as they confront problems unique to the political/economic circumstance of Third World nations. ( Dunnett, 1982) Practical Training and Return. Does the university have an obligation to develop programs and services (even if only at the basic level of information exchange akin to that provided by campus career placement offices) that can assist international students to gain practical training? At the same time, does the university have an obligation toward developing programs that would encourage and assist self-sponsored students to return home rather than remain in the host country? Alumni Contact. Should the university develop an aggressive alumni program for its international students?

8c. Health

An area of research that is woefully underrepresented in the literature (as mentioned earlier) is research pertaining to the health of international students—both physical and mental. Very little is known about the disease pattern among international students and whether the pattern is general (akin to that found among the natives) or whether the pattern is more specific to international students. For example, one can surmise that international students are prone to suffer more from diseases of stress such as stomach ulcers or high-blood pressure than do the rest of the student population. Very little is known about patterns of alcohol and drug use among international students. One again may surmise that given the high incidence of personal depression among international students their use of alcohol and drugs may be at levels higher than that for the native students. Or the reverse may also be true, given that many international students come from cultures where use of alcohol and drugs is (in comparison to Western nations) at very low levels.

While some research on the mental health of international students exists, as mentioned earlier, there is need to expand it. Mental health (to be understood here in its broad sense) is in many respects culture bound—especially when it comes to treatment. (see Prince, 1973) This, therefore, necessitates an understanding of the varied counseling needs of the different nationalities represented among international students.

8d. Postsojourn Issues

How does the international student fare after returning home? What problems does he/she encounter in terms of "counter culture-shock"?; locating a job; making use of his/her training and so on. These and other issues pertain to what may be termed as postsojourn issues, and here once again, research is still in its infancy, and requiring redress. One organization that has begun to concern itself with these matters, the National Association for Foreign Student Affairs, has published a very helpful monograph on the subject. (Hood and Schieffer, 1983) In it a number of very pertinent topics are covered such as the professional reintegration of women, developing a professional library, continuing research and publication and so on. (Other studies relevant to this area of research include Adler, 1981; Bochner, Lin, and McLeod, 1980; Gama and Pedersen, 1977; and Martin, 1984)

## 9. Political Economy of International Study

The issues of further research raised here so far, are issues that are still within the realm of traditional student research. The dramatic increase in the population of international students throughout the world over the last decade, however, has brought forth an area of research that before would not have been necessary or possible to conduct because the numbers of international students was not large enough. This new area of research may be termed "the political economy of international study." The principal objective of this research area would be twofold: to begin the examination in depth of a host of questions that pertain to the macro-level dimension of international study (in contrast to the micro-level dimension represented by such concerns as factors inhibiting satisfactory social adjustment, or evaluating the effectiveness of an orientation program for international students, etc.); and to enlist the theoretical and conceptual tools of a variety of relevant disciplines in the social sciences (economics, politics, sociology, etc.) for the task of examining phenomena pertinent to international study. In other words a political economy of international study is a research area that aims at examining the macro-level aspects of international study through an interdisciplinary approach characterized by sound methodologies. What then are the main elements for further research (since some sporadic research has already started in this area--see, for example, Williams, (1981), and Barber, Altbach, and Myers (1984) that would constitute the research agenda for this new area that we have termed political economy of international study? They include the following:

### 9a. Economic Cost-Benefit Analysis--Host-Country

As a consequence of two unrelated factors: the rapid increase in international student flows and the world economic recession experienced by many countries throughout the world, including the host nations of the West, governments and institutions among the host nations have begun to raise the issue of the cost of educating thousands of international students at the expense of the taxpayers. Several important studies relating to this theme include that issued by the Canadian Bureau for International Education in 1977; the Grubel and Scott U.S.A. study (1977) and the research by Mark Blaug (1981) in England.

### 9a.1 Costs

At the outset it is important to note, as Blaug (1981) points out, that, unlike in most other situations where costs are relatively easy to determine, in the case of international students costs are just as difficult to calculate as the benefits. Therefore, it is necessary to point out, following Blaug, the key points of economic analysis that must be considered when undertaking research in this area:

(1) The difference between marginal costs and average costs, and their relative importance must be determined. If the problem is to assess capacity in educational institutions and ways and means of using excess capacity, or conversely reducing excess pressure on limited capacity, then analysis must center on the calculation of marginal costs--that is, the additional cost incurred as a consequence of either adding or subtracting a student from the total student population. If on the other hand, the issue is to determine how much subsidy that the institutions must receive (from whatever source: public or private)-- since almost all institutions of higher education rely on some sort of subsidy--then it is the average cost that is of importance. That is, the cost calculated in terms of per capita total capital plus recurrent expenditure.

(2) The relationship between marginal costs and marginal savings is not necessarily a one-to-one relationship; that is, the relationship is not always an inverse one. The reason is that cutbacks in student enrollment cannot always be matched by corresponding cutbacks in staff--especially tenured staff.

(3) The calculation of costs and savings has to take into consideration the fact that the distribution of international students by fields of study (as well as institutions) is not an even one. For example, in the United Kingdom international students at the graduate level comprise nearly 57.6% of total enrollment in the fields of engineering and technology, while only 16.1% in education. (Williams, 1981) And it is a well-known fact that the cost of providing training in engineering is significantly higher than that of training in education.

(4) The calculation of costs and savings is further bedeviled by the problem of determining teaching costs and research costs. In all research universities it is an accepted understanding that teaching staff will devote some of their time (ranging anywhere from 50% or less, to 75% or more) to research, and it follows, therefore, that an increase or decrease in student enrollment will have an impact on research costs. These costs will also vary by field of study.

### 9a.2 Benefits

Turning now to the calculation of benefits, the research situation becomes even more complex. Thus any calculation of benefits accruing to the host country from the pressures of international students must devise appropriate methodology to measure the following key dimensions of benefits:

(1) International students at the graduate level provide benefits through the research they carry out in the process of producing their doctoral dissertations (and in some cases Masters' theses), especially considering that they tend to be concentrated in fields such as engineering sciences, computer sciences, medicine, and so on. The problem here is to determine the value to the host country of this research.

(2) A sizable number of international students provide research assistance (as well as teaching assistance) through their roles as stipended research/teaching assistants in their institutions. These assistants provide labor to their academic institutions at a lower cost than full-time professional staff.

(3) If the international research assistant or teaching assistant received his or her pregraduate level education outside the host-country, then the host-country is deriving further benefit in that it did not have to pay for this part of the student's education.

(4) The host-country derives benefits from those international students who are legitimately granted residence/work permits because of their much needed services in the economy--that is, as long as their pregraduate level education was undertaken outside the host-country.

(5) If the host-country is in a situation of a chronic balance of payments deficit (as for example the U.S. today) then the host-country benefits from the foreign exchange they bring in. The benefit can become more dramatic, however, when viewed from the perspective of a state-level economy (as in the situation of the U.S. where the economy is spatially fragmented). Thus, for example, the state of New York (a state with many international students) received for a nine-month period during the academic year of 1982/83 foreign exchange equivalent to 145 million dollars in the form of living expenses. (Institute of International Education, 1983)

(6) If the large population of international students leads to an increase in export orders for goods produced in the host-country in the long run, via alumni preference for host-country goods, then the host country will benefit. The problem here, of course, is the construction of an appropriate methodology to measure this benefit--an immensely difficult task.

(7) A benefit almost impossible to calculate (at least in monetary terms) but one that perhaps does exist, is that of cross-cultural understanding and enlightenment that the host-population would derive from the presence of international students--as long as, of course, an effort is made to produce positive contact. Much closer to the feasibility of placing a numerical figure on this type of benefit is the kind of benefit derived from a program such as that operated by the Oregon State System of Higher Education. Under this

program needy international students earn tuition assistance credit by providing 80 hours of educational service per academic year. And educational service is broadly defined to include providing assistance to local schools with their cross-cultural programs, advising the Oregon import/export business community, and so on. (See Van de Water, 1983)

To conclude this section, it is important to stress that in undertaking calculations of this type--that is, cost-benefit analysis of the presence of international students--the implication is not that there is an automatic case for doing away with international students if the finding is that the cost far outweighs the benefit (from the perspective of economics). What it does imply is that whatever other reasons that may be adduced in favor of the presence of international students (foreign aid; foreign policy, etc.), they will have to be made more explicit and convincing to the taxpayer. Thus, for example, if it is a question of foreign aid, then it may well be more sensible for the host country to provide funds for development of educational facilties within the home-country.

## 9b.   Economic Cost-Benefit Analysis--Home-Country

Just as the economic recession has impelled host-nations to subject previously unquestioned expenditures to cost-benefit calculations, the home-countries (many of which are in the Third World, and hence in even more serious economic crisis than the host countries) need to undertake cost-benefit analysis of their international student programs. To our knowledge no one has as yet done a thorough study of this area, though the work of Maliyamkono, et al. (1982) does touch on the subject.

### 9b.1 Costs

In determining the costs from the perspective of the Third World the problems that the prospective researcher would encounter would not only be those of methodology (akin to those pertaining to host-country cost-benefit calculations) but also of access to statistical data. The dearth of relevant statistical data in the Third World on many issues is legendary. Assuming that some data were available then the key elements of the calculations relating to the cost side of the equation would be the following:

(1) Marginal costs (assuming that the home-country has some comparable educational facilities available) must be calculated and compared with the cost of sending the student abroad. If the country does not have comparable educational facilties (for example, the home-country university may not have a medical department to train doctors) then the average cost must be calculated and compared with the cost of sending the student abroad. Since it is unlikely that the cost of sending the student abroad will be greater than the average cost of training him or her at home (because if this was so one can assume that the home-country would quickly establish the relevant facility) the average cost must be calculated in terms of

projections over a number of years. This of course will involve further calculations of two types: projections of economic growth and projections of person-power demand. The question then arises as to whether the number of years are too many (before the average cost begins to equal that of the cost of sending the student abroad) to warrant an immediate establishment of the facility in question, or whether the number of years are few enough to justify development of the facility.

(2) Considering the heavy reliance by Third World countries on imports for almost all of their needs (including the raw materials that go into manufacturing--given the import dependent import-substitution stategies that were pursued by many Third World countries in the late fifties and sixties) a very important cost that these countries have to take into consideration is that of foreign exchange outlays. If the shortage of foreign exchange is critical (which is the case for most nonoil-producing Third World nations today) then there arises the need for comparing costs between international study among the industrialized countries, and international study among the more advanced of the Third World countries (such as India), in order to conserve the scarce foreign exchange. This would of course entail curtailing the freedom of choice of the student (including the privately funded student) regarding which host-country to go to.

(3) The cost of nonreturning students must be taken into consideration. This involves calculating the cost of educating the student plus life-time contributions foregone, and then compared against the benefit of money sent back to relatives by the student (something that is common among Third World student nonreturnees whose relatives are still at home).

(4) The cost of sending a student to a host country using a different medium of instruction from that used by the student must also be factored in cases where this happens. (As, for example, in the case of students from Saudi Arabia going to study in the United States.)

In addition to these costs, mention must also be made of those costs that are almost impossible to measure but are never the less observable. These costs include: returnees helping to forge new personal consumption patterns learnt from the affluent host countries of the West but wholly inappropriate to the home country's level of economic development; returnees helping to implement development stategies appropriate to the circumstances of the host-country but not the home-country (for example, advocacy of capital-intensive production techniques in situations of scarce capital but abundant labor supply); returnees becoming a political liability as a result of a mismatch between their rising expectations generated through life-experience in the host-country, and the reality of the situation facing them upon returning to the home-country--consequently leading them to embark on a course of political destabilization; and so on. Many of these issues are discussed in further detail in Kumar (1980), albeit not with specific reference to the international student.

### 9b.2  Benefits

We now turn to a discussion of benefits, and here once again the methodological implications involved are without doubt daunting.  Among the benefits that require analysis are the following:

(1) The benefit of new knowledge and skills gained, and their application in employment, must be calculated.  This would require comparison with similar workers who received their training locally (that is, where such workers exist).  It should be noted that a subjective assessment by employers of the relative productive worth of the two sets of workers is a method not to be favored if one is to go by the example of Maliyamkono, et al. (1982).  (In taking this methodological route, they found an overwhelming tendency for locally trained employers to favor locally trained workers, and vice versa.)  A method that insures productivity more objectively would have to be devised—perhaps along the lines of comparing production output between those units under over-seas trained management.  (One fairly easy study, for example, that can be conducted along this principle is to compare the research output of locally trained university staff with that of the overseas trained university staff).  Another alternative would be to devise some form of time and motion study.  Of course the problem would be greatly simplified if the conventional micro-economic approach of using times and correlating them with place of training is used as a basis for calculating benefits, although this approach also has a number of problems.

(2) In those situations where the home country had no choice but to send its students abroad for higher education because of the lack of appropriate facilties, then of course benefit can be measured in terms of those workers (who invariably are foreign) that they replace after returning home.

(3) Benefits accrue to the home country in those situations where international study is funded not by the home country, but by the host country through some form of bilateral aid.  Here the only cost to be taken into consideration would be costs such as those relating to appropriateness of training received, etc.

As with the costs, there are also benefits that are almost impossible to measure.  An example is the general personal and intellectual development the individual undergoes as a result of foreign travel—an individual benefit that also has an indirect benefit for the home country.

It will be noted, for reasons that are clear, that the calculation of costs and benefits for the home country is infinitely more difficult than that for the host country.  Yet a cost-benefit analysis for the home countries of the Third World is sorely needed as their economies slowly grind to a halt as a result of a combination of past errors and malpractices, and the present global economic recession.

## 9c. International Students and Foreign Aid

An important issue that for long had remained implicit in the process of allowing Third World international students to come and study in the institutions of the advanced host country (immaterial of whether the students are self-supported of officially sponsored) has been that of providing development assistance to the Third World. However, further research is necessary to determine how best this assistance can be provided—assuming that the host country does feel obligated to provide such a form of assistance and the home country is willing to receive such aid. (A number of studies that have raised issues pertinent to this area include Danckwortt, 1980; Fry, 1984; Hunter, 1981; Jenkins, 1983; Oxenham, 1981; United Kingdom, 1980; and Williams, 1981b.) A number of pertinent issues that arise on this matter include the following:

(1) There is the issue of the relevance of training that the international student obtains that needs to be considered. It is necessary to evaluate this training and determine ways of redressing weaknesses with regard to relevance.

(2) There is need to provide opportunities for practical training—following completion of formal classroom studies—both legal measures (relax regulations that restrict work) and develop liaison programs between institutions and industry.

(3) Consideration must be given toward developing measures to dissuade international students from remaining in the country following completion of their studies—and this is especially important in the case of those students who are considered to be bright (that is, the ones who are most likely to be granted residence permits by the host-country).

(4) In keeping with the democratic traditions of the host-nations, channels must be developed to extend aid to those Third World students who would ordinarily be bypassed by bilateral scholarship programs as well as home-country state-sponsored scholarship programs. This may happen for a variety of reasons, such as political discrimination, or racial discrimination, etc. Such students would necessarily be needy, but they would also be exceptionally promising.

(5) Similarly, there is also need to focus attention on those groups of nations that are finding it incresingly difficult to finance international study for their students in the face of rising tuition costs, that is, the nonoil-producing nations such as Tanzania, or Guatemala, or Sri Lanka.

(6) A very pertinent question that requires research attention in this area is that of the benefit to the host-country of providing foreign aid of this type (that is, providing access to study facilities). Does aid here constitute merely a humanitarian gesture or can other grounds be adduced in its support? For example, such aid helps to create allies, develop (indirectly) democratic forms of government and thereby promote world peace and stability, and

perhaps most important of all assist in the economic development of these nations. The importance of the last point cannot be over-emphasized. The development of Third World nations to levels where they can play the same role for capital investment and commodity markets as do the industrialized host-nations with respect to each other, can only be in the long-term benefit of the host-nations.

Turning now to the perspective of the home-country on the issue of foreign aid, there is need for research to be directed toward consideration of matters such as the following:

(1) They must consider alternative places (that is, other Third World nations) to educate their students, and thereby lessen the problems of excessive foreign exchange costs, incompatible curricula, and even cultural dependency. Hence a bilateral aid program, for example, may be made to have provisions for students to be sent to a third country.

(2) Measures must be developed to assist in decreasing the tendency for overseas trained nationals to exacerbate inequality--international students upon returning home tend to become members of a "super-elite" within the Third World.

(3) In the case of countries such as India with fairly well-developed higher education systems, it is necessary to devise measures that prevent foreign-exchange leakage by allowing access to it only in those circumstances where there is determination of a bona fide need for the type of training the student wishes to undertake abroad.

(4) It is necessary for Third World nations to develop programs that would encourage privately sponsored students to return home rather than becoming part of the "brain drain."

## 9d. International Students and Foreign Policy

International students, for the host-country, comprise an additional element in the realm of diplomacy and foreign policy. A concrete example of this relates to Guinea-Bissau and the U.S. As soon as it became clear (following the 1980 coup in Guinea-Bissau) that the new administrators wished to realign themselves away from their long-time benefactor, the Soviet Union, the United States quickly began an aid program for Guinea-Bissau, the most important element of which included scholarships to students in Guinea-Bissau to come and study in the U.S. The U.S. thereby established both a tangible relationship--as well as an intangible one--of the sort that comes with having top-level foreign administrators as alumni of one's own institutions.

Of course the matter of furthering the foreign-policy interests of the host-country (in terms of cultivating allies, trading partners, etc.) through the education of international students is in a sense an act of faith. It is almost impossible to evaluate accurately the extent to which international students develop long-term positive attitudes toward the host-country, and thereafter translate these attitudes into positive behavior after returning home.

Of intriguing interest in this area is the question of determining the extent to which the presence of large numbers of international students from a given country acts to stabilize relations between the country and the host-country. For example, could it be that the presence of a large number of international students from Iran during the Iranian hostage crisis helped to prevent the crisis from deteriorating any further than it did?

## Conclusion

In addition to the areas of further research that we have discussed so far in Sections 7 and 8 above, it is necessary to observe that there are a number of other areas in which research of almost any kind (including the traditional socio-psychological and adaptation variety) is severely lacking. These areas include the following:

(a) International students studying in other Third World Countries. As mentioned earlier in the essay, there is a sizable flow of international students between Third World countries themselves. Do these students exhibit the same kinds of problems as do those Third World students who come to study in the industrialized nations? Do they receive a more relevant education than do those who study in the industrialized nations? These and many other questions need to be asked and answered. (One study that has been done in this area is that by Ganguli (1975) which looks at international students in India. Another relevant study is that by Hafeez-Zaidi, which examines the cross-cultural problems of social adjustment of international students in Pakistan. (see Hafeez-Zaidi (1975)

(b) International students involved in miltiary training. A significant amount of training aid via bilateral agreements takes the form of military training assistance. Very little is known about the nonmilitary aspects of this training—that is, aspects such as the attitudes and adjustment problems of the Third World trainees.

(c) International students studying in China and Eastern Bloc countries—specifically international students from the noncommunist countries. The flow of international students to the communist countries is fairly large, and yet the amount of research on such students is very meagre indeed. (See Table 4) Whatever little is known has tended to portray the experience of studying in these countries as usually less than satisfactory. (See, for example, Robinson, 1982)

(d) Female international students. The general increase in the participation in higher education by women throughout the world over the years has also been reflected in a general increase in the number of female international students to the point where, in a country such as the U.S., roughly one out of every three international students are female. Yet despite this trend very little attempt is made by researchers to disaggregate variables and data by gender. Female international students, by virtue of their gender, encounter special problems both in the host-countries, and upon return in the home-countries. Research on female international students must also include research on that group of women who do not go overseas as students but as spouses. A pertinent study to this end, for example, is that by Ntiri (1979), who discusses the efforts of wives of African international students in the U.S. to upgrade their education. (See also Rowe and Sjoberg, 1981)

(e) Informal international students. This is a category of people who are not students in the strictest sense of the word, but yet they form part of what (Vente, 1981) calls "nonorganized" exchange. These are people who go abroad on assignment by their employers (either the government, or an international organization, or a multi-national corporation). Research needs to be undertaken toward both a factual documentation of the direction and magnitude of this kind of international flow, and the similarities and dissimilarities between the cross-cultural problems they encounter, and those that ordinary international students encounter.

## TABLE 4

### The Flow of International Students from Third World Countries (Non-Communist) to China and Eastern Bloc Countries (1965 and 1967)

Countries and Region of Destination

| Home Regions | U.S.S.R. | | Eastern Europe | | China | | Total | |
|---|---|---|---|---|---|---|---|---|
| | 1965 | 1979 | 1965 | 1979 | 1965 | 1979 | 1965 | 1979 |
| Africa | 5,065 | 14,690 | 2,800 | 12,400 | 275 | 240 | 8,140 | 27,330 |
| Asia | 2,310 | 6,660 | 965 | 3,060 | 175 | 95 | 3,450 | 9,815 |
| Latin America | 935 | 2,860 | 305 | 2,150 | – | – | 1,240 | 5,010 |
| Middle East | 2,125 | 6,745 | 955 | 6,405 | 5 | 10 | 3,085 | 13,160 |
| Total | 10,435 | 30,955 | 5,025 | 24,015 | 455 | 345 | 15,915 | 55,315 |

Source: Based on data from the National Foreign Assessment Center, Central Intelligence Agency, 1980

As we conclude this essay, an issue that we need to address in terms of the future is that of international student numbers. It seems to us that the rapid increases in the numbers of international students witnessed during the past decade will inevitably slow, and indeed there is evidence from the U.S. and Britain that rates of increase have already slowed. As opportunities for domestic study in some of the large sending nations such as Nigeria, Malaysia, and Venezuela grow, more of their students will remain at home for their higher education. It is also likely that economic necessity and national priorities will cause additional countries to restrict the exit of their nationals for overseas study—as India has done in recent years. It is also possible that some of the host-nations may raise their fees so high as to deter international students from studying in these countries. Recent trends in Britain, traditionally the country of choice for many Commonwealth students, indicate that the fee increases did in fact direct students to other countries.

Similarly, as circumstances and policies change, the mix of international students is also likely to change. We observe for example that in the U.S. with fewer Iranians and Nigerians coming to study, their numbers have been partly made up by Malaysians and an ever growing number of Chinese students from Hong Kong, Taiwan, and other Southeast Asian nations. The People's Republic of China has increased the numbers of its students studying abroad dramatically.

In determining the magnitude and direction of future international student flow the orientations of the major donor agencies in the industrialized nations will also play an important role. During the 1960s, agencies such as the U.S. Agency for International Development, the Ford Foundation, Britain's Overseas Development Administration, and others placed greater emphasis on the training of high-level personnel and provided more scholarships and other assistance to higher education; and while this is no longer so, there are signs that this may be changing.

While it is difficult to predict the economic circumstances or political imperatives that might account for future shifts, given current trends, it seems unlikely that the rates of increase of recent years can be sustained, but it is also unlikely that the absolute numbers of international students will significantly decline. It is likely that numbers will modestly grow, although the configuration of sending and receiving countries may fairly significantly alter and the fields of specialization may change as well.

This essay has presented a multifaceted overview of issues related to international students and foreign study. We have pointed to some of the priorities for future research. Without question, the topic is of considerable importance as a policy issue and as a matter for applied concern by professionals working with international students. It is our conviction that research on international students has achieved some level of coherence and sophistication with a potential for yielding some fruitful generalizations. Further there is an emerging research community, consequently this is a field that has the potential to "come of age" and in this sense it would be a significant development. Of course much still remains to be done, as we have pointed out.  There is a need to temper the heavy, policy-oriented research that has been the hallmark of research on international students over the last two to three decades, with academic, theory-oriented research, if generalizations are to be generated—something that has not been easy to do with past research—and by way of providing methodological guidance.

The issue of methodology is a crucial one; it must be stressed.  For it has been among the major weaknesses of past research.  The problem has not simply been of proper or "scientific" research designs for many of the studies undertaken but also of formulation of research questions themselves—arising primarily out of the failure to perceive the fundamentally "behavorial" character of much of the data required for the purposes of the studies that were undertaken in the areas of cross-cultural contact and social adjustment.  It is the kind of data that is immensely difficult to operationalize because of the complexity of the variables involved, ranging as they do from the personality of the person to the characteristics of the cultural environment.

## REFERENCES

Adler, N.  Re-entry:  Managing Cross-Cultural Transitions.  Group and Organization Studies, 1981, 6, 341-356.

Akoff, A., Thaver, F., and Elkind, L.  Mental Health and Counseling ideas of Asian and American students.  Journal of Counseling Psychology, 1966, 13, 219-223.

Alexander, A. A., et al.  Psychotherapy and the Foreign Student.  In P. P. Pedersen, et al. (Eds.), Counseling Across Cultures.  Honolulu: University Press of Hawaii, 1981, pp. 227-246.

Altbach, P. G.  The Dilemma of Success:  Higher Education in Advanced Developing Countries.  Prospects, 1983, 12, 293-312.

Altbach, P. G.  The University as Center and Periphery.  Teachers College Record, 1981, 82, 601-621.

Altekar, A. S.  Education in Ancient India.  Benares:  Kishore, 1948.

American Council on Education.  Foreign Student and Institutional Policy: Toward an Agenda for Action.  Washington, D.C.:  Author, 1982.

Anthony, M. W.  Suspension of Deportation:  A Revitalized Relief for the Alien (Kamheangpatiyooth vs. Immigration and Naturalization Service).  San Diego Law Review, 1980, 18, 65-88.

Australian Government.  Committee of Review of Private Overseas Student Policy.  Mutual Advantage.  Canberra:  Australian Government Publishing Service, 1984.

Babiker, I. E., Cox, J. L., and Miller, P. M.  The Measurement of Cultural Distance and its Relationship to Medical Consultations, Symptomatology and Examination Performance of Overseas Students at Edinburgh University.  Social Psychiatry, 1980, 15, 109-116.

Bachman, E.  Approaches to International Education.  New York: Macmillan, 1984.

Bailey, K. M., Pialorsi, F., and Zukowski-Faust, J.  Foreign Teaching Assistants in U.S. Universities.  Washington, D.C.:  National Association for Foreign Student Affairs, 1984.

Barber, Elinor, Altbach, P. G., and Myers, R. G. (Eds.)  Bridges to Knowledge:  Foreign Students in Comparative Perspective.  Chicago: University of Chicago Press, 1984.

Baron, M.  The Relevance of U.S. Graduate Programs to Foreign Students from Developing Countries.  Washington, D.C.:  National Association for Foreign Student Affairs, 1979.

Becker, T. Black Africans and Black Americans on an American Campus: the African View. Sociology and Social Research, 1973, 57, 168-181.

Bedrosian, A. Alien Status: Legal Issues and Institutional Responsibilities. In Jenkins, H. M., et al., Educating Students from Other Nations: American Colleges and Universities in International Educational Interchange. San Francisco: Jossey-Bass, 1983, pp. 163-83.

Benson, A. G. On-the-job Behavior of College and University Foreign Student Advisers as Perceived by Knowledgeable Faculty Members. Unpublished doctoral dissertation, Michigan State University, 1968.

Berendzen, R. Ethics in International Higher Education. In M. C. Baca and R. H. Stein (Eds.), Ethical Principles, Practices and Problems in Higher Education. Springfield, Illinois: Thomas, 1983, pp. 80-98.

Bie, K. N. Norwegian Students at British Universities—A Case Study of the Academic Performances of Foreign Students. Scandinavian Journal of Education of Education Research, 1976, 20, 1-24.

Blaug, M. The Economic Cost and Benefits of Overseas Students. In P. Williams (Ed.), The Overseas Student Question: Studies for a Policy. London: Heinemann, 1981, pp. 47-90.

Bochner, S. Cultural Diversity: Implications for Modernization and International Education. In K. Kumar (Ed.), Bonds Without Bondage. Honolulu: University Press of Hawaii, 1979, pp. 231-56.

Bochner, S., Lin, A., and McLeod, B. M. Anticipated Role Conflict of Returning Overseas Students. Journal of Social Psychology, 1980, 110, 265-272.

Boer, E. E. Some Psychosocial Factors Affecting Adaptation and Orientation of Foreign Students. In S. C. Dunnett (Ed.), Factors Affecting the Adaptation of Foreign Students in Cross Cultural Settings. Buffalo: Council on International Studies, State University of New York at Buffalo, 1981, pp. 34-58.

Bourdieu, P., and Passeron, J. C. Reproduction in Education, Society and Culture. London: Sage, 1977.

Bowman, J. S. Learning About American Government: Attitudes of Foreign Students. Teaching Political Science, 1978, 5, 181-191.

Boyan, D. (Ed.). Profiles: The Foreign Student in the United States. New York: Institute of International Education, 1981.

Brickman, W. W. Foreign Students in American Elementary and Secondary Schools. Philadelphia: International House, Ogontz Plan Committee, 1967.

Brickman, W. W. Two Millenia of International Relations in Higher Education. Norwood, Pennsylvania: Norwood Editions, 1975.

Brislin, R. Outcomes, Human Relations, and Contributions to Task Effectiveness as Key Variables in Educational Exchanges. In German Academic Exchange Service, Research on Exchanges: Proceedings of the German-American Conference at Wissenschafts-Zentrum, Bonn, November 24-28, 1980. Bonn: Author, 1980.

Brown, M. A. U.S. Students Abroad. In H. M. Jenkins, et al. Educating Students from Other Nations: American Colleges and Universities in International Interchange. San Francisco: Jossey-Bass, 1983, pp. 65-86.

Business Higher Education Forum. Engineering Manpower and Education: Foundation for Future Competitiveness. Washington, D.C.: American Council on Education, 1982.

Canadian Bureau for International Education. A Question of Self-Interest: A Statement on Foreign Students in Canada. Ottawa: 1977.

Carrigan, O. The Right Mix: The Report of the Commission on Foreign Student Policy in Canada. Ottawa, Canadian Bureau for International Education, 1977.

Christensen, G. C. and Thielen, T. B. Cross-Cultural Activities: Maximising the Benefits of Educational Interchange. In Jenkins, H. M., et al., Educating Students from Other Nations: American Colleges and Universities in International Educational Interchange. San Francisco: Jossey-Bass, 1983, pp. 210-36.

Cobban, A. B. The Medieval Universities: Their Development and Organization. London: Methuen, 1975.

Coelho, G. V. An Investigation of the Consequences of International Educational Exchanges. Washington, D.C.: U.S. Department of Health, Education, and Welfare, National Institute of Mental Health, 1973.

Cole, J. B., Allen, F. C. L., and Green, J. S. Survey of Health Problems of Overseas Students. Social Science and Medicine. Pt.A, Medical Sociology, 1980, 14, 627-631.

Coleman, J. S. Professional Training and Institution Building in the Third World. Comparative Education Review, 1984, 28, 180-202.

Collin, A. E. Education for National Development: Effects of U.S. Technical Training Programs. New York: Praeger, 1979.

Coombs, P. The Fourth Dimension of Foreign Policy: Education and Cultural Affairs. New York: Harper and Row, 1964.

Cooper, K.  Increasing the International Relevance of U.S. Education.  In H. M. Jenkins, et al., Educating Students from Other Nations.  San Francisco:  Jossey-Bass, 1983, pp. 277-94.

Cowser, R. L., Jr.  Foreign Student:  New Nigger on Campus.  Community College Review 1978, 6, 4-7.

Crespi, Leo P.  The Effectiveness of the Exchange Program.  Washington, D.C.:  U.S. Information Agency, Office of Research, 1978.

Dagnino, E.  Cultural and Ideological Dependence:  Building a Theoretical Framework.  In K. Kumar (Ed.), Transnational Enterprises:  Their Impact on Third World Societies and Cultures.  Boulder, Colorado:  Westview Press, 1980, pp. 297-322.

Danckwortt, D.  Where Does Educational Aid for the Third World Stand at the End of the Second Development Decade.  In Institute for Foreign Cultural Relations, International Cultural Relations--Bridge Across Frontiers:  Symposium '80:  A Documentation.  Stuttgart:  Author, 1980, pp. 125-28.

Dedijar, S.  "Early" Migration.  In W. Adams (Ed.), The Brain Drain.  New York:  Macmillan, 1968.

Deutsch, S. E.  International Education and Exchange:  A Sociological Analysis.  Cleveland, Ohio:  Case Western Reserve University, 1970.

Dixon, R., et al.  Controversial Issues in Interpreting Foreign Academic Records.  College and University, 1976, 51, 462-468.

Dodge, B.  Al-Azhar:  A Millennium of Muslim Education.  Washington, D.C.:  Middle East Institute, 1961.

Dolibois, J. E.  Alive and Well:  International Alumni Program. International Educational and Cultural Exchange, 1976, 11, 32-34.

Dunnett, S. C.  A Study of the Effects of an English Language Training and Orientation Program on Foreign Student Adaptation.  In S. C. Dunnett (Ed.), Factors Affecting the Adaptation of Foreign Students in Cross-Cultural Settings.  Buffalo, New York:  Council on International Studies, State University of New York at Buffalo, 1981.

Dunnett, S. C.  Management Skills Training for Foreign Engineering Students:  An Assessment of Need and Availability.  Washington, D.C.:  National Association for Foreign Student Affairs, 1982.

Ebbers, K. D. and Peterson, D. M.  The Seductivity of Stereotypes: Examining American Attitudes Toward Foreign Students.  In S. C. Dunnett (Ed.), Factors Affecting the Adaptation of Foreign Students in Cross Cultural Settings.  Buffalo, New York:  Council on International Studies, State University of New York at Buffalo, 1981, pp. 176-90.

Fisher, S. H. and Dey, W. J. Forged Educational Credentials: A Sorry Tale. New York: World Education Services, 1979.

Fiske, E. B. Ethical Issues in Recruiting Students. New Directions for Higher Education, 1981, 9, 41-48.

Flack, J. Results and Effects of Study Abroad. Annals of the American Academy of Political and Social Science, 1976, 424, 107-115.

Fouad, A. A. and Jones, E. C. Electrical-Engineering Curriculum and the Education of International Students. IEEE Transactions on Education, 1979, 22, 95-98.

Fraser, S. E. Overseas Students in Australia: Governmental Policies and Institutional Programs. Comparative Education Review, 1984, 28, 279-99.

Fry, G. W. The Economic and Political Impact of Study Abroad. Comparative Education Review, 1984, 28, 203-220.

Fuenzalida, E. U.S. Education for the Third World: How Relevant? World Higher Education Communique, 1981, 4, 15-19.

Gama, E. M. P., and Pedersen, P. Readjustment Problems of Brazilian Returnees from Graduate Studies in the U.S. International Journal of Intercultural Relations, 1977, 1I, 46-59.

Galtung, J. E. The Impact of Study Abroad: A Three-by-Three Nation Study of Cross-Cultural Contact. Journal of Peace Research, 1965, 3I, 258-275.

Ganguli, H. C. Foreign Students: The Indian Experience. New Delhi: Sterling, 1975.

Glaser, W. and Habers, G. C. The Brain Drain: Emigration and Return. New York: Pergamon, 1978.

Glimm, H. and Kuper, W., (Eds.), University, Science and Development in Africa. Bonn: Deutscher Akademischer Austauschdienst, 1980.

Goodwin, C. D. and Nacht, M. Absence of Decision: Foreign Students in American Colleges and Universities. New York: Institute of International Education, 1983.

Goodwin, C. D., and Nacht, M. Fondness and Frustration: The Impact of American Higher Education on Foreign Students with Special Reference to the Case of Brazil. New York: Institute of International Education, 1984.

Gopinathan, S. Intellectual Dependency and the Indigenization Response: Case Studies of Three Disciplines in Two Third World Universities. Unpublished doctoral dissertation, State University of New York at Buffalo, 1984.

Gray, J. H.   The Status of Foreign Students Under the Immigration Act, 1976 (Canada).  McGill Law Journal, 1982, 27, 556-562.

Grubel, H. G., and Scott, A.  The Brain Drain: Determinants, Measurement and Welfare Effects.  Waterloo, Ontario:  Wilfrid Laurier University Press, 1977.

Gullahorn, J. T., and Gullahorn, J. E.   An Extension of the U-curve Hypothesis.  Journal of Social Issues, 1963, 19, 33-47.

Hafeez-Zaidi, S. M.   Adjustment Problems of Foreign Muslim Students in Pakistan.  In R. W. Brislin, S. Bochner, and W. J. Lonner (Eds.), Cross-cultural Perspectives on Learning.  New York:   John Wiley, 1975, pp. 117-30.

Hanson, J. W.  Education Nsukka:  A Study of Institution Building Among the Modern Ibo.  East Lansing, Michigan:  Michigan State University, 1968.

Harari, M.   Priorities for Research and Action in the Graduate Foreign Student Field.  Exchange, 1970, 6, 60-67.

Hasan, R.   Socialization and Cross-Cultural Education (Indo-Pakistani Students Studying in Britain).  Linguistics, 1976, No. 175, 7-25.

Haskins, C. H.  The Rise of Universities.  Ithaca, New York:  Cornell, 1966.

Hawkins, J. N.   Educational Exchanges and the Transformation of Higher Education in the People's Republic of China.  In E. G. Barber, P. G. Altbach, and R. G. Myers (Eds.), Bridges to Knowledge: Foreign Students in Comparative Perspective.   Chicago:   University of Chicago Press, 1984.

Heath, G. L.   Foreign Student Attitudes at International House, Berkeley. Exchange, 1970, 5I, 66-70.

Hegazy, M. E.   Cross-cultural Experience and Social Change:  The Case of Foreign Study.   Unpublished doctoral dissertation, University of Minnesota, 1968.

Heil, D. and Aleamoni, L.   Assessment of the Proficiency in the Use and Understanding of English by Foreign Students as Measured by the Test of English as a Foreign Language.  Urbana, Illinois:  University of Illinois, Office of Instructional Resources, Measurement and Research Division, 1974.

Hensley, T. R. and Sell, D. K.   Study Abroad Program:  An Examination of Impacts on Student Attitudes.  Teaching Political Science, 1979, 6, 387-411.

Hess, Gerhard.   Freshmen and Sophomores Abroad.   New York:   Teachers College, 1982.

Higbee, H. D. The Status of Foreign Student Advising in United States Universities and Colleges. East Lansing: Michigan State University, 1961.

Higginbotham, H. N. Cultural Issues in Providing Psychological Services for Foreign Students in the United States. International Journal of Intercultural Relations, 1979, 31, 49-85.

Hood, M. A. G. and Schieffer, K. J. Professional Integration: A Guide for Students from the Developing World. Washington, D.C.: Education for International Development, National Association for Foreign Student Affairs, 1981.

Hull, W. F., IV. Foreign Students in the United States of America. New York: Praeger, 1978.

Hunter, G. The Needs and Desires of Developing Countries for Foreign Study Facilities: Some Reflections. In P. Williams (ed.) The Overseas Student Question, London: Heinemann, 1981, pp. 135-49.

Institute of International Education. Open Doors 1981/82. New York: Institute of International Education, 1983.

International Research and Exchanges Board. A Balance Sheet for East-West Exchanges: Working Papers. Conference on Scholarly Exchanges with the USSR and Eastern Europe: Two Decades of American Experience, Washington, D.C., 1979). New York: 1980.

Jenkins, H. M. (Ed.) Foreign Student Recruitment: Realities and Recommendations. New York: College Entrance Examination Board, 1980.

Jenkins, H. M. Economics: Analyzing Costs and Benefits. In H. M. Jenkins, et al., Educating Students from Other Nations: American Colleges and Universities in International Educational Interchange. San Francisco: Jossey-Bass, 1983 (a), pp. 237-50.

Jenkins, H. M., et al. Educating Students from Other Nations. San Francisco: Jossey-Bass, 1983. (b)

Jenkins, H. M. Growth and Impact of Educational Interchanges. In H. M. Jenkins, et al. Educating Students from Other Nations. San Francisco: Jossey-Bass, 1983 (c) pp. 4-30.

Jenkins, H. M. Recruitment: Ensuring Educational and Ethical Standards. In H. M. Jenkins, et al., Educating Students from Other Nations. San Francisco: Jossey-Bass, 1983 (d) pp. 113-34.

Jenkins, H. M. (Ed.), The Role of the Foreign Student in the Process of Development. Washington, D.C.: National Association for Foreign Student Affairs, 1983. (e)

Kaplan, R. English as a Second Language: An Overview of the Literature. In E. G. Barber, P. G. Altbach, and R. G. Myers (Eds.), Bridges to

Knowledge:  Foreign Students in Comparative Perspective.  Chicago:
University of Chicago Press, 1984.

Kimmel, P., Ockey, W. C., and Sander, H. J.  Final Report:  International
Training  Assessment  Program.  Washington,  D.C.:  Development
Education and Training Research Institute, 1972.

Klineberg, O.  Mental Health Aspects of International Student Exchange.
In German Academic Exchange Service, Research on Exchanges:  Pro-
ceedings of the German-American Conference at Wissenschafts-Zentrum,
Bonn, November 24-28, 1980.  Bonn:  1980.

Klineberg, O. and Hull, W. F., IV.  At A Foreign University:  An International Study of Adaptation and Coping.  New York:  Praeger, 1979.

Kumagai, F.  The Effects of Cross-Cultural Education on Attitudes and
Personality of Japanese Students, Sociology of Education, 1977, 50,
40-47.

Kumar, K. (Ed.)  Bonds Without Bondage.  Honolulu:  University Press of
Hawaii, 1977.

Kumar, K. (Ed.).  Transnational Enterprises:  Their Impact on Third World
Societies and Cultures.  Boulder, Colorado:  Westview, 1980.

Lee, Motoko Y., et al.  Needs of Foreign Students at U.S. Colleges and
Universities.  Washington, D.C.:  National Association for Foreign
Student Affairs, 1981.

Lockett, B. A.  A Study of the Effectiveness of Foreign Student Advisers
at  American  Colleges  and  Universities  as  Reported  by  Foreign
Students Sponsored by the United States Agency for International
Development.  Unpublished  doctoral  dissertation,  American
University, 1970.

Lysgaard, Sverre.  Adjustment in a Foreign Society:  Norwegian Fulbright
Grantees Visiting the United States.  International Social Science
Bulletin, 1955, 7, 45-51.

Maliyamkono, T. L., et al., Training and Productivity in East Africa:  A
Report of the Eastern African Universities Research Project on the
Impact of Overseas Training and Development.  London:  Heinemann,
1982.

Marion, P. B., Jr. and Thomas, H., Jr.  Residence Hall Proximity to
Foreign Students as an Influence on Selected Attitudes and Behaviors
of American College Students.  Journal of College and University
Student Housing, 1980, 10, 16-19.

Markham, J. W.  International Images and Mass Communication Behavior.
Iowa City:  University of Iowa, School of Journalism, 1967.

Martin, G. M.  A Model for the Cultural and Statistical Analysis of
Academic Achievement of Foreign Graduate Students at the University

of North Carolina at Chapel Hill. Unpublished doctoral dissertation, University of North Carolina, 1971.

Martin, J. N. The Intercultural Re-entry Conceptualization and
Directions for Future Research. International Journal of Intercultural Relations, 1984, 8, 115-134.

Matross, R., et al. American Student Attitudes Toward Foreign Students
Before and During an International Crisis. Journal of College
Student Personnel, 1982, 23, 58-65.

Mazrui, A. A. The African University as a Multi-National Corporation:
Problems of Penetration and Dependency. Harvard Educational Review,
1975, 45, 191-210.

Melnendez-Craig, M. A Study of the Academic Achievement and Related
Problems Among Latin American Students Enrolled in the Major Utah
Universities. Unpublished doctoral dissertation, Brigham Young
University, 1970.

Mestenhauser, J. A. Foreign Students as Teachers: Lessons from the
Program in Learning with Foreign Students. In G. Althen (Ed.),
Learning Across Cultures: Intercultural Communication and
International Educational Exchange. Washington, D.C.: National
Association for Foreign Student Affairs, 1981, pp. 143-50.

Michii, T. N. Problems of Cross-Cultural Education: The Japanese Case.
In S. C. Dunnett (Ed.), Factors Affecting the Adaptation of Foreign
Students in Cross Cultural Settings. Buffalo, New York: Council on
International Studies, State University of New York at Buffalo,
1981, pp. 126-36.

Miller, J. C. African Students and the Racial Attitudes and Practices of
Americans. Unpublished doctoral dissertation, University of North
Carolina, 1967.

Miller, M. H., et al., The Cross-Cultural Student: Lessons in Human
Nature. Bulletin of the Menninger Clinic, 1971, 35, 128-131.

Miller, R. E. A Study of Significant Elements in the On-the-job Behavior
of College and University Foreign Student Advisers. Unpublished
doctoral dissertation, Michigan State University, 1968.

Moock, J. L. Overseas Training and National Development Objectives in
Sub-Saharan Africa. Comparative Education Review, 1984, 28,
221-240.

Myer, R. B. Curriculum: U.S. Capacities, Developing Countries' Needs.
New York: Institute of International Education, 1979.

Myers, R. G. Education and Emigration. New York: McKay, 1972.

National Association for Foreign Student Affairs. An Inquiry into Departmental Policies and Practices in Relation to the Graduate Education of Foreign Students. Washington, D.C.: 1972.

National Foreign Assessment Center, Central Intelligence Agency. Communist Aid Activities in Non-Communist Less Developed Countries 1979 and 1954-79: A Research Paper. Washington, D.C.: Photoduplication Service, Library of Congress, 1980. (Superintendent of Documents #ER80-10318U).

Neff, C. B. (Ed.), New Directions for Experiential Learning: Cross-cultural Learning, No. 11. San Francisco: Jossey-Bass, 1981.

Neville, A. Alienation from the Second Homeland: German Difficulties in Dealing with Foreigners, Western European Education, 1981, 13, 65-69.

Nitri, D. W. Continuing Education Efforts of African Students' Wives in the United States. Journal of the National Association for Women Deans, Administrators, and Counselors, 1979, 42, 16-21.

Nurullah, S. and Naik, J. P. A Student's History of Education in India. Bombay: Macmillan, 1956.

Odenyo, A. O. Africans and Afro-Americans on Campus: A Study of Some of the Relationships Between Minority Sub-communities. Unpublished doctoral dissertation, University of Minnesota, 1970.

Oxenham, J. Study Abroad and Development Policy--An Enquiry. In P. Williams (Ed.), The Overseas Student Question: Studies for a Policy. London: Heinemann, 1981, pp. 150-64.

Paige, R. M. Foreign Students as Learning Resources. In Proceedings of the Central Region Conference on International Agricultural Training. Urbana-Champaign: University of Illinois, 1978.

Parsons, E. A. The Alexandrian Library: Glory of the Hellenic World. Amsterdam: Elsevier, 1952.

Patrick, W. S. Admissions: Developing Effective Selection Practices. In H. M. Jenkins, et al., Educating Students from Other Nations: American Colleges and Universities in International Educational Interchange. San Francisco: Jossey-Bass, 1983, pp. 135-62.

Pedersen, P. Personal Problem Solving Resources Used by University of Minnesota Foreign Students. In S. C. Dunnett, Factors Affecting the Adaptation of Foreign Students in Cross Cultural Settings. Buffalo, New York: Council on International Studies, State University of New York at Buffalo, 1981.

Pierce, F. N. Foreign Student Views and Attitudes Toward Advertising in the United States. Unpublished doctoral dissertation, University of Illinois, 1969.

Prince, R. Mental Health Workers Should be Trained at Home: Some Implications of Transcultural Psychiatric Research. Paper presented at the American Psychological Association Conference, Montreal, August 1973.

Rao, G. L. Brain Drain and Foreign Students: A Study of the Attitudes and Intentions of Foreign Students in Australia, the U.S.A., Canada and France. New York: St. Martin's, 1979.

Rashdall, H. The Universities of Europe in the Middle Ages. London: Oxford University Press, 1936.

Robinson, B. E. and Hendel, D. D. Foreign Students as Teachers: An Untapped Educational Resource. Alternative Higher Education, 1981, 5, 256-269.

Robinson, L. An American in Leningrad. New York: W. W. Norton, 1982.

Roeloffs, K. International Mobility in Higher Education: the Experiences of an Academic Exchange Agency in the Federal Republic of Germany. European Journal of Education, 1982, 17, 27-36.

Rogers, K. A. Alumni Networking. In M. A. G. Hood and K. J. Schieffer, (Eds.), Professional Integration: A Guide for Students from the Developing World. Washington, D.C.: National Association for Foreign Student Affairs, 1983.

Rogers, K. A. Improving the Latin American Engineering Student's Experience in the U.S. University. Washington, D.C.: National Association for Foreign Student Affairs, 1971.

Ronkin, R. R. Modifying the Ph.D Program for Foreign Students. Science 1969, 163, 20.

Rowe, L. and Sjoberg, S. (Eds.) International Women Students: Perspectives for the 80s: Report of the International Womens Student Conference. Washington, D.C.: National Association for Foreign Student Affairs, 1981.

Sauvant, K. P., and Mennis, B. Sociocultural Investments and the International Political Economy of North-South Relations: the Role of Transnational Enterprises. In K. Kumar (Ed.), Transnational Enterprises: Their Impact on Third World Societies and Cultures. Boulder, Colorado, Westview Press, 1980, pp. 275-96.

Sharon, S. T. Test of English As a Foreign Language As a Moderator of Graduate Record Examination Scores in the Prediction of Foreign Student's Grades in Graduate School. Princeton, New Jersey: Educational Testing Service, 1971.

Shaw, R. A. The Stranger in Our Midst: Liability or Asset? Engineering Education, 1982, 72I, 310-313.

Sims, W. A., and Stelcner, M. The Costs and Benefits of Foreign Students in Canada: A Methodology. Ottawa: Canadian Bureau for International Education, 1981.

Smith, S. K. Alien Students in the United States: Statutory Interpretation and Problems of Control. Suffolk Transnational Law Journal, 1981, 5, 235-250.

Smith, A., Woesler de Panafieu, C. and Jarousse, J.-P. Foreign Student Flows and Policies in an International Perspective. In P. Williams (Ed.), The Overseas Student Question: Studies for a Policy. London: Heinemann, 1981, pp. 165-222.

Stauffer, R. B. Western Values and the Case for Third World Cultural Disengagement. In K. Kumar (Ed.), Bonds Without Bondage. Honolulu: University Press of Hawaii, 1979.

Stewart, E. C. American Culture Patterns: A Cross-cultural Perspective. Washington, D.C.: Society for International Education, Training and Research, 1975.

Stone, B. Gaps in Graduate Training of Students From Abroad. Science, 1969, p. 1118.

Story, K. E. The Student Development Professional and the Foreign Student: A Conflict of Values. Journal of College Student Personnel, 1982, 23, 66-70.

Sue, D. W. Eliminating Cultural Oppression in Counseling: Toward a General Theory. Journal of Counseling Psychology, 1978, 25, 419-428.

Sugimoto, R. A. The Relationship of Selected Predictive Variables to Foreign Student Achievement at the University of California, Los Angeles. Unpublished doctoral dissertation, University of Southern California, 1966.

Susskind, C. and Schell, L. Exporting Technical Education: A Survey and Case Study of Foreign Professionals with U.S. Graduate Degrees. New York: Institute of International Education, 1968.

Turner, S. M. (Ed.)., Evaluation of Foreign Educational Credentials and Recognition of Degree Equivalences. Boston: Northeastern University, Center for International Higher Education Documentation, 1979.

Uehara, S. A Study of Academic Achievement of F-1 Classed Aliens and Other Non-immigrant Temporary Students at Kapoilani Community College. Honolulu, Hawaii: Kapoilani Community College, 1969.

Uhlig, S. J., Crofton, H. E. M. and Thompson, J. H. Industrial Training for Kenya: An Evaluation of ODM's Technical Co-operation Programme. London: Ministry of Overseas Development, 1978.

United Kingdom. House of Commons. Foreign Affairs Committee. Overseas Development Sub-committee. Minutes of Evidence Taken Before the Overseas Development Sub-Committee and Appendices. Overseas Student Fees: Aid and Development Implications. London: Her Majesty's Stationery Office, 1980.

Van de Water, J. Financial Aid for Foreign Students: The Oregon Model. National Association for Foreign Student Affairs Newsletter, 1983, 34, pp. 97, 106.

Vente, R. The "Technological Mind" and Other Issues of Current Exchange Research. In German Academic Exchange Service, Research on Exchanges: Proceedings of the German-American Conference at Wissenschaftszentrum, Bonn, November 24-28, 1980. Bonn: 1981, pp. 74-88.

Veysey, L. The Emergence of the American University. Chicago: University of Chicago Press, 1965.

Wakita, K. Asian Studies Survey-Spring 1970. Los Angeles, Los Angeles City College, 1971.

Wallace, W. Overseas Students: The Foreign Policy Implications. In P. Williams (Ed.), The Overseas Student Question: Studies for a Policy. London: Heinemann, 1981.

Weiler, H. The Political Dilemmas of Foreign Study. Comparative Education Review, 1984, 28I, 168-179.

White, S. and White, T. G. Acculturation of Foreign Graduate Students in Relation to Their English Language Proficiency. In S. Dunnett, (Ed.), 105. Factors Affecting the Adaptation of Foreign Students in Cross Cultural Settings. Buffalo: Council on International Studies, 1981, pp. 59-70.

Williams, P. Britain's Full-Cost Policy for Overseas Students. Comparative Education Review, 1984, 28, 258-278.

Williams, P. The Emergence of the Problem: Editorial Introduction. In P. Williams, The Overseas Student Question: Studies for a Policy. London: Heinemann, 1981, pp. 1-21.

Williams, P. (Ed.), The Overseas Student Question: Studies for a Policy. London: Heinemann, 1981.

Williams, P. A Policy for Overseas Students: Analysis-Options-Proposals. London: Overseas Students Trust, 1982.

Winkler, D. R. The Economic Impacts of Foreign Students in the United States. Los Angeles: University of Southern California, School of Public Administration, 1981.

Woolston, V. Administration: Coordinating and Integrating Programs and Services. In H. M. Jenkins, et al., Educating Students from Other

Nations: American Colleges and Universities in International Educational Interchange. San Francisco: Jossey-Bass, 1983.

Yeh, D. K. Paranoid Manifestations Among Chinese Students Studying Abroad: Some Preliminary Findings. In W. P. Lebra (Ed.), Transcultural Research in Mental Health. Honolulu: University Press of Hawaii, 1972.

Zunin, L. M. and Rubin, R. T. Paranoid Psychotic Reactions in Foreign Students from Non-Western Countries. Journal of American College Health Association, 1967, 15, 220-226.

# BIBLIOGRAPHY

GUIDE TO THE USE OF THE BIBLIOGRAPHY

This bibliography is organized according to thirty-seven categories. While we have tried to make these categories as clear as possible, there is inevitable overlap in coverage. The following listing provides a brief definition of each category and an indication, where relevant, of other related categories for cross-reference usage. It is hoped that readers will look under the relevant topics for related materials.

Definitions of Categories and Guide to Cross References Searches

1. Reference and Bibliographical Materials
Includes bibliographies; foreign student handbooks, and guides for students from abroad.

2. General
Includes broad works on foreign students in several countries or in one country but from several countries or broad geographical areas (Asia, Africa, etc.); statistical compilations and analyses. See also "Specific Student Nationality Studies," "Soviet, Chinese, and Eastern European Areas," and the next subcategory and category.

3. Foreign Students in Third World Countries (General materials)
Includes items where a Third World country receives students (e.g., Americans in India.) See also, "Disciplinary Studies, e.g., Medicine and Health.")

4. Community and Junior Colleges
Includes all work specifically on community colleges. Many items here are relevant to other areas of the bibliography.

5. Historical Studies
Includes all items with mainly historical emphasis, including the recent (since 1950) time period if from a historical perspective. Many items here are relevant as background to other topics in the bibliography.

6. Policy of "Sending" Countries
Includes work on national policy and philosophy for sending students abroad, both how and why they should travel. See also, "Economics--Cost and Benefits (Home-Country)" and "Overseas Students and Development."

7. Policy of "Host" Countries
Includes work on national policy and philosophy for receiving foreign students. See also, "Economics--Cost and Benefits (Host-Country)," and "Soviet, Chinese, and Eastern European Areas."

8. Institutional Policy
Includes work on the orientation and philosophy of specific institutions. See also, "Recruitment," "Admission," and "Administration."

9. Economic Aspects: Cost-Benefit Analyses of "Sending" Countries
Includes work on broad economic consequences of sending students abroad both from national and personal perspectives. See also, "Overseas Students and Development," "Migration of Talent," and next category.

10. Economic Aspects: Cost-Benefit Analyses of "Host" Countries
Includes work on the broad economic consequences of receiving foreign students.
See also, "Migration of Talent."

11. Overseas Study and Socioeconomic Development
Attempts to isolate work linking foreign study to the development process. See also, "Attitudinal and Behavioral Studies," and "Curricula and Programs of Study."

12. Legal Issues
Attempts to isolate the technical problems of national policy and cross-cultural contact.

13. Recruitment: Policies and Procedures
Includes works on programs and abuses of recruitment. See also, "Reference," "Evaluation of Credentials," and "Language Problems."

14. Admissions: Policies and Procedures
Includes works on the admission process and standards. Also see, "Reference," "Evaluation of Credentials," and "Language Problems."

15. Evaluation of Credentials and Equivalence of Degrees
Contains works which describe the content of specific nations' educational systems and general discussions of making degrees more uniform. Also see, "Admissions."

16. Finances: Sources and Problems
Focuses on how students are able to pay for their education. Also see, more broadly, the economics section.

17. Health
Includes work on the health problems of studying in a new environment.

18. Counseling Services
Includes work on all forms of counseling—personal and academic. Also see, "Adaptation Problems."

19. Adaptation Problems (The Alien Institutional and Cultural Environment)
Includes many studies of the student fitting into a new environment. Also see, "Attitudinal and Behavioral Studies," "Soviet, Chinese, and Eastern European Areas," and next category.

20. Academic Peformance
Assessment of why students do well or badly academically. Also see, "Evaluation of Credentials," "Adaptation Problems," and "Language Problems."

21. Attitudinal and Behavioral Studies
Attempts to present the broad psychological work on foreign students. Also see, "Adaptation Problems," and "Academic Performance."

22. Cross-Cultural Issues and Activities
Includes broad works on international exchanges and their philosophy. Does not include descriptions of specific international exchange of study abroad programs.

23. Foreign Scholars
Includes work on exchange programs at the higher educational level.

24. Curricula and Programs of Study
Includes broad study of curricula and the debate on their relevance for foreign students. Also see, "Disciplinary Studies."

25. Practical Training
Includes work on nonformal and postgraduate training or work experience of students from abroad.

26. Language Problems
Attempts to include all material that deals with language training, testing, and other problems. Also see, "Admissions," and "Academic Performance."

27. International Educational Exchange and Study Abroad
Attempts to isolate the material on specific study-abroad programs and specific international exchanges primarily at the undergraduate level, including college extensions in foreign countries.

28. Disciplinary Studies (Law, Engineering, Agriculture, etc.)
Includes the curricular and special problems of specific types of disciplines for foreign students when the focus of the work is on the area of study.

29. Medical Study Abroad
Same as the above, but specifically on medical and health staff training.

30. Specific National Studies
Includes work that focuses on a single nationality group studying abroad. Also see, "General," and Attitudinal and Behavioral Studies."

31. Specific Institutional Studies
Deals with foreign students at a specific institution, hence focuses on student problems of those particular institutions.

32. Women International Students
Includes work where women are the primary focus and when the work does not fall into another category. Also see, sections like "Academic Performance," adaptation and attitudes.

33. Studies of Eastern Bloc and Chinese Students
Attempts to include all work on foreign students in these societies. Includes some work in Russian.

34. <u>Return and Re-entry Issues</u>
Includes work on fitting foreign trained personnel into both the social and economic life of their home countries. Also see, "Overseas Students and Development," and "Migration of Talent."

35. <u>Alumni</u>
Work on how institutions of higher education, primarily American, have attempted programs for foreign alumni.

36. <u>Foreign Student Advisors and Personnel</u>
Includes work of the professionalization of a growing academic staff area.

37. <u>Migration of Talent (The "Brain Drain")</u>
A selection of material on "brain drain" issues. Also see, "Problems and Issues of Return of Graduates."

## 1. REFERENCE AND BIBLIOGRAPHICAL MATERIALS

1.  American Association of Collegiate Registrars and Admissions Officers. A Bibliography of Reference Materials for Evaluating Foreign Student Credentials. Washington, D.C.: American Association of Collegiate Registrars and Admissions Officers, 1982. (3rd. ed.)

2.  American Council on Education, Overseas Liaison Committee. International Directory for Educational Liaison. Washington, D.C.: American Council on Education, 1972.

3.  American Field Service. Handbook on Selection for the Americans Abroad Programs. New York: AFS, 1964.

4.  Barnes, Gregory A. The American University: A World Guide. Philadelphia, PA: ISI Press, 1984.

5.  Brickman, William W. Foreign Students in the United States: A Selected and Annotated Bibliography. New York: College Entrance Examination Board, 1963.

6.  Canada, Department of External Affairs. Notes for the Guidance of Students Considering University Study in Canada. Ottawa: Department of External Affairs, 1965.

7.  Canada, Department of External Affairs, Information Division. University Study in Canada. Ottawa: Association of Universities and Colleges of Canada, 1976.

8.  Canadian Bureau for International Education. Guide to Foreign Student Authorization for Canada. Ottawa: CBIE, 1978.

9.  Canadian Bureau for International Education. Guide to Foreign Student Authorization for Canada. Ottawa: CBIE, 1979.

10. Canadian Bureau for International Education. The International Student Handbook. Ottawa: CBIE, 1984.

11. Claire, Elizabeth. A Foreign Student's Guide to Dangerous English. Rochelle Park, New Jersey: Eardley Publications, 1982.

12. College Entrance Guide for American Students Overseas. New York: College Entrance Examination Board, 1975.

13. Committee on International Exchange of Persons, Conference Board of Associated Research Councils. The Directory of Visiting Scholars in the United States. Washington, D.C.: CIEP, 1968.

14. Cornell University. Handbook for Families of Foreign Visitors. Ithaca, NY: Cornell University, 1964.

15. Council for European Studies. Fellowship Guide for Western Europe. Pittsburgh: Council for European Studies, 1971.

16. Council on International Educational Exchange. 1981 Student Travel Catalog. San Francisco: CIEE, 1981.

17. Council on International Educational Exchange. United States of America: Student Travelers' Information. New York: CIEE, 1972.

18. Council on International Educational Exchange. Where to Stay in United States of America. New York: CIEE, 1974.

19. Council on International Educational Exchange. Whole World Handbook, 1973-74. New York: CIEE, 1973.

20. Crabbs, Richard F. and Frank W. Holmquist. United States Higher Education and World Affairs: A Partially Annotated Bibliography. New York: Praeger, 1967.

21. Crew, Anna. Student Guide to North America 1969. New York: British Student Travel Center, 1969.

22. Danilov, Dan P. A Welcome to the United States of America. Seattle, Washington: Welcome Publications, 1978.

23. Dart, Francis, and Michael Moravcsik. The Physics Graduate Student in the United States--A Guide for Prospective Foreign Students. Washington, D.C.: AAPT Press, 1973.

24. Denby, Myrto. Facts for Foreign Students. Washington, D.C.: Foreign Student Service Council, 1965.

25. Duisberg-Gesellschaft. Progress Through Training: Information for Guests from the Third World Coming for Further Training to the Federal Republic of Germany. Bonn: Dummlet, 1977.

26. Donovan, Katherine C. Assisting Students and Scholars from the People's Republic of China: A Handbook for Community Groups. Washington, D.C.: U.S.-China Education Clearinghouse/National Association for Foreign Student Affairs, 1981.

27. Espinosa, J. Manuel. A Selected Bibliography on Educational and Cultural Exchange: With Special Reference to the Programs of the United States Department of State. Washington, D.C.: Bureau of Educational and Cultural Affairs, Department of State, 1975.

28. Felsen, W. L. United States of America West--The Foreign Traveler's Sightseeing Guide to the American West. Stinson Beach, California: Peregrination Press, 1968.

29. Garraty, J. A., L. Von Klemper, and J. H. Taylor. The New Guide to Study Abroad. New York: Harper and Row, 1981.

30. German Academic Exchange Service. Studies at Universities. Bonn: DAAD, no date.

31. Gottschang, Karen Turner. China Bound: A Handbook for American Students, Researchers and Teachers. Washington, D.C.: U.S.-China Education Clearinghouse/National Association for Foreign Student Affairs, 1981.

32. Hawes, G. R. Guide Practique de l'Enseignement Superieur aux Etats-Unis. Paris: Seghers, 1971.

33. Herman, Shirley Yvonne. Guide to Study in Europe: A Selective Guide to European Schools and Universities. New York: Four Winds Press, 1969.

34. Higher Education in the United Kingdom—A Handbook for Students From Overseas and Their Advisors. Essex: Longman, 1978.

35. Howes, Sally B. Employment Guide for Massachusetts Institute of Technology Foreign Students. Cambridge: Massachusetts Institute of Technology Placement Bureau, 1967.

36. Institute of International Education. The Community, Technical and Junior College in the United States: A Guide for Foreign Students. New York: Institute of International Education, 1979.

37. Institute of International Education. The Community and Junior College in the United States. New York: IIE, 1974.

38. Institute of International Education, Information Services Division. Fields of Study in United States Colleges and Universities: A Guide for Foreign Students. New York: IIE, 1979.

39. Institute of International Education. Guides for Foreign Students: Undergraduate Study in the United States: The Four Year College. New York: IIE, 1974.

40. Institute of International Education. Handbook on International Study. New York: IIE, 1969.

41. Institute of International Education. Scholarships and Fellowships for Foreign Study: A Selected Bibliography. New York: IIE, 1980.

42. Institute of International Education. The Two-Year College in the United States—A Guide for Foreign Students. New York: IIE, 1967.

43. Jones, Valarie A. and John Stalker, eds. Interpreting the Black Experience in America to Foreign Students: A Guide to Materials. Washington, D.C.: National Association for Foreign Student Affairs, 1976.

44. Kong, N. H., ed. Overseas Students Handbook. Wellington, New Zealand: New Zealand University Students' Association, 1974.

45. Lockyear, T. N., ed. Postgraduate Training in Australia: Handbook for Overseas Students. Canberra, Australia: Australian Vice Chancellors' Committee, 1982.

46. Miller, Vincent A. The Guidebook for International Trainers in Business and Industry. New York: Van Nostrand Reinhold, 1979.

47. Naciones Unidas, Comision Economica para la America Latina. Bibliografia sobre Emigracion de Personal Catificado en America Latina. Santiago, Chile: Comision Economica para America Latina, 1976.

48. National Association for Foreign Student Affairs. Bibliography on Study, Work and Travel Abroad. Washington, D.C.: National Association for Foreign Student Affairs, 1982.

49. National Association for Foreign Student Affairs. Foreign Student Admissions, Credentials Bibliography. Washington, D.C.: National Association for Foreign Student Affairs, 1979.

50. Organization for Economic Cooperation and Development. Inventory of Training Possibilities in Europe. New York: McGraw-Hill, 1966.

51. Paget, Roger. International Educational Exchanges: Selected Bibliography of Recent Materials. Washington, D.C.: United States International Communication Agency, 1980.

52. Potashnik, Michael. A Guide to Selected Fellowships and Grants for Research on Latin America and the Caribbean. New York: Foreign Area Fellowship Program, 1972.

53. Quigley, Thomas. Directory of United States Catholic Organizations Serving International Students and Visitors. Washington, D.C.: National Catholic Welfare Conference, 1965.

54. Roberts, Dorothy. A Scholar's Guide to Japan. Honolulu, Hawaii: Institute of Student Interchange, University of Hawaii, 1966.

55. Sasnett, Martena and Inez Sepmeyer. Graduate Study in the United States--A Guide for Foreign Students. New York: Institute of International Education, 1972.

56. Seto, Edward and K. C. Tam. Handbook for Students Going Abroad. Hong Kong: Overseas Study Service Center, 1969.

57. Spaulding, Seth and Michael Flack. The World's Students in the United States: A Review and Evaluation of Research on Foreign Students. New York: Praeger, 1976.

This comprehensive volume provides an analysis and evaluation of research on foreign students in the United States up to 1976. The authors consider research reported in 450 studies (including books, journal articles, conference reports, dissertations, sponsored studies, etc.). These items are abstracted in an annotated bibliography. In addition, they are discussed in a comprehensive essay. The essay uses five main categories: what happens to foreign students in the United States (Chapter 2); the structure, administration, and financing of foreign student programs (Chapter 3); new approaches to technical cooperation in the preparation of human resources for development (Chapter 4); the migration of talent (Chapter 5); and foreign and international organization research (Chapter 6). The largest amount of research (160 empirical studies and 44 nonempirical studies) concerned what happened to foreign students in the United States. Such topics as attitude studies, academic performance, problems of social adjustment, and the like are considered in this research. Research relating to the structure and administration of foreign student programs are covered in 35 empirical and 126 nonempirical studies. Admissions procedures, English language programs and training, advisement and counseling, and related matters are considered in this literature. The phenomenon of talent migration (sometimes called the "brain drain") is considered in 66 studies.

Structural factors in the "sending" countries such as underdevelopment, dislocations in the academic system and in the job market are found to be important in determining brain drain. Spaulding and Flack, in 1976, found that the research done outside of the United States was very small, with UNESCO providing some information. This volume provides the most comprehensive and thorough overview on the subject done up to 1976 and it remains a key resource for any study of foreign students, here in the United States or in other countries.

58. Spencer, Charles S., and Vivian R. Stahl. Bibliography of Research on International Exchanges. Washington, D.C.: Office of Research, United States Information Agency, 1983.

59. Spencer, Richard Edward, and Ruth Awe. International Educational Exchange: A Bibliography. New York: Institute of International Education, 1970.

60. Study Abroad: Handbook for Advisers and Administrators. Washington, D.C.: National Association for Foreign Student Affairs, 1979.

61. Tysse, Agnes, ed. International Education: The American Experience, A Bibliography. Metuchen, New Jersey: Scarecrow Press, 1974.

62. United States Bureau of Educational and Cultural Affairs. A Guide to United States Government Agencies Involved in International Educational and Cultural Activities. Washington, D.C.: U.S. Government Printing Office, 1968.

63. United States Department of Education, Office of International Education. A Foreign Student's Guide to Study in the United States. Washington, D.C.: U.S. Department of Education, 1982.

64. United States Department of Health, Education and Welfare. The Foreign Medical Graduate: A Bibliography. Washington, D.C.: Department of Health, Education and Welfare, 1972.

65. United States Department of State, Bureau of Intelligence and Research. Cross-Cultural Education: A Bibliography of Government-Sponsored and Private Research on Foreign Students and Trainees in the U.S. and Other Countries, 1946-1964. Washington, D.C.: Department of State, 1965.

66. United States Office of Education. American Students and Teachers Abroad: Sources of Information About Overseas Study, Teaching, Work and Travel. Washington, D.C.: U.S. Government Printing Office, 1975.

67. United States Office of Education. Opportunities Abroad for Teachers, under the International Educational and Cultural Exchange Program. Washington, D.C.: U.S. Office of Education, 1967.

68. United States Office of Education. Opportunities Abroad for Teachers 1971-72. Washington, D.C.: U.S. Government Printing Office, 1971.

69. United States Office of Education. Research and Training Opportunities Abroad, 1972-73--Higher Education Programs in Foreign Language and Area Studies. Washington, D.C.: U.S. Government Printing Office, 1971.

70. United States National Student Association. Guidebook on Student Travel in America. New York: Educational Travel Incorporated, 1966.

71. United States National Student Association. 1963 Vacation Opportunities for Foreign Students. New York: USNSA, 1963.

72. U.S.-China Education Clearinghouse. Survey Summary: Students and Scholars from the People's Republic of China Currently in the United States. Washington, D.C.: National Association for Foreign Student Affairs, 1980.

73. University of Hawaii. International Songs and Phrases. Honolulu, Hawaii: University of Hawaii, 1965.

74. von Klemperer, Lily. International Education: A Directory of Resource Materials on Comparative Education and Study in Another Country. Washington, D.C.: Newsletter Classified, 1979.

75. Wang, Sheila. Study in the United States: Orientation Handbook. Washington, D.C.: Educational Foundations, 1968.

76. Wiprud, Helen R. International Education Programs of the U.S. Government: An Inventory. Washington, D.C.: United States Federal Interagency Commission on Education, International Education Task Force/Government Printing Office, 1980.

77. Young Men's Christian Association. A Guide to Greater Boston for Foreign Nationals. Boston, Massachusetts: YMCA, 1967.

### Articles

78. Fraser, S. E. "China's International, Cultural, and Educational Relations: With Selected Bibliography." Comparative Education Review 13 (February, 1969): 60-87.

79. Glaser, William A., and G. Christopher Habers. "Bibliography about the Migration and Return of Professionals." In The Brain Drain: Emigration and Return, edited by William A. Glaser, and G. Christopher Habers, pp. 270-299. Oxford: Pergamon Press, 1978.

80. Kaplan, Robert B. "English as a Second Language: A Guide to the Literature." In Bridges to Knowledge: Foreign Students in a Comparative Perspective, edited by Elinor Barber, Philip G. Altbach, and Robert Myers, pp. 247-258. Chicago: University of Chicago Press, 1984.

81. Lulat, Y. G.-M. "International Students and Study Abroad Programs: A Select Bibliography." Comparative Education Review 28 (May, 1984): 300-339.

82. Lutman, Martha. "Introductory Bibliography for Study Abroad." National Association for Foreign Student Affairs Newsletter 29 (December, 1977): 8ff.

83. Mitchell, Pamela, and Archer Schreiber. "Advising on Study, Travel and Work in Latin America: An Advisor's Bibliography." National Association for Foreign Student Affairs Newsletter 28 (May, 1977): 11ff.

84. Webster, Dennis. "Asian, American, Black and White College Students' Preferences for Help-Giving Sources." Washington Journal of Counseling Psychology 25 (No. 2, 1978): 124-130.

## 2. GENERAL

85. Aich, Prodosh. Farbige unter Weissen. Cologne: Kiepenheuer and Witsch, 1962.

> This book is a comprehensive sociological study of non-European foreign students mainly from the developing countries who were studying in 1960 in the Federal Republic of Germany (FRG). A survey was carried out and data were collected from 386 foreign students in seven universities and other higher education institutions. The following problems are studied:
> . reasons for study abroad and in particular in the FRG;
> . social background of the foreign student population;
> . financial situation and provisions for foreign students;
> . language proficiency and problems;
> . national associations ("clubs");
> . relations with the German community in and outside of universities;
> . discriminations: its forms and consequences for foreign students;
> . problems after graduation ("nonreturning").
>
> Statistical comparison of data and survey findings is made with regard to information concerning foreign students from Egypt, India, Indonesia, Jordan, Ghana, Nigeria, Central African Republic, and Norway.
> A very elaborate questionnaire which was used for data collection is enclosed at the end of this book.

86. Australian Committee of Directors and Principals of Advanced Education. Overseas Students in Colleges of Advanced Education. Canberra: Australian Committee of Directors and Principals of Advanced Education, 1983.

87. Australian Vice Chancellors' Committee. Overseas Students Enrolled at Australian Universities. Canberra: Australian Vice Chancellors' Committee, 1983.

88. Barber, Elinor, Philip G. Altbach, and Robert Myers, eds. Bridges to Knowledge: Foreign Students in Comparative Perspective. Chicago: University of Chicago Press, 1984.

89. Blaug, Mark, and Maureen Woodhall. A Survey of Overseas Students in British Higher Education 1980. London: Overseas Students Trust, 1981.

90. Bochner, Stephen, and Peter Wicks, eds. Overseas Students in Australia. Auburn: New South Wales University Press, 1972.

There were nearly 11,000 foreign students in 1972 studying in the Australian universities, colleges and schools. This book is an anthology of 26 analytical articles written by authors intimately acquainted with this category of students, mostly in relation to their background, motives for undertaking study abroad and particularly in Australia, as well as their problems and achievements.

A wide range of topics discussed in this publication include:

No. 3.   The Cultural Background of Southeast Asian Students in Australia
No. 5.   Pacific Islands Students in Australia
No. 12.  The Psychological Problems of the Eastern Student (A)
No. 13.  The Study Methods and Academic Results of Overseas Students (A)
No. 14.  New Study Patterns
No. 15.  The Law and the Private Student
No. 16.  The Language Barrier
No. 20.  Counselling Overseas Students (A)
No. 21.  The Host Family Scheme
No. 22.  The International Student Center
No. 25.  The Effectiveness of Education Abroad.

(Articles marked with (A) are separately abstracted in this volume.)

91.  Boyan, Douglas R., ed. Profiles: The Foreign Student in the United States. New York: Institute of International Education, 1981. (annual publication)

This new publication of the Institute of International Education will appear annually and focus on specific aspects of foreign student interest. This first publication in the series reports on a survey of foreign students which was appended to the annual IIE Annual Census of Foreign students in 1979. The stress of this report is on the individual foreign student, rather than the institutional variables; 1,961 colleges and universities provided data on 160,000 individual students, or about 56% of the total number of foreign students in the United States. The IIE's "Step 3" report features data on the following topics: nationality of foreign students, field of study, academic level, sex distribution, age, and the relationship between field of study and academic level. Detailed percentage-based table provide information on the field of study according to regions, variations in the fields of study by region and sex, and other variables. The bulk of the volume consists of reports by country and by individual academic institutions of some of the variables in the questionnaire. The volume does not provide analysis, but is a valuable source of quite recent statistics concerning foreign students in the United States. It is a valuable supplement to the IIE's annual publication, Open Doors, to which this is, in fact, related.

92. Brickman, William W. Foreign Students in American Elementary and Secondary Schools. Philadelphia: International House, 1967.

93. British Council. Statistics of Overseas Students in Britain. London: British Council. (annual publication)

94. Canadian Bureau for International Education. Cross Canada Survey of Foreign Student Services. Ottawa: Canadian Bureau for International Education, 1977.

95. Canadian Bureau for International Education. Statistics on Foreign Students. Ottawa: Canadian Bureau for International Education, 1981.

96. Clarke, Helen, and Martha Ozawa. The Foreign Student in the United States. Madison, Wisconsin: University of Wisconsin, School of Social Work, 1970.

97. Cohen, Gail. The Learning Traveler. New York: Institute of International Education, 1980.

98. Council of Cultural Cooperation. Conference sur la Situation des Etudiants Etrangers dans les Etats Membres du Conseil de la Cooperation Culturelle. Strasbourg: Council of Europe, 1981.

99. Council of Europe. Second Conference on Foreign Students and Trainees in Europe. Strasbourg: Council of Europe, 1963.

100. Council of Ontario Universities, Research Division. Citizenship of Students and Faculty in Canadian Universities: A Statistical Report. Ottawa: Association of Universities and Colleges of Canada, 1979.

101. Dankwortt, Dieter. Die Junge Elite Asiens and Afrikas als Gast und Schuler Europas: Sozial-Wissenschaftliche Studie. Hamburg: Psychologisches Institut der Universitat Hamburg, 1959.

102. Deutsch, Steven. International Education and Exchange—A Sociological Analysis. Cleveland: The Press of Case Western University, 1970.

    This book is a sociological analysis of international education and exchange. It is based largely on data acquired through typical sociological survey research. The full range of constituencies involved in programs of international education and exchange were included in the surveys. The early research was conducted during the years 1963-65 at several colleges and universities in Cleveland. There is a full discussion of the survey design, sampling, and nature of the research.

As a prelude to examining the sociological survey research, this work discusses first the broader context of international education, and then the relationship between education and economic development. The primary objective of this book is to present an integrated sociological study of international education and exchange.

103. Deutscher Akademischer Austauschdienst. The Foreign Student in Germany. Bad Godesberg, West Germany: DAAD, n.d.

104. Ditmar, Eva van. "Latin American Students in United States Universities: An Exploratory Study." Unpublished Ph.D thesis, University of California, Los Angeles, 1967.

105. DuBois, Cora. Foreign Students and Higher Education in the United States. Washington, D.C.: American Council on Education, 1956.

106. East Sussex County Planning Department. Foreign Students in East Sussex: Report of Proceedings at Seminar at East Sussex College of Higher Education, Eastbourne on 8 April 1978. Lewes, England: East Sussex County Planning Department, 1978. (publication No. 162)

107. European Center for Higher Education. Statistical Study on Higher Education in Europe, 1970-75. Bucharest: European Center for Higher Education, 1978.

108. Government of Quebec, Cabinet du Ministre de l'Education. Les Frais de Scolarite des Etudiants Etrangers dans les Colleges et Universites du Quebec: Le Gouvernement Enonce une Politique Generale. Montreal: Cabinet du Ministre de l'Education, 1978.

109. Hood, Mary Ann G. 235,000 Foreign Students in U.S. Colleges and Universities: Impact and Response. Washington, D.C.: National Association for Foreign Student Affairs, 1979.

110. Hubbard, J. R. Higher Education and the International Student. Los Angeles: University of Southern California, 1978.

111. Imbert, Jacques. Les Etudiants Etrangers en France. Paris: Centre des Ouevres Universitaires et Scholares, 1980. (mimeo)

112. Institute of International Education. Overall Picture of the Distribution of Foreign Students in the Countries of the UNESCO European Region. New York: IIE, 1976.

113. Institute of International Education. Profiles: The Foreign Student in the United States. New York: Institute of International Education. (annual publication)

114. Interassociational Committee on Data Collection (ICDC). Guide to Data Collection on International Students. Washington, D.C.:

National Association for Foreign Student Affairs, 1982. (mimeo)

115. International Education of the Council of Graduate Schools in the United States. The Foreign Student in American Graduate Schools. Washington, D.C.: CGS, 1980.

116. International Student Program of the National Catholic Educational Association. Foreign Students In Catholic Colleges and Universities 1963-1964. Washington, D.C.: ISPNCEA, 1965.

117. Israel, Ministry of Immigrant Absorption, Central Bureau of Statistics. Survey on Absorption of Students from Abroad, 1972/73. Students Who Began Studies in 1969/70 (Fourth Interview) and in 1970/71 (Third Interview). Jerusalem: Ministry of Immigrant Absorption, Central Bureau of Statistics, 1975.

118. Jacqz, Jane. African Students at United States Universities. Washington: D.C.: African American Institute, 1967.

119. Jarousse, Jean-Pierre. Foreign Students in France. Paris: Institute of Education of the European Cultural Foundation, 1980.

120. Jarousse, Jean Pierre, Alan Smith, and Christine Woesler de Panafieu. Les Etudiants Etrangers: Comparaison Internationale des Flux et des Politiques, 1960-1980. Paris: European Institute of Education and Social Policy, 1983.

   This book provides findings of the research project with an international and national context. It has two parts: a general report and national case studies.
   The "general report" itself has two parts. The first concerns actual problems of foreign students (mostly in the context of admission and financial assistance policies) studying primarily in countries belonging to the European community and/or Council of Europe.
   The second part is a survey and statistical study of foreign student flows (1960-1976) in the following 24 highly industrialized countries: Austria, Belgium, Canada, Czechoslovakia, Denmark, Federal Republic of Germany, Finland, France, German Democratic Republic, Greece, Ireland, Italy, Japan, Luxembourg, Norway, Netherlands, Portugal, Spain, Sweden, Switzerland, the United Kingdom, Turkey, the United States, and the Soviet Union.
   Besides the general flow analyses, this part of the report refers to such specific issues as:
   . foreign students from OPEC countries;
   . political refugees as foreign students (with specific reference to the Vietnamese students in Western Europe and the United States);
   . migrant workers and their impact on the flow of foreign students (with special reference to the Turkish students in the FRG);
   . inter-European student mobility;

. inter-Scandinavian student mobility; and
. distribution of foreign students by sex, field, and level
  of study.

121. Jenkins, Hugh M.  A Glance Back, A Glimpse Forward:  Leafing
     Through the History and Future of the National Association for
     Foreign Student Affairs.  Washington, D.C.:  National
     Association for Foreign Student Affairs, 1979.

122. Kasprzyk, Peter.  Die Forderung afrikanischer Studenten durch den
     DAAD.  Bonn:  Deutscher Akademischer Austaushdienst, n.d.

123. Kendall, M., and P. Williams.  Overseas Students in Britain:  Some
     Facts and Figures.  London:  Overseas Students Trust, 1979.

124. Kincaid, Harry V.  A Preliminary Study of the Goals and Problems of
     the Foreign Students in the United States.  Menlo  Park:
     Stanford Research Institute, 1961.

125. Latin American Students in United States Colleges and Universities.
     Washington, D.C.:  Gordon Ruscoe, 1968.

126. Mestenhauser, Josef A., ed.  Research in Programs for Foreign
     Students:  A Report of the Waldenwoods Seminar.  New York:
     National Association of Foreign Student Advisers, 1961.

127. Meyer, Manfred.  Die Auslandischen Studenten in Osterreich.
     Vienna:  Verlag Ferdinand Berger.

128. Mills, Richard C.  Narrow is the Road.  Los Angeles:  Harbor House,
     1963.

129. National Association for Foreign Student Affairs.  Innovations and
     New  Programs  of  Special  Interest  on  Foreign  Students.
     Washington, D.C.:  National Association for Foreign Student
     Affairs, 1970.

130. National  Association  for  Foreign  Student  Affairs.  Selected
     Speeches:  27th Annual Conference of the National Association
     for Foreign Student Affairs.  Washington, D.C.:  May 7-11,
     1975.  Washington, D.C.:  National Association for Foreign
     Student Affairs, 1975.

131. National Catholic Educational Association.  Foreign Students in
     Catholic Colleges and Universities 1962-63.  Washington, D.C.:
     NCEA, 1963.

132. National Catholic Welfare Conference.  American Catholics and
     Foreign Students.  Washington, D.C.:  National Catholic Welfare
     Conference, 1966.

133. National Center for Education Statistics, Department of Education.
     Digest of Education Statistics.  Washington, D.C.:  Government
     Printing Office.  (annual publication)

134. National Liaison Committee on Foreign Student Admissions. The Foreign Graduate Student: Priorities for Research and Action. New York: College Entrance Examination Board, 1971.

135. Ndeng, James. Prix entre Deux Forces. Paris: La Pensee Universelle, 1975.

136. Neice, David C., and Peter Braun. A Patron for the World? A Descriptive Report of the CBIE Survey of Foreign Students in Post-Secondary Institutions in Canada, 1977. Ottawa: Canadian Bureau of International Education, 1977. (two vols.)

137. Nelson, Donald. Crucial Issues in Foreign Student Education. Washington, D.C.: National Association for Foreign Student Affairs, 1975.

138. Operations and Policy Research. Foreign Students in the United States: A National Survey. Washington, D.C.: Operations and Policy Research, 1966. (two vols.)

139. Otto, David. A Report on the Survey of Foreign Students. Edmonton, Alberta: Office of Institutional Research and Planning, 1975.

140. Paraskevopoulos, J., Richard Dremuk, and L. Kirstein. Factors Relating to Application Statistics and Enrollment Yield for Foreign Students. Urbana: University of Illinois, 1969.

141. Rao, G. Lakshmana. Overseas Students in Australia: Some Major Findings from a Nation-wide Survey. Canberra: Australian National University, 1977.

142. Report of the NAFSA Task Force on Intercultural Communications Workshops. Washington, D.C.: National Association for Foreign Student Affairs, 1973.

143. Report on the Task Force on Visiting International Students in Alberta. Edmonton: University of Alberta, 1979.

144. Ruscoe, C. Gordon. Latin American Students in the U.S. Colleges and Universities. Washington, D.C.: National Association for Foreign Student Affairs, 1968.

145. Salinger, Marion. The Intercultural Traveler. A Teacher's Guide. Durham: Duke University, 1977.

146. Select Committee on Economic and Cultural Nationalism. Colleges and Universities in Ontario: Interim Report. Toronto: Select Committee on Economic and Cultural Nationalism, 1973.

147. Service des Etudes Informatiques et Statistiques, Ministere de l'Education, France. Statistique des Etudiants de Nationalite Etrangere dans les Universites. Paris: Service des Etudes

Informatiques et Statistiques, Ministere de l'Education. (annual publication)

148. Stassen, M. L'enseignement Superieur dans la Communaute Europeenne: Guide pour les Etudiants. Luxembourg: Office des publications officielles des Communaute Europeennes, 1977.

149. Stassen, M. L'enseignement Superieur dans la Communaute Europeenne: Guide de l'etudiant. Luxembourg: Office de publications officielles des Communaute Europeennes, 1981.

150. Statistical Office of the European Communities. Eurostat: Education and Training. Luxembourg: Office for the Official Publications of the European Communities. (annual publication)

151. Statistical Study on Higher Education in Europe: 1971-1972 and 1972-1973. Bucharest: UNESCO/CEPES, 1975.

152. Statistics on Foreign Students. Ottawa: Canadian Bureau for International Education, 1981.

153. Studenten aus Entwicklungslandern an Deutchen Hochschulen. Bonn: Akademischer Verlag, 1963.

154. Students from Overseas in Britain. London: Central Office of Information, Reference Division, 1965.

155. UNESCO. Statistics of Students Abroad, 1962-1968: Where They Go, Where They Come From, What they Study. Paris: UNESCO, 1972.

156. UNESCO. Statistics of Students Abroad 1969-1973. Paris: UNESCO, 1976.

157. UNESCO. Statistics of Students Abroad, 1974-1978. Paris: UNESCO, 1982.

158. UNESCO. Study Abroad, 1972/1973-1973/1974: International Scholarships and Courses. Paris: UNESCO, 1972.

159. UNESCO. Study Abroad, 1981-1982/1982-1983: International Scholarships; International Courses. Paris: UNESCO, 1980.

160. United Kingdom, Overseas Development Sub-Committee, Foreign Affairs Committee, House of Commons. Supply Estimates, 1983-1984: Support for Overseas Students. London: Her Majesty's Stationery Office, 1983.

161. United States Advisory Commission on International Education and Cultural Affairs. Foreign Students in the United States: A National Survey. Washington, D.C.: U.S. Advisory Commission on International Education and Cultural Affairs, 1966.

162. United States Department of Health, Education and Welfare, Institute of International Studies. Research and Training

Opportunities Abroad, 1973–1974--Higher Education Programs in Foreign Language and Area Studies. Washington, D.C.: U.S. Government Printing Office, 1973.

163. United States General Accounting Office. Defense Action to Reduce Charges for Foreign Military Training Will Result in the Loss of Millions of Dollars. Washington, D.C.: General Accounting Office/Government Printing Office, 1977.

164. United States National Science Foundation. Scientists and Engineers from Abroad--Trends of the Past Decade: 1966–1975. Washington, D.C.: Government Printing Office, 1977.

165. Von Zur-Muehlen, Max. Foreign Students in Canada and Canadian Students Abroad. Ottawa: Statistics Canada, 1978.

This study, with an emphasis on statistical information rather than its analysis, deals with foreign students
attending Canadian educational institutions and Canadian
citizens and landed immigrants who have obtained their
university education abroad. Highlighted in the data are
several significant trends including Canada's dependence on
foreign-trained university manpower. It is indicated that
almost 20% of Canadian university graduates obtained their
degrees abroad while about 60% of doctoral graduates
obtained their degrees abroad. During the 1960s the number
of Canadian students studying abroad declined from nearly
16,000 to around 10,000 by the mid-seventies; the number,
however, has started growing again. About 75% of these
Canadians are studying in the United States while most of
the remainder are in British or French universities. An
overview of foreign students in Canada between 1973 and
1977 shows a marked growth in their number, rising from
30,000 to 56,000 but the number declined to 52,000 in 1977.
Foreign students constituted about 5.3% of total full- and
part-time enrollment in 1977–78. While the number of
foreign students from the United States declined from 30%
in 1973 to 15% in 1977, the Figures from 29 least-developed
countries grew from 1,500 to about 2,500 with that of Hong
Kong alone increasing from 21% to almost one-third (6,200
to 16,500). Chapters four to six provide data on the
geographic distribution of foreign students in Canada,
their level and place of study and their geographic origin.
Some current issues are discussed in Chapter Seven with
concluding observations in the last chapter. The appendices include sources of data (Canadian Students Abroad and
Foreign Students in Canada), explanatory notes on the
limitations of the data and tables, and a discussion of
student marginal costs.

166. Von Zur-Muehlen, Max. Foreign Students in Canada: A Preliminary Documentation for 1981–82. Ottawa: Statistics Canada, Education, Science and Culture Division, 1981.

167. Von Zur-Muehlen, Max. Foreign Students' Patterns in Canadian Universities in 1980. Ottawa: Canadian Bureau of International Education, 1980.

168. Walton, Barbara J. Foreign Student Exchange in Perspective: Research on Foreign Students in the United States. Washington, D.C.: Office of External Research, U.S. Department of State, 1967.

169. Wheeler, W. R., H. H. King, and A. B. Davidson, eds. The Foreign Student in America. New York: Association Press, 1925.

170. Wicks, P., ed. Overseas Students in Australia. Sydney: New South Wales University Press, 1972.

171. World Student Christian Federation. Foreign Students--A New Ministry in a New World. Geneva: WSCF, 1965.

172. World University Service. Overseas Student--The Dramatic Decline: The WUS Report. London: World University Service, 1981.

173. Yates, Alfred, ed. Exploring Education: Students from Overseas. London: National Foundation for Educational Research in England and Wales, 1971.

## Articles

174. Alexander, F. Q., et al. "Foreign Students in the U.S.: New Help for High Schools." College Board Review 116 (Summer, 1980): 2-6.

175. Animashawun, G. K. "African Students in Britain." Race 5 (January, 1963): 38-47.

176. Aronson, J. "Basic Techniques for International Student Research." College and University 47 (Summer, 1972): 379-386.

The workshop focused on the need to develop: (1) a common data form; (2) the need for sound research analyses; and (3) a feedback instrument for all institutions. The essential discussions involved three proposed charts. Chart 1, a data-base chart for credential analysts, specifying over 33 different data entries for the evaluation of foreign student applicants credentials; Chart 2, a research form for admitted international students, (which could be shared as a common form among educational institutions); and Chart 3, a theoretical data sheet form for admitted international students. The purpose of the forms to be developed were to provide a facility in evaluating students from other countries. The goal of the workshop was to develop a common data base.

177. "Avec un Passeport a Universite. Conditions d' Etudes pour les Etudiants Etrangers en Republique Federale d' Allemagne." Bildung und Wissenschaft/Education en Allemagne (No. 16, 1974): 233-254.

178. Bates, Kathy. "Neither Foreign Nor at Home." National Association for Foreign Student Affairs Newsletter 28 (Summer, 1977): 1ff.

179. Beecher, W. "Scrambled Scene...U.S. Students in Britain." International Journal and Cultural Exchange 8 (No. 2, 1972): 46-53.

180. Boukhris, Mohamed. "Les Etudiants Etrangers." Revue de l'Institut de Sociologie (No. 1, 1972): 97-104.

181. Boulares, Habib. "Un Yalta technologique." Jeune Afrique (April 14, 1982): 44-45.

182. Bristow, R. "Foreign Students: Trends and Developments." Coombe Lodge Reports 10 (No. 6, 1977): 245-249.

183. Burn, Barbara. "Study in Great Britain a la British." National Association for Foreign Student Affairs Newsletter 26 (December, 1974): 8ff.

184. Byers, Philip P. "Asian Invasion of American Campuses—Why?" International Educational and Cultural Exchange 6 (Spring, 1971): 58-70.

    This article is based on interviews with many Asian students conducted by the author. The purpose of the interviews was to provide information on the student's purpose and motivation, his ability to meet his financial obligations, his facility with the English language, his academic competence, and his health. The author gives some figures about the increase of Asian student enrollment in American universities during the period from 1964 to 1969:

    | | |
    |---|---|
    | Hong Kong: | 7,202 students—85 to 90% do not return to their country |
    | Taiwan: | 8,566 students—95% do not return to their country |
    | Thailand: | 4,372 students—Thai students are not emigrants |
    | India: | 11,327 students |
    | Malaysia: | 663 students |
    | Singapore: | 343 students |
    | Philippines: | The increase is very small because the Filipinos provide more higher education to their population. |
    | South Korea: | 3,991 students—an increase of 53% |

    The author concludes his paper by saying that overall, the increase in the Asian student population in the United

States was 68% during the five-year period. The greatest proportion of this increase has come from three areas:
1. Thailand:    168%
2. Hong Kong:   120%
3. Taiwan:       85%

The causes of this increase are related to:
1)  Thailand has a scarcity of university places and financially rewards those with an American degree and a knowledge of English.
2)  Hong Kong has a severe shortage of university places and an uncertain future. Its students are emigrating.
3)  Taiwanese students are using student status to emigrate to the United States.

185.  Caldwell, Geoff. "Asian Students and Professionals in Australia: Some Initial Comparisons." Education News 15 (No. 7, 1976): 27-31.

186.  Canada, Statistics Canada, Education, Science and Culture Division. "Foreign-Born University Graduates in Canada." Service Bulletin 5 (No. 5, 1976): 1-5.

187.  Carter, William D. "Study and Training Abroad in the United Nations." Annals of the American Academy of Political and Social Science 424 (March, 1976): 67-77.

188.  Crewson, John W. "International Students and American Higher Education: An Interview with Richard Berendzen." Trends 2000 1 (No. 4, 1979): 15-24.

189.  Donahue, Francis. "The International Student: His Six Roles." Clearinghouse 45 (September, 1970): 51-55.

190.  Dupeux, Genevieve. "Etudiants Etrangers au Travail." Revue de Psychologie des Peuples 23 (September, 1968): 276-287.

191.  Eddy, Margot Sanders. "Foreign Students in the United States: Is the Welcome Mat Out?" AAHE Bulletin (December, 1978): 5-8.

192.  Eliot, Alan I. A. "Foreign Students in Perspectives." Social Science Information 6 (December, 1967): 189-201.

193.  Enarson, Harold L. "Response of U.S. Higher Education to Educational Needs of Foreign Students." Higher Education in Europe 4 (April-June, 1979): 20-23.

194.  "Les Etudiants Etrangers dans les Universities Francais 1974-1975." Informations Universitaires et Professionelles Internationales (April-May, 1976): 27-49.

195.  Florin, Frits. "Refugee Students in the Netherlands." Higher Education and Research in the Netherlands 19 (No. 3, 1975): 19-23.

196.  Forster, Siegfried.  "30 Jahre Auslanderstudium in der DDR."  Das Hochschulwesen 29 (No. 12, 1981):  339-344.

197.  Freeman, S. A.  "Undergraduate Study Abroad:  Objectives and Problems."  International Journal of American Linguistics 32 (January, 1966):  185-196.

198.  Gerritz, E. M., et al.  "Rationale for International Students."  College and University 45 (Summer, 1970):  530-534.

199.  Gorakhpurwalla, H. D.  "Foreign Students in American Universities."  Journal of Engineering Education 59 (June, 1969):  1125-1126.

200.  Hoffmann, Wolfgang.  "Auslandsbeziehungen nach 1945."  Die Universitat Munster 1780-1980.  Im Auftrag-des Rektors (1980):  89-96.

201.  Holdsworth, May.  "The Commonwealth Student."  Durham University Journal 58 (December, 1965):  43-45.

202.  Ilchenko, V. J.  "The Foreign Students in the Contemporary World:  Methodological Analysis of the Problem."  Sovremennaya Vysshaya Shkola (No. 2, 1983):  161-175.  (in Russian)

> This article is mostly devoted to the (very) critical analysis of how a phenomenon of the "foreign student" is seen and studied by bourgeois social scientists. The author blames them for presenting a problem of foreign students without its class and social context and replacing it with almost total concentration on academic, pedagogical, psychological and financial issues. In addition, he criticizes the interpretation of training of foreign students as one of the forms of Western assistance to the development of qualified manpower for developing countries. He sees it as being a part in the chain of interdependency consisting of "transnational corporations--charitable foundations--foreign students," and also being one of the areas of the socioeconomic and ideological rivalries between two systems:  capitalism and socialism.  For this reason the "role and contribution of the Soviet Union and other socialist countries to the international student exchange is diminished and undervalued "in the research conducted in the West."
> The author postulates that statistical data on foreign students in the capitalist countries interpreted as the Western contribution to manpower development of other countries should be reduced by the number of students who:
> . already have immigrant status;
> . have decided not to return to their home countries while still studying;
> . do not receive training which is "expected in their home countries."
> Speaking about the "brain drain" problem, the author estimates that only 50-55% of the graduates from western

higher education institutions return to their country of origin. Contrary to this, "all without exception who completed studies in the socialist countries return to their country" and "they are never seen as a potential additional influx of the qualified personnel."

The author argues that the majority of foreign students in the capitalist countries undertake social and not technical studies, (even though the latter is of more relevance to the needs of developing countries). Out of 17,000 foreign students who graduated from the Soviet Union's educational institutions in the academic year 1981-82, 1.2 thousand were medical doctors and qualified nurses; more than one thousand agronomists and veterinary doctors; nine thousand engineers; three thousand teaching specialists in higher and secondary education; 2.5 thousand industrial managers. In addition, about 10,000 foreigners participated in different forms of upgrading and development programs.

It is estimated that about 15% of the world's foreign student population receive education in the socialist countries. The efficiency of their educational programs is at the same time higher than that of the capitalist countries, e.g., the dropout rate among foreign students in the Soviet Union is only 2-3%.

Concrete examples of the involvement of different foundations in international student exchange serve as examples of the correlation between promotion of foreign studies and foreign interest of the capitalist countries.

203. Imbert, J. "Foreign Students in France." Higher Education in Europe 6 (April-June, 1981): 46-50.

The author points out three factors for a steady tendency of growing foreign student enrollment. First, every country wants to profit from the scientific progress made by other countries. A second factor is that most young people today have a great desire to be exposed to new contacts and to change. The third one, (which refers mainly to foreign students from developing countries) is lack of sufficient study places at home. An additional factor is that some students feel that they receive inferior education in their own universities and consequently desire to study abroad in well-established and competitive institutions.

Furthermore, study abroad gives the student "an added sense of prestige in comparison with those that were unable to have such an advantage."

The author discusses enrollment trends of foreign students in France since 1970, which shows that e.g., in 1975 France had the most foreign students of any European country (93,750), and after the United States, the second largest foreign student enrollment in the world.

204. Ingold, C. T., et al. "The Overseas Postgraduate." _Overseas Universities_ (November, 1973): 14-18.

205. Jenkins, Hugh M. "International Student." In _International Encyclopedia of Higher Education_, edited by A. Knowles, pp. 1512-1518. San Francisco: Jossey-Bass, 1977.

206. Jenkins, Hugh M. "NAFSA and the Student Abroad: A Silver Anniversary Review." _International Educational and Cultural Exchange_ 8 (Spring, 1973): 1-13.

207. Jenkins, Hugh M. "The State of the Association." _National Association for Foreign Student Affairs Newsletter_ 23 (May, 1972): 4ff.

208. Jenkins, Hugh M., et al. "Data Collection Project on Foreign Student Enrollments in U.S. Colleges and Universities." _College and University_ 53 (Summer, 1978): 512-517.

209. Johnson, Dixon C. "Problems of Foreign Students." _International Educational and Cultural Exchange_ 7 (Fall, 1971): 61-68.

210. Kayser-Jones, J. S., et al. "Canadian and European Students in the United States." _Journal of Nursing Education_ 21 (September, 1982): 26-31.

211. Lansdale, David. "U.S. Universities and Third World Students." In _Bridges to Knowledge: Foreign Students in a Comparative Perspective_, edited by Elinor Barber, Philip G. Altbach, and Robert Myers, pp. 196-206. Chicago: University of Chicago Press, 1984.

212. Limbach, Hans Reiner. "Auslandische Studenten in Deutschland." _Caritas_ 70 (No. 4, 1969): 214-217.

213. Marville, Ade. "The Case of the International Student: A Foreign Student Reports." _College Board Review_ (Summer, 1981): 23-26.

214. Mayot, P., et al. "Les Etudiants." _Esprit, Changer la Culture et la Politique_ No. 11-12 (1978): 88-223.

215. Melby, John F. "The Foreign Student in America." _ORBIS_ 8 (Spring, 1964): 153-163.

216. Mumme, Martin. "Die Universitat fur Auslander in Perugia als Vorbild Einer Effizienten Kulturpolitik." _Sprache und Wahrheit_ No. 39-40 (1971): 287-291.

217. Musnik, Isabelle. "Student Flows in Higher Education 1970-1977." _Paedagogica Europaea_ 8 (No. 1, 1978): 37-70.

    This article aims to analyze some of the main trends in enrollment of the higher education systems in the following 15 countries over the period 1970-1977: Austria,

Belgium, Denmark, West Germany, Finland, France, Greece, Ireland, Italy, the Netherlands, Norway, Spain, Sweden, Switzerland and the United Kingdom. In the first place a summary of recent trends is made of (1) total enrollments, (2) new entrants, (3) female students, and (4) changes in subject choice. Secondly, the author analyzes factors underlying the trends, among them being (1) developments in the macro-economic system and, in particular, the rise of graduate unemployment, (2) the demographic factor, (3) changes in student flows/orientation inside the upper secondary school, (4) revisions and alterations in policies of admission to higher education, and (5) the possible effect of policies on "diversification" in the most secondary sector.

218. "Overall Picture of the Distribution of Foreign Students in the Countries of the Unesco European Region." Higher Education in Europe 4 (April-June, 1979): 13-17.

219. Overseas Students Trust. "Statistics." In The Overseas Student Question: Studies for a Policy, edited by Peter Williams, pp. 265-291. London: Heinemann, 1981.

220. Perkins, J. A. "The International Movement of Students and Staff." Vestes 22 (No. 2, 1979): 44-47.

221. Pfeiffer, W. M. "Probleme bei Studenten aus Enticklungslandern." In Psychische Storungen bei Studenten, edited by S. Jahnke, and H. U. Ziolko. Stuttgart: Thieme, 1969.

222. Putney, Audery. "The Foreign Student Information Clearinghouse: A Useful Resource." National Association for Foreign Student Affairs Newsletter 33 (October, 1981): 23ff.

223. Reichard, John F. "The State of Overseas Student Affairs in the United Kingdom." National Association for Foreign Student Affairs Newsletter 34 (October, 1982): 1ff.

224. Rice, G. W. "Study Abroad: Some Problems and Prospects." Vidya 2 (1968): 37-45.

225. Riddell, K. D. "From All the World They Come." University of Toronto Quarterly 3 (December, 1969): 67-74.

226. Rix, Allan. "Canada and International Education." National Association for Foreign Student Affairs Newsletter 22 (May, 1971): 1ff.

227. Rix, J. A. "Impact of Foreign Students on Graduate Education." In Proceedings of the Eighteenth Annual Meeting of the Council of Graduate Schools in the United States: Changing Patterns in Graduate Education, edited by J. W. Ryan, pp. 131-133. Washington, D.C.: Council of Graduate Schools, 1979.

228. Robert, Jacques. "Accueillir l'Etudiant Etranger. Rapport final." CRE-Information (1st Quarter, 1982): 60-67.

229. Ryten, E. "Citizenship of Graduate Students in Canadian Universities. Service Bulletin (April, 1972): 4-11.

230. Schafer, Dieter. "Auslandische Studenten vom Wintersemester 1972/73 bis zum Wintersemester 1978/79." Statische Rundschau fur das Land Nordhein--Westfalen 31 (September, 1979): 429-433.

231. Schieffer, O. "La Republic Federal d'Allemagne. Bureau Central pour l'Enseignement Etranger. Centre National d'Information en Matiere d'Equivalences." Information Universitaires et Professionalles Internationales (September-October, 1977): 18-28.

232. Schulte, H. "Probleme des Auslanderstudiums." Deutsche Universitatszeitung No. 23 (1972): 936-941.

233. Schulte, Hansgerd. "Reflexions sur le Probleme de la Mobilite des Etudiants en Europe." CRE-Information No. 34 (2nd Quarter, 1976): 11-29.

234. Schulte, Hansgerd. "Reflexion zur Probleme der Studentischen Mobilitat in Europa." Die Deutsche Universitatszeitung 76 (No. 9-10, 1976): 265-271.

235. Schulz, H. E. "Moglichkeiten Einer Fachlichen Forderung Auslandischer Germanistik Studenten." Deutsche Universitatszietung Vereinight mit Hochschule-Dienst No. 23 (1971): 769-773.

236. "Statistique des Etudiants de Nationalite Etranger dans les Universites 1973-1974." Note d'Information No. 8 (1975): 1-4.

237. "Statistique des Etudiants de Nationalite Etrangere dans les Universites. 1974-1975." Note d'Information No. 8 (1976): 1-4.

238. Stevenson, Russell. "U.S. Graduate Students from Less Developed Countries." American Journal of Agricultural Economics 56 (November, 1974): 816-818.

239. Taylor, Mary Louise. "Study Abroad." In International Encyclopedia of Higher Education, edited by A. Knowles, pp. 1518-1528. San Francisco: Jossey-Bass, 1977.

240. Teichler, Ulrich. "Trends in Higher Education with Respect to Student Population." Higher Education in Europe 5 (No. 2, 1980): 24-34.

    This article presents analyses of the basic trends with regard to the student population in Europe, Canada,

Israel, and the United States in the 1970's. It refers to such issues as: growth of enrollment, female and adult student enrollment, diversity of institutions, distribution of students by field of study and foreign students. The article points out that in absolute figures such countries as the United States, France, Canada, the Federal Republic of Germany, and the United Kingdom are the largest host countries while in countries such as Switzerland, Austrian foreign students constitute more than 10% of the total enrollment in higher education. In the years 1970-1975 the percentage of European foreign students in the European Region had increased from 24.3 to 34.6%.

241. Thomassen, F. P. "Zulasung von Auslandern zum Wissenschaftlichen Studium in den Niederlanden." Hochschule und Forschung in den Niederlanden 11 (No. 1, 1967): 34-41.

242. Torrey, E. F., F. J. Van Rheenan, and H. A. Katchadourian. "Problems of Foreign Students: An Overview." Journal of the American College Health Association 19 (December, 1970): 83-86.

243. "U.S.A. and the Foreign Student." International Educational and Cultural Exchange 10 (Fall, 1974): 4-13.

244. Vickery, B. C. "Overseas Students and Higher Degrees." In Education and Training Theory and Provision, pp. 101-104. The Hague: Federation Internationale de Documentation, 1979.

245. Walker, J. "Rationale for International Students." College and University 45 (Summer, 1970): 405-414.

Four contributors discuss the topic: "an integrated campus and community program for foreign students." One contributor outlines some aspects of foreign students' difficulties encountered on American campuses and suggests that detailed information be provided to foreign students before they leave for the U.S.; help be given in familiarizing them with the customs and activities on the campus; and an international students club be established. Another contributor argues that a more human role should be injected into the admissions procedure. The other two contributors discuss respectively the role of the foreign student adviser as the link between foreign students and all offices on the campus, and the specific ways to "treat foreign students well after they get here."

246. Walton, Barbara J. "Research on Foreign Graduate Students." International Educational and Cultural Exchange 6 (Winter, 1971): 17-29.

In 1969, 45% of the 121,362 foreign students in the United States were at the graduate level compared with 35% 10 years earlier. At the same time these students have tended to concentrate at relatively few graduate institutions.

Policy planners and administrators have been inclined to favor admission of graduate over undergraduate foreign students for many years. This emphasis on graduate-level study stems from the belief that studies at this level were more likely to contribute to the economic growth of the foreign student's home country.

The article reviews research conducted on foreign students during the 1950's and early 1960's. (That is the period in which there was very little differentiation made between graduate and undergraduate foreign students.) Research carried out at the universities as well as U.S. government sponsored studies is dealt with on the following topics:

. nationality studies;
. academic performance;
. foreign students as professionals;
. learning problems encountered by foreign students;
. courses that would be most and least useful for foreign students;
. foreign students in engineering and medical studies; and
. the "brain drain".

In conclusion, the author points out the lack of "serious study of curriculum for foreign students in general" and suggests an introduction, even on a tentative basis, of either orientation or special courses for foreign students' academic and professional development.

247.  Warmbrunn, Werner. "Our Pride and Shame." National Association for Foreign Student Affairs Newsletter 15 (December, 1963): 1ff.

248.  Winogue, W. J. D. "Distributive Justice and Foreign University Students: A New Zealand View." Canadian and International Education 1 (December, 1972): 35-43.

The author of this article discusses the conflict between administrative, political, and academic policies that exist when dealing with foreign students in New Zealand. Since the number of foreign students in New Zealand is growing rapidly, the country is developing policies to deal with them. The author discusses this treatment of the students in political and ethical terms.

The differentiation of foreign students in terms of whether they are government-aided or privately funded leads the author to raise such questions as: Why do certain rules apply to government-aided students and not to the privately funded ones? Why should universities even admit foreign students? What are the grounds for giving government-aided foreign students special treatment? As these questions illustrate, the author attempts to show how the political decisions of the New Zealand government conflict with ethical principles. The central theme of the

article is how the principle of distributive justice should
be applied to foreign students in New Zealand.

249.  Wolfgang, K. F.  "10,000 Miles from Home."  International
Educational and Cultural Exchange 11 (Winter, 1976):  11-14.

250.  Zeigler, A. L.  "Foreign Student Programs in the United Kingdom."
International Educational and Cultural Exchange 5 (Summer,
1969):  35-48.

The author spent six months in England in 1968,
investigating overseas student services in the U.K.  He
discovered several significant innovations in overseas
student programming.  The article discusses basic differences between the U.K. and the U.S. regarding problems
of overseas students.  Among the topics discussed in the
article include:  The foreign student adviser; student
government efforts; program financing; private funds
distribution; language resources pooling; job placement;
international student houses; returned overseas volunteers;
associations concerned with overseas students; and racial
problems.

251.  Zelleke, Kefelev.  "Auslandische Studenten in der Bundesrepublik
Erwartungen Hoffnungen und Wirklichkeit."  Diakonie
Mitteilungen aus dem Diakonisch--Missionarischen werk 8 (No. 3,
1971):  10-19.


Reportage


252.  "American Enrollment Increasing in Japan."  Chronicle of Higher
Education 23 (October 14, 1981):  17.

253.  Bishop, T.  "British Go Feet First into European Institutions."
Times Higher Education Supplement (January 6, 1978):  9.

254.  "Britain Offers Training."  Chronicle of Higher Education 10
(August 4, 1975):  2.

255.  Brock, A.  "Les Etudiants a l'Etranger Toujours plus Nombreux."
Information Universitaires et Professionales Internationales
(September-October, 1977):  16-17.

256.  "Canada Expects Increase in Foreign Student Enrolment.  Chronicle
of Higher Education 21 (August 25, 1980):  6.

257.  Cookson, C.  "Foreign Students Pour into U.S.A. But Government
Support Declines."  Times Education Supplement 3392 (June 26,
1981):  16.

258.  Cookson, C.  "Huge Rise in Overseas Enrolments."  Times Higher
Education Supplement (November 21, 1980):  6.

259. Crequer, N. "Drop in Overseas Numbers Unlikely." Times Higher Education Supplement (July 18, 1980): 1.

260. David, P. "DES Forecasts Overseas Drop." Times Higher Education Supplement (July 25, 1980): 1.

261. David, P. "Overseas Students Set to Treble in U.S." Times Higher Education Supplement (October 23, 1981): 1.

262. Dhombres, D. "Un Etudiante sur dix est Etranger." Le Monde de l'Education No. 17 (1976): 38-39.

263. "Echanges Universitaires avec l'Etranger. Bon Nomme de Nouvelles Priorites." Bildung und Wissenschaft/Education en Allemagne No. 9 (1974): 136-138.

264. Edgerton, Wallace B. "Number of Foreign Students Continues to Increase, but at a Slower Rate." Change 14 (November/December, 1982): 49-51.

265. Edles, N. "Foreign Students in U.S. Colleges and Universities." American Education 16 (July, 1980): back cover.

266. "Egyptian Overseas Students Leave American U." Chronicle of Higher Education 8 (June 24, 1974): 7.

267. "Enseignements Etrangers en France et Enseignements Francais a l'Etranger, dans l'Enseignement Superieur." Note d'Information No. 40 (1977): 1-4.

268. "Emfehlungen des DAAD zum Auslanderstudium." Deutsche Universitatszeitung (No. 3, 1970): 18.

269. "Etudes d'Etrangers en RFA. Espoirs et Realites." Bildung und Wissenschaft/Education en Allemagne No. 9 (1974): 135-136.

270. Farmer, Richard N., and Ronald E. Hoyt. "Foreign Students in Indiana." Indiana Business Review 50 (March-April, 1975): 7-9.

271. Felsenstein, F. "Bulgars in Britain." Times Higher Education Supplement (November 5, 1982): 14.

272. "Fewer Studying Abroad." Chronicle of Higher Education 10 (August 4, 1975): 2.

273. "Foreign Links with Students of Other Nations." Times Educational Supplement No. 2626 (September 17, 1965): 475.

274. "Foreign Students in the U.S. (1972-73)." Chronicle of Higher Education 8 (April 1, 1974): 8.

275. "Foreign Students in U.S. Colleges (1973-74)." Chronicle of Higher Education 10 (April 14, 1975): 13.

276. "Foreign Students in the United States (Fact-File)." Chronicle of Higher Education 16 (April 17, 1978): 12.

277. "Foreign Students in U.S. Institutions (Fact-File)." Chronicle of Higher Education 25 (December 8, 1982): 22.

278. "Foreign Students in U.S.--Problem and Opportunity: A Conversation with Richard Berendzen, President of the American University." U.S. News 91 (October 5, 1981): 66.

279. "Foreign Undergraduates Attending Italian Universities." Italy: Documents and Notes 17 (September/October, 1968): 429-431.

280. Greer, William S. "Foreign Students: Boon or a Threat?" New York Times (March 22, 1983): 72-73.

281. "Grundsatze zum Studium von Auslandern in der Bundesrepublik Deutschland Einschliesslich Berlin (West)." Deutsches Universitatzeitung No. 22 (1972): 906-909.

282. Hamilton, Thomas Hale. "On the Falling Short of Good Intentions." National Association for Foreign Student Affairs Newsletter 15 (November, 1963): 1ff.

283. Herbert, Wray. "Abroad in the U.S.--Foreign Students on American Campuses." Educational Record 62 (No. 3, 1981): 68-71.

284. "Inscription des Etudiants Etrangers dans les Universites en France." Information Universitaires et Professionelles Internationales (September-October, 1978): 20.

285. "Italy: Reprieve for Foreign Students." Newsletter (Council of Europe) (No. 3, 1977): 24-26.

286. Kuhn, Anslem. "Loving Our Third World Neighbors--Western Education for Foreign Students." Times Higher Education Supplement (June 10, 1983): 34.

287. "Learning More About Foreign Students: Selected Readings." College Board Review 116 (Summer, 1980): 7.

288. Maass, K. J. "Die Mobilitat der Hochschullehrer--ein Europeisches Problem." Deutsche Universitatszeitung No. 20 (1972): 819-821.

289. Makins, V. "Asian Preferences to be Met." Times Education Supplement (October 1, 1982): 8.

290. Massing, M. "Visible Imports." New Statesman 93 (May 6, 1977): 598.

291. "Mobilite des Etudiants Europeens." Informations Universitaires et Professionelles Internationales (September-October, 1978): 17-19.

292. More, D. "Foreign Students in U.S. Colleges." American Education 11 (June, 1975): back cover.

293. Neave, G. "Forecast of Many More Foreigners." Times Higher Education Supplement (September 30, 1977): 11.

294. Neave, G. "Foreign Intake Increasing." Times Higher Education Supplement (March 7, 1980): 6.

295. Neave, G. "Foreign Student Cuts Start to Bite." Times Higher Education Supplement (November 24, 1978): 6.

296. "New Woes for Foreign Students." Chronicle of Higher Education 8 (August 5, 1974): 24.

297. "1979-80 Enrolment of Foreign Students." Chronicle of Higher Education 22 (May 11, 1981): 14.

298. "Number (of Foreign Students) in U.S." Chronicle of Higher Education 23 (December 9, 1981): 17.

299. "Oil-Rich Countries Supply 1 in 3 Foreign Students in U.S. Colleges." Chronicle of Higher Education 20 (April 7, 1980): 17.

300. O'Leary, J. "Bitter Home Truths About Overseas Students." Times Higher Education Supplement (February 8, 1980): 7.

301. O'Leary, J. "Dead Debate Revived." Times Higher Education Supplement (May 9, 1980): 7.

302. O'Leary, J. "Non-Commonwealth Students Pour in." Times Higher Education Supplement (August 11, 1978): 1.

303. O'Leary, J. "Overseas Students Hold Up." Times Higher Education Supplement 455 (July 24, 1981): 1.

304. Passmore, B. "Enrollments by Overseas Students Fall by 30%." Times Higher Education Supplement (January 23, 1981): 8.

305. Passmore, B. "Overseas Enrollment Down 25%." Times Education Supplement 3424 (February 12, 1982): 7.

306. "Les Pays Europeens a la Recherche d'un Consensus pour Favoriser la Mobilite des Etudiants." Informations Universitaires et Professionelles Internationales 25 (November-December, 1981): 29-31.

307. Reid, S. "DES Considers Overseas Students' Body." Times Higher Education Supplement (September 30, 1977): 1.

308. Reid, S. "Sharp Increase in Poly Applicants from Overseas." Times Higher Education Supplement (July 1, 1977): 1.

309. Rogler, Gunther. "Manipulation Auslandischer Studenten?" Die Deutsche Universitatszeitung 24 (No. 4, 1969): 7-8.

310. Rosenbaum, Ulrich. "'Auslanderstudium als Funktion des Kulturimperialismus'. Zum Auslanderprogram und Auslandergesetzenwurf des VDS." Die Deutsche Universitatszeitung 24 (No. 9, 1969): 18.

311. Roth, M. "Doors Open for Foreigners." Times Higher Education Supplement (April 30, 1982): 7.

312. Ryan, Edmund G. "STEP Toward Solving a Problem of Higher Education." College Management 8 (November/December): 23-25.

313. Schmetzer, U. "Foreign Students Bring Their Troubles to Perugia." Times Higher Education Supplement (January 4, 1980): 5.

314. Scully, M. G. "Foreign Enrollment at U.S. Colleges: The Pace Slows." Chronicle of Higher Education 25 (October 20, 1982): 2.

315. Scully, Malcolm G. "1 Million Foreign Students at U.S. Colleges, Triple Present Number, Seen Likely by 1990." Chronicle of Higher Education 23 (October 21, 1981): 1.

316. Semas, Philip W. "Foreign Students: More Coming." Chronicle of Higher Education 10 (March 24, 1975): 1.

317. Spencer, D. "High Hopes Among Asian Young [Report of Research]." Times Higher Education Supplement 3389 (June 5, 1981): 9.

318. "Studium von Auslandern Sole Durch Internationale Konsultation Verbessert Werden." Die Deutsche Universitatszeitung (No. 4, 1974): 139-142.

319. "Study-abroad Programs Continue to Grow." Chronicle of Higher Education, 14 (May 21, 1977): 2.

320. "Studying Abroad: Old Custom Takes on New Importance; In Huge Numbers, Students Are Crossing the Globe in Search of College Education; It's a Trend Paying Dividends--and Raising Problems, Too." U.S. News and World Report 82 (January 24, 1977): 57-58.

321. "286,000 in U.S." Chronicle of Higher Education 21 (October 20, 1980): 18.

322. "U.S.-Soviet Exchanges: A Chronology." Chronicle of Higher Education 27 (September 14, 1984): 1.

323. Walker, R. M. "Statistics of the Month: Number of Foreign Students Enrolled in American Institutions of Higher Education, by Area of Origin: 1948/49-1964/65." American Education 1 (Summer, 1965): back cover.

324. Watson, Alan. "Ways to Help Our Poor Relations--Serving Unful-
     filled Educational Needs in the Third World." Times Higher
     Education Supplement (July 16, 1982): 26.

325. Wheen, F. "Visiting Judgement--Foreign Students in Great Britain."
     New Statesman 97 (February 9, 1979): 171.

326. Willis, F. "Absence Makes the Tongue Grow Swifter." Times Higher
     Education Supplement (November 18, 1977): 12.

327. Winker, Karen J. "New Woes for Foreign Students." Chronicle of
     Higher Education 8 (August 5, 1974): 24.

328. Woodcock, Lynda. "Influx of Foreign Students: An Issue in
     Canada." Chronicle of Higher Education 16 (March 13, 1978):
     3.

329. Woodcock, Lynda. "Number of Foreign Students in Canada Grows."
     Chronicle of Higher Education 23 (January 27, 1982): 15.

330. Wright, L. "Foreign Students Review." Times Higher Education
     Supplement (October 13, 1978): 6.

331. Wright, L. "Political Gag on African Scholarship Students." Times
     Higher Education Supplement (September 1, 1978): 5.

332. Zamoyska, B. "Rush for Overseas Work." Times Education Supplement
     (June 24, 1977): 8.

## 3. FOREIGN STUDENTS IN THIRD WORLD COUNTRIES (GENERAL MATERIALS)

333. Boewe, Charles E. The Green Book: American Scholar in Pakistan.
     Islamabad, Pakistan: United States Educational Foundation in
     Pakistan, 1977.

334. Ganguli, H. C. Foreign Students: The Indian Experience. New
     Delhi: Sterling Publishers, n.d.

335. International Research Associates. The Effectiveness of the
     Exchange Program: Africa-Uruguay. New York: International
     Research Associates, 1963.

### Articles

336. Cormack, Margaret. "American Students in India: Ambassadors or
     Cultural Polluters?" International Studies Quarterly 17
     (September, 1973): 337-358.

This discussion focuses on the specific question of sending American undergraduate students to India, using the case of the Callison-in-Bangalore program. It discusses problems that led to Indian Government regulations on foreign academic programs--regulations that will deny scholars and students freedoms they previously enjoyed. As of 1973 foreign scholars and students are subject to the same requirement regarding registration, evaluation, and supervision as Indians. The author examines Indian criticisms that led to the restrictions and found: (1) Scholars and graduate students engaged in high-level research were more task-oriented than younger students; (2) their independence on research topics and modes was questioned more than their life-styles; (3) those more experience-oriented were particularly criticized for their independence as regards residence, travel, and general behavior. After describing the effects of the experience on American students and the effects of American students on India, the author examines the aims of intercultural programs. He suggests a clear intercultural aim, appropriate selection and orientation in relation to this aim, a continuous intercultural seminar in the field, and an integration of the intercultural experience in the ensuing college curriculum to make education "higher" in today's terms.

337.  Hafeez-Zaidi, S. M. "Adjustment Problems of Foreign Muslim Students in Pakistan." In Cross-Cultural Perspectives on Learning, edited by Richard Brislin, Stephen Bochner, and Walter Lonner, pp. 117-130. New York: John Wiley, 1975.

This study is unique in the sense that an attempt has been made to analyze problems of adjustment of a group of Asian and African students in a country whose degree of development is similar to that of their own country and, in certain aspects may even be less. At the time of this study there were about one thousand foreign students in Pakistan, most of them being males and majoring in medicine and engineering, or science. This study examined 102 male and 21 female foreign students in Karachi, and a 43-item questionnaire was administered to each participant individually. Seventy-three % of the respondents indicated that their choice was determined by the fact that Pakistan is a Muslim country and therefore psychologically attractive. Other considerations were easy admissions, desire to improve English, academic attraction and received scholarship. It is assumed that the major difficulties faced by foreign students fall within the categories of physical, academic, and sociocultural differences. To reduce the constant limitations of social psychological research methodology, the author suggests the use of unobtrusive and nonreactive techniques of data collection in combination with direct questions.

338. Maud, R. "Racism in Rag Time; Apartheid." <u>University Quarterly</u> 27 (August, 1973): 407-419.

339. Maxwell, W. E. "Ethnic Identity of Male Chinese Students in Thai Universities." <u>Comparative Education Review</u> 18 (February, 1974): 55-69.

   The major thesis of this study is that a great deal of the variation among societies in the ethnic consequences of schooling is due to the interplay of school factors and societal constraints and that an important category of these contingencies concerns the opportunities in nonschool institutions open to members of a given ethnic group. The study is grounded on the theories of ethnic assimilation, and ethnic pluralism. The history of Chinese immigration and the maintenance of distinctive Chinese traditions in Thailand is explored. Three sets of hypotheses were proposed and these were investigated mainly on the responses to questionnaire surveys of Chinese students in three fields of study: political science, medicine, and business in Thailand. The questionnaire surveys were administered in the Thai language by Thai research assistants to the students during classroom sessions in 1966 and 1971. The ethnic classification in the report shows that 61% of all students are of families engaged in private business, and that almost all the students who identified themselves as Chinese are from business families where nearly all the fathers designated by the category of "self-employed and employers" are independent retail merchants. Seventy-four percent of the male medical students are from homes where the dominant culture is Chinese with 89% reporting at least some recent Chinese ancestry. These and other findings reported in the study provide support for the three hypotheses proposed from the assimilationist perspective. Many Chinese students show an interest in assimilation into the Thai bureaucratic elite, and would welcome marriage with a Thai. On the question of pluralism only little support is provided by the data for predictions that most of the Chinese will become Thai within two or three generations. It is suggested that though the assimilation of the Chinese is continuing, the pace of assimilation is likely to be rather slow unless the number of work opportunities in the elite and upper-middle status levels of Thai society increases.

340. Pyle, K. K. International Cross-Cultural Service/Learning. "American Students in Jamaica: Impact on Student Development." <u>Journal of College Student Personnel</u> 22 (November, 1981): 509-514.

Reportage

341. "Countries with Largest Number of Americans." Chronicle of Higher Education 23 (December 16, 1981): 10.

## 4. COMMUNITY AND JUNIOR COLLEGES

342. Bloom, Joyce Neimark Mauser. "Students from Other Lands in the American Two-Year College." Unpublished Ed.D thesis, Columbia University, 1970.

343. Brender, Robert L. A Statewide Study: Identified Problems of International Students Enrolled in Public Community/Junior Colleges in Florida. Tallahassee, Florida: Center for State and Regional Leadership, Florida State University and University of Florida, 1972.

344. Cooney, David Thomas. "A Foreign Student Program in Florida Public Community Colleges: Present Status and Future Development." Unpublished Ph.D thesis, Florida State University, 1973.

345. Elliot, Frederick George. "Foreign Student Programs in Selected Public California Junior Colleges: An Analysis of Administrative Policies and Practices." Unpublished Ed.D thesis, University of California, Los Angeles, 1967.

346. Farrokhshahab, Mohammad Reza. "Opinions of Students and Faculty at Iranian Technical Institutes on the Importance of Modifying Their Institutes in Terms of Selected Characteristics of American Community Colleges." Unpublished Ph.D thesis, American University, 1980.

347. Fersh, Seymour, and Edward Fitchen. The Community College and International Education: A Report of Progress. Cocoa, Florida: Brevard Community College, 1981.

348. Gassman, Cletus Robert. "A Study of Foreign Student Advisors in Two-Year and Four-Year Colleges and Universities in Texas." Unpublished Ed.D thesis, East Texas State University, 1982.

349. Georgiades, John George. "Identified Problems of International Students: Public New Jersey Community Colleges and Rutgers—The State University of New Jersey." Unpublished Ed.D thesis, Rutgers University, 1980.

350. Gleazer, J. Edmund, Jr., et al. The Foreign Student in United States Community and Junior Colleges. New York: College Entrance Examination Board, 1978.

This colloquium was attended by a group of representatives of United States higher education, government,
professional groups, and foreign students. The purpose of
the colloquium was to explore the impact of the thousands
of foreign students enrolled in the U.S. community and
junior colleges and to plan ways to help institutions,
government, and other agencies improve the quality of their
experience. This book is a collection of the opening
address, three background papers, and a public statement
expressing the opinions and recommendations of the members.
One paper presents information about the characteristics of
the more than 60,000 foreign students in the two-year
institutions in the U.S. It describes where they come
from, what they study, how they are financed, and other
specific information. Another paper deals with constraints
and issues in planning and implementing programs for
foreign students in those institutions. The third paper
considers effective programming for foreign students in
community and junior colleges. The public statement summarizes points regarding the purpose of international education in U.S. community colleges, and the need for foreign
student involvement as a facet of an international education program, as well as the conclusions reached at the
colloquium.

351. Greene, William Edwin. "International Education Programs in
      Selected Florida Community Colleges." Unpublished Ed.D thesis,
      Florida Atlantic University, 1980.

352. Gwynne, Margaret Ann. "The Effects of Study Abroad on Community
      College Students." Unpublished Ed.D thesis, Teachers College,
      Columbia University, 1981.

353. Hart, Roy Harold. "Problems of International Students Enrolled in
      Texas Public Community Colleges as Perceived by International
      Students and International Student Advisors." Unpublished Ed.D
      thesis, East Texas State University, 1974.

354. Hess, Gerhard. Freshmen and Sophomores Abroad: Community Colleges
      and Overseas Academic Programs. New York: Teachers College
      Press, 1982.

355. Holwerda, Thomas. "A Comprehensive Policy for a Foreign Student
      Program at Orange Coast Community College." Unpublished Ed.D
      thesis, University of Southern California, 1980.

356. Lammers, Patricia Ann. "Four Perspectives of the Proper Role of
      Foreign Student Education at Ten Selected Community and Junior
      Colleges in the United States." Unpublished Ed.D thesis,
      University of Northern Colorado, 1982.

357. Marsh, Harriet Louise. "Foreign Student Advisors in Community
      Colleges: A Study of Role and Function in Community Colleges

of Washington State." Unpublished Ed.D thesis, Columbia University, 1972.

358. Sjogren, Clifford Frank, Jr. "Foreign Students in Michigan Community and Junior Colleges: An Analysis of Present Conditions, Experiences, and Expectations." Unpublished Ph.D thesis, University of Michigan, 1972.

359. Yarrington, Roger, ed. Internationalizing Community Colleges. Washington, D.C.: American Association of Community and Junior Colleges, 1978.

## Articles

360. Adams, A. H., G. Ellyson, and W. Greene. "Effective Programming for Foreign Students in Community and Junior Colleges." In The Foreign Student in United States Community and Junior Colleges, edited by J. Edmund Gleazer, Jr., et al., pp. 53-74. New York: College Entrance Examination Board, 1978.

361. Adams, A. Hugh. "Foreign Students in Community and Junior Colleges." In The Foreign Student in United States Community and Junior Colleges, edited by J. Edmund Gleazer, Jr., et al., pp. 53-74. New York: College Entrance Examination Board, 1978.

This paper first reviews briefly the increasing involvement of two-year colleges in international education. Then it concentrates on the effective programming for foreign students in these institutions. Suggestions are made as to the implementation of an effective program for foreign students, among them being the utilization of the expertise and resources of NAFSA for consultation in program development, the establishing of a data bank on campus, the devising of a system of class role identification, and the establishment of a faculty/student 'pal' system and an international/intercultural club. The author maintains that the investment in time, energy, and resources in the foreign student program is more than paid back through benefits accruing to the institution via participation in the international and intercultural dimension of higher education.

362. Cowser, R. L., Jr. "Foreign Student: New Nigger on Campus." Community College Review 6 (Summer, 1978): 4-7.

363. Davis, James M. "Foreign Students in the 2-Year College." International Educational and Cultural Exchange 7 (Fall, 1971): 25-32.

364. Diener, Thomas. "Foreign Students and U.S. Community Colleges." Community College Review 7 (Spring, 1980): 58-65.

365. Diener, Thomas. "Profile of Foreign Students in United States Community and Junior Colleges." In The Foreign Student in United States Community and Junior Colleges, edited by J. Edmund Gleazer, Jr., et al., pp. 14-31. New York: College Entrance Examination Board, 1978.

Foreign students are enrolling in U.S. community and junior colleges in record numbers. Students from Third World countries are playing a dominant role in this increase. The two-year institutions find themselves offering studies appropriate to many foreign nationals. At the same time foreign students do present a number of special issues and problems. This paper presents information about the characteristics of the more than 60,000 foreign students in two-year institutions in the U.S. It describes where these foreign students come from, what they study, how they are financed, and other specific information about them. In 1976-77, 68% of foreign students in two-year U.S. colleges were male, most of them not married; 66% were full-time students and enrolled in transfer programs. Fifty-two percent of them were financed personally, 80% of them pursued the associate degree, most of them were from developing countries, and concentrated on such popular majors as engineering, business/management, general and interdisciplinary studies, education, health, data processing, and computer science.

366. Diener, T. J., and L. Kerr. "Institutional Responsibilities to Foreign Students." New Directions for Community Colleges No. 26 (1979): 49-56.

367. Gleazer, J. Edmund, Jr. "To Transcend the Boundaries." In The Foreign Student in United States Community and Junior Colleges, edited by J. Edmund Gleazer, Jr., et al., pp. 4-13. New York: College Entrance Examination Board, 1978.

368. Hagey, A. R. and J. Hagey. "The International Student and the Junior College: Academic and Social Needs." Journal of College Student Personnel 13 (March, 1972): 140-144.

369. Kastner, Harold H., Jr. "Modifying the Open-Door Policy." Community College Review 6 (Spring, 1979): 28-33.

370. Kerr, L., and T. J. Diener. "Two-Year Colleges: New Pioneers?" International Educational and Cultural Exchange 10 (Spring, 1975): 12-15.

371. Lambert, Jonathan. "International Students and the Community College." National Association for Foreign Student Affairs Newsletter 33 (October, 1981): 19ff.

372. Martorand, S. Y. "Constraints and Issues in Planning and Implementing Programs for Foreign Students in Community and Junior Colleges." In The Foreign Student in United States

Community and Junior Colleges, edited by J. Edmund Gleazer, Jr., et al., pp. 32-51. New York: College Entrance Examination Board, 1978.

The purpose of this paper is twofold: first, to provide a general description of the constraints—the problems and hindrances—community colleges encounter in developing programs and services for foreign students and in acquiring an international dimension; second, by identifying issues related to these constraints, to set the stage for further discussion, decision and action in removing the constraints. It first describes the background in community college education of foreign student enrollment. Then it examines the assumption that community colleges need to make more and better efforts in serving foreign students and developing an international dimension. The third and fourth section present respectively the constraints that seem generally recognized and issues that community colleges must face and resolve if the constraints are to be attacked effectively.

373.  Matthewson, D. E.  "International Students in the Junior College." College and University 43 (Summer, 1968): 497-512.


Reportage


374.  "1 in 3 Students from Abroad is Attending a Two-Year College." Chronicle of Higher Education 9 (December 16, 1974): 2.

375.  Silny, Josep. "It's not Surprising that Community Colleges Enroll Many Foreign Students." Chronicle of Higher Education 9 (January 20, 1975): 11.


# 5. HISTORICAL STUDIES


376.  Board of Foreign Scholarships. A Quarter Century: The American Adventure in Academic Exchange. Washington, D.C.: Board of Foreign Scholarship, 1971.

377.  Buchloh, Paul G., and Walter T. Rix, eds. American Colony of Gottingen: Historical and Other Data Collected Between the Years 1855 and 1888. Gottingen: Vandenhoeck and Ruprecht, 1976.

378.  Diehl, Carl. Americans and German Scholarship, 1770-1870. New Haven: Yale University Press, 1978.

379.  Faruqi, Ashraf. "European Involvement in the Aligarh Movement: The Role and Influence of the European Faculty in the Social

and Political Aspects of the Mohamedan Anglo-Oriental College, 1875-1920." Unpublished Ph.D thesis, Duke University, 1978.

380. Green, Donald G. "Characteristics of International Alumni, Cornell University, 1935-1959." Unpublished Ph.D thesis, Cornell University, 1964.

381. Hayes, Mary. "Irish Scholars in the Universities at Paris and Oxford Before 1500." Unpublished Ph.D thesis, City University of New York, 1979.

382. Johnson, Walter, and Francis Colligan. The Fulbright Program--A History. Chicago: University of Chicago Press, 1966.

    In 1952 and 1953 the Committee on Foreign Relations undertook a study of the overseas information programs of the United States. The committee examined all the means by which the U.S. was seeking to improve worldwide appreciation of the values of a free society and to encourage international understanding. The authors of this study give a detailed account of the Fulbright Program, and the venture into international educational and scholarly interchange between the U.S. and other countries. They provide a definitive and fascinating history and reveal some of the trials and tribulations of getting exchange programs started, keeping them going, and maintaining morale during the dark and discouraging days of the McCarthy period. The book also puts into perspective problems on which able and conscientious educators and administrators differed, and recorded some of the spectacular successes of educational exchange programs that stood the test of time.

383. Kellermann, Henry J. Cultural Relations as an Instrument of U.S. Foreign Policy: The Educational Exchange Program Between the United States and Germany, 1945-1954. Washington, D.C.: Bureau of Educational and Cultural Affairs, U.S. Department of State/Government Printing Office, 1978.

384. Miller, Olive. Creating a World of Friends: A Twenty Year History of the Community Section of the National Association for Foreign Student Affairs. Washington, D.C.: National Association for Foreign Student Affairs, 1981.

385. Munro, Dana Gardner. A Student in Central America, 1914-1916. New Orleans: Middle American Research Institute, Tulane University, 1983.

386. Obergottsberger, Hugo. 25 Jahre Fulbright--Programm in Osterreich. Vienna: Osterreiches--Amerikan Erziehungskommission, 1975.

387. Ohl, Ronald Edward. "The University of Padua, 1405-1509: An International Community of Students and Professors." Unpublished Ph.D thesis, University of Pennsylvania, 1980.

388. Roth, Lois. Public Diplomacy and the Past: The Studies of U.S. Information and Cultural Programs (1952-1975). Washington, D.C.: Foreign Service Institute, Department of State, 1981.

389. Sloan, R. C., and I. G. Cumings. A Survey of African Students Studying in the United States. New York: Phelps-Stokes Fund, 1949.

390. Smith, Kent Warner. "The United States Cultural Crusade in Mexico, 1938-1945: A Case Study in Person-to-Person Peacemaking." Unpublished Ph.D thesis, University of California, 1972.

391. Tomaszewski, Viktor, ed. The University of Edinburgh and Poland: An Historical Review. Edinburgh: The University of Edinburgh, 1968.

392. United States Board of Foreign Scholarships, Department of State. International Educational Exchange--The Opening Decades, 1946-1966. Washington, D.C.: U.S. Government Printing Office, 1967.

393. United States Department of State. Reviews and Evaluation of Inter-American Cultural Programs and Activities Undertaken by the United States, prior to 1956. Washington, D.C.: Department of State, 1956.


## Articles

394. Brickman, William W. "International Exchange in Higher Education: Europe and the United States, 1700-1900." Notre Dame Journal of Education 3 (Spring, 1972): 10-21.

This article examines higher educational relations involving Europe and the United States during the period 1700-1900. By higher education the author does not only refer to universities and colleges; he includes any kind of advanced studies, structured institutionally or carried out independently by such personalities of American political and scientific life as Benjamin Franklin and Abraham Lincoln.

Brickman points out that international relations in the field of higher learning are in the roots of American higher education. English roots, mainly through relationship of graduates of Cambridge and Oxford with Harvard, are obvious. But the links with universities in Leiden, Geneva, Paris, or Louvain were no less important for the process of development of higher education in the Colonial America.

Americans in large numbers went to Europe at the end of the 18th century to study medicine in the Universities of Leiden, Paris, Edinburgh, Vienna, London, Oxford, Uppsala, and in the Italian universities.

The 19th century brought again interest in studies in Europe, mainly in medical education offered in German universities. From 1820 to 1920, it has been estimated that between 9,000 to 10,000 Americans studied in Germany, many of them coming back with a Ph.D. (The first Ph.D was granted in the United States in 1861 at Yale University.)

American higher education institutions were throughout the 19th century also recipients of students from other countries such as Germany or Japan.

395. Carroll, L. "Sea Voyage Controversy and the Kayasthas of North India, 1901-1909." Modern Asian Studies 13 (April, 1979): 265-299.

396. Cross, A. G. "Russian Students in Eighteenth-Century Oxford." Journal of European Studies 5 (June, 1975): 91-110.

397. Diaconescu, M. "Foreign Students in Romania--A Short Historical Survey." Romanian Review No. 12 (1980): 103-111.

398. Frijhoff, Willem. "Etudiants Etrangers a l'Academie d'Congers au 17$^{eme}$ Siecle." Lias [Amsterdam] 4 (No. 1, 1977): 13-84.

399. Frijhoff, Willem. "Etudiants Hollandais dans les Colleges Francais, 17$^{eme}$ et 18$^{eme}$ Siecles." Lias [Amsterdam] 3 (No. 2, 1976): 301-312.

400. Gish, O. "Foreign-born Graduates of British Medical Schools 1948-1966." British Journal of Medical Education 5 (No. 1, 1971): 22-29.

401. Jenkins, Hugh M. "International Education and The National Association for Foreign Student Affairs, 1948-1978." International Educational and Cultural Exchange 14 (No. 1, 1978): 17-21.

402. Jewsbury, George F. "Russian Students in Nancy, France, 1905-1914: A Case Study." Jahrbuch fur Geschichte Osteuropas 23 (No. 2, 1975): 225-228.

403. King, Kenneth J. "African Students in Negro American Colleges: Notes on the Good African." Phylon 31 (Spring, 1970): 16-30.

The first World War led to a great explosion of interest of Africans in higher education. It developed links between black people in Africa and the U.S. on an unprecedented scale, and this led a body of Africans to feel that the most relevant overseas education might be acquired in the black colleges and universities of the Southern states of the U.S. This article gives an account and analysis of the case of Tuskegee Institute, Alabama in enrolling black students from Uganda during the 1920s.

404. Koloko, E. M. "Origins of Overseas Training for Zambians 1900-1975." In Policy Developments in Overseas Training, edited by T. L. Maliyamkono, pp. 80-98. Dar es Salaam: Black Star Agencies and Eastern African Universities Research Project, 1980.

405. Leonhardt, F. "Hollister at Purdue University--Remembrances of a Foreign Exchange Student." In Perspectives on the History of Reinforced Concrete in the United States 1904-1941--Solom Cady Hollister Colloquium, edited by J. F. Abel, and D. P. Billington, pp. 223-226. Princeton, New Jersey: Princeton University, Department of Civil Engineering, 1980.

406. McNeil, W. A. "Scottish Entries in the Acta Rectoria Universitatis Parisiensis 1519-1633." Scottish Historical Review 43 (April, 1964): 66-86.

407. Muller, Wolfgang. "Schweizer Studenten der Universitat Freiburg in Breisgau im 19 Jahrhundert." Allemannica. Landeskundliche Beitrage (Festschrift fur Bruno Boesch zum 65 Geburstag). Alemannisches Jahrbuch 1973/75 (Buhl/Baden: 1976): 590-596.

408. Ninkovich, F. "Chinese Students in the United States: Cultural Relations and American China Policy, 1942-1945." Pacific Historical Review 49 (August, 1980): 471-498.

409. Schmoker, John. "The First Twenty-Five Years." National Association for Foreign Student Affairs Newsletter 24 (May, 1973): 1ff.

410. Schultz, Gisela. "Gegenseitigkeit in der Auswartigen Kulturpolitic durch Austrausch von Studenten und Wissenschaftlern--Versuch Einer Historischen Bestands-Aufnahme aus Anlass des 50 Jahrigen Jubilaums der Deutschen Akademischen Austrauschdienstes." Zeitschrift fur Kulturaustausch 25 (No. 3, 1975): 51-58.

411. Silvera, Alain. "The First Egyptian Student Mission to France under Muhammad Ali." Middle Eastern Studies 16 (May, 1980): 1-22.

412. Stafford, F. "In Search of the Practical: Colombian Students in Foreign Lands, 1845-1890." Hispanic American Historial Review 52 (No. 2, 1972): 230-249.

One index of a growing Latin American interest in technical study after the middle of the 19th century can be found in the records of New York state's Rensselaer Polytechnic Institute. In the 25 years between 1850 and 1875 some 90 youths from the Hispanic world studied there, accounting for more than 10% of the graduates. In the next decade another 60 Latins attended Rensselaer, making up more than 9% of the student body. While many upper-class Colombians sent their sons to the U.S. because they identified it with practicality, others turned to Europe because of its established scientific superiority. The results of the 19th-century experiments in foreign training must be judged in terms of the parents' aim and in the context of contemporary educational patterns. In general, Colombian investment in foreign study produced their best return in commerce and medicine. After 1870 the conditions determining study abroad and its possible fruits became more favorable, and the return was better.

413. Stewart, Gordon M. "British Students at the University of Gottingen in the Eighteenth Century." German Life and Letters 33 (No. 1, 1979): 32-41.

414. Trevelyan, M. "Yesterday and Today; Thirty Years with International Students." International Education and Cultural Exchange 8 (Summer, 1972): 1-15.

415. United States International Communication Agency. "Quarter Century of Educational Exchange." International Educational and Cultural Exchange 13 (Spring, 1978): 28-32.

416. Watt, D. E. R. "Scottish Student Life Abroad in the Fourteenth Century." Scottish Historical Review 59 (April, 1980): 3-21.

417. Williams, W. L. "Ethnic Relations of African Students in the United States with Black Americans, 1870-1900." Journal of Negro History 65 (Summer, 1980): 228-249.

418. Yates, B. A. "Educating Congolese Abroad: An Historical Note on African Elites." International Journal of African Historical Studies 14 (No. 1, 1981): 34-64.

This study identifies the first generation Congolese elite as composing three groups: preacher-teachers, soldiers, and artisans and examines how three study-abroad programs helped in the emergence of these first generation, nontraditional elites and their connection to social, political, and economic policy. How the study-abroad schemes provided the intimate link between Belgian domestic politics and Belgian colonial policy and practice is also explored.

The Congolese nationals who went abroad in the nineteenth century, the nature of the formal programs available in those years and the role of the colonial government and Congo Missions are covered. The projects to educate Congolese nationals overseas did not represent the prevailing policy of either the mission societies or the colonial government, therefore no wonder these projects were terminated by the colonial regime. The state as well as the missionaries favored educating Congolese in Africa. Reasons are advanced as to why the Congolese returnees were inducted into the militia and why the government failed to train other secular elites. On the legacy of the nineteenth century, it is concluded that 80 years of Belgian Catholic domination of the Congo educational system resulted in few secular elites but scores of problems for independent Zaire.

## 6. POLICY OF "SENDING" COUNTRIES

419. Maliyamkono, T. L., ed. Policy Developments in Overseas Training. Dar es Salaam, Tanzania: Black Star Agencies and Eastern African Universities Research Project, 1980.

420. Torres Padilla, Oscar. La Formacion de Recursos Humanos en el Exterior; Un Estudio para la Determinacion de Prioridades. San Jose, Costa Rica: Universidad de Costa Rica, 1972.

421. Young, Robert L. "Study Abroad and National Purpose in the Middle East." Unpublished Ph.D thesis, Stanford University, 1965.

### Articles

422. Adam, H. M. "Somali Policies Towards Education, Training and Manpower." In Policy Developments in Overseas Training, edited by T. L. Maliyamkono, pp. 99-122. Dar es Salaam: Black Star Agencies and Eastern African Universities Research Project, 1980.

423. Arnstein, G., and C. R. Foster. "Big Lift nach Amerika: Ein Kommentar aus Washington." Bildung und Erziehung 27 (No. 6, 1974): 399-406.

424. Gee, T. W. "Policy on Overseas Students in Post-Colonial Period." In Policy Developments in Overseas Training, edited by T. L. Maliyamkono, pp. 229-289. Dar es Salaam: Black Star Agencies and Eastern African Universities Research Project, 1980.

425. Kinjanjui, K., M. Adholla, and P. Anaminyi. "Evolution of Overseas Training Policy in Kenya." In Policy Development in Overseas Training, edited by T. L. Maliyamkono, pp. 58-79. Dar es Salaam: Black Star Agencies and Eastern African Universities Research Project, 1980.

426. Maliyamkono, T. L., and S. Wells. "Impact Surveys on Overseas Training." In Policy Development in Overseas Training, edited by T. L. Maliyamkono, pp. 1-37. Dar es Salaam: Black Star Agencies and Eastern African Universities Research Project, 1980.

427. Similane, V. M. "Analysis of Training Policies in Swaziland." In Policy Development in Overseas Training, edited by T. L.

Maliyamkono, pp. 123-130. Dar es Salaam: Black Star Agencies and Eastern African Universities Research Project, 1980.

428. Sumra, S., and A. G. Ishumi. "Trends in Tanzania's Policies Towards Higher Training." In Policy Development in Overseas Training, edited by T. L. Maliyamkono, pp. 38-57. Dar es Salaam: Black Star Agencies and Eastern African Universities Research Project, 1980.

429. Walgren, Doug, et al. "Taiwan Surveillance and Harassment of Taiwanese University Students in the U.S." In Taiwan Agents in America and the Death of Professor Wen-Chen Chen, pp. 22-59. Washington, D.C.: Government Printing Office, 1981.

430. Wells, S., and P. Boogaard. "Policy Issues in Overseas Training." In Policy Development in Overseas Training, edited by T. L. Maliyamkono, pp. 195-228. Dar es Salaam: Black Star Agencies and Eastern African Universities Research Project, 1980.


## Reportage

431. B. T. W. "West Germany Will Send 'Surplus' Students to 25 U.S. Colleges If Plan Goes Through." Chronicle of Higher Education 8 (December 9, 1973): 2.

432. "South Korea Eases Study-abroad Requirements." Chronicle of Higher Education 23 (February 24, 1982): 31.


# 7. POLICY OF "HOST" COUNTRY

433. American Association of State Colleges and Universities. Trends and Issues in Globalizing Higher Education. Washington, D.C.: AASCU, 1977.

During the academic year 1975-76 AASCU organized, in collaboration with a number of U.S. universities five workshops devoted to an examination of the international role and responsibility of U.S. higher education. This publication represents a summary of highlights of these workshops and it covers the following main themes:
. mission, commitment, institutional change: The education of students for a highly multicultural and inter-dependent world is endorsed.
. academic content and faculty development: This must be used to encourage international/intercultural education.
. international exchanges, development, and linkages: This must be encouraged for students and especially for faculty because it is "critical to globalizing of

education on campus" and it is necessary for continuous
rejuvenation of higher education.

. foreign students: Their number in the U.S. universities and colleges is steadily growing, especially among
those coming from developing countries. This trend
should not result in the curriculum modifications to
suit the needs of foreign students at the expense of
U.S. students. It is pointed out that there are "still
too many doctoral students from developing countries
writing library dissertations that have no relevance or
real usefulness to the role they will play in their home
countries."

. international development: The evolution of African and
Asian universities demonstrate interest in moving away
from the European model towards a more flexible curriculum, an area in which U.S. higher education institutions
are particularly experienced. This development offers a
great opportunity to strengthen international and intercultural programs currently functioning at U.S. universities and colleges.

434.  American Council on Education, Overseas Liaison Committee. Future
Nigerian-U.S. Linkages in Higher Education. Washington, D.C.:
American Council on Education, 1977.

435.  Barber, Elinor G.  A Survey of Policy Changes: Foreign Students in
Public Institutions of Higher Education. New York:  Institute
of International Education, 1983.

In 1981, the IIE queried all public two-year and
four-year public institutions concerning their policies
toward foreign students, with an emphasis on finding out
if changes in policy had taken place. In 1983, a second
study of these institutions was undertaken. Emphasis in
the analysis was placed on those institutions with the
largest numbers of foreign students. About 61% of the
institutions surveyed responded to the questionnaire.
Overall, the following results were reported: (a) foreign
students will find somewhat decreased services provided
for them; (b) changes with regard to financial assistance
and qualifications for admission are more likely to be
adverse than favorable; (c) changes in policy introduced
by the institutions with the largest numbers of foreign
students depart from the norm, but the direction of their
impact is not consistently positive or negative; (d) among
the states with the largest concentrations of foreign
students, only New York stands out as having made it more
difficult, through the decrease in tuition waivers and
stiffer admissions requirements, for foreign students to
come; and (e) the institutions where the foreign student
population is growing at a relatively rapid rate appear to
be inclined to encourage this growth and are clearly not
taking actions to restrict it.

436. Bristow, R., and J. E. C. Thornton. <u>Overseas Students and Govern-ment Policy 1962-1979</u>. London: Overseas Students Trust, 1979.

437. Canadian Bureau for International Education. <u>A Question of Self-Interest: A Statement on Foreign Students in Canada</u>. Ottawa: Canadian Bureau for International Education, 1977.

This publication represents a statement approved by the CBIE Board of Directors the purpose of which was "to provoke discussion" on foreign students' issues in the Canadian higher education.
The authors consider that:
. Canadian post-secondary educational institutions benefit from the presence of non-Canadian students;
. reception of foreign students has an impact on Canada's future foreign relations;
. foreign students policies should be designed to reflect Canada's self-interest first, since the primary respon-sibility of Canadian governments is to Canadians;
. the process and mechanics of development in the Third World are best decided by the people and governments of the Third World; and
. Canadians have an obligation to share their educational resources with less developed countries to promote better international understanding. Recent developments and trends in receiving foreign students and "exporting" Canadians to study abroad are discussed.
Finally, the statement addresses a question of Canada's self-interest in receiving foreign students. It considers that such interest can be served if any one or more of the following conditions is satisfied:
. If the presence of foreign students improves the quality of the educational experiences offered by the institu-tion, or
. If the reception of foreign students furthers the long-or short-range economic and political interest of Canada abroad, or
. If there is an immediate financial return from the pre-sence of foreign students in Canada.
In three sections of the statement these three conditions are discussed.
In conclusion, CBIE believes there is the need for a re-examination of Canada's motives and methods if Canadians and foreign students are to gain maximum benefit from their stay.

438. Canadian Bureau for International Education. <u>The Right Mix: Report of the Commission on Foreign Student Policy</u>. Ottawa: Canadian Bureau for International Education, 1981.

In 1981, CBIE Board of Directors, concerned with the lack of coherent policies related to foreign students especially in the context of their growing numbers, approved the establishment of a Commission on Foreign Student Policy. This publication is the first report of this commission, which contains a large number of recommendations to Canadian educational institutions, provincial and federal governments, and to other interested organizations and institutions.

The two-track structured report which analyzes the situation and provides a series of recommendations deals with the following:

. foreign students: definition and jurisdiction;
. analysis of the foreign student population in Canada, its social, economic, and educational background as well as motivations for studying in Canada;
. a framework of the present institutional policies with regard to recruitment, testing, and enrollment of foreign students;
. policies related to costs and tuition fees for foreign students as well as the Canadian taxpayers.

Overall, the report gives two basic reasons to support the presence of foreign students in Canada. One is a moral one and emphasized Canada's "obligations to the international community of nations." The other is founded on practical considerations and emphasizes Canada's economic and political interest. It also makes recommendations concerning "the management of foreign student enrollment" which will result in imminent restriction on enrollment growth of foreign students in the Canadian higher education institutions. Some of these recommendations include introduction of:

. enrollment limits for foreign students, using geographically determined quotas; and
. coherent and coordinated federal and provincial governments policies regarding tuition fees and funding of programs directed towards foreign students.

The authors of the report stress the importance of the development of the coordinated and coherent policy on foreign students. In this context it also recommends that CBIE serve as "a clearinghouse for information on institutional foreign student enrollment and recruiting policies, and that it coordinate the establishment of cooperative networks among those institutions."

439. Canadian Federation of Students. A Decade of Dishonor: Patterns of Fees and Quotas for International Students. Toronto: CFS, 1983.

440. Cleveland, E., G. Mangove, and J. C. Adams. The Overseas American Agenda for Action. New York: McGraw-Hill, 1960.

441. College Entrance Examination Board. University, Government, and the Foreign Graduate Student. Princeton: CEEB, 1969.

442. Committee on Educational Interchange Policy. The Foreign Student: Exchangee or Immigrant? New York: Committee on Educational Interchange Policy, 1958.

443. Committee on the Foreign Student in American Colleges and Universities. The College, the University, and the Foreign Student. Washington, D.C.: National Association for Foreign Student Affairs, 1979.

   This is a report of leading educators' recommendations for strengthening educational exchange programs in U.S. colleges and universities. The report calls for a complete re-examination of the philosophy, objectives, and operation of the foreign student programs at most institutions in this country. The basic point of this report is that the exchange programs cannot be strengthened in any meaningful or lasting way unless they are seen in the context of the total international activities, at home and abroad, of any given institution. The second point is that the responsibility for defining those activities rests squarely on the leaders of education. The third point is that the international commitments of the American college and university are permanent. The report discusses education's stake in international exchange, the university's responsibilities to the foreign student, and the administration of services for foreign students.

444. Education and World Affairs. The Foreign Student: Whom Shall We Welcome? New York: EWA, 1965.

445. Frey, James S. "The Development of a Criterion Instrument for Evaluating Agency-Sponsored Study Abroad Programs." Unpublished Ed.D thesis, Indiana University, 1976.

446. Gass, J. R., and R. F. Lyons. International Flows of Students: Policy Conference on Economic Growth and Investment in Education. Paris: Organization for Economic Cooperation and Development, 1962.

447. Gerstein, H. Auslandische Studenten in der Bundesrepublik Deutschland. Bad-Godesburg: Deutscher Akademischer Austauschdienst, 1974.

448. International Education and Cultural Affairs, Department of State. Is Anyone Listening? The Sixth Annual Report of the U.S. Advisory Commission on International Educational and Cultural Affairs. Washington, D.C.: IECA, 1969.

449. International Educational Exchange Liaison Group. Enhancing American Influence Abroad: International Exchanges in the National Interest. Washington, D.C.: National Association for Foreign Student Affairs, 1981.

450. International Research Associates. A Study of Relations to the State Department Exchange Program among Returned Mexican Grantees. Mexico City: International Research Associates, 1959.

451. International Research Associates. The Thai Student Exchange: An Evaluation Report. New York: International Research Associates, 1955.

452. Loccumer Arbeitskreis Auslanderstudium. Auslanderstudium, Fragen und Empfehlungen zu einer Reform. Loccum: Pressestelle der Evangel Akademie, 1969.

453. Meyersohn, Rolf. Development of an Evaluation System for Fulbright Students' Program. New York: Institute of International Education, 1973.

454. Mutual Advantage: Report of the Committee of Review of Private Overseas Student Policy. Canberra: Australian Government Publishing Service, 1984.

455. National Board of Universities and Colleges. Higher Education for Visiting Students. Stockholm: Utbildnings Forlaget, 1980.

456. National Board of Universities and Colleges. Higher Education for Immigrants and Political Refugees. Stockholm: Utbildnings Forlaget, 1980.

457. National Liaison Committee on Foreign Student Admissions. The Foreign Undergraduate Student: Institutional Priorities for Action. Princeton: College Board Publications, 1975.

This book is the result of a colloquium which was held in June 1979 in Racine, Wisconsin. It deals with the impact that undergraduate foreign students and United States postsecondary education have on each other. The meeting was organized around the following three papers, which dealt with the ideal, the real, and the practical approaches to undergraduate foreign student programs:
1. "In Quest of the Ideal" by Alister W. McCrone.
2. "The Now Reality" by A. Lee Zeigler.
3. "A Practical Approach to the Development of Institutional Priorities" by Hugh M. Jenkins.
At the end of this publication, a summary of recommendations formulated during this colloquium is presented. They include:
. provision of adequate information about higher education institutions in the United States to be carried out by reliable professional counseling centers overseas. These centers can be binational or sponsored by the U.S. government or local governments;
. due regard for the students' qualifications and the appropriateness of their institutions' programs;

. establishment of clearinghouses in the United States to
ease the application process and assure good match;
. study of how to broaden undergraduate curriculums that
include an international dimension;
. efforts to be made to lobby for legislation advan-
tageous to foreign students, e.g., relaxing restrictions
on summer employment;
. recommendation that each institution with a substantial
number of foreign students form a task force to examine
its international higher education programs;
. encouragement of alumni contacts and participation in
their professional development after they have returned
to their countries; and
. strengthening of ties among existing foreign student
associations which could eventually make possible the
creation of an international association of foreign
student organizations.

458. Overseas Students Trust. Overseas Students and Government Policy.
London: Overseas Students Trust, 1979.

An inquiry into possible policies for the regulation
and funding of foreign (overseas) students in Britain,
this volume provides a full scale analysis of the financial and policy aspects of the issue in light of the
current situation in Britain. The research team collected
statistics concerning the financial aspects of overseas
students, their numbers in Britain and in several other
countries, and various policy options. The study concludes by accepting the government's "full fee" policy,
but also recommends various options for alternative
funding for students from countries of importance to
British foreign and trade policy while taking recognition
of Britain's "special relationship," not only with the
European Community but with such countries as those in the
Commonwealth and with Hong Kong and Cyprus.

459. Political and Economic Planning. New Commonwealth Students in
Britain: With Special Reference to Students from East Africa.
London: Allen and Unwin, 1965.

This study examines policies of the United Kingdom in
the early 1960's, especially in the context of the
recommendations of the Robbins Committee on Higher
Education, toward education and training of students from
the four East African countries; Kenya, Tanganyika,
Uganda, and Zanzibar. (The union of Tanganyika and
Zanzibar took place after the research was done.)
The volume is divided into three parts: Part I is
concerned with trends in the admission of overseas
students to British institutions of higher education and
with an estimate of future demand for study places by
students from East Africa. Part II is concerned with
policies relating to the academic and formal educational

aspects of these students' lives in England, and Part III deals with the students' experiences, outside their courses.

Two interviews were carried out to provide data. The problems which East African students face in British universities and colleges include:
. lack of academic and career advice;
. study difficulties;
. problems of English;
. problems of practical training;
. problems of adjustment.

This report is mostly addressed to those "whose work gives them direct responsibility for overseas students in the United Kingdom and accordingly each recommendation made in the report suggests who should, in the author's view, carry it out." These recommendations are addressed to:
. the British Government;
. the overseas governments;
. institutions receiving students;
. Universities Central Council on Admissions;
. the General Nursing Council;
. voluntary organizations concerned with overseas students; and
. private trusts with emergency funds for students.

460. Reed, Ruth, Jean Hutton, and John Bazalgette. Freedom to Study: A Report Prepared by the Grubb Institute for the Overseas Students Trust. London: Overseas Students Trust, 1978.

In 1976 the Overseas Students Trust commissioned the Grubb Institute to make recommendations concerning the facilities which overseas students required if they were to make the most effective use of their study period in the United Kingdom. The Overseas Student Trust, established in 1961 and registered as an educational charity, seeks to expand and improve the services made available to overseas students in the United Kingdom. In this study the Grubb Institute gathered evidence from overseas students on how they viewed their experience in Britain. Students in the survey were drawn from universities, polytechnics, and colleges of further education in different parts of the country. The report, which analyzes the students' criticisms of the provisions made available to them, points out that many of the provisions are based on the assumption that the overseas students are poor and disadvantaged. It is suggested that the students are not welfare objects and to regard them as such is an avoidance of the need to restructure some of the systems which serve the educational process. To show that the overseas student is part of the educational process, three different but overlapping systems are examined, namely: the academic system, in which the student takes up his fundamental role as a student; the selection system, in which he enters into professional relationship between himself and his college; and the U.K. boundary control system, in which he will be treated as a visitor and not an intruder or an immigrant. The report concludes that overseas students' bad experiences have more to do with the unsatisfactory nature of these systems and less to do with the students' personal problems. The report provides several recommendations to the various authorities and institutions on how they could act more responsibly toward overseas students. The key recommendation is that the academic staff in educational institutions should take greater responsibility for overseas students. "Academic tutors," whose task would be to help students concentrate on their studies, and changes in the role of advisers of overseas students are considered necessary. The report places emphasis on the sense of power and dignity of the overseas student and makes proposals on how this awareness could be achieved. To avoid the difficulties overseas students face at the port of entry, it is suggested that the regulations covering the admission of overseas students to the United Kingdom be standardized and made mandatory for all countries. The Grubb Institute calls for public discussion of the issues raised in the report, beginning with the publication of this report and the setting up of conferences around its significant themes.

461. Roberts, Stanley C. and Kogila Adam-Moodley. Institutional Policies: Admissions, Fees and Quotas for Foreign Students at Canadian Post-Secondary Institutions. Ottawa: Canadian Bureau for International Education, 1977.

462. Social Security Administration, Department of Health, Education and Welfare. Social Security Coverage of Foreign Students and Exchange Visitors. Baltimore, Maryland: Social Security Administration, 1979.

463. Splett, Oskar. Die Politik des Kulturaustausches; Was Fehlt in der Bundesrupublik Deutschland? Munich: Olzog Verlag, 1977.

464. Stacey, Dorothy. Commitment to Learning: Thirty Years of U.S. Public Health Service International Fellowships, 1946-76. Washington, D.C.: International Health Fellowship Branch, Public Health Service, Department of Health, Education and Welfare, 1978.

465. Stine, Dorothy Pearce. "The Role of the United States in the International Educational Exchange of Teachers and Students." Unpublished Ed.D thesis, University of Houston, 1954.

466. United Kingdom, Department of Education and Science. Government Observations on the First Report from the Education, Science and Arts Committee [of the House of Commons]. London: Her Majesty's Stationery Office, 1980.

467. United States Congress, House Subcommittee on Africa. African Students and Study Programs in the United States: Report and Hearings. Washington, D.C.: Government Printing Office, 1965.

468. Von Zur-Muehlen, Max. Foreign Student Issues in 1976-77. Ottawa: Canadian Bureau for International Education, 1977.

469. Williams, Peter, ed. The Overseas Student Question: Studies for a Policy. London: Heinemann, 1981.

470. Williams, Peter, ed. A Policy for Overseas Students. London: Overseas Students Trust, 1982.

471. Winks, Robin W. A Report on Some Aspects of the Fulbright-Hays Program. New Haven, Connecticut: Yale University, 1977.


## Articles

472. Arnold, Ruth, and Harold Adams. "Rationale for International Students I." College and University 45 (Summer, 1970): 530-544.

473. Bayer, Alan E. "Foreign Students in American Colleges: Time for Change in Policy and Practice." Research in Higher Education 1 (No. 4, 1973): 389-400.

    Institutional characteristics for the total population of more than 2,300 U.S. colleges and universities are related to the proportionate foreign student enrollment through stepwise, multiple-regression analysis. Comprehensive data (for 1967) developed through the Cooperative Institutional Research Program (CIRP) of the American Council of Education are used to define the percentage of foreign students among the total enrolled student body (dependent variable). Fifteen measures of institutional characteristics were derived from the CIRP file as predictor variables and were selected to assess their relationship to the proportionate foreign student enrollment. Overall, about three-fourths of U.S. higher education institutions have less than 2% of foreign students in their student population, almost one-fifth have 2 to 6%, and one-twentieth have more than 6% foreign students. Relatively large numbers of foreign students are enrolled in universities, in private and sectarian institutions, in predominantly white institutions located in the West, generally considered to be of "high quality" (as measured by affluence, selectivity, percent of faculty with Ph.D's, and library holdings).
    In conclusion, the author points out that, due to the overall supply-demand situation in U.S., higher education in early 1970s, foreign students are not necessarily in direct competition with U.S. students for available

student positions. He also sees signs of the "reverse brain drain" with regard to the U.S. qualified manpower as a consequence of the overall economic situation in the United States.

474. Berendzen, Richard. "Ethics in International Higher Education." In Principles, Practices and Problems in Higher Education, edited by M. C. Baca, and R. H. Stein, pp. 80-98. Springfield, Illinois: Thomas, 1983.

475. Blaug, Mark, and Maureen Woodhall. "A Survey of Overseas Students in British Higher Education 1980." In The Overseas Student Question: Studies for a Policy, edited by Peter Williams, pp. 239-264. London: Heinemann, 1981.

476. Dubbeldam, L. F. B. "Policies of the Netherlands International Education: Origins and Trends." In The Impact of Overseas Training on Development, edited by T. L. Maliyamkono, pp. 131-152. Arusha, Tanzania: Eastern African Publications, 1979.

477. Fraser, Stewart E. "Overseas Students in Australia: Government Policies and Institutional Support." Comparative Education Review 28 (May, 1984): 279-299.

478. Gieseke, Ludwig. "Discussion of a Foreign Student Policy in the Federal Republic of Germany." Higher Education in Europe 8 (No. 1, 1983): 101-104.

479. Glimm, H. "Training Foreign Students in the Federal Republic of Germany." In Policy Developments in Overseas Training, edited by T. L. Maliyamkono, pp. 302-337. Dar es Salaam: Black Star Agencies and Eastern African Universities Research Project, 1980.

480. Harari, M. "Priorities for Research and Action in the Graduate Foreign Student Field." International Educational and Cultural Exchange 6 (Fall, 1970): 60-67.

481. Hayden, Rose Lee. "U. S. Government Exchanges: The Quest for Coordination." Annals of The American Academy of Political and Social Science 449 (May, 1980): 114-128.

482. Hetland, A. "Policy Regarding Training Programmes for Students from Developing Countries." In Policy Development in Overseas Training, edited by T. L. Maliyamkono, pp. 290-301. Dar es Salaam: Black Star Agencies and Eastern African Universities Research Project, 1980.

483. Ilchman, Alice S. "Standards and Responsibilities: New Challenges for International Educators." National Association for Foreign Student Affairs Newsletter 31 (Summer, 1980): 1ff.

484. Kann, U. "Policy and Training Programmes for Students from Developing Countries." In Policy Development in Overseas Training, edited by T. L. Maliyamkono, pp. 153-194. Dar es Salaam: Black Star Agencies and Eastern African Universities Research Project, 1980.

485. Kaplan, Robert B. "Meeting the Educational Needs of Other Nations." In Educating Students from Other Nations, edited by Hugh Jenkins, pp. 253-276. San Francisco: Jossey-Bass, 1983.

486. Lamarsh, J. R., and M. M. Miller. "Weapons Proliferation and Foreign Students." British Atomic Scientist 36 (No. 3, 1980): 25-30.

487. Leestima, R. "U.S. Office of Education Programs Abroad." International Educational and Cultural Exchange 8 (No. 2, 1972): 32-45.

488. Lefever, Ernest W. "The Military Assistance [Educational Exchange] Training Program." Annals of the American Academy of Political and Social Science 424 (March, 1976): 85-95.

489. McLaughlin, M. M. "AID Training and Self-Help." International Educational and Cultural Exchange 5 (Summer, 1969): 60-69.

490. Oxenham, John. "Study Abroad and Development Policy—An Enquiry." In The Overseas Student Question: Studies for a Policy, edited by Peter Williams, pp. 150-164. London: Heinemann, 1981.

491. "Rationale for International Students, I." College and University 45 (No. 4, 1970): 530-544.

> This is a discussion of on-campus philosophy and objectives as they relate to foreign students, which took place during the 56th annual meeting of the American Association of Collegiate Registrars and Admissions Officers.
> The presentations emphasize the importance of U.S. economic and political interests in continuing or even expanding its educational exchange program and point out that full-scale involvement of U.S. institutions in international educational exchange is a relatively new phenomenon. In formulating exchange programs, the following factors have to be taken into account: (1) the size of the institution; (2) its private or public status; (3) its undergraduate or graduate character; (4) its fields of specialization; (5) its overseas involvement through exchange programs, government contracts, inter-university, and other programs.
> An educational institution which accepts foreign students assumes obligations such as:
> (1) providing adequate pre-admission information to prospective foreign students;

    (2)   assuming careful procedures for selection, admission, academic placement, reception, orientation, housing and food service without discrimination on the basis of national, ethnic, or cultural background;
    (3)   providing a good standard of classroom education;
    (4)   providing competent staff to advise foreign students.
Statistical data and trends on foreign students enrolled in U.S. institutions are also presented.

492.  Renken, Gerg. "University Places for Foreign Passport Holders." Bildung und Wissenschaft No. 16 (1974): 233-254.

493.  Smith, Alan, Christine V. Woesler de Panafieu, and Jean-Pierre Jarousse. "Foreign Student Flows and Policies in an International Perspective." In The Overseas Student Question: Studies for a Policy, edited by Peter Williams, pp. 165-223. London: Heinemann, 1981.

494.  Spaulding, S., and G. V. Coelho. "Research on Students from Abroad--The Neglected Policy Implications." In Uprooting and Development: Dilemmas of Coping with Modernization, edited by G. V. Coelho, and P. I. Ahmed, pp. 321-339. New York: Plenum Press, 1980.

The authors of this paper [chapter 15] review the cross-cultural educational activities of several U.S. government branches and other institutions, e.g., International Communications Agency, Agency for International Development, National Institute of Education, NAFSA and the participation of the United States in international organizations such as UNESCO in internationalization of education and its implications for U.S. policy in this area.

The authors stress the valuable contribution of foreign study both to the student's host-country and to his/her home-country. In this context they make several recommendations, which should assure that:

. transnational communication could exist on a continuing basis between former students and their teachers;
. the counseling and advising of potential foreign students would not be under the "propaganda arm" of the host government;
. government agencies collaborate in recruiting foreign students, with specific attention to the possibility of eventual employment in the home country; and
. legislative authority and support are advocated in the United States in order to promote the activities of international organizations and institutions which deal with programs of student exchange.

Finally, the authors argue that the social impact of the uprooting of students is largely determined by educational agencies and cultural institutions which establish priorities in policy. The role of national policy is therefore central in the developing of the

organizational infrastructure and institutional supports
that are necessary for an effective contribution of study
abroad for technological, social, and cultural development
of the foreign students' host countries.

495. Stassen, Manfred. "Interchanges, Internationalism and Ideology: A
     Case for Policy and Research." National Association for
     Foreign Student Affairs Newsletter 35 (March, 1984): 116-118.

496. Thomas, A. "Rationale for International Students: A Hidden
     Educational Resource." College and University 45 (Summer,
     1970): 622-625.

497. United States, Advisory Commission on International Educational and
     Cultural Affairs. "Unfinished Agenda; Summary and
     Recommendations of the 14th Report." International
     Educational and Cultural Exchange 13 (Spring, 1978): 3-5.

498. Vroman, Clyde, Lee Wilcox, and Robert Tschan. "Research on
     AID-Sponsored Students." College and University 45 (Summer,
     1970): 717-723.

499. Wallace, William. "Overseas Students: The Foreign Policy
     Implications." In The Overseas Student Question: Studies for
     a Policy, edited by Peter Williams, pp. 111-134. London:
     Heinemann, 1981.

500. Watson, Barbara M., and David Crosland. "Review of U.S. Policy on
     Iranian [including students] Immigration in Light of November
     1979 Takeover of the American Embassy in Iran." In U.S.
     Immigration Policy Regarding Iranian Nationals, pp. 2-33.
     Washington, D.C.: Government Printing Office, 1980.

501. Wicks, P. "Asian Students in Australia: Policies and Issues."
     Unicorn 4 (July, 1978): 135-141.

502. Williams, Peter. "Britain's Full-Cost Policy for Overseas
     Students." Comparative Education Review 28 (May, 1984):
     258-278.

503. Williams, Peter. "The Emergence of the Problem." In The Overseas
     Student Question: Studies for a Policy, edited by Peter
     Williams, pp. 1-21. London: Heinemann, 1981.

504. Williams, Peter. "Look West? Asian Attitudes to Study Abroad and
     Britain's Response." Asian Affairs 14 (February, 1983):
     15-26.

     This essay is the result of a revision to a lecture
given on October 5, 1982.
     The essay reviews the unfortunate nature of the
current policy of the government since 1980 which has
caused an increase in student fees for foreign visiting

students and thereby a steadily diminishing number of foreign students studying in the United Kingdom.

The problem faced by the declining number of students, particularly students from Asia in Britain, and the need for the British educational institutions to continue to recruit students from other countries, particularly the Third World, are discussed. The rationale for this recruitment of foreign students is based on the following areas of concern: first, it is in the interest of the British national policy to recruit students; secondly, foreign students are a vehicle to maintain international communication links; thirdly, the foreign students studying in Britain are a political asset both in the short term and the long term, and may serve as a system of rewarding countries for maintaining good relations with the United Kingdom; fourth, there is a trade and economic benefit potential from exposing foreign students to the British society; and lastly, foreign students comprise a dimension of continued overseas political and economic assistance as part of Britain's responsibility to the commonwealth.

A major portion of the article is devoted to a summary of the overseas student trust report developed in part by the author, entitled, "Policy for Overseas Students, Analysis, Options, Proposals." Basically, the report is broken down into three major areas. One, that there can be full-cost fees reinterpreted to mean "no subsidy." Secondly, a discussion of the report's concessions "for special territories such as Hong Kong and Bermuda and students from there." Third, recommendations for a unique award scheme to attract distinguished and meritorious students who are unable, for political or personal reasons, to study in Britain.

Lastly, the report recommends that the discretionary budget funds of approximately 10% be set aside for students to be recruited directly by British universities. Basically, the article contends that it is in the long-term interest of the United Kingdom to recruit select foreign students, particularly from the Third World, to study in Britain.

505. Williams, Peter. "Overseas Students in Britain: the Background." In The Overseas Student Question: Studies for a Policy, edited by Peter Williams, pp. 22-46. London: Heinemann, 1981.

506. Williams, Peter. "The Way Ahead." In The Overseas Student Question: Studies for a Policy, edited by Peter Williams, pp. 223-238. London: Heinemann, 1981.

Reportage

507. Abraham, A. S. "India Applies New Entry Rules." Times Higher Education Supplement (September 26, 1980): 6.

508. Abraham, A. S. "India Catches the Overflow from the Western Squeeze." Times Higher Education Supplement 471 (November 13, 1981): 9.

509. "American Medical Student Expelled from Poland." Chronicle of Higher Education 24 (July 14, 1982): 18.

510. "Anglo-French Accord on Student Exchange." Times Education Supplement (March 19, 1976): 8.

511. Bristow, Rupert. "A Recipe for Inertia--Government Policy on Overseas Students." Times Higher Education Supplement (October 9, 1981): 14.

512. "British Universities Warned About Foreign Influence." Chronicle of Higher Eduction 26 (July 20, 1983): 10.

513. "Canadian Commission on Foreign Students." Chronicle of Higher Education 22 (April 20, 1981): 19.

514. "Canadians Drop Move to Oust Foreigners." Times Higher Education Supplement (September 29, 1978): 5.

515. Casey, A. "Foreigners to Get Less of a Welcome." Times Education Supplement 3496 (July 1, 1983): 15.

516. Clough, P. "Government Papers to Ban Students from Abroad." Times Higher Education Supplement (July 15, 1977): 13.

517. Cohen, L. "New Deal in Sight for Holland's Foreign Students." Times Higher Education Supplement 474 (December 4, 1981): 7.

518. "Common Market Approves Joint Education Projects." Chronicle of Higher Education 21 (August 25, 1980): 25.

519. Cookson, C. "Canada Limits Foreign Recruits." Times Higher Education Supplement 449 (June 12, 1981): 6.

520. Dahlby, T. "Japanese Obstacle Course." Far East Economic Review 108 (May 23, 1980): 70.

521. David, P. "Call for National Policy as Balance Shifts from Poor to Rich." Times Higher Education Supplement 471 (November 13, 1981): 8.

522. David, P. "Quota Policy Brings Course Closure Fear." Times Higher Education Supplement (September 1, 1978): 1.

523. "Deportation of Palestinian Reaffirmed." Chronicle of Higher Education 21 (January 12, 1981): 13.

524. Dickson, D. "New Pentagon Rules on Overseas Students—Secrecy Threat to Sensitive Research Plans." Nature 289 (1981): 736.

525. Dickson, D. "Universities Complain at Pentagon Policy—Restrictions on Foreign Students Cause Alarm." Nature 290 (1981): 435-436.

526. Dickson, D. "French Minister to Probe Mutiny at Cultural-Exchange Agency." Chronicle of Higher Education 25 (November 17, 1982): 21.

527. Downings, J. "Race Quotas Put Polys in Classic Dilemma." Times Higher Education Supplement (March 3, 1978): 9.

528. Dubin, Joel. "U.S. Criticizes Israel's Expulsion Policy for Foreign Professors on West Bank." Chronicle of Higher Education 25 (November 24, 1982): 15.

529. "Grande-Bretagne: Restrictions pour l'Universite." Le Monde de l'Education No. 55 (1979): 24.

530. Hovey, J. A., Jr. "Coordination of International Exchange and Training Programs; the Opportunities and Limitations." International Educational and Cultural Exchange 14 (Summer, 1978): 33-35.

531. Hutchinson, J. "Drive to Improve Intake." Times Higher Education Supplement 439 (April 3, 1981): 4.

532. Hutchinson, J. "Ministers Aim to Improve Condition." Times Higher Education Supplement 471 (November 13, 1981): 9.

533. Hutchinson, J. "Overseas Drop-out Problem." Times Higher Education Supplement 447 (May 29, 1981): 6.

534. Judd, J. "Penalties for Breaking Overseas Totals." Times Higher Education Supplement (December 1, 1978): 1.

535. Judd, J. "Poly Overseas Number Can Be Cut: DES." Times Higher Education Supplement (June 16, 1978): 1.

536. Kahne, Stephen. "Does the U.S. Need a National Policy on Foreign Students?" Engineering Education 74 (October, 1983): 54-56.

537. Karpen, V. "Das vorlautige Eude des Studentenex-port—Plans und ein neues Auslands-Studienprogramm. Ein Diskussionsbeitrag zum/Schwarz—Schilling—Plan." Die Deutsche Universitatszeitung No. 7 (1974): 276-278.

538. Kasprzyk, Peter. "Zum Auslanderstudium in der Bundesrepublik--ein neues Beratungsmodell." _Die Deutsche Universitatszeitung_ 23 (No. 4, 1968): 21-24.

539. Maslen, G. "Australia Clamps Down on Foreigners." _Times Higher Education Supplement_ (July 1, 1983): 6.

540. Maslen, G. "Australian Academics Lose Out on Home Ground." _Times Higher Education Supplement_ (July 4, 1980): 6.

541. Maslen, G. "Australian Charges Idiotic." _Times Higher Education Supplement_ 471 (November 13, 1981): 8.

542. Maslen, G. "Australians Worry About Big Increase in Asian Students." _Chronicle of Higher Education_ 26 (June 1, 1983): 23-24.

543. Maslen, G. "Worry Over Increase in Aliens." _Times Higher Education Supplement_ 549 (May 13, 1983): 6.

544. McDonald, Kim. "AAAS Challenges Defense Department Claim That Exchanges Harm U.S. Security." _Chronicle of Higher Education_ 23 (October 28, 1981): 1.

545. McDonald, Kim. "Pentagon Bars 100 Scientific Papers at San Diego Meeting; State Department Eases Monitoring of Chinese Scholars." _Chronicle of Higher Education_ 25 (September 15, 1982): 12.

546. McDonald, Kim. "Pentagon Eases Restriction on Contract." _Chronicle of Higher Education_ 24 (June 30, 1982): 10.

547. McDonald, Kim. "U.S. Bars Campus Visits of Soviet Robotics Experts." _Chronicle of Higher Education_ 24 (April 14, 1982): 13.

548. McDonald, Kim. "U.S. to Restrict Visas for Visitors Likely to Obtain Technical Data Illegally." _Chronicle of Higher Education_ 26 (May 18, 1983): 21.

549. McQuaid, E. P. "Clamp on Foreign Researchers." _Times Higher Education Supplement_ (June 17, 1983): 7.

550. McQuaid, E. P. "Technology Leaks Prompt U.S. Clampdown on Exit Visas." _Times Higher Education Supplement_ 551 (May 2, 1983): 6.

551. Middleton, Lorenzo. "Curbs Put on Enrollment of Iranians." _Chronicle of Higher Education_ 20 (June 9, 1980): 5.

552. Middleton, L. "New Rules Would Tighten U.S. Control Over Foreign Students." _Chronicle of Higher Education_ 20 (March 31, 1980): 11.

553. Middleton, Lorenzo. "Programs Threatened by House Approval of International Communication Agency Cuts." Chronicle of Higher Education 23 (November 11, 1981): 16.

554. Neave, G. "Call for Curbs on Foreign Students." Times Higher Education Supplement (July 7, 1978): 6.

555. Neave, G. "Circular Tightens Up Conditions for Foreign Students." Times Higher Education Supplement (June 9, 1978): 6.

556. Neave, G. "Government Breaks Promise on Overseas Student Rules." Times Higher Education Supplement 459 (August 21, 1981): 6.

557. Neave, G. "Students Protest over Entry Regulations." Times Higher Education Supplement (April 11, 1980): 5.

558. "New Agency to Run Overseas Exchanges." Chronicle of Higher Education 16 (March 27, 1978): 13.

559. "New Life for Nash Crescent; International Students House." Times Educational Supplement (May 7, 1965): 1411.

560. O'Leary, John. "Loud Reports from Commons. Government Committees' Findings on the Overseas Students Question." Times Higher Education Supplement (May 10, 1980): 10.

561. O'Leary, J. "Pair of Loud Reports in the Commons." Times Higher Education Supplement (May 30, 1980): 10.

562. "Reagan Reviewing Restrictions on Iranians." Chronicle of Higher Education 21 (December 8, 1980): 16.

563. Reid, S. "Polys Forced to Comply on Overseas Levels." Times Higher Education Supplement (December 16, 1977): 1.

564. Reid, S. "ILEA Adopts Overseas Student Quota." Times Higher Education Supplement (August 12, 1977): 1.

565. Roth, M. "Japan Decides to Go for Higher Number." Times Higher Education Supplement 457 (August 7, 1981): 6.

566. Schmetzer, U. "Italy Closes Its Door to Foreigners." Times Higher Education Supplement (February 20, 1981): 6.

567. Scully, Malcolm. "Americans Criticized Arrests in Poland, Half of Exchanges." Chronicle of Higher Education 23 (January 13, 1982): 17.

568. Scully, Malcolm G. "Carter Sends Congress His Plan for Reorganizing Overseas Exchange." Chronicle of Higher Education 15 (October 25, 1977): 13.

569. Scully, M. G. "Europe Restricts Foreign Students." Chronicle of Higher Education 17 (October 10, 1978): 10.

570. Scully, Malcolm G.  "Italy Bars Foreign Students."  Chronicle of Higher Education 14 (July 5, 1977):  9.

571. Scully, M. G.  "Senate Eases 2 Year Rule on Foreigners at U.S. Colleges."  Chronicle of Higher Education 26 (May 25, 1983): 18.

572. Scully, Malcolm G.  "U.S. Colleges Lack Coherent Policies on Foreign Students, Report Says."  Chronicle of Higher Education 25 (February 16, 1983):  19.

573. Semas, Philip W.  "Foreign Students Face Restrictions in Canada." Chronicle of Higher Education 14 (April 11, 1977):  7.

574. Shaw, J.  "End to Backdoor Immigration."  Far East Economic Review 105 (September 7, 1979):  26-27.

575. "Soviet Student in Japan Granted Asylum in U.S."  Chronicle of Higher Education 26 (August 10, 1983):  18.

576. T. H.  "Austria's Universities Place Tight Control on Foreign Enrollments."  Chronicle of Higher Education 15 (September 26, 1977):  6.

577. "Two-Year Rule Worries High Tech Industries."  Times Higher Education Supplement 512 (August 27, 1982):  6.

578. "U.S. Bars New Exchange with Poland."  Chronicle of Higher Education 24 (May 26, 1982):  21.

579. "U.S. Cracks Down on Immigrants."  Times Higher Education Supplement (April 4, 1980):  5.

580. "U.S. Said to Restrict Activities of Foreign Scholars."  Chronicle of Higher Education 23 (December 8, 1981):  1.

581. "U.S. Students Denied Entry to Soviet Union."  Chronicle of Higher Education 15 (October 11, 1977):  2.

582. Wehrwein, Austin.  "Minnesota Fights State Department Limits on Chinese Students."  Chronicle of Higher Education 23 (November 11, 1981):  1.

583. Winkler, Karen J.  "Closing the Books of Foreign Students." International Educational and Cultural Exchange 9 (Fall-Winter, 1973-74):  17-18.

## 8. INSTITUTIONAL POLICY

584. American Association of Collegiate Registrars and Admissions Officers; the Council of Graduate Schools; the Institute of International Education. The Foreign Graduate Student: Priorities for Research and Action. Princeton: College Board Publications, 1971.

585. American Council on Education. Foreign Students and Institutional Policy. Washington, D.C.: American Council on Education, 1982.

586. Burn, Barbara B., ed. Higher Education Reform: Implications for Foreign Students. New York: Institute of International Education, 1978.

587. Canadian Bureau for International Education. Existing Institutional Policies and Practices Regarding Foreign Students: Existing Institutional Services for Foreign Students. Ottawa: Canadian Bureau for International Education, 1981.

588. Canadian Bureau for International Education. Foreign Student Policies in Canadian Universities and Colleges. Ottawa: Canadian Bureau of International Education, 1981. (mimeo)

589. College Entrance Examination Board. The Foreign Undergraduate Student: Institutional Priorities for Action. New York: College Entrance Examination Board, 1975.

590. Committee on Foreign Students and Institutional Policy. Foreign Students and Institutional Policy: Toward an Agenda for Action. Washington, D.C.: American Council on Education, 1982.

591. Committee on International Education of the Council of Graduate Schools in the United States. The Foreign Student in American Graduate Schools. Washington, D.C.: Council of Graduate Schools, 1980.

592. Fiedler, Judith. Allocation of Services and Activities Fees and Opinion on International Students at the University of Washington. Seattle, Washington: University of Washington, 1975.

593. The Foreign Undergraduate Student: Institutional Priorities for Action. A Colloquium Held at Wingspread, Racine, Wisconsin, June 20-21, 1974. New York: College Entrance Examination Board, 1975.

594. Garrett, Larry Neal. "The Foreign Student in American Higher Education: A Study of the Policies and Practices of Selected Host Institutions as They Relate to English Language Proficiency and Academic Advisement." Unpublished Ph.D thesis, George Peabody College for Teachers, 1979.

This study which investigated the stated policies and actual practices of selected American host institutions with regard to certain prescribed academic foreign student affairs covered 1,908 post-secondary institutions reporting the enrollment of foreign students or visiting foreign scholars in 1974-75. Answers were sought to such questions as to why there were foreign students in American higher education, why there were foreign student academic policies and whether selected host institutions had prescribed student policy as regards English Language (ESL) proficiency and academic advisement. Questionnaires covering demographic data, ESL and academic advisement were mailed to the Foreign Student Advisers in the various institutions. The major findings in the field survey showed that there were certain "target" areas in which most colleges and universities surveyed did provide foreign student policies and practices. While, for example, ESL proficiency was a requirement for foreign student admission, some evident "gaps" were noticed in the policy provisions on academic advisement. It is recommended that institutions engaged in international education should reassess the rationales for recruiting foreign students and the policies and practices which actualize those rationales through daily decision-making. Careful planning based on resource and needs assessment techniques should also be considered.

595. Goodwin, Crauford D., and Michael Nacht. Absence of Decision: Foreign Students in American Colleges and Universities: A Report on Policy Formation and Lack Thereof. New York: Institute of International Education, 1983.

The purpose of this research report is to discuss "how U.S. institutions that deal directly with foreign students view the presence of those students today, what problems they perceive, and how they do, in fact, go about forming policy and directing action in this arena." The researchers chose three states (Florida, Ohio, and California) and spoke to a variety of individuals in policy-making positions—state legislators, aides to governors, senior university officials, state higher education planners, and others. The basic conclusions of this study are:
(a) Most college and university officials place the foreign student low on their list of priorities. Knowledge and interest in the issue is significant only when the percentage of foreign students is in excess of 15 to 20% of the student body.

    (b)  Most institutions have not thought through in much
detail the economic, educational, political, and
organizational issues associated with the presence of
large numbers of foreign students.

    (c)  The marginal cost of the foreign student has rarely
been computed and a generalizable methodology for
such computations would be welcome.

    (d)  The consideration of different pricing approaches to
the foreign student requires serious examination.

    (e)  The "humanist presumption" that foreign students are
an enriching presence in American higher education
needs to be supported with stronger evidence.

    (f)  There is little basis at present for determining the
optimum number of foreign students in particular
education settings.

    (g)  Public institutions are particularly sensitive to
legislative pressures concerning foreign students.

    (h)  Issues of economic protectionism and national
security are becoming highly salient in relations
between government and the major research
universities.

    (i)  Institutions could benefit from "self-study" of their
own foreign student issues that could answer
questions of pricing, numbers, quotas, etc.

596.  Hughbanks, Corinne Neubauer. "A Study to Ascertain Administrative
Policy and Faculty Opinions About Foreign Students in Public
Universities and Private Colleges of the Midwest."
Unpublished Ph.D thesis, University of Nebraska, 1980.

597.  Institute of International Education. Report on the Survey of
Policy Changes toward Foreign Students in Public Institutions
of Higher Education. New York: Institute of International
Education, 1981. (mimeo)

598.  Institute of International Education. Survey of U.S. Public
Institutional Policies Regarding Foreign Students. New York:
Institute of International Education, 1981.

599.  National Association for Foreign Student Affairs. The College, the
University and the Foreign Student. Washington, D.C.:
National Association for Foreign Student Affairs, 1979.

600.  Zikopoulos, Marianthi and Elinor G. Barber. The ITT International
Fellowship Program: An Assessment After Ten Years. New York:
Institute of International Education, [1984].

## Articles

601.  Baume, C. A. "United States University and the Foreign Student."
In Proceedings: 1979 Frontiers in Education Conference,
edited by L. P. Grayson, and J. M. Biedenbach. Washington,
D.C.: American Society for Engineering Education.

602. Corry, Anne. "Political Intimidation of Foreign Students and Academic Freedom." National Association for Foreign Student Affairs Newsletter 28 (March, 1977): 7ff.

603. Iglinsky, C., et al. "Is Your Institution Really Ready to Admit Foreign Students? Are You?" College and University 48 (Summer, 1973): 601-619.

604. Matson, M. B., and R. Kirkwood. "Study the Issues Before Offering Study Abroad." Educational Record 64 (Spring, 1983): 48-51.

605. Sharp, T. E. "Institutional Administration and the Foreign Student Program." College and University 57 (No. 3, 1982): 323-326.

606. Van Wart, M. R. "Affordable and Quality International Programming for the 1980s." Liberal Education 68 (Fall, 1982): 193-199.

607. Woolston, Valerie. "Administration: Coordinating and Integrating Programs and Services." In Educating Students From Other Nations: American Colleges and Universities in International Educational Interchange, edited by Hugh M. Jenkins, et al., pp. 184-209. San Francisco: Jossey-Bass, 1983.

### Reportage

608. Biemiller, L. "Louisiana Tech University Sued for Maintaining Separate Housing for Some Foreign Students." Chronicle of Higher Education 26 (July 6, 1983): 2.

609. Chapman, C. "Japanese Internationalization Plan Stymied by Conservative Universities." Chronicle of Higher Education 21 (November 10, 1980): 13.

## 9. ECONOMIC ASPECTS: COST-BENEFIT ANALYSIS OF "SENDING" COUNTRIES

610. Abellatif, Ragab Abdelwahab. "A Study of Economic and Social Costs and Benefits of Egyptians Studying at American Universities." Unpublished Ph.D thesis, George Peabody College for Teachers, 1978.

611. Canadian Bureau for International Education. The Costs and Benefits of Foreign Students in Canada. Ottawa: CBIE, 1981.

612. Dorai, Gopalakrishnan. "Economics of the International Flow of Students: A Cost-Benefit Analysis." Unpublished Ph.D thesis, Wayne State University, 1968.

613.  Fry, Gerald W.  "The Economic and Political Impact of Study
      Abroad."  Comparative Education Review 28 (May, 1984):
      203-220.

614.  Harbison, Ralph W.  "Economic Returns of Graduate Education; A Case
      Study of Colombians Trained in the United States."
      Unpublished Ph.D thesis, Princeton University, 1973.

615.  Najmul, Hossain.  "The Economics of U.S. Higher Education for
      Foreign Students."  Unpublished Ph.D thesis, Virginia
      Polytechnic Institute and State University, 1981.

          This is an application of human capital theory model
      to decision-making by foreign students seeking to study in
      the United States.  The assumption was that foreign
      students will study in the United States: (1) because
      studying in the United States is of greater value 'than
      studying in their country of origin'; and (2) that there
      are nonmonetary benefits and costs of studying in the
      United States.  The findings were based upon primary data.
      The author concludes that students' rate of return from
      U.S. education are high monetarily not only for engineers
      but also for other students from India and Taiwan.  The
      nonmonetary costs associated with American education
      varies according to the country of origin or region.
          Factors that affect the student's stay in the United
      States include:  country of origin, political stability,
      and job opportunities within the country of origin as well
      as family ties.  These variables will determine a length
      of study in the United States and, in point of fact, the
      length of stay in the country.

## Articles

616.  Brinley, Thomas.  "The International Circulation of Human Capital."
      Minerva 4 (Summer, 1967):  479-506.

617.  Comay, Y.  "Benefits and Costs of Study Abroad and Migration."
      Canadian Journal of Economics 3 (May, 1970):  300-308.

618.  Grubel, Herbert G.  "Non-returning Foreign Students and the Cost of
      Student Exchange."  International Education and Cultural
      Exchange (Spring, 1966):  20-29.

619.  Kidd, Charles V.  "The Economics of the Brain Drain."  Minerva 4-1
      (1965):  105-107.

620.  Watson, Roy J., Jr.  "The Simpson-Mazzoli Bill:  An Analysis of
      Selected Economic Policies."  San Diego Law Review 20
      (December, 1982):  97-116.

Reportage

621.  Schneider, Dieter. "Auslander studium. Weniger Studenten aus Entwicklungslandern und mehr aus Industrienationen." VDI-- Nachrichten 25 (No. 38, 1971): 12.

622.  Scully, Malcolm G. "Nigeria Promises $10-Million to Pay Debts of Students in U.S. Colleges." Chronicle of Higher Education 27 (September 21, 1983): 29.

---

## 10. ECONOMIC ASPECTS: COST-BENEFIT ANALYSIS OF "HOST" COUNTRY

623.  Chadwick, John. The Unofficial Commonwealth. The Story of the Commonwealth Foundation 1965-1980. London: Allen and Unwin, 1982.

624.  DeVine, Bruce Frederic. "The U.S. Student Exchange Program: Reverse Foreign Aid?" Unpublished Ph.D thesis, Claremont Graduate School and University Center, 1971.

This study attempts to test the hypothesis that the United States, despite its provision of higher education resources for vast numbers of students from developing countries, gains financially on student exchange with these countries as a result primarily of the nonreturn of a minority of such students. Techniques of cost-benefit analysis were applied to data for the 1964-65 academic year to test the hypothesis that foreign student self-support is represented by program costs for education, travel, and maintenance while the residual represents costs of higher education borne by residents of the United States. The benefits identified and measured were: subsidized education of American college students in developing countries and voluntary nonreturn of a percentage of developing country students entering the United States in 1964-65.

A nonreturning student is considered as a capital asset the value of which is computed by discounting to the present (1965) his expected life-time earnings in the United States. Part I provides a theoretical framework for the evaluation of the results while Part II deals with the empirical work on costs and benefits, a comparison of the overall exchange balance with various measures of U.S. foreign aid, and an evaluation of the effects of the balance on the welfare of all participants. The conclusions were that when low rates are used to discount human capital values the United States is a net beneficiary on the exchange transaction; effects of the dollar balance on participant welfare depend on the particular standards set by each when the exchange was entered. A comparison of net balance figures with assistance given by the United States in other forms indicates a range of from −1.5 to +4.6% with the latter depending both on the discount rate used to compute student values and on how foreign aid is defined. The study suggests the inclusion of similar calculations in international balance of payments accounting.

625. Hossain, N. "The Economics of U.S. Higher Education for Foreign Students." Unpublished Ph.D thesis, Virginia Polytechnic Institute and State University, 1981.

626. Limbird, H. M. Foreign Students in Iowa: A Preliminary Estimate of Social and Economic Benefits and Costs. Ames, Iowa: Office of International Educational Services, Iowa State University, 1979.

627. London Conference on Overseas Students. Overseas Students: A Subsidy to Britain. London: United Kingdom Council for Overseas Students Affairs, 1979.

628. New Zealand Students Association. Submission to the Minister of Education on the Effects of the $1500 Discriminatory Fee for Private Overseas Students. Wellington: New Zealand Student Association, 1980.

629. Rives, Janet McMillan. "The International Market for Higher Education: An Economic Analysis with Special Reference to the United States." Unpublished Ph.D thesis, Duke University, 1971.

This study is concerned with the way in which the operation of an international market for higher education contributes to international flows of human capital on a temporary basis and on a permanent basis. The aim of the study is to develop and analyze, theoretically and empirically, the international market for higher education. The relationship between the market for higher education and international flows of human capital is stressed. Particular emphasis is placed on trade in United States education and on movement of human capital into the United States.

The conclusion of the study is that the interaction of international markets for higher education and for human capital services suggests a nonoptimal allocation of human resources under a variety of welfare criteria. The implication of this conclusion for policy depend on the welfare goals of the policy-making body and on the expected feedback effect of the policy on trade in education and human capital migration.

630. Sims, A., and M. Stelcner. The Costs and Benefits of Foreign Students in Canada: A Methodology. Ottawa: Canadian Bureau for International Education, 1981.

631. United Kingdom, Foreign and Commonwealth Office. Overseas Student Fees: Aid and Development Implications. Government Observations on the Report of the Sub-Committee on Overseas Development of the Select Committee on Foreign Affairs. [of the House of Commons]. London: Her Majesty's Stationery Office, 1980.

632. United Kingdom, House of Commons Education, Science and Arts Committee. The Funding and Organization of Courses in Higher Education: Interim Report on Overseas Student Fees. London: Her Majesty's Stationery Office, 1980.

633. United Kingdom, Overseas Development Sub-Committee, Foreign Affairs Committee, House of Commons. Enquiry into the Implications for Aid and Development of the Government's Decision to Increase Overseas Students Fees--Council for Education in the Commonwealth, et al. London: Her Majesty's Stationery Office, 1980: 1-37.

634. United Kingdom, Overseas Development Sub-Committee, Foreign Affairs Committee, House of Commons. Enquiry Into the Implications for Aid and Development of the Government's Decision to Increase Overseas Students Fees--Institute of Science and Technology, University of Manchester, et al. London: Her Majesty's Stationery Office, 1980: 50-76.

635. United Kingdom, Overseas Development Sub-Committee, Foreign Affairs Committee, House of Commons. Minutes of Evidence Taken Before the Overseas Development Sub-Committee and Appendices. Overseas Student Fees: Aid and Development Implications. London: Her Majesty's Stationery Office, 1980.

636. United Kingdom, Overseas Development Sub-Committee, Foreign Affairs Committee, House of Commons. Overseas Students Fees: Monitoring of Effects on Aid and Development--National Union of Students. London: Her Majesty's Stationery Office, 1981: 1-20.

637. United Kingdom, Overseas Development Sub-Committee, Foreign Affairs Committee, House of Commons. Overseas Student Fees: Monitoring of Effects on Aid and Development--Derby College of Further Education. London: Her Majesty's Stationery Office, 1981: 21-51.

638. United States Congress. Current Health Manpower Issues. [Prepared for the Use of the Committee on Interstate and Foreign Commerce, House of Representatives and its Subcommittees on Health and the Environment, Ninety-Sixth Congress, First Session]. Washington, D.C.: Government Printing Office, 1979.

639. United States General Accounting Office. Millions of Dollars of Costs Incurred in Training Foreign Military Students Have not Been Recovered. Washington, D.C.: Government Printing Office, 1978.

640. Winkler, D. R. The Economic Impacts of Foreign Students in the United States. Los Angeles: School of Public Administration, University of Southern California, 1981.

641. Winkler, D. R. The Fiscal Consequences of Foreign Students in Public Higher Education: A Case Study of California. Los Angeles: School of Public Administration, University of Southern California, 1982.


                              Articles


642. Blaug, Mark. "The Economic Costs and Benefits of Overseas Students." In The Overseas Student Question: Studies for a Policy, edited by Peter Williams, pp. 47-90. London: Heinemann, 1981.

643. Carman, D. Gary. "The Cost of Foreign Students at Public Universities in Texas." Texas Business Review 55 (September-October, 1981): 234-237.

644. Grubel, H. G., and A. D. Scott. "The Costs of U.S. College Student Exchange Programs." Journal of Human Resources 1 (1966): 79-98.

645. Hanisch, Thor Einar. "A Case of Nordic Assistance in Higher Education to Developing Countries." Higher Education in Europe 7 (January-March, 1982): 5-12.

646. Hossain, Najmal. "Why So Many Foreign Students in Graduate School?: A Cost Benefit Analysis." Journal of the Association of International Education Administrators 3 (May, 1983): 23-30.

647. Jenkins, Hugh. "Economics: Analyzing Costs and Benefits." In Educating Students from Other Nations, edited by Hugh Jenkins, pp. 237-250. San Francisco: Jossey-Bass, 1983.

648. Johnson, Alan W. "Costs of International Education: Who Pays?" International Educational and Cultural Exchange 6 (Spring, 1971): 32-43.

        This paper was originally written in the early 1970's. The case study primarily focuses on the role of California and its treatment of foreign students in the decade of the 1970's.
        If it is becoming increasingly difficult and costly to provide higher education for growing numbers of

American students. What then are the prospects for foreign students in the United States? The paper discusses two aspects of this problem which have recently come to the fore in the California state colleges: the effects of rising tuition for foreign students and the question of who will bear the cost of foreign student programs--the students themselves, the state government, the federal government, or some combination of all three.

649. Landers, Thomas. "The Effects of Financial Difficulties on International Educational Exchange." National Association for Foreign Student Affairs Newsletter 23 (February, 1972): 1ff.

650. Lyman, Richard. "The Costs and Values of International Education." National Association for Foreign Student Affairs Newsletter 32 (Summer, 1981): 165ff.

651. O'Leary, J. "Britain Puts up the Fees for Overseas Students." Round Table 278 (April, 1980): 167-171.

652. Overseas Students Trust. "Overseas Students and British Commercial Interests." In The Overseas Student Question: Studies for a Policy, edited by Peter Williams, pp. 91-110. London: Heinemann, 1981.

653. "Portugal-Afrique - La Cooperation du Portugal avec les Pays Africains." Jeune Afrique (April 28, 1982): 63-66.

654. Schlesinger, Philip. "No Foreigners, Please--Driving Out Overseas Students and Their Money." National Association for Foreign Student Affairs Newsletter 31 (January, 1980): 99ff.

655. Ulivi, Ricardo M., and Thomas W. Jones. "The Economic Impact of International Students on Northwest Arkansas, 1977." Arkansas Business and Economic Review 12 (Spring, 1979): 22-31.

## Reportage

656. "Academics Press for Fees U-Turn." Times Higher Education Supplement (February 27, 1981): 1.

657. Boyson, Rhodes. "Britain is Hit by Overseas Fees Policy. Prescription for Cuts." Times Higher Education Supplement (November 16, 1979): 9.

658. "Faltering Steps to Altruism?--Higher Fees for Foreign Students." Times Higher Education Supplement (December 12, 1975): 16.

659. "Federal Government Aids Some 1500 Foreign Students." University Affairs 10 (September, 1969): 9.

660. Feinmann, J. "Britain: A Renegade on Overseas Student Fees." Times Higher Education Supplement (January 13, 1978): 4.

661. Geddes, D. "High Fees Produce Intake Variations." Times Higher Education Supplement (November 7, 1980): 1.

662. Gibb, Francis. "Overseas Students and Fees Increase." Times Higher Education Supplement (December 19, 1975): 24.

663. "Higher Foreign-student Fees in Alberta." Chronicle of Higher Education 24 (May 19, 1982): 18.

664. Houser, M. "Buying the Cow to Get Some Milk." Times Higher Education Supplement (July 1, 1983): 8.

665. Kloss, Gunther. "Clampdown on Overseas Entrants." Times Higher Education Supplement (September 26, 1975): 13.

666. McGhie, J. "Courses Collapse as Foreign Students are Priced Out." Times Higher Education Supplement (February 15, 1980): 11.

667. Ndirangu, I. "How Britain Lost Its Student Appeal [Kenya Students]." Times Educational Supplement 3391 (June 19, 1981): 14.

668. "Nigerian Students Said to Owe $6-Million in Great Britain." Chronicle of Higher Education 26 (August 10, 1983): 13.

669. O'Leary, J. "Britain under EEC Pressure on Student Fees." Times Higher Education Supplement (March 21, 1980): 1.

670. O'Leary, J. "Cuba Helps Students Outpriced by Britain." Times Higher Education Supplement 462 (September 11, 1981): 1.

671. O'Leary, J. "Foreign Office Shifts Its Approach to Overseas Fees Policy." Times Higher Education Supplement 446 (May 22, 1981): 1.

672. O'Leary, J. "Ministers Consider Fee Changes." Times Higher Education Supplement 523 (November 12, 1982): 1.

673. O'Leary, J. "Riches from Overseas Fees Rethink." Times Higher Education Supplement 536 (February 11, 1983): 1.

674. "Overseas Fees in the Lords." Times Educational Supplement No. 2700 (February 17, 1967): 540.

675. "Overseas Fees Policy May Be Softening." Times Higher Education Supplement (September 12, 1980): 1.

676. "Overseas Fees to Rise Again." Times Higher Education Supplement (January 23, 1981): 1.

677. "The Overseas Student Question—Ramifications of the Government's Full-Cost Fees Policy." Times Higher Education Supplement (May 1, 1981): 31.

678. "Overseas Students' Fees." Times Educational Supplement No. 2695 (January 13, 1967): 92.

679. "Overseas Students Fees: Differential Between Home and Overseas Students Fees." Times Higher Education Supplement (March 19, 1976): 16.

680. "Overseas Students Likely to Drop by Half." Times Higher Education Supplement (November 14, 1980): 1.

681. Parker, A. "Will Overseas Numbers Be Squeezed As We Tunnel the Hump?" Times Higher Education Supplement (July 28, 1978): 10.

682. Pedley, Frank. "Costing our Paternalism: Overseas Students." Municipal and Public Service Journal 83 (August 22, 1975): 1079-1080.

683. Price, Christopher. "Package Tour Lessons of Student Fees." Times Higher Education Supplement (June 6, 1980): 29.

684. "Quebec Plans Rise in Foreign-Student Fees." Chronicle of Higher Education 22 (March 30, 1981): 18.

685. "Quebec to Raise Foreign-Student Charges." Chronicle of Higher Education 23 (February 24, 1982): 18.

686. Reid, S. "Fee Waiver For Many Foreign Students Likely." Times Higher Education Supplement (November 11, 1977): 1.

687. Reid, S. "Overseas Fee Level May Hit Immigrants." Times Higher Education Supplement (October 28, 1977): 1.

688. Schmetzer, U. "Reprieve for Foreign Students." Times Higher Education Supplement (October 14, 1977): 5.

689. Walker, D. "Britain to Lower Tuition Rates for Foreign Students." Chronicle of Higher Education 26 (March 2, 1983): 19-20.

690. Wallington, Peter. "How the Policy on Overseas Fees Policy Bends the Law." Times Higher Education Supplement (April 18, 1980): 10.

691. Wilby, P. "What Price Foreign Students?" New Statesman 91 (February 27, 1976): 255.

692. Wilce, H. "British Fees Now Higher Than Harvard." Times Higher Education Supplement (November 23, 1979): 13.

693. Williams, Peter. "How to Lose Friends and Influence Abroad--
      Britain's Overseas Student Fees Policy." _Times Higher
      Education Supplement_ (July 17, 1981): 14.

694. Wright, L. "Overseas Enrollment Drop in Face of New Government
      Policy." _Times Higher Education Supplement_ (May 12, 1978): 6.

---

## 11. OVERSEAS STUDY AND SOCIOECONOMIC DEVELOPMENT

695. Buffenmyer, Jay Ralph. "Emigration of High-Level Manpower and
      National Development: A Case Study of Jamaica." Unpublished
      Ph.D thesis, University of Pittsburgh, 1970.

696. Collin, A. E. _Education for National Development: Effects of U.S.
      Technical Training Programs_. New York: Praeger, 1979.

697. Elpheikh, Nadia Hussein. "Graduate Education for Economic Develop-
      ment: An Evaluation of Patterns and Trends of Specialization
      of Latin American Students in the United States." Unpublished
      Ph.D thesis, Oklahoma State University, 1972.

698. Gollin, Albert. _The Transfer and Use of Development Skills_.
      Washington, D.C.: Agency for International Development, Office
      of International Training, 1967.

699. Greenblat, Cathy Stein. "Orientation to Modernization and the
      Sojourn Experience: A Study of Foreign Students from Four
      Developing Countries." Unpublished Ph.D thesis, Columbia
      University, 1968.

The purpose of this study was to test part of the
theory which states that the foreign student's relationship to the program of change in his home-country is
related to sojourn and post-sojourn factors. A cross-
national sample of students from Chile, Colombia, Greece,
and Turkey enrolled at accredited colleges and universities in New York City (N=140) was studied to test the
hypothesis that differences in "orientation to modernization" would be related to differences in academic,
social, cultural, and personal adjustment during the
sojourn. The interview schedule which contained forced-
choice and open-ended questions dealt with: (1) the
student's evaluation of the speed with which change was
taking place in his home-country; (2) the place he felt
should be accorded to tradition in the modernization
process; and (3) the degree of change that he felt to be
desirable in programs of economic development. While
"Constrictors," "Adjustors," and "Ideologists" had approximately the same scores on measures of contact with

Americans, differences in academic performance and satisfaction showed only a slight relationship to the construct. Orientation to modernization was found to be related to differences in the nature and bases of attitudes toward the host country and to attitude change. Explanation of some of the variance in the experiences and attitudes of foreign students will require knowledge of their socio-political orientations. A further study of the predictive value of the construct "orientation to modernization" for both sojourn and post-sojourn adjustments is therefore suggested.

700. Grieswelle, Detlef. Studenten aus Entwicklungslandern: Eine Pilot-Studie. Munich: Minerva, 1978.

701. Hodgkin, Mary C. The Innovations: The Role of Foreign Trained Persons in Southeast Asia. Sydney: Sydney University Press, 1972.

Since World War II Australia has played an increasing role in the education of Asian students, particularly those from Southeast Asia. In early 1970's more than 10,000 were in educational institutions at all levels and great emphasis was placed on the importance of this aspect of government foreign policy in the overall picture of aid to developing countries. But what is being achieved? This book explores the influence that graduates, particularly from Australia, are exerting on the economic growth of three very different areas: the sophisticated, commercial city of Singapore; Malaysia, with its industrializing towns and rural hinterland; and Sarawak, Sabah, and Brunei, which are in the early stages of development. It looks also at the impact of the returnees in terms of their cultural background, traditional roles, opportunities for leadership, and abilities and inclinations. It makes some critical comments on the future of this form of cross-cultural training and the role which the industrialized nations must play if future educational aid to underdeveloped countries is to live up to the claims of the donors.

702. Jenkins, Hugh M., ed. The Role of the Foreign Student in the Process of Development. Washington, D.C.: National Association for Foreign Student Affairs, 1983.

703. Klineberg, Otto, and J. Ben Brika. Etudiants du Tiers Monde en Europe. Paris: Mouton, 1972.

704. Maliyamkono, T. L., A. G. M. Ishumi, and S. J. Wells. Higher Education and Development in Eastern Africa: A Report of the Eastern African Universities Research Project on the Impact of Overseas Training and Development. London: Heinemann Educational Books, 1982.

705. Maliyamkono, T. L., ed. Overseas Training: Its Impact on Development. Arusha, Tanzania: Eastern African Publications, 1979.

706. Maliyamkono, T. L., et al. Training and Productivity in East Africa: A Report of the Eastern African Universities Research Project on the Impact of Overseas Training and Development. London: Heinemann Educational Books, 1982.

707. Myer, Richard, and M. L. Taylor, eds. Curriculum: U.S. Capacities, Developing Countries' Needs. New York: Institute of International Education, 1979.

708. Ogunbi, A. J. "The Perceived Relevance of Foreign Students' Training to Their Role as Future Change Agents in National Development (An Evaluation)." Unpublished Ph.D thesis, Michigan State University, 1978.

709. Stifel, Laurence D., et al. Education and Training for Public Sector Management in Developing Countries. New York: The Rockefeller Foundation, 1977.

710. United States Agency for International Development. A.I.D. Participant Training Program: The Transfer and Use of Development Skills. Washington, D.C.: Agency for International Development, 1966.

711. Wood, Richard. United States Universities: Their Role in Aid-Financed Technical Assistance Overseas. New York: Education and World Affairs, 1968.

712. Yesufu, Tijani M., ed. International Seminar on Manpower Problems in Economic Development, Lagos, 1964. Ibadan: Oxford University Press, 1969.

### Articles

713. Abreu-Vale, Jose. "Studenten aus der Dritten Welt." Civitas 30 (No. 9-10, 1974-75): 669-676.

714. Adwere-Boamah, J. "Intellect and Commitment: A Potential for Educational Change in the New Nations." International Journal of Comparative Sociology 13 (No. 2, 1972): 99-112.

This study was a preliminary attempt to provide some needed information about the prospective African elites in the U.S. colleges and universities. The specific objective of the study was to investigate the educational orientations and concerns of African students in the U.S. and to assess the relationship of such orientations to the perceptions of problems facing the African countries. The study was designed to discover how the different orientations among and within the study sample may relate to demographic factors, choice of academic discipline, and other variables. The research data were drawn from the total population of African students enrolled in 44 higher educational institutions in the U.S. Pacific Coast Region. Questionnaires were sent to 390 African students, and 250 of them responded. Among the many problems confronting African countries, a large proportion (66%) of African students in the study consider economic development, educational needs (55%), and living conditions in the African countries as very serious problems. The author also analyzes the samples' educational orientations and their correlates, and discusses the results in terms of ideological, social, and educational implications to these prospective African elites.

715. Annabi, Mohammed. "North-South University Co-operation--Tunisian Case Study." Higher Education in Europe 7 (January-March, 1982): 22-25.

716. Coleman, James S. "Professorial Training and Institution Building in the Third World: Two Rockefeller Foundation Experiences." Comparative Education Review 28 (May, 1984): 180-202.

717. Cormack, Margaret L. "International Development through Educational Exchange." Review of Educational Research 38 (June, 1968): 293-302.

718. Cussler, Margaret. "The Foreign Student--Innovator of the Future." International Review of Sociology (April, 1971): 651-663.

719. Davis, F. J. "Problems of Development in Turkey as Seen by Turks Returned Home from Study in American Universities." Sociology and Social Research 57 (No. 4, 1973): 429-442.

This study concerns the views on modernization of Turks who have returned home from university or college study in the United States. The focus of attention is on what they consider Turkey's major problems to be; how they perceive the speed of development; their own perceived capacity to influence the process, and the nations they consider most appropriate models for Turkey.

Data were gathered both by interview and question-naire. There were 222 questionnaire respondents and 111 people were interviewed representing returnees to Turkey who studied in American universities from 1957 to 1968. The major finding of the study was that most of the re-turnees were dissatisfied with the pace of change, which they considered was slow, but were confident that they could personally contribute to the development of their homeland. They felt that their study in the United States helped to increase this confidence. On the issue of the nations they considered most appropriate models for Turkey, several of the returnees refused to list any national model on the ground that Turkey must not copy any other nation or that she should select the best features of various countries. The United States, however, was one of the most-listed "guideline countries."

720. Djao, A. W. "Industrialization and Education: Influx of Hong Kong Students to Canadian Universities." Journal of Contemporary Asia 12 (No. 2, 1982): 216-225.

721. Gollin, Albert. "Foreign Study and Modernization: The Transfer of Technology Through Education." International Social Science Journal 19 (No. 3, 1967): 359-377.

    The important role played by education in the development of human resources has engaged the attention of both planners and theorists over the years. When it comes to transferring knowledge and technology, foreign study is considered one of the most important means. The study deals with transfer of knowledge and technology by recipients of United States technical training from 29 countries. Concepts and programs of technical training as development assistance and the antecedents and elements of participant training are treated. On the participants and their instructional programs, the survey revealed that administrative problems had few results of any consequence; "social adjustment" was found to be an inconsequential problem area for participants and there was little or no relationship between the few available measures of social adjustment in the surveys and participants' evaluations of the worth or occupational outcomes of their training. In general, underlying institutional arrangements emerge as significant influences upon the outcomes of this method of inducing technological change.

722. Groves, Marion H. "Contributions to Development by Asians Who Have Studied Abroad." International Educational and Cultural Exchange (Summer, 1967): 13-19.

723. Hara, Y. "From Westernization to Japanization: Replacement of Foreign Teachers by Japanese Who Studied Abroad." Developing Economies 15 (No. 4, 1977): 440-461.

    The author first traces the history of the government-employed foreigners in Japanese industry, commerce, government, and educational institutions. The number of these employed foreigners reached its peak during 1873-76 (over 500), and decreased sharply with the beginning of the 1880s. During 1867-1912 there were 348 foreign instructors in Japan, among whom, by nationality there were more teachers from Germany (136) than from any other country. With respect to specialization, persons from Great Britain were most numerous in the humanities; Americans and Germans were dominant in social sciences; and Germans were most numerous in fields of natural sciences. Secondly, the author provides an overview of the history of Japanese students sent abroad, dating back to years before Meigi Restoration. From 1875 to 1908 the Japanese Ministry of Education sent 446 students to Europe and America.

It is argued that the replacement of foreigners by returned Japanese students as agents in Japan's modernization had a significance that went beyond a mere replacement of personnel. It meant a change from "direct Westernization" to a process of "indirect Westernization," and therein lay the foundation for the transition from imitation to adaptation and then to creativity. However, one of the far-reaching effects of the process of "Japanization" was a weakening of the Japanese people's foreign-language capabilities and its international adaptability.

724. Heft, David. "The Foreign Student: His Problems, His Impact [on United States Society and on the Economics and Social Development of His Own Country]." Americas 16 (February, 1964): 17-21.

725. Hodgkin, Mary C. "The Communication of Innovations: The Influence of the Foreign Trained Returnee on Socio-Cultural Change in Developing Countries." Southeast-Asian Journal of Sociology 4 (1971): 53-71.

726. Hunter, Guy. "The Needs and Desires of Developing Countries for Foreign Study Facilities: Some Reflections." In The Overseas Student Question, edited by Peter Williams, pp. 135-149. London: Heinemann, 1981.

727. Jacobel, R. W. "Resources and Technology in Developing Nations; A Semester Study Abroad." Journal of College Science Teaching 9 (March, 1980): 193-196.

728. Lambo, T. A. "International Exchange and National Development." International Educational and Cultural Exchange 12 (Winter, 1977): 25-33.

729. Mallakh, Ragaei El, and Tapan Mukerjee. "The Education Dimension of U.S. Aid to Africa: African Students Enrolled in American Colleges." Africa Today 17 (May/June, 1970): 22-24.

730. Moock, Joyce Lewinger. "Overseas Training and National Development Objectives in Sub-Saharan Africa." Comparative Education Review 28 (May, 1984): 221-240.

731. Okoh, Nduka. "Education, Attitudes, and Development." Education and Development 5 (No. 1, 1978): 53-70.

732. Overton, Edward W., Jr. "Can the Developing Nations Afford American Higher Education?" College and University 42 (Summer, 1967): 427-432.

733. Profeta, Lydia, and Robert S. Davie. "Regional Approaches to the Development of Human and Economic Resources: Asia." Journal of Cooperative Education 17 (No. 3, 1981): 62-69.

734. Raman, N. Pahabhi. "Training of Nationals of Developing Countries: Two Proposals." International Development Review 19 (No. 2, 1977): 19-21.

735. Ravenswaay, C. A. "International Students and Technical Assistance." Higher Education and Research in the Netherlands 11 (January, 1967): 38-45.

736. Rawls, James R., and Moses Akpanudo. "Training Obtained in Developed Countries and Needs of a Developing Country." International Review of Applied Psychology 30 (No. 4, 1981): 535-552.

737. Schmidt, S. C., and J. T. Scott, Jr. "Advanced Training for Foreign Students: The Regional Approach." Journal of Developing Areas 6 (No. 1, 1971): 39-50.

   The authors discuss in broad outline the five major concerns in early 1970s of the impact of training of Third World students in developed countries. They list the concerns in the following areas:
   (1) the inappropriateness of training needs for the home countries
   (2) the long and costly training periods
   (3) paternal attitudes of host institutions
   (4) dissertation research topics often based on the host-country's problems
   (5) brain drain
   After extensive discussion of the above concerns, the authors focus on the need to establish regional training institutions and recommend that these institutions have a relationship to the United Nations. They specifically feel that having regional institutions in the following areas: Northeast Asia, Southeast Asia, Central America, South America, West Africa, East Africa, North Africa and the Middle East would effectively alleviate some of the difficulties faced by foreign students coming to the United States and also more realistically address educational needs in an interdisciplinary fashion relevant to Third World countries. They specifically feel that these regional institutes, once established, should not be supported more than 10 or 15 years by the United Nations or other agencies and suggest that foundations endow chairs similar to the Chair Endowment Program that occurs in the United States.

738. Useem, John, and Ruth Useem. "American Educated Indians and Americans in India: A Comparison of Two Modernizing Roles." Journal of Social Issues 24 (October, 1968): 143-158.

This study is based on the socialization factors affecting Americans living in India and Indians who study in the United States. The authors posit three dominant aspects of modernity: (1) In a global interdependent society "expectations for the bi-national and multi-national endeavors...transcend national relationships; (2) that modernity entails complex organizational structures that affect the participants not only in terms of their individual culture but the culture that they encounter; (3) there are consequences of post-independence changes on the individual's social life when he/she comes from a developing country. They delineate these effects as emerging from the development of transnational goals for living and expectations of life-styles, as well as the diminishment or calling into question of communal loyalties and changing status of women in traditional religious affiliations. The authors review changes in the number of Indians studying in the United States, the recipient of the major influx of foreign nationals, particularly Indians, and the role of Americans studying or teaching in India. They find a trend of fewer missionaries and more business-men and governmental employees with a quickening of the pace, and expansion in magnitude, of interchange of persons between the two countries. They also find a shared outlook among the two groups and a moderate amount of interaction between them. The study concludes with a summary of the modernizing functions Americans perform in their work roles and a speculation about the future.

739. van der Horst, G. I. C. "The Involvement of Dutch Universities in Development Co-operation: The Current Situation." Higher Education and Research in the Netherlands 20 (No. 4, 1976): 4-14.

740. Vielle, D., Jean-Pierre. "Las Migraciones Educativas a Nivel Superior: Su Importancia en el Estudio del Desarrollo Socio-Economico Regional y de la Distribucion de la Fuerza de Trabajo." Revista del Centro de Estudios Educativos 7 (No. 3, 1977): 79-95.

741. Wang, Lawrence K., and James R. Rawls. "The Transfer of Training Obtained Abroad to Taiwan." Industry of Free China 43 (February, 1975): 11-25.

742. Weiler, Hans N. "The Political Dilemmas of Foreign Study." Comparative Education Review 28 (May, 1984): 168-179.

## 12. LEGAL ISSUES

743. Australian Government. <u>Overseas Students Charge Collection Act</u>.
Canberra. Australian Government Publishing Service, 1979.

744. Danilov, Dan. <u>U.S. Immigration and Naturalization Law Citator</u>.
Seattle: Butterworth Legal Publishers, 1982.

745. Guglielmo, Hector. "Rights and Obligations of Foreign Students in
an American University." Unpublished Ph.D thesis, University
of Arizona, 1967.

The purpose of the study is to attempt to discover
what factors in the foreign students' background and
experience have a positive or negative relationship to his
knowledge of civil regulations regarding: (1) Immigration
regulations; (2) Automobile operator's responsibilities;
(3) Income tax and Social Security; (4) Housing regulations; (5) Employment responsibilities; and (6) Purchasing
and installment buying. These factors were compared,
relative to:
1. The amount of time the student had been in the United
States.
2. The amount of contact the foreign student had with
Americans.
3. The amount of formal orientation the student received.
The population was 146 foreign students at the
University of Arizona.
Results:
. A definite positive relationship was noted between length
of time in the United States and scores on the
questionnaire.
. The amount of orientation had little bearing on how well
the students scored on the questionnaire.
. The number of countries in which the student lived for at
least three months was positively related to how well he
answered the questionnaire.
. Participants with experience of part-time or full-time
employment scored much higher than students without the
experience of employment.

The study ends with some recommendations such as:
. Initial orientation may be useful to the students'
adjustment.
. Universities and communities should provide means for
more interpersonal contacts between foreign and American
students.
. Adequate counseling should be made available to the
foreign students.

746. Jacqz, Jane. Refugee Students from Southern Africa. Washington, D.C.: African American Institute, 1967.

747. Kapner, Harold, and Irving Field. Not for Illegal Aliens Only: How to Get a Green Card. New York: Golden Door Publications, 1978.

748. Matthewson, Douglas E., Jr., ed. Immigration Rules, Regulations, and Requirements and Foreign Student Enrollments. Southeast Florida Education Consortium Workshop, Miami, Florida, February 18, 1981. Miami, Florida: Southeast Florida Education Consortium, 1981.

749. National Association for Foreign Student Affairs. Adviser's Manual of Federal Regulations Affecting Foreign Students and Scholars. Washington, D.C.: National Association for Foreign Student Affairs, 1982. (revised edition)

750. National Association for Foreign Student Affairs. Update to Adviser's Manual of Federal Regulations Affecting Foreign Students and Scholars. Washington, D.C.: NAFSA, 1978.

751. Permanent Residence and Other Immigration Benefits for the Foreign Student. Washington, D.C.: Allen and Jones, 1979.

752. Smith, Eugene H., and Marvin Boron. Faculty Member's Guide to U.S. Immigration Law. Washington, D.C.: National Association for Foreign Student Affairs, 1980.

753. United States, Comptroller General. Report to the Congress: Better Controls Needed to Prevent Foreign Students from Violating the Conditions of Their Entry and Stay While in the United States. Washington, D.C.: General Accounting Office, 1975.

754. United States, Social Security Administration, Department of Health Education and Welfare. Social Security Coverage of Foreign Students and Exchange Visitors. Baltimore, Maryland: Social Security Administraton, 1979.

## Articles

755. Anthony, Mark W. "Suspension of Deportation: A Revitalized Relief for the Alien." San Diego Law Review 18 (December, 1980): 65-88.

756. Baron, Marvin. "The Impact of the Buckley Amendment on Foreign Student Offices." National Association for Foreign Student Affairs Newsletter 28 (November, 1976): 6ff.

757. Bedrosian, Alex. "Alien Status: Legal Issue and Institutional Responsibilities." In Educating Students From Other Nations: American Colleges and Universities in International Educational

_Interchange_, edited by Hugh M. Jenkins, et al., pp. 163-183. San Francisco: Jossey-Bass, 1983.

758. Bedrosian, Alex. "Social Security Coverage of Foreign Students and Exchange Visitors." _National Association for Foreign Student Affairs Newsletter_ 26 (June, 1975): 4ff.

759. Castillo, Leonel J. "I.N.S. Arrests and Detention of 180 Unidentified Iranian Students in Chicago, Illinois, (May 1978 memo)." In _Departments of State, Justice, and Commerce, The Judiciary and Related Agencies Appropriations for 1980. Part 5. Department of Justice [Congressional Hearings]_. Washington, D.C.: Government Printing Office, 1979.

760. Cook, Paul A. "Government Regulations Concerning International Exchange." In _International Encyclopedia of Higher Education_, edited by A. Knowles, pp. 1551-1557. San Francisco: Jossey-Bass, 1977.

761. Cooper, Timothy T. "Educating the Foreign and Illegal Alien Student." In _School Law in Contemporary Society_, edited by M. A. McGheney. Topeka, Kansas: National Organization on Legal Problems of Education, 1980.

762. Dilley, Steven C., and Debra McGilsky. "United States and Foreign Tax Ramifications for a Student Studying or Working Abroad." _Taxes: The Tax Magazine_ 57 (March, 1979): 170-173.

763. Fortunato, Joseph A. "Constitutional Law--Equal Protection Does Not Protect Nonimmigrant Iranian Students from Selective Deportation--Narenji v. Civiletti." _Seton Hall Law Review_ 2 (No. 2, 1980): 230-242.

764. Gray, Julius H. "The Status of Foreign Students under the Immigration Act, 1976 [Canada]." _McGill Law Journal_ 27 (Summer, 1982): 556-562.

765. Hass, James, and Jerry Wilcox. "The Form I-20 Revisited." _National Association for Foreign Student Affairs Newsletter_ 31 (April, 1980): 171ff.

766. Johnston, Tony. "The Law and the Private Overseas Student." In _Overseas Students in Australia_, edited by S. Bochner, and P. Wicks, pp. 119-128. Auburn: New South Wales University Press, 1972.

767. Joshi, Joan H., et al. "Fulbright Act of 1946." _College and University_ 51 (Summer, 1976): 555-560.

768. Lindsey, Robert B. "The Rights of Foreign Students in the United States." _Interpreter Releases_ 51 (June 24, 1974): 163-171.

769. Lowenstein, Edith. "Foreign Student Advising and the Use of Immigration Lawyers." National Association for Foreign Student Affairs Newsletter 25 (October, 1973): 1ff.

770. McAnally, Mary. "The Plight of Student Exiles in the U.S.A." Africa Today 17 (May/June, 1970): 1-10.

   Essentially this article deals with the problem of over 100 former South African black students who study in the United States and have become "stateless individuals." The author reviews United States immigration policies and quotes extensively from the American Immigration and Naturalization Service of 1968 and the Federal Register of 1970. The most salient part of the article deals with recommendations from South African students on what Americans can do to improve the students' situation.

771. McDonald, Nancy J. "Selective Enforcement of Immigration Laws on the Basis of Nationality as an Instrument of Foreign Policy [with Reference to the Case of Narenji v. Civiletti, a Class Action Filed on Behalf of Non-Immigrant Iranian Students]." Notre Dame Lawyer 56 (April, 1981): 704-718.

772. "1965-66 Fulbright-Hays Grantees: 10 Years Later." International Educational and Cultural Exchange 11 (No. 1, 1975): 37-41.

773. Olson, Heather. "Immigration Regulations Affecting Practical Training [of Foreign Students]." In Resources for Practical Training [of Foreign Students], pp. 15-20. Washington, D.C.: National Association for Foreign Student Affairs, 1983.

774. Smith, Eugene. "Guidelines for the Release of Information from the Files of Foreign Students and Visitors." National Association for Foreign Student Affairs Newsletter 23 (June, 1972): 10ff.

775. Smith, Eugene. "Revisions to the Adviser's Manual of Federal Regulations Affecting Foreign Students and Scholars." National Association for Foreign Student Affairs Newsletter 28 (Summer, 1977): 5ff.

776. Smith, Shelagh Kiley. "Alien Students in the United States: Statutory Interpretation and Problems of Control." Suffolk Transnational Law Journal 5 (June, 1981): 235-250.

777. Trakman, L. E. "Need for Legal Training in International Comparative and Foreign Law--Foreign Lawyers at American Law Schools." Journal of Legal Education 27 (No. 4, 1976): 509-551.

778. Wicks, Peter. "Diplomatic Perspectives." In Overseas Students in Australia, edited by S. Bochner, and P. Wicks, pp. 10-21. Auburn: New South Wales University Press, 1972.

Reportage

779. Hutchinson, J. "Court Rules Against Entry Guidelines." Times Higher Education Supplement 516 (September 24, 1982): 7.

780. Hutchinson, J. "Entry Rules Hamper Exchange." Times Higher Education Supplement (June 24, 1983): 6.

781. "Immigrant Laws Said to Hurt Foreign Students." Chronicle of Higher Education 8 (June 24, 1974): 4.

782. "Iranian-Student Policy Upheld." Chronicle of Higher Education 20 (April 7, 1980): 14.

783. Jackson, M. "Heads Breaking Law on Jobs." Times Education Supplement (April 18, 1975): 4.

784. "Judge Bars Rules on U.S. Aid to Medical Students Abroad." Chronicle of Higher Education 26 (July 27, 1983): 8.

785. "Libyan Students May Stay in U.S." Chronicle of Higher Education 22 (June 1, 1981): 9.

786. "Limits Proposed on Foreign Student Employment." Chronicle of Higher Education 24 (June 9, 1982): 20.

787. Link, Mary. "Congress Easing Law Making Medical Schools Admit Foreign Students." Congressional Quarterly Weekly Report 35 (October 29, 1977): 2327-2328.

788. Middleton, L. "INS Urged to Fine Colleges Over Foreign Student Reports." Chronicle of Higher Education 22 (March 23, 1981): 14.

789. Middleton, Lorenzo. "Status of Iranian Students in Doubt." Chronicle of Higher Education 20 (April 21, 1980): 8.

790. Middleton, Lorenzo. "U.S. to Require Annual Registration of Foreign Students." Chronicle of Higher Education 21 (February 2, 1981): 16.

791. Middleton, Lorenzo. "U.S. Seeks Tighter Control Over Foreign Students." Chronicle of Higher Education 20 (March 3, 1980): 12.

792. Middleton, Lorenzo. "U.S. Stops College's Foreign-Student Program." Chronicle of Higher Education 18 (May 21, 1979): 4.

793. Middleton, Lorenzo. "White House Urged to Ease Visa Restrictions on Iranians." Chronicle of Higher Education 20 (June 2, 1980): 6.

794. Middleton, Lorenzo, and M. Scully. "Most Iranian Students Can Stay in U.S. Despite Severing of Diplomatic Relations." Chronicle of Higher Education 20 (April 14, 1980): 1.

795. Morris, B. "Academics Expelled Over Anti-PLO Understanding." Times Higher Education Supplement (November 5, 1982): 7.

796. Morris, B. "Foreign Dons Refuse to Sign Anti-PLO Pledge." Times Higher Education Supplement (October 1, 1982): 7.

797. O'Leary, J. "Lords Rule on Overseas Status." Times Higher Education Supplement 529 (December 24, 1982): 1.

798. "Students from Abroad to Find Job Rules Tighter this Summer." Chronicle of Higher Education 8 (May 6, 1974): 4.

799. "Tax Rules Hit Foreign Students in Canada." Chronicle of Higher Education 21 (September 8, 1980): 16.

800. Tender, P. de "Le Nouveau Statut Administratif des Etudiants Etrangers en Belgique." Informationes Universitaires et Professionelles Internationales 25 (September–October, 1981): 31-33.

801. "U.S. Lifts Visa Restrictions on Iranians." Chronicle of Higher Education 22 (March 30, 1981): 15.

802. "U.S. Probes Visa-Fraud Charges." Chronicle of Higher Education 22 (May 26, 1981): 10.

803. Walker, D. "Many Countries Placing Restrictions on Foreign Students, Researchers Say." Chronicle of Higher Education 22 (June 8, 1981): 15.

804. Winokur, Marshall. "Foreign Students' Toughest Test: Getting a Visa." Chronicle of Higher Education 24 (March 24, 1982): 56.

805. Woodcock, Lynda. "Restrictions on Visa Students are Increasing." University Affairs 18 (No. 1, 1977): 2-4.

## 13. RECRUITMENT: POLICIES AND PROCEDURES

806. Agarwal, Vinod Bhushan. "Foreign Students' Demand for U.S. Higher Education." Unpublished Ph.D thesis, University of California at Santa Barbara, 1977.

807. College Entrance Examination Board. Guidelines for the Recruitment of Foreign Students. New York: College Entrance Examination Board, 1978.

808. Commission on Voluntary Service and Action. Invest Yourself—1971. New York: Commission on Voluntary Service, 1971.

809. Jenkins, Hugh M., ed. Foreign Student Recruitment: Realities and Recommendations. New York: College Entrance Examination Board, 1980.

   This is a report of the colloquium held in March, 1980 on foreign students, sponsored by the National Liaison Committee on Foreign Student Admission (NLC), which is composed of the American Association of Collegiate Registrars and Admission Officers (AACRAO), the College Board, the Council of Graduate Schools in the United States (CGS), the Institute of International Education (IIE), and the National Association for Foreign Student Affairs (NAFSA). Problem areas discussed include:
   . "Foreign Student Recruitment – Why? Demographic and Financial Factors, Present and Future"
   . "Current Practice in the Recruitment of Foreign Students"

   Besides the discussions on the problems raised, the participants took part in two working group projects, to explore the feasibility of establishing a clearinghouse for information on foreign student recruitment to U.S. universities and colleges, and to set down criteria for ethical recruitment practices and suggest ways in which these might be disseminated to relevant U.S. institutions.
   A number of recommendations made were directed toward the enhancement of positive approaches to the function of foreign student recruitment in the United States.

810. Johnston, James Boyd. "A Marketing Approach to Increase Foreign Student Enrollment in American Higher Education." Unpublished Ed.D thesis, University of Pennsylvania, 1976.

811. Kasprzyk, Peter. Die Forderung afrikanischer Studenten durch den DAAD. Bonn-Bad Godesberg: DAAD, 1974.

812. Putman, Ivan, Nancy Young, and Leo Sweeney. Guidelines for the Recruitment of Foreign Students. Washington, D.C.: College Entrance Examinations Board, 1979.

813. Simerville, Clara. The Foreign Student as Your Customer. Corvallis, Oregon: Oregon State University Press, 1965.

Articles

814. Armenio, Joseph A. "Back to the Agora: Marketing Foreign Admissions." Journal of the National Association of College Admissions Counselors 22 (No. 4, 1978): 30-34.

815. "Buffalo Sets Program for Foreign Students." Journal of American Dentist Association 82 (January, 1971): 77-79.

816.  Fiske, Edward B.  "Ethical Issues in Recruiting Students."  New
      Directions for Higher Education 33 (1981):  41-48.

          The author argues that demographic changes (the
      decline in the number of college-age youth in the United
      States) mean "the shift from a seller's to a buyer's mar-
      ket."  In this context he also discusses the abuse in
      recruiting foreign students, pointing out problems linked
      with:
      . insufficient information on possibilities as well as con-
        ditions for studying in the United States;
      . "headhunting" practices in some South American countries;
      . presigning of 1-20 forms by some colleges (necessary for
        foreign students to obtain U.S. visa);
      . lack of adequate counseling for foreign students.

817.  Hammond, E., et al.  "Responsible Enrollment Philosophy."  College
      and University 51 (Summer, 1976):  494-496.

818.  Hoover, Gary.  "Recruiters:  Getting Your Share?  Third Party
      Recruitment/Placement--Is It Ethical?"  National Association
      for Foreign Student Affairs Newsletter 31 (November, 1979):
      33ff.

819.  Hoover, Jack, Ronald E. Thomas, and Phillip P. Byers.  "Should
      Admissions Officers Attempt to Balance Institutional Budgets by
      Recruiting Foreign Students?"  College and University 49
      (Summer, 1974):  690-701.

820.  Hopkins, Gary W.  "Recruitment of Foreign Students:  Reality or
      Myth?"  National ACAC Journal 23 (February, 1979):  28-30.

821.  Klein, Richard B.  "New Sources of Students for Short-Term
      Study-Abroad Programs."  Bulletin of the Association of
      Departments of Foreign Languages 13 (No. 2, 1981):  20-23.

822.  Nelson, L. M., and J. E. Dotibois.  "Public Relations and the
      Foreign Student."  College and University Journal 11
      (September, 1972):  28-31.

823.  Sharp, T. E.  "Recruiters and Recruiting."  National Association
      for Foreign Student Affairs Newsletter 33 (March, 1982):
      105ff.

824.  Stedman, Joann.  "Professional Concerns in International
      Recruitment."  National Association for Foreign Student Affairs
      Newsletter 35 (March, 1984):  110-122.

825.  Thomas, Ronald E.  "So You Want to Recruit Foreign Students."
      National ACAC Journal 19 (November, 1974):  11-13.

Reportage

826. Cookson, C. "Business of Recruitment, U.S.-style." Times Higher Education Supplement (December 7, 1979): 1.

827. "Denver: Colleges Told to Seek Students From Abroad." Chronicle of Higher Education 21 (September 15, 1980): 5.

828. "Ethical Aspects of Foreign Student Recruitment." College and University 54 (Summer, 1979): 319-320.

829. Hapgood, David. "The Competition for Africa's Students." Reporter 29 (September 12, 1963): 41-42.

830. Jacobson, Robert L. "Community Colleges Seek a Global Perspective: Strategies for Enrolling More Students from Overseas." Chronicle of Higher Education 15 (November 28, 1977): 5.

831. Scully, M. G. "Abuses in Foreign-Student Recruiting Tarnish U.S. Colleges' Image Abroad." Chronicle of Higher Education 20 (April 7, 1980): 1.

832. Simon, E. "Who Needs Foreign Students?" Chemtech 12 (No. 4, 1982): 208-210.

833. Walker, David. "Scottish University Is Recruiting American High-School Students." Chronicle of Higher Education 24 (May 19, 1982): 19.

## 14. ADMISSIONS POLICIES AND PROCEDURES

834. Australian Vice Chancellor's Committee. Admission of Students from Interstate and Overseas. Canberra: Australian Vice Chancellor's Committee, 1974.

835. Campos-Arcia, M. A. "Graduate Foreign Student Admissions Decision-Making: An Application of the "JAN" Technique." Unpublished Ed.D thesis, North Carolina State University at Raleigh, 1978.

836. Craven, Thomas Fenner. "A Comparison of Admissions Criteria and Performance in Graduate School for Foreign and American Students at Temple University." Unpublished Ed.D thesis, Temple University, 1981.

837. Deluga, Marvin Raymond. "An Analysis of the Selection Procedures of Foreign Students, at the Undergraduate Level, in the United States." Unpublished Ed.D thesis, University of Idaho, 1970.

838. Dube, W. F. Trend Study of Coordinated Transfer Application System (COTRANS) Participants, 1970 through 1976: Final Report. Washington, D.C.: Division of Student Studies, Association of American Medical Colleges, 1977.

839. Fisher, S. H., and W. J. Dey. Forged Educational Credentials: A Sorry Tale. New York: World Education Services, 1979.

840. Gharavi, Ebrahim. "Admission of Foreign Graduate Students: An Analysis of Judgements by Selected Faculty and Administrators at North Texas State University. Unpublished Ph.D thesis, North Texas State University, 1977.

841. Higbee, Homer, and Marjorie K. Winters, eds. The Admission and Placement of Students from Hong Kong, Malaysia, Philippines, Singapore. Report of a Workshop (Baguio, Philippines, February 1979). Washington, D.C.: American Association of Collegiate Registrars and Admissions Officers, and National Association for Foreign Student Affairs, 1980.

842. Homan, James Cornelius. "Foreign Student Admissions: A Discriminant Analysis Approach." Unpublished Ed.D thesis, University of Colorado at Boulder, 1973.

843. Jacqz, Jane W., ed. Guidelines for the Admission and Placement of Students from the Middle East and North Africa. New York: Institute of International Education, 1966.

844. Jacqz, Jane W., ed. Workshop on the Admission of Students from Taiwan and Hong Kong, Minneapolis, 1966. Guidelines for the Admission and Placement of Students from Taiwan and Hong Kong; Report of Information Presented at a Conference. New York: Institute of International Education, 1966.

845. Larsen, John Arnold. "A Survey of Foreign Student Admissions Officers to Ascertain Academic Criteria for Selection of Freshman Foreign Students." Unpublished Ph.D thesis, University of Wyoming, 1969.

846. Merva, George E. Admissions Criteria for Foreign Students and Graduates of Curricula other than Agricultural Engineering. St. Joseph, Michigan: American Society of Agricultural Engineers, 1978.

847. National Association for Foreign Student Affairs. Admission and Selection of Foreign Students: Guideline Series 2. Washington, D.C.: NAFSA, 1978.

848. National Association for Foreign Student Affairs. Students Abroad: A Guide for Selecting a Foreign Education. Washington, D.C.: NAFSA, 1979.

849. National Commission on Accrediting. Maintenance of Academic Standards Through Accreditation in the United States of

America. Washington, D.C.: National Commission on Accrediting, Department of State, 1965.

850. The Overseas Selection of Foreign Students. New York: Education and World Affairs, 1966.

851. Peisch, Mark L. The Foreign Graduate Student at Twenty-Two American Universities--Admissions and Financial Aid. New York: Institute of International Education, 1965.

852. Peisch, Mark. Overseas Selection of Foreign Students. New York: Education.and World Affairs, 1966.

853. United States, Agency for International Development. No Two Alike: The Comparability Question in Foreign Student Admissions. Washington, D.C.: Office of International Training, U.S. Agency for International Development, 1983.

854. Willard, Frances. A Study of the Educational System of India and Guide to the Academic Placement of Students from India in United States Educational Institutions. Washington, D.C.: American Council on Education, 1964.

855. Woolston, Valerie, ed. Foreign Educational Credentials Required for Consideration of Admission to Universities and Colleges in the United States. Washington, D.C.: Office of International Training, U.S. Agency for International Development, 1981.


Articles

856. Abadzi, Helen. "The Use of Multivariate Statistical Procedures in International Student Admissions." Journal of College Student Personnel 21 (May, 1980): 195-201.

857. "Admission and Placement of Foreign Undergraduate Students: Panel Discussion." College and University 40 (Summer, 1965): 429-432.

858. Aleamoni, Lawrence M. "The Vagaries of Selection - I. Selection, Placement, and Proficiency in American Colleges and Universities." National ACAC Journal 17 (August, 1972): 7-12.

859. American Association of Collegiate Registrars and Admissions Officers. "Proceedings of the 63rd Annual Meeting, Houston, Texas, 1977." College and University 52 (Summer, 1977): 355-364.

860. Barker, Billy W. "The Foreign Transfer Student: Feel and Fact." College and University 50 (Spring, 1975): 243-246.

861. Beale, Andrew V. "The Vagaries of Selection - II. How College Admissions Officers Rate Applicants." National ACAC Journal 17 (August, 1972): 13-14.

862. Bradshaw, J. R., and G. F. McKinnon. "Foreign Students and Placement." Journal of College Placement 40 (Winter, 1980): 48-50.

863. Burns, W. A. D., et al. "Admission of Scandinavian Students." College and University 49 (Summer, 1974): 669-682.

864. Dart, Francis E. "Observations on an Obstacle Course [Facing Asian Physics Students Seeking Admission to Graduate Schools in the U.S.]." International Educational and Cultural Exchange 11 (No. 2, 1975): 29-32.

865. Dixon, Rebecca, et al. "Controversial Issues in Interpreting Foreign Academic Records." College and University 51 (Summer, 1976): 462-468.

866. Elliot, G. F. "The Dilemma of Foreign Student Admissions." Junior College Journal 40 (October, 1969): 17-20.

867. Fisher, Stephen H. "Handling Forged Credentials." National Association for Foreign Student Affairs Newsletter 26 (February, 1975): 6ff.

868. Fisher, S. H. "Should There Be a Spectrum of Foreign Student Admissions Standards?" College and University 50 (Summer, 1975): 502-505.

869. Fisher, S. H. "Sleuthing Against Swindlers of Foreign Academic Credentials." National Association for Foreign Student Affairs Newsletter 30 (February, 1979): 101ff.

870. Groenewold, Roger. "International Admissions: A Self-Taught Course in World Geography." College and University 59 (No. 1, 1983): 70-73.

871. Haas, G. J. "Foreign Student Admissions." College and University 50 (Summer, 1975): 505-512.

872. Jameson, Sanford C. "The Challenge to Foreign Student Admissions in the 70's." National Association for Foreign Student Affairs Newsletter 21 (May, 1970): 7ff.

873. Johnson, A. W., and J. R. Gotcher. "Priorities System for Admitting International Students." International Education and Cultural Exchange 13 (Spring, 1978): 41-47.

874. Jones, E. W., et al. "Admissions Policies and Procedures: United Kingdom." College and University 53 (Summer, 1978): 481-488.

875. Kellog, T. G., et al. "Progress Report on the AACRAO-AID Participant Selection and Placement Study." College and University 43 (Summer, 1968): 465-468.

876. Kelson, D. S., and G. J. Haas. "So You Know Nothing about Foreign Admissions." College and University 48 (Summer, 1973): 578-585.

877. Krivy, G. J., et al. "Guidelines for Foreign Student Admissions." College and University 49 (Summer, 1974): 630-637.

878. LaBerge, Bernard E. "Towards an Integrated Approach to Foreign Student Placement." National Association for Foreign Student Affairs Newsletter 26 (February, 1975): 3ff.

879. LaBerge, Bernard E., and Bernadette Leary. "Can Placement Serve Foreign Students?" Journal of College Placement 36 (No. 4, 1976): 51-54.

880. Lewis, J., et al. "Comparison of International Admissions Systems at Four Universities." College and University 47 (Summer, 1972): 284-287.

881. McNeely, S. S., Jr. "Academic Credentials of Indian Applicants." College and University 42 (Spring, 1967): 365-382.

882. Miller, W. "Die Probleme der Harmonisierung des Schulwesens in der EWG." Erziehung und Unterricht (No. 4, 1971): 279-286.

883. Neal, Fern. "Placing Peter [A Foreign Student]." Journal of College Placement 37 (No. 4, 1977): 52-54.

884. Oakeshott, M. F. "Activities of the National Equivalence Information Centre for the United Kingdom." Higher Education in Europe 14 (April-June, 1979): 36-37.

885. Patrick, William S. "Admissions: Developing Effective Selection Practices." In Educating Students from Other Nations: American Colleges and Universities in International Educational Interchange, edited by Hugh M. Jenkins, et al., pp. 135-162. San Francisco: Jossey-Bass, 1983.

886. Pyle, C. A. "Trends in International Student Admissions--Needs and Responses." In Proceedings: 1979 Frontiers in Education Conference, edited by L. P. Grayson, and J. M. Biedenbach, pp. 62-64. Washington, D.C.: American Society for Engineering Education, 1979.

887. Pyle, C. A., et al. "Resources, Personnel, and Agencies to Assist in Credential Analysis." College and University 47 (Summer, 1972): 359-367.

888. Silny, J., and N. W. Young. "Fraudulent Foreign Student Credentials." College and University 53 (Summer, 1978): 490-498.

889. Sjogren, Cliff. "Admissions Techniques. Minority Group Students—Foreign Students." National Association for Foreign Student Affairs Newsletter 22 (December, 1970): 12.

890. Slocum, J., et al. "Granting Advanced Standing and Transfer Credit to International Students." College and University 47 (Summer, 1972): 687-698.

891. Strain, W. H. "Which Foreign Students Should U.S. Institutions Admit?" Phi Delta Kappan 46 (March, 1965): 332-335.

892. Sweeney, L. J., et al. "Admission and Placement of Students from Australia, New Zealand, Hong Kong, Malaysia, Singapore." College and University 45 (Summer, 1970): 843-849.

893. Sweeney, L. J., et al. "Admission and Placement of Students from Ceylon, India, Pakistan." College and University 45 (Summer, 1970): 838-843.

894. Swenson, F. G. "Should Admissions Officers Attempt to Balance Institutional Budgets by Recruiting Foreign Students?" College and University 49 (Summer, 1974): 690-701.

895. Thompson, R., et al. "Admission and Placement of Graduate Foreign Students." College and University 43 (Summer, 1968): 570-575.

896. Tyler, Varro E. "Admission and Placement of Foreign Graduate Students." American Journal of Pharmaceutical Education 41 (No. 4, 1977): 385-388.

897. Vaudioux, Jacques. "Les Politiques Nationales d'Acces des Etudiants Etrangers." CRE - Information No. 57 (1st Quarter, 1982): 7-24.

898. Vold, R. D., and P. Mukerjee. "Correlation of Indian Training with American School Requirements." Journal of Chemical Education 46 (No. 12, 1969): 833-837.

899. Walker, J., et al. "Reducing Multiple Foreign Applications; A Proposal." College and University 45 (Summer, 1970): 506-513.

### Reportage

900. Butts, Thomas A. "College Admissions for the Culturally Distinct." CAPS Capsule 4 (Winter, 1971): 7-9.

901. "Enseignement Superieur et Recherche." Bulletin d'Information—Conseil de l'Europe (No. 1, 1974): 5-6.

902. Mould, D. "How to Get into an American University." Times Higher Education Supplement (June 16, 1978): 10.

903. Papke, David R. "Capitalizing on the Premed Dream: Foreign School Placement." New Leader 61 (January, 1978): 22-24.

904. "U.S. Institutions Urged to Adopt Standards on Foreign Students." Chronicle of Higher Education 22 (June 8, 1981): 5.

905. Williken, R. "Doors to the West Open Wide." Times Higher Education Supplement (September 8, 1978): 7.

## 15. EVALUATION OF CREDENTIALS AND EQUIVALENCE OF DEGREES

906. Abadzi, Helen. "Evaluation of Foreign Student Admission Procedures Used at the University of Alabama." Unpublished Ph.D thesis, the University of Alabama, 1975.

907. American Association of Collegiate Registrars and Admissions Officers. Switzerland: A Guide to the Academic Placement of Students from Switzerland in United States Educational Institutions. Washington, D.C.: AACRAO, 1963.

908. American Association of Collegiate Registrars and Admissions Officers-AID Study Committee. The AACRAO-AID Participant Selection and Placement Study. A Report to the Office of International Training Agency for International Development, U.S. Department of State. Washington, D.C.: AACRAO, 1971.

909. American Association of Collegiate Registrars and Admissions Officers. Committee on Evaluation of Foreign Student Credentials. Afghanistan: A Guide to the Academic Placement of Students from Afghanistan in Educational Institutions in the U.S.A. Washington, D.C.: AACRAO, 1961.

910. American Association of Collegiate Registrars and Admissions Officers. Committee on Evaluation of Foreign Student Credentials. Caribbean: A Guide to the Academic Placement of Students from European Affiliated Areas of the Caribbean in Educational Institutions in the U.S.A. Washington, D.C.: AACRAO, 1961.

911. American Association of Collegiate Registrars and Admissions Officers. Committee on Evaluation of Foreign Student Credentials. Hong Kong: A Guide to the Academic Placement of Students from Hong Kong in Educational Institutions in the U.S.A. Washington, D.C.: AACRAO, 1961.

912. American Association of Collegiate Registrars and Admissions Officers. Committee on Evaluation of Foreign Student Credentials. Rumania: A Guide to the Academic Placement of

Students from Rumania in Educational Institutions in the U.S.A. Washington, D.C.: AACRAO, 1961.

913. American Association of Collegiate Registrars and Admissions Officers. Committee on Evaluation of Foreign Student Credentials. Tanganyika: A Guide to the Academic Placement of Students from Tanganyika in Educational Institutions in the U.S.A. Washington, D.C.: AACRAO, 1961.

914. American Association of Collegiate Registrars and Admissions Officers. Austria: A Survey of Austrian Education and Guide to the Academic Placement of Students from Austria in Educational Institutions in the United States of America. Washington, D.C.: AACRAO, 1961.

915. American Association of Collegiate Registrars and Admissions Officers. Czechoslovakia: A Guide to the Academic Placement of Students from Czechoslovakia in Educational Institutions in the United States. Washington, D.C.: AACRAO, 1964.

916. American Association of Collegiate Registrars and Admissions Officers. Chile: A Guide to the Academic Placement of Students from Chile in Educational Institutions in the United States. Washington, D.C.: AACRAO, 1965.

917. American Association of Collegiate Registrars and Admissions Officers. Iran: A Guide to the Academic Placement of Students from Iran in Educational Institutions in the United States. Washington, D.C: AACRAO, 1964.

918. American Association of Collegiate Registrars and Admissions Officers. The Philippines: A Guide to the Academic Placement of Students from the Republic of the Philippines in Educational Institutions in the U.S.A. Washington, D.C.: AACRAO, 1962.

919. American Association of Collegiate Registrars and Admissions Officers. The Soviet Zone of Germany: A Guide to the Academic Placement of Students from the Soviet Zone of Germany in Educational Institutions in the United States. Washington, D.C.: AACRAO, 1964.

920. American Association of Collegiate Registrars and Admissions Officers. Spain: A Study of the Educational System of Spain and a Guide to the Academic Placement of Students from Spain in United States Educational Institutions. Washington, D.C.: AACRAO, 1967.

921. American Association of Collegiate Registrars and Admissions Officers. U.S.S.R.: A Guide to the Academic Placement of Students from the U.S.S.R. in Educational Institutions in the United States. Washington, D.C.: AACRAO, 1966.

922. American Association of Collegiate Registrars and Admissions Officers. Hungarian People's Republic: A Guide to the

Academic Placement of Students from the Hungarian People's Republic in Educational Institutions in the United States. Washington, D.C.: AACRAO, 1972.

923. American Association of Collegiate Registrars and Admissions Officers. New Zealand: A Guide to the Academic Placement of Students from New Zealand in Educational Institutions in the United States. Washington, D.C.: AACRAO, 1965.

924. American Association of Collegiate Registrars and Admissions Officers. Peru: A Guide to the Academic Placement of Students from Peru in Educational Institutions in the United States. Washington, D.C.: AACRAO, 1966.

925. American Association of Collegiate Registrars and Admissions Officers. Poland: A Guide to the Academic Placement of Students from Poland in Educational Institutions in the United States. Washington, D.C.: AACRAO, 1964.

926. American Association of Collegiate Registrars and Admissions Officers. Saudi Arabia: A Study of the Educational System of the Kingdom of Saudi Arabia and Guide to the Academic Placement of Students in the United States Educational Institutions. Washington, D.C.: AACRAO, 1968.

927. American Association of Collegiate Registrars and Admissions Officers. Taiwan: A Guide to the Academic Placement of Students from Taiwan in Educational Institutions in the United States. Washington, D.C.: AACRAO, 1967.

928. Arnold, Ruth. Do It-Yourself Evaluation of Foreign Student Credentials. Washington, D.C.: American Council on Education Publications, 1966.

929. Chapman, Eunice. Italy: A Survey of Italian Education and Guide to the Academic Placement of Italian Students in Educational Institutions in the U.S.A. Washington, D.C.: American Association of Collegiate Registrars and Admissions Officers, 1962.

930. Chapman, Eunice. Lebanon: A Study of the Educational System of Lebanon and Guide to the Academic Placement of Students from Lebanon in Educational Institutions in the U.S.A. Washington, D.C.: American Association of Collegiate Registrars and Admissions Officers, 1964.

931. Chavels, Samuel G. Mexico: A Study of the Educational System of Mexico and a Guide to the Academic Placement of Students from Mexico in United States Educational Institutions. Washington, D.C.: American Association of Collegiate Registrars and Admissions Officers, 1968.

932. Coffman, William E. Evidence of Cultural Factors in Responses of African Students to Items in an American Test of Scholastic Aptitude. New York: College Entrance Examination Board, 1963.

933. Cote, Michel. Admission des Etudiants dans les Universites du Quebec: Evaluation des Dossiers Etrangers par Comparaison avec le Systeme Collegial Quebecois. Montreal: Service Regional d'Admission du Montreal Metropolitain, 1980.

934. Dickey, Karlene. Switzerland--Educational System and a Guide to the Academic Placement in U.S. Educational Institutions. Washington, D.C.: American Association of Collegiate Registrars and Admissions Officers, 1981.

935. Federal Republic of Germany. Secretariat of the Standing Conference of Ministers of Education and Cultural Affairs of the Lander. The Educational System in the Federal Republic of Germany. Bonn: Foreign Office of the Federal Republic of Germany, no date.

936. Fish, Cynthia, ed. Workshop on the Admission and Academic Placement of Students from the Caribbean Area. The Admission and Academic Placement of Students from the Caribbean: A Workshop Report. San Juan: The North-South Center, 1972.

937. Fisher, Stephen H. The United Kindgom of Great Britain and Northern Ireland. A Study of the Educational System of the United Kingdom and a Guide to the Academic Placement of Students from the United Kingdom in United States Educational Institutions. Washington, D.C.: American Association of Collegiate Registrars and Admissions Officers, 1976.

938. Frey, James S. Turkey: A Study of the Educational System of Turkey and a Guide to the Academic Placement of Students from Turkey in United States Educational Institutions. Washington, D.C.: American Association of Collegiate Registrars and Admissions Officers, 1972.

939. Frey, James S., and Stephen H. Fisher. Israel: A Guide to the Academic Placement of Students from Israel in Educational Institutions of the United States. Washington, D.C.: American Association of Collegiate Registrars and Admissions Officers, 1976.

940. Guiton, Jean. From Equivalence of Degrees to Evaluation of Competence: Present Procedures. Paris: UNESCO, 1977.

941. Hefling, Robert J. Libya: A Study of the Educational System of the Libyan Arab Republic and a Guide to the Academic Placement of Students from Libya in United States Educational Institutions. Washington, D.C.: American Association of Collegiate Registrars and Admissions Officers, 1972.

942. Herriott, J. Homer. Venezuela: A Guide to the Academic Placement of Venezuelan Students in Educational Institutions in the United States of America. Washington, D.C.: American Association of Collegiate Registrars and Admissions Officers, 1961.

943. Hoover, Gary. Venezuela: A Study of the Educational System of Venezuela and a Guide to the Academic Placement of Students from Venezuela in Educational Institutions of the United States. Washington, D.C.: American Assocation of Collegiate Registrars and Admission Officers, 1978.

944. Hyslop, Beatrice F. France: A Study of French Education and Guide to the Academic Placement of Students from France in Educational Institutions in the U.S.A. Washington, D.C.: American Association of Collegiate Registrars and Admissions Officers, 1964.

945. Institute of International Education. Evaluating Foreign Students' Credentials. New York: Institute of International Education, 1981.

946. International Association of Universities. Methods of Establishing Equivalence Between Degrees and Diplomas. Paris: UNESCO, 1970.

947. Jarmon, Hattie, Ellsworth Gerritz, and William S. Patrick. Vietnam: A Study of the System of Higher Education of Vietnam and Guide to the Admission and Academic Placement of Vietnamese Students in Colleges and Universities in the United States. Washington, D.C.: American Association of Collegiate Registrars and Admissions Officers, 1970.

948. Johnson, Johnny K. Thailand: A Study of the Educational System of Thailand and a Guide to Academic Placement of Students from Thailand in Educational Institutions in the United States. Washington, D.C.: American Association of Collegiate Registrars and Admissions Officers, 1978.

949. Kennedy, Patrick J. New Zealand: A Guide to the Academic Placement of Students from New Zealand in United States Educational Institutions. Washington, D.C.: American Association of Collegiate Registrars and Admissions Officers, 1981.

950. Kennedy, Patrick J. The Republic of China (Taiwan): A Study of the Educational System of the Republic of China and a Guide to the Academic Placement of Students from the Republic of China in United States Educational Institutions. Washington, D.C.: American Association of Collegiate Registrars and Admissions Officers, 1977.

951. Margolis, Alan M. Nigeria: A Study of the Educational System of Nigeria and a Guide to the Placement of Students from Nigeria

in Educational Institutions in the United States. Washington, D.C.: American Association of Collegiate Registrars and Admissions Officers, 1977.

952. Masclet, Jean Claude. La Mobilite Intraeuropeenne des Etudiants non Diplomes. Paris: Institute of Education, 1975.

953. Mayer, M. Diploma: International Schools and University Entrance. New York: Twentieth Century Fund, 1968.

954. Mize, David W. Algeria: A Study of the Educational System of Algeria and a Guide to the Academic Placement of Students from Algeria in Educational Institutions of the United States. Washington, D.C.: American Association of Collegiate Registrars and Admissions Officers, 1978.

955. Oliver, Eugene. Greece: A Study of the Educational System of Greece and a Guide to the Academic Placement of Students from Greece in Educational Institutions of the United States. Washington, D.C.: American Association of Collegiate Registrars and Admissions Officers, 1982.

956. Pearce, Beatrice. United Kingdom: A Study of the Educational System of the United Kingdom and Guide to the Academic Placement of Students from the United Kingdom in United States Educational Institutions. Washington, D.C.: American Association of Collegiate Registrars and Admissions Officers, 1963.

957. Phelps, Reginald Henry. Germany: A Study of the Educational System of Germany and Guide to the Academic Placement of Students from Germany in United States Educational Institutions. Washington, D.C.: American Association of Collegiate Registrars and Admissions Officers, 1966.

958. Sharp, Theodore, Inez Sepmeyer, and Martena Sasnett. The Country Index—Interpretations for Use in the Evaluation of Foreign Secondary Academic Credentials. Alhambra, California: Severy Publishing, 1971.

959. Sweeney, Leo J. Islamic Republic of Pakistan: A Study of the Educational System of Pakistan and a Guide to the Academic Placement of Students from Pakistan in Educational Institutions of the United States. Washington, D.C.: American Association of Collegiate Registrars and Admissions Officers, 1977.

960. Thomas, Alfred. Guides to the Academic Placement of Students from Foreign Countries in Educational Institutions in the United States of America. Washington, D.C.: American Association of Collegiate Registrars and Admissions Officers, 1969.

961. Trudeau, Edouard. Selected French Speaking Sub-Saharan African Countries: Burundi, Cameroon (Eastern), Chad, Congo-Brazzaville, Dahomey, Gabon, Ivory Coast, Mali, Mauritania,

Niger, Rwanda, Senegal, Togo, Upper Volta, Zaire: A Guide to the Academic Placement of Students from these Countries in Academic Institutions of the United States. Washington, D.C.: American Association of Collegiate Registrars and Admissions Officers, 1975.

962. Turner, Solveig M., ed. Evaluation of Foreign Educational Credentials and Recognition of Degree Equivalences. Boston: Center for International Higher Education, Northeastern University, 1979.

963. Villa, Kitty Maker. Mexico: A Study of the Educational System of Mexico and a Guide to the Academic Placement of Students from Mexico in Educational Institutions of the United States. Washington, D.C.: American Association of Collegiate Registrars and Admissions Officers, 1982.

964. Vroman, Clyde. Japan: A Guide to the Academic Placement of Students from Japan in United States Educational Institutions. Washington, D.C.: American Association of Collegiate Registrars and Admissions Officers, 1966.

965. Wanner, Raymond E. France: A Study of the Educational System of France and a Guide to the Academic Placement of Students from France in Educational Institutions of the United States. Washington, D.C.: American Association of Collegiate Registrars and Admissions Officers, 1975.

966. Willard, Frances M. The Republic of India: A Guide to the Academic Placement of Students from the Republic of India in United States Educational Institutions. Washington, D.C.: American Association of Collegiate Registrars and Admissions Officers, 1964.

## Articles

967. Adam, Roy. "Prufung Auslandischer Studenten fur die Zulassung zu Universitaten." In Moglishkeiten und Grenzen der Testanwendung in der Schule. Bericht uber Erste Internationale Arbeitstagung uber Testanwendung in der Schule. Berlin, 16-24 Mai 1967, pp. 789-795. Weinheim: Pedagogisches Zentrum Veroffentlichungen, 1968.

968. "Adoption of the Convention on the Recognition of Studies, Diplomas and Degrees in Higher Education in the Arab and European States Bordering on the Mediterranean." Higher Education in Europe 1 (No. 2, 1977): 3-5.

969. Arrighi, P. "Recognition of Diplomas in the European Community." Western European Education 14 (Spring/Summer, 1982): 131-136.

970. Campos, C. "Students and Europe." Universities Quarterly 26 (Summer, 1972): 280-309.

971. Cole-Baker, D. "Towards an International University Entrance Examination." Comparative Education 2 (November, 1965): 43-45.

972. "Conclusions of the Conference on Academic Mobility in Europe." CRE-Information No. 57 (1982): 75-82.

973. Crow, John T. "Admissions Criteria for Algerian High School Graduates and the Performance of Sonatrach-Sponsored Undergraduate Students at Various Universities in the State of Texas: A Contrastive Analysis." International Education 7 (Fall, 1977): 18-24.

974. Cuevas Cancino, F. "Une Convention Regional sur la Reconnaissance des Diplomes." Perspectives 5 (No. 2, 1975): 279-282.

975. Dremuk, R., and J. Frey. "Report on Feasibility for Foreign Credential Evaluation Service." College and University 44 (Summer, 1969): 418-421.

976. "Les Equivalences de Diplomes Etrangers aux Pays-Bas." Informations Universitaires et Professionelles Internationales (January-February, 1978): 16-23.

977. "Les Equivalences d'Etudes Franco-Allemandes et la Cooperation Universitaire." Informations Universitaires et Professionelles Internationales (August-September, 1976): 17-21.

978. "Evaluating Foreign Students' Credentials: Parts 1, 2 and 3." World Higher Education Communique 2 (Fall, 1980): 24-27; 3 (Winter, 1980): 19-21; 3 (Spring, 1981): 26-28.

979. "Foreign Credential Evaluation." College and University 52 (Summer, 1977): 518-521.

980. Frey, James S. "The Evaluation of Foreign Student Credentials: A Proposal." National Association for Foreign Student Affairs Newsletter 17 (December, 1965): 2ff.

981. Gerritz, G. M., et al. "Evaluation of Credentials from Brazil, Colombia, Venezuela, and Central America." College and University 44 (Summer, 1969): 578-585.

982. Griff, E. R., et al. "Foreign Credential Evaluation." College and University 51 (Summer, 1976): 474-482.

983. Howell, John. "On the Meaning of SAT Scores Obtained by Foreign Students of Non-English Language Background." College and University 43 (Winter, 1968): 225-232.

984. Huntley, S., et al. "GRE and Its Applicability to Foreign Students." College and University 47 (Summer, 1972): 621-624.

985. Lockyear, Fred. "Iranian Students: 37,000 or 75,000? Dealing with Academic Credentials Outlined." National Association for Foreign Student Affairs Newsletter 30 (January, 1979): 73ff.

986. Mulligan, Agnes C. "Evaluating Foreign Credentials." College and University 41 (Spring, 1966): 307-313.

987. National Liaison Committee on Foreign Student Admissions." Report on Feasibility for Foreign Credential Evaluation Service." College and University 44 (Summer, 1969): 414-418.

988. Patrick, W. S., et al. "Centralized Foreign Document Evaluation Center." College and University 43 (Summer, 1968): 546-549.

989. Perkins, J. A. "Mobility of Students and Staff Internationally." In Pressures and Priorities, edited by T. Craig, pp. 365-371. London: Association of Commonwealth Universities, 1979.

990. Saurwein, V. "Evaluation and Placement of International Engineering Students in United States Universities--United Nations Connections." In Proceedings: 1979 Frontiers in Education Conference, edited by L. P. Grayson, and J. M. Biedenbach, pp. 69-72. Washington, D.C.: American Society for Engineering Education.

991. Seaton, Ian. "Principes de la Conception de Tests Destines a l'Evaluation Prealable d'Etudiants Etrangers Venant Etudier en Grande-Bretagne." Etudes de Linguistique Appliquee 43 (July-September, 1981): 67-78.

992. Sjogren, C., et al. "Evaluation of Education Credentials from Turkey and the United Arab Republic." College and University 44 (Summer, 1969): 418-421.

993. Stassen, Manfred. "Academic Mobility and Interuniversity Cooperation." Higher Education in Europe (No. 2, 1980): 40-48.

994. Trapero Ballesteros, A. "De l'Equivalence des Diplomes a l'Evaluation de l'Homme." Informations Universitaires et Professionelles Internationales (June-July, 1974): 10-15.

995. Turner, Solveig M. "Directory of Equivalency Centers." World Higher Education Communique 4 (Spring, 1982): 8-11.

Reportage

996. "(U.S.) Educational Testing Service to Offer Exams in China." Chronicle of Higher Education 22 (May 18, 1981): 16.

## 16. FINANCES: SOURCES AND PROBLEMS

997. Breitenbach, Dieter, and Dieter Danckwortt. Studenten aus Afrika und Asien als Stipendiaten in Deutschland. Berlin: DAAD, 1961.

998. College Entrance Examination Board. Financial Planning for Study in the United States--A Guide for Students from Other Countries. Princeton: CEEB, 1973.

999. Council for International Studies and Programs. The CISP International Studies Funding Book. New York: CISP, 1979.

1000. Dremuk, Richard. How Foreign Monetary Exchange Affects Foreign Students. New York: College Entrance Examination Board, 1967.

1001. Dunlop, Fergus. Europe's Guests: Students and Trainees: A Survey on the Welfare of Foreign Students and Trainees in Europe. Strasbourg: Council for Cultural Cooperation of the Council of Europe, 1966.

1002. Greater New York Council for Foreign Students. Factors Related to Financial Problems of Foreign Students. New York: Greater New York Council, 1964.

1003. Heffich, Walter. Foreign Student Costs: A Report on the Costs of Educating Foreign Students at Canadian Universities. Ottawa: Canadian Bureau for International Education, 1977.

1004. Hendricks, Glenn L., and Kenneth A. Skinner. Economic and Social Coping Strategies of Foreign Students. Minneapolis, Minnesota: Office for Student Affairs, University of Minnesota, 1975.

1005. Institute of International Education. Costs at U.S. Educational Institutions. New York: Institute of International Education. (annual publication)

1006. Phillips, A. British Aid for Overseas Students. London: World University Service, 1980.

1007. Stecklein, J. E., and H. C. Liu. Study of Foreign Student Employment Financial Resources. Washington, D.C.: National Association for Foreign Student Affairs, 1974.

1008. Taylor, Graham R. Financial Aid for Non-Sponsored African Students. New York: College Entrance Examinations Board, 1963.

1009. UNESCO. Training Abroad--A Study of UNESCO Fellowships and Travel Grants, 1948-1968. Paris: UNESCO, 1971.

1010. United States, National Institutes of Health. NIH International Research Fellowships Program: An Evaluation, 1958-1977. Bethesda, Maryland: NIH, 1980.

Articles

1011. Ackerman, William C. "Private Support Activities in International Education." International Educational and Cultural Exchange 6 (Fall, 1970): 1-13.

1012. Arum, Stephen, and Gary Althen. "Foreign Student Enrollment and Full Tuition Dollar." National Association for Foreign Student Affairs Newsletter 29 (May-June, 1978): 20ff.

1013. Baumer, E. F. "Visas, Financial Support, and Fees for International Students." In Proceedings of the Eighteenth Annual Meeting of the Council of Graduate Schools in the United States: Changing Patterns in Graduate Education, edited by J. W. Ryan, pp. 271-277. Washington, D.C.: Council of Graduate Schools, 1979.

1014. "Bourses et Mobilite Accrue pour les Etudiants de la Communaute Europeenne." Informations Universitaires et Professionelles Internationales (March-April, 1979): 33-35.

1015. Dickey, K. N., and Lovelace, H. D. "Financial Verification for Foreign Students." College and University 53 (Summer, 1978): 477-481.

1016. Eberly, Donald. "Overseas Scholarships as Seen from Nigeria." National Association for Foreign Student Affairs Newsletter 16 (March, 1965): 3ff.

1017. "Educational Exchange in the Seventies. Statement by the Board of Foreign Scholarships, August 1971." International Educational and Cultural Exchange 7 (No. 2, 1971): 1-9.

1018. Henry, David D. "The Latin American Scholarship Program of American Universities." International Educational and Cultural Exchange 7 (Winter, 1972): 30-55.

    The author of this article is the director of the Latin American Scholarship Program of American Universities (LASPAU), which offers Latin American universities assistance with their staffing problems as well as means for their candidates to enter "the complex world of U.S. higher education." This program is a cooperative undertaking of more than 300 North American and Latin American institutions of higher education. The article itself is a report on the program's operations for the academic years 1969-70 and 1970-71.
    This report is constructed in an interesting way. On the one hand it presents tasks and realizations of the LASPAU and on the other hand it is addressed to U.S.

universities in the form of requests, and sometimes even of demands within the context of rationalization of the admission and financial support for foreign graduate students from participating Latin American universities who are undertaking their education in the United States.

A substantial part of the article is devoted to presentation of a series of targets adopted by LASPAU's Board of Trustees which may be viewed as "guideposts or measuring rods" along the road towards the realization of the program's objectives. These targets are:

1. Focus increased attention [of LASPAU] on Latin American institutions that come forward with carefully developed long-range staffing plans and regularly employ returned LASPAU graduates to assist in the realization of those plans.
2. Maintain and, if possible, expand the number of U.S. universities willing to cover the cost of tuition and fees for LASPAU scholars.
3. Reduce to 2½ years the average length of time a LASPAU scholar is away from his home-country.
4. Expand participation in LASPAU of Brazilian universities and Brazilian students.
5. Increase the percentage of LASPAU graduates who enter the teaching profession.
6. Encourage the creation of alumni groups in each cooperating country.
7. Enlist the support of the Organization of American States (OAS) in financing the repayment of loans to LASPAU students.
8. Attempt to include other foreign universities outside the United States in the training and financial support of LASPAU-selected scholars.
9. Encourage the development of a nucleus of LASPAU-trained professors on the faculties of provincial universities in Latin America.
10. Assist in the establishment of Latin American university "centers of excellence."
11. Concentrate LASPAU resources on those Latin American university faculty and/or departments that reflect national and area requirements of the greatest importance.
12. Respond affirmatively to Latin American initiatives in changing the thrust of the program from a predominantly undergraduate to a predominantly postgraduate program.

Activities of LASPAU in the academic years 1969-70 and 1970-71 toward realization of the above targets are presented in detail. At the end, the author presents the structure and a composition of the program's Board of Trustees and LASPAU's supporting organizations.

1019. Johnson, Dixon. "Financial Aid and the Nigerian Student." National Association for Foreign Student Affairs Newsletter 27 (March, 1976): 1ff.

1020. Joshi, Joan H. "Finances: Finding the Funds for International Study." In Educating Students From Other Nations: American Colleges and Universities in International Educational Interchange, edited by Hugh M. Jenkins, et al., pp. 91-112. San Francisco: Jossey-Bass, 1983.

1021. Malone, V., et al. "Agency Sponsored International Students." College and University 49 (Summer, 1974): 638-646.

1022. Margolis, A., et al. "Educational Patterns in Mexico; Latin American Scholarship Program of American Universities." College and University 43 (Summer, 1968): 413-418.

1023. Maxwell, Janette Fenn. "An Alien's Constitutional Right to Loan, Scholarship and Tuition Benefits at State Supported Colleges and Universities." California Western Law Review 14 (No. 3, 1979): 514-562.

1024. Myers, Robert. "External Financing of Foreign Study: The Case of the Ford Foundation in Peru." In Bridges to Knowledge: Foreign Students in a Comparative Perspective, edited by Elinor Barber, Philip G. Altbach, and Robert Myers, pp. 147-163. Chicago: University of Chicago Press, 1984.

1025. "Des Offres de Bourses pour l'Etranger." Informations Universitaires et Professionelles Internationales (November-December, 1977): 22-35.

1026. Oh, Tai Keun. "The Asian Students in Our Labor Force: Who, What, Where and Why." Business and Society 9 (Spring, 1969): 16-23.

1027. Rahn, H. "Aid to Study Abroad [for German Students]: Experiences and Implications." Western European Education 11 (Fall-Winter, 1979-80): 150-164.

1028. Ryan, A. "Welfare Problems and Induction of Overseas Students." Coombe Lodge Reports 10 (No. 6, 1977): 256-260.

1029. Smith, Gerald. "Student Employment Abroad." In International Encyclopedia of Higher Education, edited by A. Knowles, pp. 1557-1565. San Francisco: Jossey-Bass, 1977.

1030. Steele, M. H. "AHEA's 1968-1969 International Scholarship Students." Journal of Home Economics 61 (April, 1969): 265-268.

1031. Tigreat, M. "Les Bourses da FAC." Cooperation et Developpement No. 46 (1973): 40-45.

1032. Water, Jack. "Financial Aid for Foreign Students: The Oregon Model." National Association for Foreign Student Affairs Newsletter 34 (March, 1983): 97ff.

### Reportage

1033. Bayliss, B. "New Attempt to Save Foreign Students from Fee Rises." Times Higher Education Supplement (January 25, 1980): 3.

1034. Binyon, M. "All This, and Grants Too." Times Higher Education Supplement 471 (November 13, 1981): 8.

1035. Bridges, B. "Malays Look Toward U.S. for Tuition." Times Higher Education Supplement (May 30, 1980): 6.

1036. Bristow, Rupert. "An 'I am All Right Jack' Fees Policy." Times Higher Education Supplement (October 3, 1980): 10.

1037. "British Charges to Rise." Chronicle of Higher Education 21 (February 17, 1981): 16.

1038. "Bursary Switch for Foreign Students?" Times Education Supplement (August 25, 1978): 3.

1039. Cohen, S. "Commons Committee to Review Rise in Foreign Student Fees." Times Higher Education Supplement (December 28, 1979): 3.

1040. Cohen, S. "Overseas Students: Universities Want Cut in Fees But Curb on Numbers." Times Higher Education Supplement (June 25, 1976): 6.

1041. "Colleges in the Marketplace: Forcing Foreign Students to Pay Full Cost Will Give British Universities a Needed Jolt." Economist 273 (November 10, 1979): 18.

1042. "Commonwealth Concern About Foreign Student Tuition." Chronicle of Higher Education 23 (November 25, 1981): 21.

1043. "Concern at Higher Fees." Times Educational Supplement (January 27, 1967): 272.

1044. Cookson, C. "Foreign Students Face Higher Fees in Backlash over Iran." Times Higher Education Supplement (December 14, 1979): 5.

1045. David, P. "Foreign Fee Charging Plan Drawn Up." Times Higher Education Supplement (August 25, 1978): 1.

1046. "8 Foreign Students Indicted for Aid Fraud." Chronicle of Higher Education 25 (October 6, 1982): 2.

1047. "Foreign Students in Ontario Protest Fee Increases." Chronicle of Higher Education 26 (April 20, 1983): 19.

1048. "Foreign Students Indicted in Loan Fraud." Chronicle of Higher Education 23 (September 16, 1981): 2.

1049. "Foreign Students' Job Waivers May Be Taken from Colleges." Chronicle of Higher Education 9 (November 25, 1974): 4.

1050. "Foreign Students on U.S. Campuses Top 218,000." Chronicle of Higher Education 10 (July 21, 1975): 7.

1051. "Foreign Students Will Pack Their Bags." Times Educational Supplement (January 20, 1967): 176.

1052. Hencke, David. "Cypriot Students Caught in the Crossfire-- Financial Difficulties." Times Higher Education Supplement (September 13, 1974): 7.

1053. "Private Group to Assist Libyan Students in U.S." Chronicle of Higher Education 23 (September 2, 1981): 2.

1054. Scully, Malcolm. "Money Woes Afflict Iranian Students; Colleges Fear Most Will Drop Out." Chronicle of Higher Education 26 (June 8, 1983): 1.

1055. "Supreme Court Ruling Opens Up Public Funds for Student Aliens." Times Higher Education Supplement (July 1, 1977): 13.

1056. Veale, Sarah, and John Murray. "Chaos for Overseas Students-- Tuition Fees and Grants." Times Higher Education Supplement (April 22, 1983): 35.

1057. Vienet, R. "Scholarships Pour la Presence Francaise--Later." Far East Economic Review 104 (April 27, 1979): 42-43.

1058. Wright, L. "Overseas Fees Break Law." Times Higher Education Supplement (June 24, 1983): 6.

## 17. HEALTH

1059. Cooper, Elizabeth Wood. "Analysis of International Student's Perceptions of Convenience Relative to University Health Center Services." Unpublished Ed.D thesis, Texas Southern University, 1981.

1060. Oghojafor, Lucky. "Psychiatric and Traditional Healing Modalities for 'Brain Fag Syndrome': Preferences for Use by Westernized Nigerian Students in Selected American Universities." Unpublished Ph.D thesis, Southern Illinois University at Carbondale, 1979.

1061. Osueke, Samuel Onyemauchechukwa. "Relation of Type of Reported Illnesses to Pattern of Use of the Student Health Center by the International Students at Texas Southern University."

Unpublished Ph.D thesis, University of Texas at Houston, School of Public Health, 1980.

1062. Rice, Robert L., Jr. "Characteristics of University Health Center Infrequent and Frequent Visitors: A Comparison of Foreign and American Students at Two Colorado Universities." Unpublished Ph.D thesis, University of Northern Colorado, 1974.

1063. Smiley, Russell Frederick. "A Comparison of Selected Health Practices Among Foreign and American College Students." Unpublished Ph.D thesis, Southern Illinois University at Carbondale, 1978.

1064. Zwingmann, Charles A. A., and A. D. G. Gunn. Uprooting and Health: Psycho-social Problems of Students from Abroad. Geneva: Division of Mental Health, World Health Organization, 1983.


### Articles

1065. Anumonye, A. "Psychological Stresses among African Students in Britain." Scottish Medical Journal 12 (September, 1967): 314-319.

1066. Anumonye, Amechi. "Ten Years After Psychotic Illness in Nigerian Students." African Journal of Psychiatry 4 (September, 1978): 85-90.

1067. Asuni, T. "The Review of Nigerian Students Repatriated on Psychiatric Grounds." West African Medical Journal 17 (February, 1968): 3-7.

1068. Babiker, I. E., J. L. Cox, and P. M. Miller. "The Measurement of Cultural Distance and Its Relationship to Medical Consultations, Symptomatology and Examination Performance of Overseas Students at Edinburgh University." Social Psychiatry 15 (No. 3, 1980): 109-116.

1069. Bourne, Peter G. "The Chinese Student: Acculturation and Mental Illness." Psychiatry 38 (No. 3, 1975): 269-277.

1070. Cole, J. B., F. C. L. Allen, and J. S. Green. "Survey of Health Problems of Overseas Students." Social Science and Medicine 14A (December, 1980): 627-631.

1071. Cox, J. L., I. E. Babiker, and P. McMiller. "Psychiatric Problems and First Year Examinations in Overseas Students at Edinburgh University." Journal of Adolescence 4 (No. 3, 1981): 261-270.

1072. Furnham, Adrian, and Lorna Trezise. "The Mental Health of Foreign Students." Social Science and Medicine 17 (No. 6, 1983): 365-370.

1073. Huang, Ken. "Campus Mental Health: The Foreigner at Your Desk." Journal of the American College Health Association 25 (February, 1977): 216-219.

1074. Itouanga, A. F. "Study of Digestive Parasitism in Lille among Foreign Students." Lille Medical 23 (No. 1, 1978): 25-32. (in French)

1075. Ko, Y. H. "Mental Health of the Overseas Chinese Students in the New Environment." Acta Psycologica Taiwanica 20 (No. 2, 1978): 1-7.

1076. Kurdina, A. A. "Some Data on Biliariasis Recorded in Leningrad among African Students." Meditsinskaia Parazitologiia i Parazitarnye Bolezni 37 (May-June, 1968): 351-354. (in Russian)

1077. Maka, G. E. "Health Survey of New Asian and African Students at the University of Illinois." Journal of the American College Health Association 12 (No. 1, 1963): 303-310.

1078. Miller, D. F., and D. J. Harwell. "International Students at an American University: Health Problems and Status." School Health 53 (January, 1983): 45-49.

1079. Posen, S. "The Asian Undergraduate in Australia." Medical Journal of Australia 2 (September, 1968): 483-489.

1080. Ray, M. M. "Health and Disease Among International Students in the United States." Journal of the American College Health Association 15 (1967): 361-364.

1081. Rice, Robert L. "Foreign Student Health Center Visitation: Where Does the Anomaly Lie?" Journal of the American College Health Association 23 (December, 1974): 134-137.

1082. Shore, Eleanor G. "Medical Preparations for Students Traveling Abroad." National Association for Foreign Student Affairs Newsletter 24 (June, 1973): 7ff.

1083. Thompson, Mary, and Daniel Fung. "Health Care of Foreign Students." National Association for Foreign Student Affairs Newsletter 29 (May-June, 1978): 12ff.

1084. Wild, Patricia B. "A Comparative Study of the Members and Non-members of a Prepaid Pediatric Health Care Plan for Children of University Students." Journal of the American College Health Association 24 (February, 1976): 139-145.

1085. Zunin, L. M. "The Return Home of Foreign Students with Emotional Problems." Journal of the American College Health Association 16 (December, 1967): 201-206.

Reportage

1086. Martin, R. W., J. O'Palka, and J. R. Mitchell. "Nutrition Education for International Students." Journal of the American College Health Association 30 (December, 1981): 148.

1087. O'Leary, J. "Health Blow to Foreigners." Times Higher Education Supplement (July 18, 1980): 1.

1088. Williamson, Geraldine. "Impediments to Health Care for the Foreign Student." Journal of the American College Health Association 30 (No. 4, 1982): 189-190.

## 18. COUNSELING SERVICES

1089. Africa Service Institute. Hints on Summer Employment for African Students. New York: Africa Service Institute, 1964.

1090. Baron, M. J., ed. Advising, Counseling, and Helping the Foreign Student. Washington, D.C.: National Association for Foreign Student Affairs, 1975.

1091. Bohn, Ralph Carl. "An Evaluation of the Educational Program for Students from Foreign Countries: Emphasis on Orientation Procedures, Individual Problems and Psychological Variables." Unpublished Ed.D thesis, Wayne State University, 1957.

1092. Center for International Educational Exchange. Guidelines on Developing Campus Services for Students Going Abroad. New York: CIEE, 1972.

1093. Coelho-Oudegeest, Maria de Lourdes Ivonne. "Cross-Cultural Counseling: A Study of Some Variables in the Counseling of Foreign Students." Unpublished Ph.D thesis, University of Wisconsin, 1971.

   A series of tests were administered to foreign students to determine their receptivity to counseling from Americans in the counseling office. It was determined that, on the basis of this pilot study, considering the factors of demographic and academic characteristics of the foreign student, including the student's language skills and cultural-bound attitudes that in relationship to counseling and factoring in variables of the foreign students age, sex, academic level, and length of stay in the United States, it was found that the age, sex, training, and experience of the counselor are significantly related to successful counseling of foreign students.

In particular, it was determined that young, female
counselors holding a Master's degree are the most effective
counselors, even factoring for counselors who are male and
hold higher levels of academic training.

1094. Fleg, John P., and Lenore Yaffee. Adjusting to the United States
of America: Orientation for International Students.
Washington, D.C.: Meridian House International, 1978.

1095. Hendricks, Glenn L., and David Zander. Impact of an Orientation
Program for Foreign Students. Minneapolis, Minnesota: Office
for Student Affairs, University of Minnesota, 1975.

1096. Ho, Man Keung. "The Effect of Group Counseling on the Academic
Performance, Study Habits and Attitudes, and the Interpersonal
Adjustment of Foreign Students." Unpublished Ph.D thesis,
Florida State University, 1969.

An evaluation of the effect of group counseling on the
academic performance, study habits, and attitudes, and the
interpersonal adjustment of foreign students. The study
included 32 first-term freshmen foreign students who were
randomly selected from the University of Tulsa and Oklahoma
State University in the Fall of 1968. The students were
divided into two groups, one experimental and one control,
in the two universities. The students were asked to take
two different tests: Survey of Study Habits and Attitudes
(SSHA) and Index of Adjustment and Values (IAV).
Prior to the experimental stage, there were no differences between the experimental groups and the control
groups in both universities. But there was a significant
difference in the experimental group between pre- and
post-testing.
Conclusions:
. Attitude change as measured by SSHA was significantly
greater in the experimental group than in the control
group between the pre- and post-experimental stages.
. Attitude change as measured by IAV was significantly
greater in the experimental group than the control group.
. There was no correlation between change in attitude as
measured by SSHA and IAV and change in grade-point
average.

1097. Hull, William Franklin. "The Influence of a Random Sample of
International Students Upon American Students in a Sensitivity
Group Experience." Unpublished Ph.D thesis, Pennsylvania State
University, 1970.

1098. Ingram, J. C. New Approaches to Training in the Overseas Aid
Program [Training Centers for Foreign Students]. Canberra:
Australian Development Assistance Bureau, 1980.

1099. Marsella, A. J., and P. B. Pederson, eds. Cross Cultural
Counselling and Psychotherapy. London: Pergamon Press, 1981.

1100. Mestenhauser, Josef, and Dietmar Barsig. Foreign Student Advisers and Learning with Foreign Students. Washington, D.C.: National Association for Foreign Student Affairs, 1977.

1101. Montgomery, Wanda Lucille. "An Exploratory Investigation of Factors Related to Academic Advising of Foreign Graduate Students in Home Economics." Unpublished Ph.D thesis, University of Minnesota, 1973.

1102. National Association for Foreign Student Affairs. Guidelines: Academic and Personal Advising. Washington, D.C.: National Association for Foreign Student Affairs, 1975.

1103. National Association for Foreign Student Affairs. Orientation of Foreign Students. Washington, D.C.: National Association for Foreign Student Affairs, 1980. (Guideline Series No. 4)

1104. Olayinka, Moses Siyanbola. "Effectiveness of Two Modes of Counseling in Assisting African Students to Adjust to the General University Environment." Unpublished Ph.D thesis, University of California-Los Angeles, 1970.

   This study examines the effectiveness of two methods of counseling in assisting African students to cope with their problems of adjusting to American university life. There were two different modes of counseling: the Guided Inquiry Mode (Mode I) and the Advisory Mode (Mode II) learning theories constituted the independent variables in this study. The dependent variable consisted of affective and behavioral process and outcome measures designed to assess efficacy of counseling.
   The results indicated that counselees in the Experimental group reported fewer problems of adjustment than control group subjects. Counselees perceived white counselors as more effective and more genuine than black counselors.

1105. Overhold, William. Some Observations on Student Personnel Practice in Selected Overseas Universities. Boston: Boston University, 1966.

1106. Owen, Wyn F. Academic Orientation for Foreign Graduate Students-- A Study of the Economics Institute. New York: IIE, 1968.

1107. Pine, W. S. "The Effect of Foreign Adult Student Participation in Program Planning on Achievement and Attitude." Unpublished Ed.D thesis, Auburn University, 1980.

1108. Report of the Conference of College and University Administrators and Foreign Student Advisors. New York: Institute of International Education, 1946.

1109. Robinson, Richard Adair. "A Comparative Study in the Areas of Student Personnel Services as Perceived by Puerto Rican, North

American, and Latin American Students Attending the Florida State University in 1977." Unpublished Ph.D thesis, Florida State University, 1978.

1110. Salimbene, Suzanne. Strengthening Your Study Skills: A Guide for Overseas Students. London: Institute of Education, University of London, 1982.

1111. Sukamto. "The Role of Foreign Graduate Student Advising as Perceived by Indonesian Students and Their Major Advisors in Selected American Campuses and Its Relationship to the Students' Predeparture Orientation and Expressed Training Satisfaction." Unpublished Ph.D thesis, University of Wisconsin-Madison, 1981.

1112. Tashijian-Brown, James Emerson. "A Study of Student Services for International Students in the Virginia Community College System." Unpublished Ed.D thesis, University of Virginia, 1978.

1113. Tucker, Lois Compton. "A Survey of the Foreign Students and Participative Staff of the George Washington University Concerning Supportive Services." Unpublished Ed.D thesis, George Washington University, 1975.

1114. Van Niekerk, Andre Bernard. "An Analysis of the Perceptions Held by Faculty and Staff, Foreign Alumni, and Foreign Students of the Services Available to Foreign Students at Andrews University." Unpublished Ph.D thesis, Michigan State University, 1975.

1115. Walz, Gary R., ed. Transcultural Counselling: Needs, Programs and Techniques. New York: Human Sciences Press, 1978.

1116. Wilkening, Walter. "Factors Associated With Adjustment of Foreign Students Studying Extension Education at Selected Land-Grant Institutions." Unpublished Ph.D thesis, University of Wisconsin, 1965.

1117. Zeigler, Lee. Overseas Student Services in the United Kingdom: Some Observations. Stanford, California: Bechtel International Center, Stanford University, 1969.

## Articles

1118. Alexander, A. A., et al. "Psychotherapy and the Foreign Student." In Counseling Across Cultures, edited by Paul Pedersen, W. J. Lonner, and J. G. Draguns, pp. 227-246. Honolulu: University of Hawaii Press, 1976.

The experiences of the foreign student in the United States who seeks psychotherapeutic help are explored in this chapter. A summary of the implications of research findings for psychotherapeutic contact with non-Western foreign students is provided. On physical and psychological health during the sojourn, it is argued that students in emotional or physical trouble regard themselves as deviant in two worlds: they have lost ties with the home world and are unable to function in the new world. The authors found the discussion on the relationship between motivational background and personal resource patterns, and a variety of health problems. From their own research and clinical experiences they show how certain factors, including communication, serve as barriers to the entrance of the foreign patient to the North American mental health system. Therapists should be aware of these factors since they are essential to a successful therapeutic beginning. Behavioral therapy approaches instituted with considerable orientation and explanation can also be of value in the treatment of foreign student patients. Some suggestions are advanced on the issue of whether the student should stay or must return home before the completion of studies.

1119. Anumonye, A. "Understanding African Students in the United States." Journal of the Medical Society of New Jersey 69 (December, 1972): 1017-1022.

1120. Arkoff, Abe, Falak Thaver, and Leonard Elkind. "Mental Health and Counseling Ideas of Asian and American Students." Journal of Counseling Psychology 13 (Summer, 1966): 219-223.

1121. Bang, Katherine. "Community Service and the Foreign Student." National Association for Foreign Student Affairs Newsletter 20 (December, 1968): 1ff.

1122. Brinkerhoff, D. B., and P. E. Sullivan. "Concerns of New Students: A Pretest-Posttest Evaluation of Orientation." Journal of College Student Personnel 23 (Summer, 1982): 384-390.

1123. Brislin, Richard W., and Paul Pedersen. "Potential Audiences for Cross-Cultural Orientation Programs: Foreign Students in United States." In Cross-Cultural Orientation Programs, edited by Richard W. Brislin, and Paul Pedersen, pp. 133-138. New York: Gardner Press, 1976.

1124. Brislin, Richard W., and Paul Pedersen. "Potential Audiences for Cross-Cultural Orientation Programs: United States Students and Faculty Abroad." In Cross-Cultural Orientation Programs, edited by Richard W. Brislin, and Paul Pedersen, pp. 138-142. New York: Gardner Press, 1976.

1125. Cormack, M. L. "Three Steps to Better Orientation." Overseas 3 (Summer, 1963): 11-15.

1126. Dadfar, Sohrabi, and Myran L. Friedlander. "Differential Attitudes of International Students toward Seeking Professional Psychological Help." Journal of Counseling Psychology 29 (No. 3, 1982): 335-338.

1127. DeAntoni, Edward. "Foreign Student Career Counselling: A Personal View." International Educational and Cultural Exchange 7 (Winter, 1972): 91-102.

1128. DeArmond, Murray M. "Mental Health and International Students." National Association for Foreign Student Affairs Newsletter 34 (April/May, 1983): 137ff.

1129. Dieffenbacher, T., J. Etish-Andrews, and L. Rowe. "Female/Male Dimensions of Cross-Cultural Counseling: A Workshop for Advisers of International Students." In International Women Students: Perspectives for the 80s. Report of the International Women Student Conference (Boston, Mass., August 1981), edited by Leslie Rowe, and Steve Sjoberg, pp. 49-59. Washington, D.C.: National Association for Foreign Student Affairs, 1981.

1130. Dillard, J. M., and G. B. Chisolm. "Counseling the International Student in a Multicultural Context." Journal of College Student Personnel 24 (March, 1983): 101-105.

1131. Domingues, P. M. "Student Personnel Services for International Students." National Association of Women Deans and Counselors Journal 33 (Winter, 1970): 82-89.

1132. Duffy, C. G. "Individualized Overseas Program for Undergraduates." International Educational and Cultural Exchange 7 (No. 1, 1971): 40-45.

1133. Eddy, John. "Factors and Guidelines in Foreign Student Guidance." Journal of College Student Personnel 13 (May, 1972): 252-254.

1134. Garrett, Larry, and C. Joanne Garrett. "The International Student and Academic Advisement: The Bus Stops Here." International Education 10 (Spring, 1981): 20-24.

1135. Gray, George. "Counselling Overseas Students." In Overseas Students in Australia, edited by S. Bochner, and P. Wicks, pp. 163-168. Auburn: New South Wales University Press, 1972.

The experiences in student counselling provided for Australian versus overseas students at the University of New South Wales from 1960 to 1970. Analyzing enrollments and interview attendances data for counseling, the author finds that there is no significant difference between the two groups in willingness to approach counsellors for help either voluntarily or when referred by fellow students or other university personnel. However, reports from the counseling unit indicate the following specific to overseas student problems which were prevalent:

. Language deficiencies in: (a) Formal academic activities mostly linked with writing essays, reports, and examination papers; (b) more informal communications and in interpersonal situations where accurate understanding of personal opinions and expressions is important; e.g., in professional training situations between medical student and patient.

. socio-cultural and assimilation problems, linked mostly with achieving a degree of successful assimilation into the university socio-cultural setting to the extent that the university becomes the main focus of the foreign student's life during his/her period of study.

. anxiety and avoidance of contacts with university administration, preoccupation with eligibility rather than suitability, reinforced by intense competition to win a university place; e.g., many Asian students elect to study Chinese for their N.S.W. Higher School Certificate Examination in order to enhance their admission prospects. Some other foreign students apply to enter a quota course which is reputed to be less difficult to enter competitively, rather than select suitable entry subjects and a degree course that suits their long-range goals.

. disproportionately high failure rates in later years, particularly noticeable in professional courses like medicine.

. accommodation problems

. fear of action by Australian government, which might affect his/her presence in Australia, in connection with granting visas or permanent residency.

In order to cope with these problems, the author suggests early and systematic arrangements for counseling, especially for undergraduate foreign students. He also confirms U.S. and Canadian experiences that one full-time counsellor is needed for each 1,000 equivalent of full-time students enrolled.

1136. Hauch, C., et al. "Agency Services for International Students." College and University 53 (Summer, 1978): 524-533.

1137. Higginbotham, H. N. "Cultural Issues in Providing Psychological Services for Foreign Students in the United States." International Journal of Intercultural Relations 3 (1979): 49-85.

With the unprecedented influx of foreign students into American colleges, serious attention must be given to providing psychological services congruent with the needs of these sojourners. In this review, key issues and dilemmas facing personnel as they attempt to set up helping services are delineated. Considered first are the patterns of foreign student adjustment, including typical stresses, the role of co-national groups in mediating stress, and patterns of clinic use. Second, ethical implications of

cross-cultural counseling are discussed; these implications
include the problem of therapy as a process that imparts
values, counselor competency, and the value of transporting
a therapy across cultures. The third section considers the
dilemma as to which treatment goals should be followed.
Next, the thorny problem of low success rates in therapy is
re-examined from a social psychological perspective. The
last section aims towards a resolution of these issues
through a proposed model for psychological services that
incorporates four domains of culture assessment. Lastly,
several criteria are offered as ethical guidelines for the
provision of psychological services.

1138. Ho, Man Keung. "Cross-Cultural Career Counseling." Vocational
Guidance Quarterly 21 (March, 1973): 186-190.

1139. Horner, David, et al., eds. "Cross-Cultural Counseling." In
Learning Across Cultures: Intercultural and International
Educational Exchange, edited by Gary Althen, pp. 30-50.
Washington, D.C.: National Association for Foreign Student
Affairs, 1981.

1140. Jameson, S. C. "Counseling Counselors Abroad on U.S. Higher
Education." International Educational and Cultural Exchange 8
(Fall, 1972): 13-18.

1141. Levitov, Peter. "Counseling Foreign Students Accused of a Crime."
National Association for Foreign Student Affairs Newsletter 29
(Summer, 1978): 7ff.

1142. Levitov, Peter. "Health Insurance: Mandatory or Optional?"
National Association for Foreign Student Affairs Newsletter 32
(April-May, 1981): 135.

1143. MacArthur, James D. "Career Services for University International
Students." Vocational Guidance Quarterly 29 (No. 2, 1980):
178-181.

1144. McCann, C. J. "Major Issues in Advising Foreign Students: A
Review." National Association of Woman Deans and Counselors
Journal 27 (Summer, 1964): 172-178.

1145. Osborne, M. M., Jr., et al. "Medical Care and Foreign Student
Families." Journal of American College Health Association 18
(June, 1970): 350-355.

1146. Overholt, William A. "The Influence of Cultural Backgrounds on
Attitudes Toward Counseling." NASPA Journal 5 (July, 1967):
12-15.

1147. Owen, Wyn F., and James L. Colwell. "Orientation for Foreign
Students: The Lesson of the Summer Economics Institute."
International Educational and Cultural Exchange (Winter, 1968):
48-54.

1148.  Pasricha, Prem. "Counseling India's Non-sponsored Students." World Higher Education Communique 4 (Winter, 1981): 3-4.

1149.  Sainsbury. "The Work of the Overseas Students Advisory Bureau." ARS Journal of the Royal Society of Arts 118 (1970): 566-567.

1150.  Schulz, H. E. "Tutorenarbeit des Akademischen Auslandsamtes der Universitat Freiburg." Deutsche Universitatszeitung (No. 4, 1970): 5-9.

1151.  Shahmirzadi, A. "Counseling Iranians." Personnel and Guidance Journal 61 (April, 1983): 487-490.

1152.  Torrey, E. F. "Problems of Foreign Students: An Overview." Journal of American College Health Association 19 (December, 1970): 83-86.

1153.  Walter-Samli, J. H., and A. C. Samli. "A Model of Career Counseling for International Students." Vocational Guidance Quarterly 28 (September, 1979): 48-55.

1154.  Watkins, David, and Estela Astilla. "Self-Esteem and Causal At-tribution of Achievement: A Filipino Investigation." Australian Psychologist 15 (No. 2, 1980): 219-225.

1155.  Weill, L. V. "Advising International Students at Small Colleges." NACADA Journal 2 (No. 1, 1982): 52-56.

1156.  Yuen, R. K., and H. E. A. Tinsley. "International and American Students' Expectancies About Counseling." Journal of Counseling Psychology 28 (January, 1981): 66-69.

1157.  American College Health Association Committee on the Health Needs of International Students. "Statement of Perspectives on the Mental Health Needs of International Students." Journal of the American College Health Association 25 (April, 1977): 280-281.

## Reportage

1158.  Binyon, M. "New Body to Look After Overseas Students." Times Educational Supplement (November 15, 1968): 1086.

1159.  Grantley, David. "OSAB on the Job." Education and Training 16 (April/May, 1974): 87 and 94.

1160.  Salimi, L., H. Lin, and E. Amateo. "Career Counseling and the Foreign Student." Journal of College Placement 38 (Fall, 1977): 30-31.

## 19. ADAPTATION PROBLEMS (THE ALIEN INSTITUTIONAL AND CULTURAL ENVIRONMENT)

1161. Akpan-Iquot, Efiong David. "An Investigation of Foreign Students' Problems in Selected Oklahoma Institutions of Higher Learning." Unpublished Ed.D thesis, Oklahoma State University, 1980.

1162. Anumonye, A. African Students in Alien Cultures. New York: Black Academy Press, 1970.

1163. Asch, Susan McCellan. "Transnational Networks: A Multi-Method Study of the American Associates of Foreign Students." Unpublished Ph.D thesis, Michigan State University, 1975.

> A sociological study of networking which examined the ongoing process of generating understandings and interpersonal relationships between foreign students and Americans, when they are brought together on an American university campus.
> It was conducted in a Midwestern university campus during 1965-1972. It grouped two samples of populations: foreign students on the campus and American students and nonstudents named by these foreign students and considered to be "close American associates."
> The findings indicate that the foreign students on this American campus are probably involved in an early stage of transnationalization. People who appear to be most likely transnationals are adults who are established in their professional careers, who have stable family lives, and who have undergone a "sensitization" to foreign persons and places.
> They do not become true transnationals until they have:
> (1) lived abroad, in a professional capacity.
> (2) returned to their native land.

1164. Bochner, Stephen. Overseas Students in Australia: Problems in Culture Learning. Honolulu: East-West Center, 1972.

1165. Claire, Elizabeth. What's So Funny?--A Foreign Student's Introduction to American Humor. New Rochelle, N.Y.: Eardley Publications, 1984.

1166. Cluff, Helene N. "Cross-Cultural Food Problems of Iranian College Students." Unpublished Ph.D thesis, Columbia University, 1963.

1167. Collins, Paul Leon. "Self-Perceived Problems of International Students Attending Howard University." Unpublished Ed.D thesis, George Washington University, 1976.

1168. Correa, Joseph M. "Intercultural Interaction and the Worldminded-
ness of College Students." Unpublished Ph.D thesis, University
of Washington, 1970.

1169. Culha, M. "Needs and Satisfactions of Foreign Students at the
University of Minnesota." Unpublished Ph.D thesis, University
of Minnesota, 1974.

Two evaluative instruments developed in connection
with this study were: (1) the foreign student importance
questionnaire (FSIQ); and (2) the foreign student
satisfaction questionnaire (FSSQ). Ninety students were
randomly selected and ninety American students were
utilized to determine attitudes. The ninety foreign
students sampled were Chinese, Indian, European, and
Canadian students attending the University of Minnesota.
It was found that both foreign and American students
are concerned about career development, academic environment and social and emotional well-being. Significant
variation was found between Canadian, European, and Chinese
student groups in terms of the opportunity to become
familiar with American culture and friends. Those students
who were least likely to have satisfaction with being
involved in American culture and having American friends
were the Chinese group, followed second by the Indian
group, thirdly by the Europeans and lastly, the Canadians.
Significance of this is that those students who were from
similar cultures to that of the host-country have greater
academic satisfaction than those who come from dissimilar
cultural backgrounds.
In other words, Canadian students were least
dissatisfied with the American institutions and Chinese
students the most dissatisfied, in terms of the cultural
adjustment at the University of Minnesota.

1170. Danckwortt, Dieter. Anpassungsprobleme von Studenten und
Praktikanten aus Entwicklungslandern in Westdeutschland: Eine
Sozial-psychologische Untersuchung. Hamburg: Psychologisches
Institut der Universitat Hamburg, 1958.

1171. Demoze, F. "A Preliminary Survey of the Relationships of Foreign
Students' Self-Concept and Personality Characteristics to Their
Region of Origin." Unpublished Ph.D thesis.

1172. Dunnett, Steven Charles. "The Effects of an English Language
Training Program and Orientation on Foreign Students at the
State University of New York at Buffalo." Unpublished Ph.D
thesis, State University of New York at Buffalo, 1977.

This is a longitudinal study that investigated the
effects of an English-language training and orientation
program on foreign student adaptation by examining two
groups of foreign students:

(a) one group which had completed a six-week intensive English language training and orientation program (ELTO) and then entered a degree program.

(b) a group which had not experienced an ELTO program but entered degree programs immediately upon arrival in the United States.

Principal Hypothesis:
Foreign students who have participated in a six-week ELTO program will have fewer difficulties in adaptation in their first academic semester than those students who come directly to the university without benefit of an ELTO program.

The two groups of students studied, were from four geographic areas: Latin America, Africa, Middle East, and Asia. A questionnaire was used to gather data.

Results:
. The adaptation of foreign students at Buffalo is eased by participation in an ELTO program.
. The ELTO program has the least effect on emotional adjustment.
. The ELTO program has a significant effect on socialization.
. There are differences in adaptation between geographic groups; in particular between Latin Americans and Middle Easterners, compared to Africans and Asians.

1173.   Ekaiko, Uko Thomas.   "The Effects of Selected Cultural and Environmental Adjustment of African Students in United States Universities."   Unpublished   Ph.D   thesis,   Wayne   State University, 1981.

The purpose of this study was to investigate the effects of selected cultural and environmental factors on the social and academic adjustment of African students in Michigan universities.

The data were collected from 161 questionnaires that were distributed to African students randomly selected from two suburban and two urban universities in the state of Michigan.

The study reached conclusions:
(1)   Communication seems to affect the academic adjustment of African students.
(2)   The climate does not seem to affect either the social or the academic adjustments of African students.
(3)   Communication, climate, and housing seem to have significant effects only on the academic adjustment.
(4)   There is a negative pattern in the social adjustment of African students in the United States.
(5)   There is an upward pattern in the academic adjustment of African students.

1174.   Ellis, Malcolm Eugene.   "Perceived Problems of Non-Canadian and Non-European   Foreign   Students   at   a   Major   University." Unpublished Ed.D thesis, Indiana University, 1978.

Based upon personal interviews, an attempt was made to determine the nature and extent of academic, personal, and social difficulties experienced by non-Canadian and non-European foreign students who attended Indiana University during the second semester of 1977-78.

A total of 54 personal interviews were conducted with students from the university. The interviews were based upon an adaptation of the Michigan International Student Programs Inventory. Of the 62 personal interviews arranged, 54 were completed, giving a response rate of 87%. The findings included the following:

Over 74% of the respondents indicated in personal interviews difficulties with English and descending orders of concerns were expressed in the following areas: (a) academic advising and record keeping; (b) social problems; (c) personal problems; (d) student activities; and (e) placement services. Students experience the least amount of difficulty in the following areas: living, dining, health services, religious services, and with the general quality of education at Indiana University. The major conclusion of the study was that one of the most difficult problems for foreign students is the English language, coupled with a need for satisfactory orientation programs to the United States and the university. Students have a negative feeling toward both the quality of their orientation and the quality of the advising offered to them by foreign student advisors. Significantly, financial considerations were not found to be a serious problem for foreign students, in general, and not a problem for many.

1175. Faehner, David Allen. "Perceptions of Campus Life at Loma Linda University According to Five Ethnic-International Student Groups." Unpublished Ph.D thesis, University of Northern Colorado, 1980.

1176. Fahrlander, Rebecca Sue. "Social Participation and Adjustment of Foreign Students at the University of Nebraska-Lincoln." Unpublished Ph.D thesis, The University of Nebraska-Lincoln, 1980.

1177. Farzad, Valiollah. "The Measurement and Analysis of Iranian Student Satisfaction in Selected California Universities." Unpublished Ed.D thesis, University of the Pacific, 1981.

1178. Galioridis, George. "A Perceptual Study of International Students' Satisfaction at the University of Alabama." Unpublished Ph.D thesis, University of Alabama, 1980.

1179. Geuer, Wolfgang, and Rita Breitenbach. Psychische Probleme Auslandischer Studenten in der BRD: Bericht uber Eine Studie i. A. DAAD. Saarbrucken: Universitat Saarlandes, Fachrichtung Psychologie, 1983.

1180. Group for the Advancement of Psychiatry. Working Abroad: A Discussion of Psychological Attitudes and Adaptation in New Situations. New York: GAP, 1964.

1181. Gruneberg, Lutz. Die Soziale Lage Auslandischer Studenten in der BRD. Konstanz: 1978.

1182. Hadwen, Charles T. M. "The Early Stages of Foreign Student Adjustment." Unpublished Ph.D thesis, Yale University, 1964.

1183. Hagey, Abdulla Rashid. "Academic and Social Adjustment of Middle Eastern Students Attending Oregon Colleges and Universities." Unpublished Ph.D thesis, University of Oregon, 1968.

1184. Heilpern, Florence. "A Case Study of the Effects of Visiting in American Homes on the Opinions of a Selected Group of Students from Abroad." Unpublished Ph.D thesis, Columbia University, 1965.

1185. Hill, Jarvis Harley. "An Analysis of a Group of Indonesian, Thai, Pakistani, and Indian Student Perceptions of Their Problems While Enrolled at Indiana University." Unpublished Ed.D thesis, Indiana University, 1966.

1186. Hughbanks, Corinne Neubauer. "A Study to Ascertain Administrative Policy and Faculty Opinions about Foreign Students in Public Universities and Private Colleges of the Midwest." Unpublished Ph.D thesis, University of Nebraska-Lincoln, 1980.

1187. Hull, W. Frank, IV. Foreign Students in the United States of America: Coping Behavior within the Educational Environment. New York: Praeger, 1978.

1188. Hull, W. F., W. H. Lemke, and R. T. Houang. Students in Sojourn. Washington, D.C.: National Association for Foreign Student Affairs, 1976.

1189. Israel, Central Bureau of Statistics. Survey on Absorption of Students from Abroad: Students who Began Their Studies in 1970/71; First Interview. Jerusalem: Central Bureau of Statistics, 1973.

1190. Israel, Central Bureau of Statistics. Survey on Absorption of Students from Abroad: Students who Began Their Studies in 1970/71; Second Interview. Jerusalem: Central Bureau of Statistics, 1973.

1191. Israel, Central Bureau of Statistics. Survey on Absorption of Students from Abroad: Students who Began Their Studies in 1969/70; Third Interview. Jerusalem: Central Bureau of Statistics, 1974.

1192.  Kaase, Max. Studenten und Auslandsstudium. Einstellungen der Deutschen Studentenschaft zum Auslandsstudium. Mannheim: Institut fur Sozialwissenschaften, 1969.

1193.  Kasraian, Abbas. "Adaptation Processes Utilized by Foreign Students in Coping with Academic Programs and Procedures in American Colleges and Universities." Unpublished Ph.D thesis, University of Denver, 1978.

1194.  Katz, B. Survey on Absorption of Students from Abroad: Final Results of a Follow-Up Study of Students Who Began Studies in 1969/70. Jerusalem: Central Bureau of Statistics, 1980.

1195.  King, Nancy B. "Case Study of a Latin American Sojourner: Crossing Hard Times." Unpublished Ph.D thesis, Wayne State University, 1981.

1196.  Kiyuna, Kenneth Mitsugi. "The Effect of Two Group Treatments on the Relationship Between Asian and American University Students." Unpublished Ph.D thesis, Pennsylvania State University, 1972.

1197.  Klineberg, Otto, and W. Frank Hull. At a Foreign University: An International Study of Adaption and Coping. New York: Praeger, 1979.

1198.  Konwinski, Tina. Stand und Perspektiven der Forschung uber Interkulturellen Personenaustausch in der BRD Protokoll, Arbeitstagung SSIP. Regensburg: Universitat Regensburg, Psychologisches Institut, 1983.

1199.  Karjewski, Frank Richard. "A Study of the Relationship of an Overseas-Experienced Population Based on Sponsorship of Parent and Subsequent Academic Adjustment to College in the United States." Unpublished Ph.D thesis, Michigan State University, 1969.

1200.  LaFrieda, Dorothea Faith. "The Relationship Between Special Programs and the Community Adaptation and Marital Adjustment of Wives of Foreign Students." Unpublished Ph.D thesis, University of Miami, 1973.

1201.  Lam, Man Ping. "The Problems of Chinese Students at the University of Illinois at Urbana-Champaign." Unpublished Ph.D thesis, University of Illinois at Urbana-Champaign, 1979.

This study has three purposes:
(1)  To ascertain the personal problems of Chinese students at the University of Illinois;
(2)  To explore the possibilities that the problems of Chinese students differ according to a number of variables;
(3)  To find out the similarities and differences between Chinese and American students.

The study was done in two phases. First, the Mooney
Problem Checklist was distributed to 755 Chinese students
and to 42 American students. Second, a questionnaire was
used in structured interviews with 48 students, 24 with
many problems and 24 with few problems.

Findings:

. There were statistically significant differences between
the percentage of problems mentioned by the students from
the Republic of China and the students from Hong Kong.
Differences also existed according to marital status and
gender.

. Significant differences were found between problems
mentioned by American students and Chinese students.

. There were statistically significant differences in ego
strength and adjustment between Chinese students with
many problems and those with few problems.

1202. Lather, Francis. "Foreign Student Perceptions of Four Critical
Components Related to Educational Experiences at Western
Michigan University." Unpublished Ed.D thesis, Western
Michigan University, 1978.

1203. Lede, Naomi, and Elaine Williams. "A Study of the Effects of
Demographic and Institutional Factors on the Cross-Cultural
Experiences of Foreign Students Attending Selected State-
Supported Universities in Texas." Unpublished Ed.D thesis,
University of Houston, 1979.

1204. Lee, Hie Sung. "International Students' Self-Concept and it's
Relationship to Academic and Non-Academic Adjustment."
Unpublished Ed.D thesis, University of Virginia, 1973.

The purpose of this study is to evaluate the responses
to a survey questionnaire of the international student
population enrolled at the University of Virginia in the
Graduate Schools of Arts and Sciences, Architecture,
Education, Engineering and Applied Science, Business
Administration, Law and Medicine during the Academic Year
1972-73.

The study put emphasis on:

(1) The relationship between the self-concept and the
degree of academic and social involvement of
international students in a culturally different
environment.

(2) The relationship between the international students'
self-concept and their attitudes towards the
university counseling center and the international
center.

The data analyzed were collected from the answers of
101 students to the questionnaires that were mailed to
them. The study came to some conclusions such as:

. There is a significant correlation between the
international student's self-concept and his nonacademic
adjustment at the university.

. There is a significant negative correlation between the international student's self-concept and his frequency of participation in the various activities held by American students.
. There is no correlation between the international student's self-concept and his intention of using the Counseling Center whenever he needs its assistance. The Counseling Center was not known to the majority of the students.

1205.   Lee, Motoko Y., M. Abd-Ella, and L. A. Burks. Needs of Foreign Students From Developing Nations at U.S. Colleges and Universities. Washington, D.C.: National Association for Foreign Student Affairs, 1981.

A national survey of 1,900 concerning the needs of students from developing countries in American universities. In every category, needs were not satisfied to the level of students' expectations, even though most of the needs were satisfied to a degree. Needs for practical experience (work experience and opportunities to apply knowledge), and anticipated postreturn needs both for material rewards and for professional opportunities and facilities were among the least met. The following profile of a student is most likely to be satisfied:
(a)   a student who is from Latin America or Europe
(b)   a student who has a job waiting for him or her at home
(c)   a student who is residing with a U.S. student
(d)   a student who is on an assistantship
(e)   a graduate student, rather than an undergraduate
(f)   a student who perceives himself or herself as having a good command of English

1206.   Lee, Motoko, Mokhtar Abd-Ella, and Linda Burks Thomas. Need Assessment of Foreign Students from Developing Nations: A Research Design. The Final Report of Phase I. Sociology Report No. 144. Ames, Iowa: Iowa State University, 1979.

1207.   Leinwand, Adrienne Sue. "The Relationship Between Micronesian Education and Culture and the Adjustment Problems of Micronesian Students at an American College." Unpublished Ph.D thesis, University of Oregon, 1981.

1208.   Leitner, Penelope Sue. "The Effects of Demographic and Interactional Factors on the Satisfaction of Foreign Graduate Students at the University of Wisconsin-Madison." Unpublished Ph.D thesis, University of Wisconsin-Madison, 1982.

A study of the similarities and differences in reported levels of satisfaction between American and foreign graduate students in a university setting and components which have immediate and long-range impacts on the satisfaction experienced by foreign graduate students. The sample for the study comprised 120 East Asian graduate students, 110 Southeast Asian graduate students, and 120 American graduate students, randomly selected at the University of Wisconsin-Madison. Survey techniques were used to collect data during the spring semester of 1982. With regard to total satisfaction and compensation for work, it was found that significant differences existed between the foreign and American student groups. Significant differences were also found to exist between the two foreign student groups concerning the quality of education, social life, and recognition of work. Native area was the only demographic variable which had a significant influence on the level of total satisfaction while academic participation and social participation significantly influenced the level of total satisfaction perceived by foreign graduate students.

1209. Lim, F. "Storungen Indonesischen." Unpublished Ph.D thesis, Universitat Erlangen-Nurnberg, 1975.

1210. Lopulisa, R. P. "The Foreign Student as a Resolver of Conflict: An Exploratory Study of His Emergent Behavior." Unpublished Ph.D thesis, University of Southern California, 1977.

1211. Mirkamali, Said-Mohammad. "Organizational Change: An Investigation with the Relationship between Culture and Resistance to Change in Organizations among Iranian and American University Students in Nashville." Unpublished Ph.D thesis, George Peabody College of Teachers of Vanderbilt University, 1980.

1212. Mithen, P. A. J. "The Foreign Student's First Academic Year: Twelve Case Studies." Unpublished Ph.D thesis, St. Louis University, 1981.

1213. Moftakhar, Hossein. "A Descriptive Study of Some of the Problems of Iranian Students Attending Oklahoma State University." Unpublished Ed.D thesis, Oklahoma State University, 1975.

1214. Morgan, Gordon D. "The Adjustment of Nigerian Students in American Colleges." Unpublished Ph.D thesis, Washington State University, 1964.

1215. Morris, Richard T. The Two-Way Mirror: National Status in Foreign Students' Adjustment. Minneapolis, Minnesota: University of Minnesota Press, 1960.

The aim of this research is: (1) to inform the research sociologist about some of the theoretical and technical problems and solutions encountered; (2) to present to the practitioner some suggestions for the counseling of foreign students; (3) to let foreign students know how other, earlier foreign students have felt. Foreign students from some 60 American universities provided data. The author deals, in one chapter, with the specific difficulties encountered in setting up instruments and interview techniques for foreign students, and other related procedures; the report describes the characteristics of the students in the study as a basis for generalization; three chapters present the distribution of responses on the main dependent and independent variables. A check on interpretation is made by comparing foreign students' and American students' responses. The book also outlines the distribution of foreign students' responses on the main dependent variables of attitude toward the U.S., and present some of the implications and limitations of the study for the foreign-student advisor.

1216. Motarassed, Ahmad. "Adaptation of Foreign Students to a Land-Grant University in the United States." Unpublished Ed.D thesis, West Virginia University, 1981.

1217. Nash, Mary L. "A Study of Adjustment Problems of Sister Students from Kerala, India, Attending Liberal Arts Colleges in the United States." Unpublished Ph.D thesis, Catholic University of America, 1963.

1218. Nenyod, Boonmee. "An Analysis of Problems Perceived by Foreign Students Enrolled in State Colleges and Universities in the State of Texas." Unpublished Ed.D thesis, East Texas State University, 1975.

1219. Ng, James T. P. "Use of the 'Mooney Problem Check List' for Identifying Psychosocial Adjustment Problems of International Students at Four Universities in Colorado." Unpublished Ph.D thesis, University of Northern Colorado, 1981.

The study was based on an attempt to identify the extent of psychological and social adjustment faced by international students in the United States at four universities in Colorado through the use of a stratified random sampling technique.
Two instruments were utilized in the study:
(1) the Mooney Problem Check List
(2) the Demographic Survey Form
Five hundred students attending the four universities in Colorado received copies of these two instruments. The rate of return was 58%, or 290 responses.
The most significant variables indicated by the respondents with troubling problems were the following:
(1) age; (2) marital status; (3) living with family; (4) year in college; (5) sources of financial support; (6) host family participation; (7) number of years employed in student's country; (8) number of years lived in the United States; (9) religion; (10) University Counseling Center visits, and (11) campus location.
The following variables were differentiated between students who reported statistically significant problems:
(1) geographic region; (2) year in college; (3) host family participation; (4) religion, and (5) campus location.

Overall findings were: (a) students who were older, were graduate students, had a greater length of stay in the United States, and had worked for a longer time in their home country were better adjusted than those who did not have the above four characteristics. Secondly, married students and students who participated with host families reported less adjustment problems than single students and those students who did not participate with host family programs.

Recommendations included:

(1) institutions should more actively integrate both the foreign students into the mainstream of the community;

(2) counseling centers should actively reach out to foreign students in an attempt to coordinate both campus and community activities on behalf of the foreign students;

(3) orientation programs be carried out by the student's home government before coming to the United States. These orientations should be in conjunction with the sponsoring institutions in the United States. Students need factual and realistic information concerning the American experience.

1220. Niyekawa, Agnes M. Adjustment Problems of Male Students from Japan in Hawaii. Honolulu: University of Hawaii Press, 1952.

1221. Odenyo, Amos Otieno. "Africans and Afro-Americans on Campus: A Study of Some of the Relationships between Two Minority Sub-communities." Unpublished Ph.D thesis, University of Minnesota, 1970.

1222. Porter, John Wilson. "The Development of an Inventory to Determine the Problems of Foreign Students." Unpublished Ph.D thesis, Michigan State University, 1962.

1223. Pruitt, France J. The Adaptation of African Students to American Education. Buffalo: Council on International Studies, State University of New York at Buffalo, 1979.

1224. Rai, Rampertapsingh. "A Study of the Academic and Social Problems of a Selected Group of Foreign Graduate Students in the Doctoral Program in the Department of Physics at the University of Oregon." Unpublished Ph.D thesis, University of Oregon, 1982.

1225. Ramirez-Better, Maria Victoria. "The Adjustment Problems of Latin American Students Attending Selected California Universities." Unpublished Ed.D thesis, University of the Pacific, 1980.

Selected Latin American students at the undergraduate level were sampled in California at "selected California universities." It is not known of the 240 undergraduate students in the sample population how many responded to the questionnaire. The basic findings are, regardless of sex, undergraduate Latin American students encountered academic problems, mostly in the areas of basic communication, writing, reading, oral skills, and English. Secondly, students did not receive sufficient help in academic program planning efforts, particularly planning academic programs that would be useful to them in terms of the national goals of their respective countries.

Significant problems related to financial aid; lack of international news, particularly about their native country available in the United States; other areas of concern were social interaction, food, time orientation, and household chores. There were not significant differences between males and females in perception of either academic or nonacademic problems, nor were there significant differences on the part of females and males concerning anticipated problems of re-entry to their home environments. Both groups who responded, male and female, were particularly concerned that their countries would not look favorably on newer "innovations" learned in the United States.

The recommendations for change include: preorientation offered in the native country by the governments or sponsoring institutions; the need for American universities to provide extensive orientation programs in both nonacademic and academic areas of concern; foreign students should be assigned American student sponsors to assist the foreign student in finding housing and facilitating adjustment to American culture. Academic curricula in American universities should include "practical training and field work experiences" for Latin American students.

1226. Rising, Murriel, and Barbara Copp. Adjustment Experiences of Non-Immigrant Foreign Students at the University of Rochester. Rochester: University of Rochester, 1968.

1227. Roudiani, Iraj. "Foreign Students: A Comparative and Correlational Study in Frames of Reference, Length of International Experience, and Patterns of Interaction in a Multi-Cultural Environment." Unpublished Ph.D thesis, Indiana University, 1976.

1228. Sabie, Taha. "Foreign Students Coping with the American Culture At Eight Selected American Universities." Unpublished Ph.D thesis, George Peabody College for Teachers, 1975.

This study was concerned with the improvement of conditions of foreign students studying in the United States. A survey instrument was designed and utilized, testing the needs of foreign students in eight universities in Kentucky. Three populations were sampled: foreign students, faculty members, and administrators from each of the eight universities. However, the total number of groups sampled and the rate of return to the surveys are not indicated.

The findings are the following:

(1) most foreign students selected their own university and attend American universities with personal funds;

(2) transcripts are evaluated by a variety of individuals at the institutions, ranging from the dean of the school, admissions officer, to registrar to foreign student advisers.

Most of the eight institutions were found not to be prepared to accommodate foreign students; in particular, the institutions failed to provide for prearrival arrangements, or welcoming committees for the students. In most instances, international houses were not available for the students, nor were orientation programs available on American culture for foreign students at the eight institutions. Degree requirements for both American and foreign students were the same at the institutions. A need was found for English-as-a-second-language courses for foreign students and on-the-job training experiences for foreign students. Foreign students felt negatively about living arrangements in the United States and also felt discriminated against because of their religion and nationality. However, it is not clear in what way they felt discriminated against, whether it was living conditions or other conditions. Most foreign students felt that both academic and cultural environments and situations in the United States required big adjustments. Foreign students felt that there was a need for special library orientation.

Recommendations included the establishment of foreign student advisers at the eight institutions and extensive university orientation and welcoming efforts. Additional recommendations include the establishment of psychological counseling services for foreign students.

1229. Samaan, Anne J. "An Autobiographical Profile Analysis of Ibo Nigerian College Students and Their Health Stress." Unpublished Ph.D thesis, Ohio University, 1971.

1230. Sewell, Marianna Beck. "An Evaluation of Food Habits of Nigerian Students in American Colleges and Universities." Unpublished Ed.D thesis, New York University, 1965.

1231. Shandiz, M. T. "Factors Influencing Foreign Students' Adjustments and Attitudes in the Community of Oklahoma State University." Unpublished Ph.D thesis, Oklahoma State University, 1981.

1232. Sharma, Sarla. "A Study to Identify and Analyze Adjustment Problems Experienced by Foreign Non-European Graduate Students Enrolled in Selected Universities in the State of North Carolina." Unpublished Ed.D thesis, University of North Carolina at Greensboro, 1971.

1233. Shattuck, Gerald. "Trans-Cultural Adaptation: A Study of Foreign Graduate Students at Cornell University." Unpublished Ph.D thesis, Cornell University, 1964.

1234. Shearer, Roberta. "A Comparative Study of American Graduate Student Friends of Foreign Students." Unpublished Ph.D thesis, Indiana University, 1965.

1235. Si-Tayeb, Said. "Nature and Distribution of Problems Encountered by Foreign Students at the University of Alabama." Unpublished Ph.D thesis, University of Alabama, 1982.

1236. Smith, Betty Jo. "Home Economics Program Development Related to Problems of Foreign Student Wives and Families in Cultural Adaptation." Unpublished Ph.D thesis, Kansas State University, 1979.

1237. Snipes, Paul David. "Communication Behavior and Personal Adjustment Among American and Foreign Students at Indiana University." Unpublished Ed.D thesis, Indiana University, 1969.

1238. Snitwongse, Chutima. "Life and Academic Adjustment Problems of Foreign Students at the University of Missouri-Columbia (Education, Curriculum, and Instruction)." Unpublished Ph.D thesis, University of Missouri-Columbia, 1979.

1239. Snyder, B. R. M.I.T. Student Adaptation Study. Cambridge: Education Research Center, Massachusetts Institute of Technology, 1967.

1240. Suchu, Zhang. A Letter from America. Garden City: Adelphi University, 1983.

1241. Surdam, Joyce Anne Caldwell. "A Study of International Student Adaptation at the University of Wyoming." Unpublished Ph.D thesis, University of Wyoming, 1980.

1242. Swan, Norman Raymond Sam, Jr. "Intercultural Communication Patterns, Problems, and Trends of International Students at the University of Missouri-Columbia. Unpublished Ph.D thesis, University of Missouri-Columbia, 1978.

1243. Swatdipong, Pongswat. "Sojourner Alienation: An Exploratory Study of Foreign Student Alienation." Unpublished Ph.D thesis, Iowa State University, 1979.

The researcher designed an exploratory model of sojourner alienation and tested it with foreign students attending Iowa State University. A total of 356 questionnaires were administered to 30% of the foreign student body at the Iowa State University. In all, 177 responses were usable for the study, a 50% response rate.

The findings of this study were the following: Length of time in the United States and the level of social participation were enhanced in particular by the length of stay and the level of participation. Length of stay, modernity, socialization, role conflict, and also role adjustment, significantly affected alienation. Role adjustment had the strongest effect on the individual with role conflict second and length of the sojourn the least significant factors.

1244. Tharpe, Gertrude Addis. "The Identification of the Essential Elements of a Predeparture Orientation Program for Hong Kong College Students." Unpublished Ed.D thesis, George Peabody College for Teachers, 1972.

1245. Tjioe, Loan Eng. Asiaten uber Deutsche Kulturkonflikte Ostasiatischer Studentinnen in der Bundesrepublik. Frankfurt-am-Main: Thesen Verlag, 1972.

1246. Valdes, Thusnelda Mencio. "Psychological and Behavioral Characteristics and Adjustment of Latin American International Students to U.S. College Life." Unpublished Ed.D thesis, University of Houston, 1979.

1247. Von Dorpowski, Horst. "The Problems of Oriental, Latin American, and Arab Students in U.S. Colleges and Universities as Perceived by These Foreign Students and by Foreign Student Advisors." Unpublished Ph.D thesis, Pennsylvania State University, 1977.

        The study attempts to determine the perceptions of both the foreign students and the foreign student advisers vis-a-vis the problems of foreign students, particularly those male and female students from Latin America, Saudi Arabia and the Orient. Survey instruments were the Michigan National Student Problems Inventory, which was mailed to 174 foreign student advisers and 350 foreign students.
        Foreign student advisers tended to perceive the problems of foreign students to be greater than foreign students did in their own perceptions of the problems. Significantly, however, the foreign student advisers' perception of the real problems of the foreign students and those critical problems viewed by the foreign students were remarkably congruent. Basic problems agreed to by both foreign students and their advisers are in the following areas: (1) financial aid; (2) English language and placement, (3) health service and religious services, the least concern of the foreign student and their advisers. In essence, the foreign student advisers apparently have, based upon this research, significantly positive understanding of the needs of foreign students.

1248. Wilson, W. Douglas. "Social Relationships of International Students Attending Oklahoma State University." Unpublished Ed.D thesis, Oklahoma State University, 1975.

1249. Win, U. Kyaw. "A Study of the Difficulties Indian and Japanese Students Encountered in Six Problem Areas at the University of

Southern California." Unpublished Ph.D thesis, University of Southern California, 1971.

1250. Yamamura, Douglas S. The Evaluations of the Japanese and Thai Grantees of Their Orientation Experiences. Honolulu: University of Hawaii, 1955.

1251. Yeung, Andrew Yue-Yan. "A Study of the Adjustment Problems Anticipated and Those Actually Experienced by International Students Enrolled at North Texas State University." Unpublished Ph.D thesis, North Texas State University, 1980.

1252. Zain, Elias K. "A Study of the Academic and Personal-Social Difficulties Encountered by a Selected Group of Foreign Students at the University of Oregon." Unpublished Ph.D thesis, University of Oregon, 1965.

## Articles

1253. "Attitudes and Adjustment in Cross-Cultural Contact: Recent Studies of Foreign Students." Journal of Social Issues 1 (May, 1956). (special issue)

The studies described in this special issue of the journal form part of a substantial research program. The initial phase of the program consisted of exploratory investigations of particular nationality groups. Four studies, dealing with relationships between a student's cultural background and his experiences in the U.S., were carried out on American university campuses. At the same time, parallel studies were carried out in the native countries of the students in question. In the second phase of the research program, four new investigations were undertaken, but each concentrated on a particular variable or set of variables which the findings of the first phase of the program suggested might be important for the adjustment of all foreign students. The issue presents the frame of reference for analyzing cross-cultural education, brief reports on three of the four studies, and an account of one study from the first phase of the research program.

1254. Benson, Philip G. "Measuring Cross-Cultural Adjustment: The Problem of Criteria." International Journal of Intercultural Relations 2 (Spring, 1978): 21-37.

The nature of the adjustment process for individuals crossing cultural boundaries has not been adequately described in past research, and this leads to difficulty in selection and training of personnel for overseas assignments. This article critically reviews research on criterion measures of overseas adaptation, and raises a series of theoretical issues to be considered in future research. In addition, methods for measurement of cross-cultural adjustment are proposed, and it is suggested that practitioners and researchers in this field could benefit from a careful definition of criteria.

1255. Blood, R. O., and S. O. Nicholson. "Experiences of Foreign Students in Dating American Women." Marriage and Family Living 24 (August, 1962): 241-248.

1256. Bochner, Stephen. "Problems in Culture Learning." In Overseas Students in Australia, edited by S. Bochner, and P. Wicks, pp. 65-81. Auburn: New South Wales University Press, 1972.

1257. Bochner, S., E. A. Bucker, and B. M. McLeod. "Communication Patterns in an International Student Dormitory: A Modification of the 'Small Wool' Method." Journal of Applied Social Psychology 6 (July-September, 1976): 275-290.

1258. Bork, Uwe. "The Shock of Studying in Germany: Students from Developing Countries in Germany." Western European Education 13 (No. 3, 1981): 57-64.

1259. Bourne-Vanneck, R. P. "Toward Another World: A West Indian at Yale." Crisis 81 (February, 1974): 43-46.

1260. Bulhan, H. A. "Reactive Identification, Alienation and Locus of Control Among Somali Students." Journal of Social Psychology 104 (1975): 69-80.

1261. Burn, Barbara. "Foreign Students and Community Action." National Association for Foreign Student Affairs Newsletter 25 (January, 1964): 4ff.

1262. Buttner, F. "Die Erwartung der Auslandischen Studenten und die Wirklichkeit der Deutschen Hochschulen." Die Deutsche Universitatszeitung (No. 9, 1974): 363-366.

1263. Calvert, Robert, and Colette Samuelsen. "Employment Problems of Foreign Students." National Association for Foreign Student Affairs Newsletter 15 (January, 1964): 5ff.

1264. Carey, Philip, and Alemaheyu Mariam. "Minoritization: Toward an Explanatory Theory of Foreign Student Adjustment in the United States." Negro Educational Review 31 (No. 3-4, 1980): 127-136.

1265. Carey, P., and A. G. Mariam. "Socialization and the Process of Migration--Case of the International Student in the United States." In Sourcebook on the New Immigration, edited by R. S. Brycelaporte, pp. 361-372. New Brunswick, New Jersey: Transaction Books, 1980.

1266. Chevrolet, Daniel. "Les Problemes d'Adaptation des Etudiants Etrangers au Systeme Universitaire Francais." Revue Francaise de Pedagogie 40 (1977): 30-44.

1267. Chu, Godwin C. "Student Expatriation: A Function of Relative Social Support." Sociology and Social Research 52 (January, 1968): 174-184.

1268. Chu, Hung-ming, et al. "A Study of Chinese Students' Adjustment in the U.S.A." Acta Psychologica Taiwanica 13 (March, 1971): 206-218.

1269. Church, A. T. "Sojourner Adjustment." Psychological Bulletin 91 (May, 1982): 540-572.

1270. Coelho, G. V. "The Foreign Students' Sojourn as a High-Risk Situation--The Culture Shock Phenomenon Reexamined." In Uprooting and Surviving: Adaptation and Resettlement of Migrant Families and Children, edited by R. C. Nann, pp. 101-108. Dordrecht: D. Reidel, 1982.

1271. Das, S. Sunder. "The Psychological Problems of Eastern Students." In Overseas Students in Australia, edited by S. Bochner, and P. Wicks. Sydney: New South Wales University Press, 1972.

1272. Davis, F. James. "Cultural Perspectives of Middle Eastern Students in America." Middle East Journal 14 (Summer, 1960): 250-264.

This study aims to explore cultural contact as experienced by foreign students in America. The subjects were Middle Eastern students at the Universities of Minnesota and Michigan, and the major purpose was to elicit their views of American life. Increasing numbers of students are coming to the U.S. from the Middle East, defined in this study as including Turkey, Iran, the United Arab Republic, the countries of the Fertile Crescent and the Arab Peninsula. The interview findings through a pilot study were used as general hypotheses to be tested by the questionnaire, which was sent to 196 students from the Middle East. The major findings include: (1) Middle Eastern students experience some surprise upon contact with American life; (2) they have favorable views of some aspects of American life and unfavorable views of others, (a) as to some general characteristics of American life, (b) with regard to education, and (c) as to marriage and family life; (3) they experience problems of cultural contact; (4) there are differences in cultural perspectives among Middle Eastern students in America by sex, marital status, native country, field of study, and length of time spent in the U.S. The questionnaire results confirmed these general hypotheses; however, differences by length of stay were not related to cultural perspectives in any consistent manner, and there were too few females to permit meaningful comparisons by sex.

1273. Dawson, Belinda. "The International Student Centre." In Overseas Students in Australia, edited by S. Bochner, and P. Wicks, pp. 198-202. Auburn: New South Wales University Press, 1972.

1274. Donvez, J. "Necessite des Stages a l'Etranger." Revue Francaise de Elite Europeenne No. 257 (1973): 6-9.

1275. Drury, D. W., and J. D. McCarthy. "Social Psychology of Name Change: Reflections on a Serendipitous Discovery." Social Psychology Quarterly 43 (September, 1980): 310-320.

1276. Dupeux, Genevieve. "Etudiants Etrangers au Travail." Revue de Psychologie des Peuples (September, 1968): 276-287.

1277. Eng-Kung-Yeh. "Cross-Cultural Adaptation and Personal Growth: The Case of Chinese Students." Acta Psychologica Taiwanica (1976): 95-104.

1278. Fanai, F. Die Psychosozialen Probleme Auslandischer Studenten in Deutschland. Zeitschrift fur Psychologie 21 (No. 3, 1971): 100-107.

1279. "Felicitations, Docteur! Une interview de James Onobiono recueillier par Jean-Pierre N'Diaye." Jeune Afrique No. 915 (July 19, 1978): 52-53.

1280. Fong, Stanley, L. Mand, and H. Peskin. "Sex-Role Strain and Personality Adjustment of China-Born Students in America." Journal of Abnormal Psychology 74 (1969): 563-567.

1281. "Foreign Students' Positive Impression of the Netherlands." Higher Education and Research in the Netherlands 18 (No. 1, 1974): 19-23.

1282. Foust, Stephen, et al., eds. "Dynamics of Cross-Cultural Adjustment: From Pre-arrival to Re-entry." In Learning Across Cultures: Intercultural and International Educational Exchange, edited by Gary Althen, pp. 7-29. Washington, D.C.: National Association for Foreign Student Affairs, 1981.

    This chapter deals with cross-cultural adjustment and the changes that are required when moving from one cultural milieu to another. The authors consider three major periods in cross-cultural adjustment:
    (1) Preparing to enter a new culture
    (2) Living in a new culture
    (3) Reentering the primary culture

    Each of these periods has its own characteristics. The emphasis was put on what happened to cross-cultural sojourners in each of these periods. The results were that the success of orientation for a cross-cultural experience, whether it involves going to a new culture or returning to an original one, depends on sensitizing participants to possible violations of expectations and to ways of coping when their expectations have been violated. This requires identifying the components of the adjustment process and their interrelationships; providing so-called "survival information"; increasing communication skills; and developing a stable social support system.

1283. Furnham, Adrian, and Stephen Bochner. "Social Difficulty in a Foreign Culture: An Empirical Analysis of Culture Shock." In Cultures in Contact: Studies in Cross-Cultural Interaction, edited by Stephen Bochner, pp. 161-198. New York: Pergamon Press, 1982.

1284. Gandhi, R. S. "Conflict and Cohesion in an Indian Student Community." Human Organization 29 (Summer, 1970): 95-102.

The concern of this study is the problem of typical community formation among a large number of Indian students at the University of Minnesota, where they seek to keep alive the culture of their homeland. A total of 147 self-administered questionnaires were distributed to all the Indian students at the University of Minnesota in the academic year of 1965-66. 134 questionnaires, about 91% of the total universe (of male students) were analyzed. Statistics were supplemented by participant observation and interviews. The main findings were that students from India formed one of the largest contingents of foreign students at the University of Minnesota. Most of the Indian states were represented with some 14 of the national languages being spoken by the students. On living and eating arrangements, certain clusters were formed as a result of regional differences and preferences for certain types and styles of cooking. On caste groups, there was not sufficient evidence to claim that caste was the center of the social life of the Indian student community. Despite different religious practices, religion was found to unite all the Indians in community-like form, setting them apart from the majority community, which was mainly Christian. The most important characteristic emerging from all observations was that the regional ties based on linguistic affiliations cut across and dominated living and eating arrangements, as well as caste and religious differences among the Indian students at Minnesota. Observation of the common activities of the community as a whole and the interpretation of facts as reported could not bear out a generalization that the Indian student community was divided into regional factions and that it could not exhibit solidarity.

1285. Gandhi, R. S. "Some Contrasts in the Foreign Student Life-Styles." International Journal of Contemporary Sociology 9 (January, 1972): 34-43.

This study focuses on the differences in the life-styles of 147 Indian students at the University of Minnesota in the mid-1960s. Questionnaires were designed to test the hypotheses that contrasting patterns of life-styles of the Indian students were due to their differences in orientations; the "old style" Indian students would be oriented inwardly toward "traditional" Indian culture while the "new style" Indian students would be oriented outwardly toward the Western world. The results show that the attitude contrasts were statistically significant. The differences in orientations and life-styles were further investigated on making a living, distribution of power and influence, and their social and cultural life.

1286. Gezi, K. I. "Factors Associated with Student Adjustment in Cross-Cultural Contact." California Journal of Educational Research 16 (May, 1965): 129-136.

1287. Golden, J. S. "Student Adjustment Abroad: A Psychiatrist's View." International Educational and Cultural Exchange 8 (Spring, 1973): 28-36.

1288. Graham, Morris A. "Acculturative Stress Among Polynesian, Asian and American Students on the Brigham Young University—Hawaii." International Journal of Intercultural Relations 7 (No. 1, 1983): 79-104.

Research was conducted over five years to determine effects upon students from nine cultural groups attending a multiracial, American university setting. It was hypothesized that acculturative stress would be greater among cultural groups of students where the gap between traditional and imposed (host) culture was greater. Data collected from Hawaiian, Samoan, Tongan, New Zealand Maori, Fijian, Chinese, Japanese, Filipino, and American Caucasian first-year students showed significant differences in assimilation patterns, affective contingencies, points of conflict and cultural stereotyping. Findings identify: (1) acculturative stress is significantly greater among Samoan students; (2) Chinese students are academically the most successfully adaptive cultural group; and (3) English language usage imposes the greatest discrimination barrier to all non-American cultures. Cultural configurations relative to Samoan students and recommendations to minimize acculturative stress are discussed.

1289. Hagey, A. R., and J. Hagey. "Meeting the Needs of Students from Other Cultures." Improving College and University Teaching 22 (Winter, 1974): 42-44.

1290. Haller, A. O., and B. Bray. "Attitudes of American Students Differently Liked by Latin American Students." Personal and Guidance Journal 38 (November, 1959): 217-221.

1291. Hamilton, J. T. "Comparison of Domestic and International Students' Perceptions of the University Environment." Journal of College Student Personnel 20 (September, 1979): 443-446.

1292. Hasan, R. "Socialization and Cross-Cultural Education." Linguistics No. 175 (1976): 7-25.

1293. Heath, G. L. "Berkeley's Community Programs for International Students." International Educational and Cultural Exchange 5 (Summer, 1969): 30-34.

1294. Hebson, C. C. "Academic Wastage Among Overseas Students." Educational Research 11 (November, 1968): 62-65.

1295. Heft, David. "The Foreign Student: His Problems, His Impact (on United States Society and on the Economic and Social Development of His Own Country)." Illustrated Americas 16 (February, 1964): 17-21.

1296. Henderson, John S. "Creating a Meaningful Foreign Experience for Students." National Association for Foreign Student Affairs Newsletter 30 (January, 1979): 92ff.

1297. Hendricks, G. L., and K. A. Skinner. "Adaptive Social Patterns of Foreign Students." Journal of College Student Personnel 18 (March, 1977): 124-127.

1298. Henry, C. J., and E. F. Wheeler. "Dietary Patterns Among Overseas Students in London." Proceedings of the Nutrition Society 39 (No. 2, 1980): A47.

1299. Hertz, R. N. "Foreign Students and the American Co-education." Phylon 25 (September, 1964): 65-71.

1300. Hodgkin, Mary C. "Acculturative Stress Among Asian Students in Australia." Australian Journal of Social Issues 13 (May, 1978): 139-150.

When foreign students from Southeast Asia come to Australia, they encounter many problems of norm conflict and cultural misunderstanding. In some cases these stresses, together with academic failures, social isolation and the strains of living in lodgings away from the supportive family, lead to emotional disturbances.

Students fall into a different category from migrants. They must make a selection from the host cultural norms and exercise restraint in identification with Australian ways because they face eventual return to their home socio-cultural environment.

Examples from a number of case histories have been chosen. They appear to follow a regular pattern of academic failure, inability to cope with relationships with the opposite sex, and eventual mental breakdown which required hospitalization.

1301. Hoeh, J., and D. Spuck. "Effects of Acculturation Process...French Students." Foreign Language Annals (1975): 220-226.

1302. Hojat, M. "Loneliness As a Function of Selected Personality Variables." Journal of Clinical Psychology 38 (January, 1982): 137-141.

1303. Hojat, M. "Psychometric Characteristics of the U.C.L.A. Loneliness Scale: A Study with Iranian College Students." Educational and Psychological Measurement 42 (No. 3, 1982): 917-925.

1304. Hull, W. Frank, IV, and Kevin P. Finney. "Longitudinal Case Studies of Foreign Students During their Initial Educational Sojourn." In Foreign Students in the United States of America: Coping Behavior within the Educational Environment, edited by W. Frank Hull, IV, pp. 196-224. New York: Praeger, 1978.

1305. Idrus, Faridah K., and L. B. Hendry. "Student Problems in Further Education: Some Home-Overseas Comparisons." Journal Pendidikan (Malaysia) (October, 1976): 39-45.

1306. James, Newton E. "Student Abroad: Expectations Versus Reality." Liberal Education 62 (December, 1976): 599-607.

    This article assesses educational goals and outcomes of American students studying in Europe. The research included a series of questions were used to delineate personal goals, aspirations, and values. Fifty-two U.S. students in study programs in Europe during the winter of 1972-73 were tested and interviewed. The author examines their intellectual disposition, relationships with other persons, political orientation, career goals, religious orientation, life goals, and most important developments in study abroad. As a whole the students interviewed were reasonably accomplished in their interpersonal relations and secure in their feelings about themselves, and that each overseas program contained a sufficient number of secure, socially competent students to provide a favorable environment for construcative personality development.

1307. Johnson, Dixon C. "Ourselves and Others: Comparative Stereotypes." International Educational and Cultural Exchange 9 (Fall-Winter, 1973-76): 24-28.

1308. Johnson, Dixon C. "Plight of Nigerians in United States as Viewed from Lagos." National Association for Foreign Student Affairs Newsletter 30 (April, 1979): 153ff.

1309. Johnson, D. C. "Problems of Foreign Students." International Educational and Cultural Exchange 7 (Fall, 1971): 61-68.

1310. Johnson, K., and K. Marow. "Meeting Some Social Language Needs of Overseas Students." Canadian Modern Languages Review 33 (No. 5, 1977): 694-707.

1311. Kahne, Merton J. "Cultural Differences: Whose Troubles Are We Talking About?" International Educational and Cultural Exchange 11 (No. 4, 1976): 36-40.

1312. Kang, Tai S. "A Foreign Student Group as an Ethnic Community." International Review of Modern Sociology (March, 1971): 2.

From a sociological viewpoint, an important aspect of social life of foreign students is formation of strong in-group oriented ethnic communities among some foreign student groups, particularly those from non-European countries. This category of foreign students has "considerable adjustment difficulties." The author of this article, using a sociological concept of ethnic community, analyzes the above-mentioned problem by studying the social life of Chinese students at the University of Minnesota.

The Chinese students are set apart in the host society by their physical characteristics, language, symbols, and unique culture; therefore, they sometimes experience problems of making psychological and behavioral adjustment.

The author considers that Chinese students form a highly in-group-oriented ethnic enclave to provide an array of institutionalized solutions to their common problems that they face as part of a plurality of aliens residing in a wider host community. Results of the survey carried out by the author among 118 randomly selected Chinese students at the University of Minnesota in 1967 indicated that the Chinese students founded their own associations, largely maintained primary relations among themselves, and sustained rather limited associations with the members of the host society. Furthermore, they mainly adhered to their own food habits, kept strong emotional ties with their homeland, and supported their own religion. In a short time, these students formed an ethnic enclave of their own and "operated very much like a first-generation immigrant group."

The author considers that these findings may be generalized to Chinese students enrolled in the other higher education institutions in the United States and the concept of the ethnic community can be extended to other non-European student groups who are set apart by their physical characteristics, language, and culture; e.g., Indians, Arabians, Japanese, or Koreans.

1313. Kang, Tai. S. "Name Change and Acculturation: Chinese Students on an American Campus." Pacific Sociological Review 14 (October, 1971): 403-412.

In a study of the social life of Chinese students at the University of Minnesota in 1967 it was discovered that of 262 Chinese students registered, 36.2% of them had anglicized their first names. The preliminary examination of this phenomenon suggested an analytical scheme to examine such aspects of social life of the group as: acculturation, group identification, and patterns of interpersonal interaction. This paper examines the social psychological implications of identity change through name change.

1314.  Kedem, Peri, and Mordechai Bar-Lev.  "Is Giving up Traditional Religious Culture Part of the Price to be Paid for Acquiring Higher Education?  Adaptation of Academic Western Culture by Jewish Israeli University Students of Middle Eastern Origin." Higher Education 12 (No. 4, 1983):  373-388.

This research was designed to investigate whether the Middle Eastern student feels that attaining the status of a "Western modern man" is incomplete with maintaining a traditional, religious way of life.  In 1980, a representative sample of the Jewish University student population (N = 1250) responded to a questionnaire aimed at measuring religious attitudes, beliefs, and practices.  The students of Middle Eastern origin proved to be more religious than their Western counterparts.  However, their feeling about themselves is that not only are they less religious than their parents and grandparents but that they are less religious than they themselves have previously been.  This feeling stemmed from their having discarded or having become lax in carrying out some of the more fundamental religious practices, even though they still maintain many of the same religious practices, attitudes, and beliefs as their forefathers.  Factors influencing the degree of religiosity are examined.  The findings show that as a whole there is no revolt against home or tradition and the students have found the way to the "new life" without breaking off from the "old ways" of the parental culture.

1315.  Kim, Hae A.  "Transplantation of Psychiatrists from Foreign Cultures."  Journal of the American Academy of Psychoanalysis 4 (No. 1, 1976):  105-112.

1316.  Kirstein, L.  "Community Services for Foreign Students in Metropolitan Areas."  International Educational and Cultural Exchange 6 (Winter, 1971):  55-61.

1317.  Klein, Marjorie H.  "Adaptation to New Cultural Environments."  In Overview of Intercultural Education, Training and Research, Volume 1: Theory, edited by David S. Hoopes, Paul B. Pedersen, and George W. Renuick, pp. 49-55.  Washington, D.C.:  Society for Intercultural Education, Training and Research, Georgetown University, 1977.

1318. Klein, Marjorie H., et al. "Far Eastern Students in a Big University--Subcultures within a Subculture." Science and Public Affairs 27 (January, 1971): 10-19.

1319. Klein, Marjorie H., et al. "The Foreign Student Adaptation Program: Social Experiences of Asian Students in the U.S." International Educational and Cultural Exchange 6 (Winter, 1971): 77-90.

This article written by a group of psychiatrists and psychologists concerns foreign students' educational adjustment and certain aspects of their personal, lived-life experience, moods, concerns, social world, and general style of life.

Data for this study were collected in 1966 and 1967 on the basis of a background questionnaire distributed to 580 students from 35 foreign countries as they passed through the Foreign Student Reception Center at the University of Wisconsin.

Analyses of the collected data for 40 Asian students from Taiwan and Hong Kong showed that during their first year of study there were seasonal differences in the incidence of health problems, and there was evidence that the rate of illness at certain times in the academic year, such as the Christmas holidays, was predictable from the amount of anticipated homesickness.

With regard to the psychiatric problems of foreign students, complaints have ranged from severe psychotic episodes, depressions through milder anxiety to neurotic states.

The study also found that the nature and background of the barriers that existed between Asian and American students stem from basic functional differences in social roles. The Chinese culture--traditional and authoritarian--gives young people a great deal of structure and support both from family and from peers. American culture stresses opposite values. Taking into account the findings of the above study, an experimental orientation program in Taiwan was carried out which focused on teaching specific techniques for overcoming interactional difficulties in relation with Americans.

A part of the study presented in this article was devoted to the contribution of situational factors and traditional values to the Indian student's decision to remain in the United States. It has been found, for example, that many students at the point of graduation show a kind of ambivalent behavior: they categorically assert that they will return home, and at the same time they actively seek employment in the United States, or seem to engage in a series of delaying maneuvers.

In conclusion, the authors suggest that the progress can best be made in solving foreign students' adaptation problems by shifting focus from the foreign aspect of the problems to their human aspects.

1320. Klineberg, Otto. "Stressful Experiences of Foreign Students at Various Stages of Sojourn: Counseling and Policy Implications." In Uprooting and Development: Dilemmas of Coping with Modernization, edited by G. V. Coelho, and Paul I. Ahmed, pp. 271-293. New York: Plenum Press, 1980.

   An important aspect of modernization is the planned movement of students across cultures for advanced training abroad. The author of this paper examines the phases of the adaptation process from the initial selection procedures in the home country, to the student's decisions in planning his/her sojourn abroad, through the decisions that lead to permanent residence in the host-country, or to the more common case of return to, and employment in, the home-country.
   Drawing upon a general review of research on foreign students in France and in other countries, the author focuses on the potential stressful issues at various stages of the sojourn abroad and considers means for mitigating them. He finds that foreign student selection procedures to screen candidates to study abroad are designed to find their level of competency in technical skills or academic work, but pay little attention to personality characteristics and degree of maturity. He recommends increased attention to preparatory activities such as language training, provision of information about the institution to be attended, and an introduction to the cultural norms and customary social behavior in the host-country.
   He also emphasizes that foreign student advisers should pay attention to areas in which a student is likely to experience a blow to his/her self-esteem. At the same time, Klineberg reiterates that the resident population must also be sensitized to the presence of the "uprooted" students, and must learn to appreciate some of the cultural and social resources that the foreign students bring to the community.

1321. Martins, D. "L'isolement Pedagogique et Social des Etudiants Etrangers." Revue Francaise de Pedagogie No. 26 (1974): 18-22.

1322. Maxwell, M. J. "Foreign Students and American Academic Ritual." Journal of Reading 17 (January, 1974): 301-305.

1323. McLaughlin, G. W. "Some Variables Interacting with Media Exposure Among Foreign Students." Sociology and Social Research 53 (July, 1969): 511-522.

1324. McMahon, Jean, and Irene Reuter. "The Host Family Scheme." In Overseas Students in Australia, edited by S. Bochner, and P. Wicks, pp. 187-190. Auburn: New South Wales University Press, 1972.

1325. Meleis, Afaf I. "Arab Students in Western Universities: Social Properties and Dilemmas." Journal of Higher Education 53 (July- August, 1982): 439-447.

Thousands of Arab students have in the past completed their education in the USA, and many more are being sent yearly. This article describes some of the major properties that characterize Arabs, and the dilemmas that Arab students, trainees, scientists, and health professionals face when they come to the United States to further their education. Differences between the Arabs and the Americans in social properties and educational systems mainly lead to difficulties felt by the Arab students in adjusting to American life and study. The article also suggests some strategies that could be devised to help them cope with that transition and enhance their potential for success: (1) an extensive ongoing orientation program be provided; (2) the Arab student's new role be supported by direct sponsorship or the establishment of a social network; (3) a list of resources and personal contacts be provided to help free the student's energy to deal with other educational challenges.

1326. Miller, M. H., et al. "The Cross-Cultural Student: Lessons in Human Nature." Bulletin of the Menninger Clinic 35 (March, 1971): 128-131.

1327. Minogne, W. J. D. "Distributive Justice and Foreign University Students: A New Zealand View." Canadian and International Education 1 (December, 1972): 35-43.

1328. Mood, T. A. "Foreign Students and the Academic Library." RQ-- Reference and Adult Services Division 22 (No. 2, 1982): 175-180.

1329. Morgan, E. E., Jr. "Study Abroad: A Process of Adaptation and Change." International Review of Education 21 (No. 2, 1975): 207-215.

This article is based on the study of three Junior Year Abroad groups who participated in the Regional Council for International Education's Study Abroad Program in Switzerland over a three-year period (1968-1970), using the methods of participant observation and written questionnaire.

The major assumption of the study was that individuals differ in their methods for adapting to the behavior patterns associated with the cross-cultural experience. The assessment of adaptation was made by focusing on individual learning and development. A multi-dimensional scaling procedure was used with a hierarchical clustering scheme to arrive at a typology of student adaptation. Five types were extracted but only two are reported in this article--the "cultural relativists" and the "cultural opposites."

The author points out that the valued outcome of study abroad is: "to help acquire a deep understanding of another culture, and to begin to appreciate and develop empathy for people who are different."

In conclusion, he points out that the overall success or failure of a study-abroad program does not rest only with the students. Thus administrators of these programs must possess an expertise and understanding of the implications of the cultural encounter and differences in adaptation to this encounter.

1330. Morgan, G. D. "Exploratory Study of Problems of Academic Adjustment of Nigerian Students in America." Journal of Negro Education 32 (Summer, 1963): 208-217.

1331. Mowlana, H., and G. W. McLaughlin. "Some Variables Interacting With Media Exposure Among Foreign Students." Sociology and Social Research 53 (July, 1969): 511-522.

1332. Okamura, Jonathan, and Richard Coller. "The Social Adjustment of Filipino Nonmigrants, Emigrants and Immigrants to Hawaii." International Journal of Intercultural Relations 2 (Fall, 1978): 295-308.

1333. Opalka, J., J. Mitchell, and R. Martin. "Introducing International Students to the American Food-Supply." Journal of the American Dietetic Association 82 (No. 5, 1983): 531-533.

1334. Ordonez, J. "Problems of Foreign Graduate Students and Factors Limiting Their Expectations." Journal of Animal Science 45 (No. 4, 1977): 919-922.

1335. Oshodin, O. G. "Alcohol Abuse Among Nigerian College Students in New York Area of the United States." College Student Journal (Summer, 1982): 153-157.

1336. Owie, Ikponmwosa. "A Comparative Study of Alienation: American vs. Foreign Students." International Education 11 (No. 2, 1982): 35-38.

1337. Owie, Ikponmwosa. "Social Alienation among Foreign Students." College Student Journal 16 (No. 2, 1982): 163-165.

1338. Palmer, E. K., and G. L. Zimmerman. "Helping Foreign Students to Adjust." Overseas 3 (Summer, 1963): 20-24.

1339. Parker, O. D. "Cultural Clues to the Middle Eastern Student." International Educational and Cultural Exchange 12 (Fall, 1976): 12-15.

1340. Payind, Mohammad Alam. "Academic, Personal and Social Problems of Afghan and Iranian Students in the United States." Educational Research Quarterly 4 (Summer, 1979): 3-11.

This study is about Afghan and Iranian students in the United States. The objective of the study is to analyze the nature and the extent of the academic, personal, and social problems of Afghan and Iranian students and to what these problems are related.

The study showed that the students had academic problems mostly related to a lack of proficiency in English and to a certain extent to the differences between the educational systems of their home countries and those of the United States. The social problems were related to the cultural background of the students and their lack of information about the United States. The study concludes with recommendations (targeted at appropriate authorities) designed to help the students overcome these problems:

. To the Ministry of Education and Other Related Authorities of both Afghanistan and Iran: There is a great need for more organized predeparture orientation programs for both sponsored and nonsponsored students going to the United States. It is also suggested that both sponsored and nonsponsored students take, in their respective countries, intensive English courses before departing for the United States.

. To the American Colleges and Universities: American colleges and universities should avoid a stereotyped conception of the international student and attempt to identify and recognize the major handicaps of different subgroups within the total group of international students.

1341. Pedersen, Paul. "Personal Problem Solving Resources Used by University of Minnesota Foreign Students." In Topics in Culture Learning, Volume 3, edited by Richard W. Brislin, pp. 55-65. Honolulu: East-West Center, 1975.

1342. Pedersen, Paul B. "Role Learning as a Coping Strategy for Uprooted Foreign Students." In Uprooting and Development: Dilemmas of Coping with Modernization, edited by G. V. Coelho, and P. I. Ahmed, pp. 295-319. New York: Plenum Press, 1980.

A major task of adaptation for foreign students in a new culture is that of recognizing the diverse roles in which one is interacting with his/her university and community members. The author of this paper [chapter 14 in the book] suggests that an identity crisis may be accentuated because the foreign student must learn to handle multiple new roles. His/her role as a student may, for example, be complicated by being perceived as a "cultural ambassador," who needs to explain and sometimes justify the policies of his/her country. The foreign student must learn to be able to differentiate and yet integrate these conflicting roles.

The author points out that the adaptation process is easier if the individual's role conflict is minimized, and if prior expectations prove to be more in accordance with the real situation. He also emphasizes the importance of the "conational" in providing support, advice, and reassurance.

1343. Penn, J. R., and M. L. Durham. "Dimensions of Cross-Cultural Interaction." Journal of College Student Personnel 19 (No. 3, 1978): 264-267.

1344. Perkins, Carolyn S., et al. "A Comparison of the Adjustment Problems of Three International Student Groups." Journal of College Student Personnel 18 (September, 1977): 382-388.

1345. Phipps, Michael. "American Society and the Foreign Students." Community College Social Science Quarterly 6 (Spring, 1976): 19-23.

1346. Pruitt, France J. "The Adaptation of African Students to American Society." International Journal of Intercultural Relations 2 (Spring, 1978): 90-118.

This report summarizes the results of a questionnaire study involving 296 sub-Saharan students from a representative set of nine American campuses. Some of the results suggest that African students in this country in the middle 1970s are predominantly Christian and middle-class in origin, coming mostly from cities of over 10,000; Nigerians vastly outnumber those from any other country; two-thirds are undergraduates and one-third graduate students, with at least a third having started their American education in a community college; and they are mostly supported by their families or themselves. Their major problems at first are in the areas of climate, communications with Americans, discrimination, homesickness, depression, irritability, and tiredness. Only a minority feel comfortable with the basic elements of American culture, though the vast majority are pleased with the education they are receiving. It was possible to identify several correlates of adjustment, defined as happiness and freedom from various problems. Students have a more positive attitude toward American values if they are from more prominent families, have attended an orientation to American education, and spend time with Americans rather than other Africans. Contacts with the foreign student office seem to be effective.

1347. Pruitt, France J. "The Adaptation of Foreign Students on American Campuses." Journal of the National Association for Women Deans, Administrators, and Counselors 41 (Summer, 1978): 144-147.

1348. Pyle, C., and J. Thompson. "Foreign Students: Minority Students? Or Both?" National ACAC Journal 15 (August, 1970): 14-18.

1349. Quigley, T. "Community and the Foreign Student." National Catholic Educational Association Bulletin 61 (August, 1964): 207-210.

1350. Ramberg, E. G., III. "The Foreign Student on the American Campus." National ACAC Journal 21 (June, 1977): 20-22.

1351. Reich, A. A. "International Understanding: The Foreign Student and the Community." College and University Journal 13 (January, 1974): 23-26.

1352. Robinson, Cynny. "First a King, then Prince, Then Forgotten-- Foreign Student and Friendship in the United States." National Association for Foreign Student Affairs Newsletter 28 (March, 1977): 12ff.

1353. Ronan, E. "Lessons from Students; Vietnamese, This Time." Journal of Reading 20 (April, 1977): 563-566.

1354. Saunder Das, S. "The Psychological Problems of the Eastern Student." In Overseas Students in Australia, edited by S. Bochner, and P. Wicks, pp. 82-94. Auburn: New South Wales University Press, 1972.

The most common mistake made by many people in the Australian higher education institutions is to "consider all students from Eastern [Asian] countries as belonging to one culture." The first part of this article deals with psychological problems some foreign students coming from the countries belonging to the "Eastern cultures" might have, when exposed and confronted with "Western" values and thinking which is predominant in Australia. Some of the issues discussed in this context are:
. concept of living;
. concept of normality, suffering, thinking; and
. values deriving from the differences in the respective social systems, e.g., "Western" system with tremendous value placed on individual life, competition and initiative versus "Eastern" system emphasizing community and/or family obligations and rights.
The second part of the article deals with the types of psychological problems of the Eastern students in Australia in light of the cultural differences brought out in the first part. The author classifies them into two broad categories, the intrinsic and the extrinsic.
The intrinsic ones are defined as "the cultural residues present within the Eastern student seen to be the determinants of behavior." The most important of these are: basic attitudes; food habits and preferences; difficulties relating to social situations; sexual

expression and inhibition, homesickness; religious beliefs and practices; the manifestations of cultural shock.

The extrinsic factors include: the attitudes of the host country; complaints raised about the behavior of the students; distractions; relations perceived as lack of warmth, pressure towards rapid acculturation and continuing interceptions.

In conclusion, the author considers ways of avoiding maladjustment among Eastern students and points out that there is no single solution to the problem but probably the most effective one would be to launch a comprehensive program of educating Australians, especially those dealing with the foreign students, regarding the cultures of other countries.

1355.  Schild, E. O.  "Foreign Student As Stranger, Learning the Norms of the Host Culture."  Journal of Social Issues 18 (No. 1, 1962): 41-54.

The extent to which the encounter with the host society enables the student to learn its norms is crucial for his adjustment.  In this study of 59 American Jewish students visiting Israel in 1955, the author examines the consequences which flow from their position as strangers in the host society, with particular emphasis on how they learn the norms of the host culture.  The research took the form of a panel study, and the data were obtained from questionnaires, intensive interviews, systematic observations, and personal diaries.  The author examines ways of learning and their effectiveness, and change of attitudes. From the discussion four hypotheses were made:  (1) in terms of scope of learning, observation is superior; (2) in terms of the effectiveness of a given learning situation, participation seems superior; (3) in terms of ease of learning, explicit communication seems most effective.  As for factors responsible for the more durable change of attitudes, the following can be suggested in order of effectiveness:  participation is the most effective means for inducing change, then observation, and then explicit communication.

1356.  Selby, Henry, and Clyde Woods.  "Foreign Students at a High Pressure University."  Sociology of Education 39 (Spring, 1966):  138-154.

1357.  Selltiz, C.  "Social Contacts of Foreign Students in the United States."  School and Society 91 (Summer, 1963):  261-266.

1358.  Semlak, William D.  "Effect of Media Use on Foreign Student Perceptions of U.S. Political Leaders."  Journalism Quarterly 56 (No. 1, 1979):  153-156, 178.

1359. Sepmeyer, I. H., and T. E. Sharp. "What's His Other Name? A Guide to the Usage of Names in 112 Countries of the World." College and University 56 (Spring, 1981): 292-298.

1360. Sewell, William H., and Oluf M. Davidson. "The Adjustment of Scandinavian Students." Journal of Social Issues 12 (No. 1, 1956): 9-19.

1361. Shaffer, Robert H., and Leo R. Dowling. "Foreign Students and Their American Student Friends." School and Society 96 (April, 1968): 245-249.

1362. Sharma, S. "Study to Identify and Analyze Adjustment Problems Experienced by Foreign Non-European Graduate Students Enrolled in Selected Universities in the State of North Carolina." California Journal of Educational Research 24 (May, 1973): 135-146.

1363. Simon, P. "Understanding Foreign Cultures." International Educational and Cultural Exchange 14 (Summer, 1978): 2-4.

1364. Singh, B. Krishna, R. Lewis Donohew, and G. Lynne Lackey. "Foreign Students as Minority Group Members in the American Society: An Exploration." International Journal of Contemporary Sociology 11 (No. 4, 1974): 207-217.

   This study analyzes the types of 193 foreign students at the University of Kentucky, aiming at assessing the social marginality of foreign students through determining the typologies existing on that campus. The findings closely parallel typologies of minority groups and give further support to suggested impact of interactive situations. The study suggests that the patterns of assimilation, pluralism, and isolation are as valid for the foreign students as they are for other minority groups.

1365. Smart, Reginald. "Intercultural Dimension of Foreign Student Affairs." In Overview of Intercultural Education and Research, edited by D. S. Hoopes, et al., pp. 44-65. Washington, D.C.: Georgetown University, 1978.

1366. Smith, Eugene H. "Campus Activism and Foreign Students." International Educational and Cultural Exchange 4 (Winter, 1969): 39-43.

1367. Smith, R. J., et al. "When is a Stereotype a Stereotype? (American Students in West Germany)." Psychological Report 46 (April, 1980): 599-608.

1368. Stafford, Thomas, Paul Marion, and M. Lee Salter. "Adjustment of International Students." NASPA Journal 18 (Summer, 1980): 40-45.

1369. Straub, J. S., et al. "Academic Freedom for International Students on American Campuses." National Association of Women Deans and Counselors Journal 33 (Winter, 1970): 77-81.

1370. Surdam, Joyce C., and James R. Collins. "Adaptation of International Students: A Cause for Concern." Journal of College Student Personnel 25 (No. 3, 1984): 240-244.

1371. Tan, A. S. "Television Use and Social Stereotypes (Chinese Students in the United States]." Journalism Quarterly 59 (Spring, 1982): 119-122.

1372. Jarrahi-Zadeh, A., and W. J. Eichman. "Impact of Sociocultural Factors on Middle-Eastern Students in the U.S.A." International Educational and Cultural Exchange 5 (Winter, 1970): 82-94.

1373. Teoh, J. "Psychological Problems Among University Students in an Area of Rapid Socio-cultural Change." Australian and New Zealand Journal of Psychiatry 8 (No. 2, 1974): 109-120.

1374. Thomas, H., Jr., et al. "Adjustment of International Students." National Association of Student Personnel Administrators Journal 18 (No. 1, 1980): 40-45.

1375. Trevelyan, M. "The Welfare of Overseas Commonwealth Students in the United Kingdom." Journal of the Royal Society of Arts (April, 1962): 333-344.

1376. Vornberg, J. A., and R. T. Grant. "Adolescent Cultural Acquaintance Experiences and Their Ethnic Group Attitudes." Adolescence 11 (Winter, 1976): 601-608.

1377. Waters, Brent, and Dennis Peterson. "Religious Groups and International Students." National Association for Foreign Student Affairs Newsletter 34 (February, 1983): 92ff.

1378. Wolfang, Aaron, and David S. Weiss. "A Locus of Control and Social Distance Comparison of Canadian and West Indian-Born Students." International Journal of Intercultural Relations 4 (No. 3/4, 1980): 295-306.

1379. Wray, Herbert. "Abroad in the U.S.: Foreign Students on American Campuses." Educational Record 62 (Summer, 1981): 68-71.

## Reportage

1380. "British Student in China Punished for Prank." Chronicle of Higher Education 22 (July 13, 1981): 13.

1381. "China Orders U.S. Student to Leave Country." Chronicle of Higher Education 24 (June 9, 1982): 22.

1382. "Chinese Taught by Student Detained." Chronicle of Higher Education 24 (June 30, 1982): 13.

1383. "Convictions in Colorado Shooting of Libyans." Chronicle of Higher Education 23 (December 16, 1981): 3.

1384. Cookson, C. "Moves to Help Victims of Culture Shock." Times Higher Education Supplement 451 (June 26, 1981): 6.

1385. Das, K. "Axed Out of Oxbridge." Far East Economic Review 118 (October 8-14, 1982): 44.

1386. Das, K. "Paper Chases New Hurdles." Far East Economic Review 107 (March 7, 1980): 21.

1387. Dubin, Joel. "Israelis Shut Down West Bank University After Demonstrations." Chronicle of Higher Education 26 (June 15, 1983): 23.

1388. "Foreign Students Help Canadians." Canadian Vocational Journal 9 (Summer, 1973): 18-19.

1389. "Former Hostages Honored at Iowa, Iranians Object." Chronicle of Higher Education 23 (October 21, 1981): 2.

1390. "Friendship for Foreign Students." Times Educational Supplement No. 2537 (January 3, 1964): 14.

1391. Grafton, Clive L. "Foreign Student Patterns in American Community Colleges." Junior College Journal 40 (March, 1970): 32-33.

1392. Hansen, Evelyn Unes. "A Brief Statement of Some Needs of Nontraditional Foreign Students in American Colleges and Universities." Alternative Higher Education 6 (No. 3, 1982): 139-141.

1393. Holmes, D. "Another Taste of Hospitality--Rhodesian Students in Great Britain." New Statesman 100 (August 8, 1980): 2-3.

1394. Honey, Charles. "Iranians in Oklahoma: Learning the Hard Way." Change 10 (1978): 21-23.

1395. "Iranian, Iraqi Students Clash." Chronicle of Higher Education 21 (October 20, 1980): 2.

1396. "Iranian Student Acquitted in Denver Death." Chronicle of Higher Education 21 (January 2, 1981): 22.

1397. "Iranian Students Attack Embassy in Vienna." Chronicle of Higher Education 22 (August 3, 1981): 6.

1398. "Iranian Students Clash in Arizona and Oklahoma." Chronicle of Higher Education 23 (September 16, 1981): 2.

1399. "Iranians Arrested after Southern Methodist University Clash." Chronicle of Higher Education 24 (August 11, 1982): 2.

1400. "Iranians Arrested at Tennessee State." Chronicle of Higher Education 23 (September 23, 1981): 3.

1401. "Iraqi Factions Clash at University of Pittsburgh." Chronicle of Higher Education 25 (December 1, 1982): 2.

1402. Johnstone, M. "Students Go on Hunger Strike." Times Higher Education Supplement (March 20, 1981): 6.

1403. Judd, J. "Fears of Bar Restricting Foreign Dons." Times Higher Education Supplement (October 28, 1977): 1.

1404. "Michigan State Student Convicted in Israel." Chronicle of Higher Education 16 (June 19, 1978): 2.

1405. "Middle Eastern Students Convicted in Protest." Chronicle of Higher Education 16 (June 19, 1978): 2.

1406. "94 Iranian Students Arrested at Texas College." Chronicle of Higher Education 16 (March 27, 1978): 2.

1407. "Oshkosh, Wisconsin: 60 Saudi Students to Transfer After Clashes in Oshkosh." Chronicle of Higher Education 19 (October 1, 1979): 7.

1408. Parker, A. "Dilemma Facing the Refugee and Overseas Student." Times Higher Education Supplement (March 14, 1980): 13.

1409. Ramoultar, Sukhu. "Racism: Where Too Few Fear to Tread." Times Higher Education Supplement (November 21, 1980): 29.

1410. "Retention of Foreign Students: Why They Stay, Why They Leave, What Happens to Them." College and University 56 (Summer, 1981): 322-323.

1411. Vjlaky, Charlotte. "Auslander Dritte Klasse. Wie Schlecht Werden Auslandische Studenten in der Bundesrepublik Behandelt?" Die Zeit 26 (No. 8, 1971): 13-14.

## 20. ACADEMIC PERFORMANCE

1412. Australia, Department of Education, Education Planning Group. Academic Progress of Private Overseas Students Who First Enrolled in a Tertiary Course in 1977. Canberra: Education Planning Group, Commonwealth Department of Education, 1982.

1413. Australia, Department of Foreign Affairs, Australian Development Assistance Bureau. Conference on Educational Difficulties of Overseas Students, 11-12 December, 1980, Canberra. Canberra: Australian Development Assistance Bureau, 1980.

1414. Canada, Government of Quebec, Cabinet du Ministre de l'Education. Les Frais de Scolarite des Etudiants Etrangers dans les Colleges et Universites du Quebec: Le Gouvernement Enquete une Politique Generale. Montreal: Cabinet du Ministre de l'Education, 1978.

1415. Chongolnee, B. "Academic, Situational, Organismic and Attitudinal Factors Affecting the Academic Achievement of Foreign Graduate Students at Iowa State University." Unpublished Ph.D thesis, Iowa State University, 1978.

1416. De Wolf, Virginia A. Predictability of First-Year University of Washington Performance for Foreign Undergraduates Entering Autumn 1978. Seattle, Washington: Educational Assessment Center, 1980.

1417. Elting, Robert Arthur. "The Prediction of Freshman Year Academic Performance of Foreign Students from Pre-Admission Data." Unpublished Ph.D thesis, New York University, 1970.

1418. Farsad, Massoud. "A Comparison of the Study Habits of Foreign and American Graduate Students at the University of Northern Colorado." Unpublished Ed.D thesis, University of Northern Colorado, 1980.

1419. Gerstein, Hannelore. Auslandische Stipendiaten in der Bundesrepublik Deutschland. Eine Empirische Erhebung uber Studiengang und Studienerfolg der DAAD-Stipendiaten. Bonn-Bad Godesberg: DAAD, 1974.

1420. Grady, William Ellis. "Selected Variables Related to Academic Achievement of American and Canadian Male Freshmen at the University of North Dakota." Unpublished Ph.D thesis, University of North Dakota, 1969.

1421. Greenall, G. M., and J. E. Price, eds. Study Modes and Academic Development of Overseas Students. London: British Council, 1980.

1422. Hennyng, Anne Marie. "History and Problems of Cross-Cultural University Education: A Case-Study of Norwegian Students and Their Academic Performance at the University of Colorado." Unpublished Ph.D thesis, University of Colorado at Boulder, 1980.

1423. Hoff, Bernadine Lorraine Ryan. "Classroom-Generated Barriers to Learning: International Students in American Higher Education." Unpublished Ph.D thesis, United States International University, 1979.

1424.  Hrommen, Clifford Harley.  "The Relationship of Noncognitive Variables to the Degree of Academic Achievement of Foreign Students at the University of Houston."  Unpublished Ed.D thesis, University of Houston, 1981.

1425.  Jensen, Margaret.  The Individual and His Learning Problems in an Unfamiliar Culture:  The Contributions of Psychology. Washington, D.C.:  National Association for Foreign Student Affairs, 1964.

1426.  Kadi, Sobhi Abdulhafeez.  "Determination and Analysis of the Bases Used by Faculty to Evaluate and Grade the Performance of Foreign Students in American Universities."  Unpublished Ph.D thesis, University of Denver, 1976.

1427.  Lehrfield, Evelyn Sklar.  "Culture Shock as a Factor Affecting the Academic Performance of American Students Abroad."  Unpublished Ph.D thesis, Northwestern University, 1974.

1428.  Mehrinfar, N.  "Academic Performance of Selected Undergraduate Foreign Students as Affected by Age, Sex and Self-Concept." Unpublished Ed.D thesis, Texas Southern University, 1981.

1429.  Melendez-Craig, Mario.  "A Study of the Academic Achievement and Related Problems Among Latin American Students Enrolled in the Major Utah Universities."  Unpublished Ed.D thesis, Brigham Young University, 1970.

        The Michigan International Student Problem Inventory was utilized in the measurement of the academic achievement of Latin American students in the major Utah universities and other related problems.  Latin Americans were found to be achieving acceptably with many of them being outstanding scholars.  No significant difference was found between academic achievement and marital status or sex among the group.  Class level and English proficiency as related to academic achievement were other variables tested.  While English proficiency was highly correlated with academic achievement there was no significant difference in grade point average among the three schools; upper division and graduate students were, however, found to achieve better than lower division students.  It was felt among most Latin Americans that the greatest problems students faced were financial, followed by academic problems, with religious and attitudinal problems of least importance.

1430.  Moghrabi, Kamel M.  "An Analysis of Factors that Influence the Degree of Success or Failure of Foreign Students at Texas A & M University."  Unpublished Ph.D thesis, Texas A & M University, 1966.

1431.  Ohuche, Romanus Ogbonna.  "Scholastic Factors Pertaining to the Academic Achievement of Nigerian Students in the United States."  Unpublished Ph.D thesis, Iowa State University, 1967.

1432. Pavri, Dina Mehervanji. "A Study of the Scholastic Achievement and Related Problems of Graduate Students at the University of Virginia." Unpublished Ed.D thesis, University of Virginia, 1963.

This study was designed to describe the academic achievement of foreign graduate students and to ascertain some of the personal, scholastic, and cultural factors that were related to and responsible for the failure or transfer of these students from the University. A total of 319 foreign students from 53 countries who were enrolled in the graduate schools of the University of Virginia from 1957 to 1961 were the subjects of the study. Data were obtained from information available from the records of the Registrar's Office, the Records Office, and the Foreign Student Office and from the returns of questionnaires sent to the students on the campus and within the country during the period of the study. The major findings include the following: (1) No significant difference was found between the scholastic performance of men and women. (2) Married students living with their families achieved at a higher level and experienced fewer difficulties than those who lived alone. (3) Students with scholarships were more successful than the self-supporting ones. (4) Eighty-eight percent of the students were satisfied with the education received at the university. (5) Fifty-five percent of foreign graduate students were above average scholastically, 25% were average, and 20% were below average. (6) Eighty-five percent of the students considered themselves capable of performing their professional tasks upon their return home.

1433. Sadeghi, Ahmad. "Important Factors that Affect Academic Success or Failure of Foreign Students at Selected Institutions of Higher Education in Tennessee." Unpublished Ph.D thesis, George Peabody College for Teachers, 1980.

1434. Salve, Ujjwala. "A Study of Selected Factors as Partial Predictors of Academic Success of Indian Graduate Students at Wayne State University from September, 1959 to December, 1962." Unpublished Ph.D thesis, Wayne State University, 1965.

1435. Sokari, H. "Predictors of College Success Among Foreign Students from Various Ethnocultural Backgrounds." Unpublished Ed.D thesis, University of San Francisco, 1980.

1436. Strommen, Clifford Harley. "The Relationship of Noncognitive Variables to the Degree of Academic Achievement of Foreign Students at the University of Houston." Unpublished Ed.D thesis, University of Houston, 1981.

1437. Sugimoto, Roy Atsuro. "The Relationship of Selected Predictive Variables to Foreign Student Achievement at the University of

California, Los Angeles." Unpublished Ph.D thesis, University of Southern California, 1966.

This study provides a description and analysis of the relationship between certain items found on forms in admission offices with foreign students and the eventual academic success or lack of success of these students. The sample consisted of 2,075 foreign students (1,375 with F-1 or J-1 visas) enrolled at the University of California, Los Angeles during 1964-65. It was hypothesized that: (1) no significant differences would be found between the success criterion and any of the 18 variables selected; (2) no predictors of academic success could be identified among the 18 variables; and (3) there was no need to improve the admission and information forms currently in use. English-language proficiency is one of the most important factors associated with academic success. Variability in the selection and admission standards among institutions of higher learning, are characteristics on which there was widespread consensus among educational authorities. Of the eight variables selected only two (sex and country of origin) were less significant. Overall grade-point average, graduate standing, first semester grade-point average and the number of terms at UCLA were factors most closely correlated with academic success. While about 15% of the foreign students experienced academic difficulties, age, date of enrollment at UCLA, type of visa and English examination scores had no significant predictive value. Improved selection criteria and careful screening procedures are among the recommendations made.

1438. Tan-Ngarmtrong, T. "The Relationship of Selected Variables to Academic Achievement of Foreign Graduate Students at Mississippi State University." Unpublished Ed.D thesis, Mississippi State University, 1979.

1439. Telleen, Judy G. Johnson. "A Predictive Model of the Cumulative Academic Achievement of Graduate Students from India: Based upon Data Collected in a Longitudinal Study of 300 Indian Graduate Students that Attended the University of Michigan." Unpublished Ph.D thesis, University of Michigan, 1970.

This study, which examined the academic and background characteristics of 300 Indian graduate students, was designed to describe those characteristics, and to create a predictive model which could be used to predict the academic achievement of the students seeking admission at the University of Michigan. All five of the basic assumptions of the study, which were stated in the form of null-hypotheses, were rejected, while only 15 of the 54 variables were found to be significantly related to academic achievement. Eight variables which were selected for the predictive model accurately predicted the cumulative letter grade of Indian students who were not a part of the original 300 students in the study. Other major findings of the study include the following: (1) Over three-fourths (76%) of the nondegree earners had a cumulative grade point of 4.99 or below (probationary status). More than one-half (62%) of the students were unmarried while over three-fourths (84%) were in the age range 21-30 years old. A chart, entitled the "Relationship of Academic Achievement with Various Factors," which summarizes the findings of 41 authors on the subject of academic achievement for the period 1924 to 1969, is provided.

1440. Thomas, Mary Michelle B. "A Descriptive Analysis of Foreign Graduate Students and the Relationship of their Characteristics to Academic Achievement at University of Mississippi." Unpublished Ph.D thesis, University of Mississippi, 1972.

1441. Tower, Gael Wells. "The International Transfer of Students from Community Colleges to Senior Institutions: Canada and United States." Unpublished Ph.D thesis, University of Arizona, 1979.

1442. Tuso, Hamdesa. "The Academic Experience of African Graduate Students at Michigan State University." Unpublished Ph.D thesis, Michigan State University, 1981.

This study was designed: (1) to develop a profile of African graduate students at Michigan State University; (2) to examine their educational experiences while studying at the university, and (3) to determine the effect of academic level and area of speculation on their educational experiences. A questionnaire and a structured interview schedule were used to gather the data. Approximately half of the 96 African graduate students at MSU were involved in the study the field work of which was undertaken between the summer of 1978 and winter of 1979. The adviser and the student were found to play key roles in the development of individualized academic programs. The pedagogical approaches at MSU were rated as "effective" by a majority of the students and while a majority indicated that they could write term papers on issues related to Africa they found they were handicapped by lack of relevant data/literature not to mention goal conflicts between given courses. While the quality of interaction between Africans and professors in general was moderate the interaction between them and their advisers in academic-related matters was high. Substantial differences were also found in the participants' interactions with their fellow graduate students (Americans, internationals, and other Africans) in academic-related matters. Some differences, depending on level and curriculum, and in educational experience, were evident.

1443. Udosen, Nnah William. "Cultural Characteristics and Humanistic Excellences: Some Dilemmas of the Foreign Student of Art

Education in America." Unpublished Ph.D thesis, Ohio State University, 1980.

1444. Wetzel, Norman Rodney. "A Study of the Academic Needs of African Students at the University of Illinois." Unpublished Ed.D thesis, University of Illinois at Urbana-Champaign, 1974.

The identification of academic needs of African students at the University of Illinois is the concern of this study. Special services, materials, experiences, activities, and skills or areas of knowledge which could help promote the success of Africans while enrolled as students at the University of Illinois, and after returning to Africa, were defined as the needs. African students enrolled at the University of Illinois; the faculty members at the university with some African experience; and African returnees who returned to Africa after completing their studies at the University of Illinois, were surveyed during the study. The conclusions are that even though African students and returnees made up a homogenous group concerning their attitudes toward the items of "need," neither environmental orientation nor length of academic or professional experience was a factor which contributed to variability in the attitudes of Africans toward the items of "need." Respondent status group and academic orientation contributed to variability in the attitudes toward the items of need but the nature or the extent of African experience of faculty members was not a contributing factor to variability in the attitudes of faculty members toward the items of need. Some programs of study which African students pursued were found to be inapplicable to African situations but both students and faculty members were unaware of the available resources which could be utilized to make the studies more applicable. Even though African students had difficulty in adapting to the American system of class assignments they rejected the notion that they should be given "special" help. Recommendations are made for the planning of programs for African students and the revisions of the instruments for further study.

1445. Wilcox, Lee Owen. "The Prediction of Academic Success of Undergraduate Foreign Students." Unpublished Ph.D thesis, University of Minnesota, 1974.

Several measures of secondary school academic performance and test scores of verbal aptitude, mathematical aptitude, subject matter achievement, and English proficiency were studied individually and in combinations in order to predict the academic success of undergraduate foreign students. Eighty-four Vietnamese freshmen enrolled at several United States institutions, and 99 Hong Kong freshmen studying at the University of Wisconsin-Madison, were the subjects of this study. The relationship of secondary school performance to freshman grades was found to be about .50 in each sample. While the mathematical aptitude scores predicted freshman grades equally well and the combination of the two predictors increased the correlation with freshman grades by about .10, neither verbal aptitude nor English proficiency contributed to prediction. It was also found that achievement test scores were better predictors of freshman grades in the Hong Kong sample while first-semester grades were less predictable than second-semester grades. Prediction in the two samples was therefore comparable to prediction with U.S. students (R = .60) with regression equations relatively stable. Bayesian m-group regression analysis was considered an appropriate model for prediction research with foreign students.

## Articles

1446. Althen, Gary. "Should Foreign Students Face Double Standards?" National Association for Foreign Student Affairs Newsletter 30 (November, 1978): 25ff.

1447. Barnes, Leslie R. "The Negotiation of Grades as a Central Feature of an Educational Exchange Program." College and University 59 (Winter, 1984): 136-149.

1448. Barrientos, Ivan, and Frank W. Schufletowski. "The Questionable Foreign Student." School and Society 96 (April, 1968): 243-245.

1449. Beswick, D. G., and G. Lakshmana Rao. "Cultural Differences and Similarities in Academic Motivation: A Comparison of Indian and Australian Student Attitudes." Australian Journal of Education 20 (1976): 184-201.

1450. Bie, Karen Nossum. "Norwegian Students at British Universities-- Case Study of the Academic Performances of Foreign Students." Scandinavian Journal of Educational Research 20 (No. 1, 1976): 1-24.

This article is based on the author's doctoral dissertation concerning academic performance of the foreign students at 16 higher education (universities, universities of technology and polytechnics) in England, Scotland, and Wales.

Generalizations about foreign students' academic performance conclude that this group does worse than British students. The author compares foreign students' performances with those of British students in the 1950s and 1960s in the following fields: architecture, business administration, dentistry, engineering, and medicine.

It was found that Norwegian students had a lower failure rate than British, and their final examination results and the means in annual examinations compared favorably with their British counterparts. General statements about foreign students' performances are thus not confirmed by Norwegian students' performances. Language difficulties in the early period of study, social adjustment and possible deficiencies in the Norwegian school background do not seem to have seriously influenced Norwegian academic performance at British higher education institutions. The question of motivation as an explanation for high standard of achievement by the Norwegian students is also discussed. In this context the author points out that "the Norwegian students may have constituted a particular group" as special conditions existed in postwar Norway insofar as there was a shortage of educational facilities in certain fields within a highly developed country, and a great demand for qualified personnel in these same fields. The Norwegians may, therefore, have had particularly high achievement motives.

1451. Cieboter, Frank. "Factors Relating to the Performance of Foreign Graduate Students." Journal of Educational Research 62 (April, 1969): 360-365.

This study examines the interrelationship between the Graduate Record Examination (GRE) scores, grade-point averages (GPA), geographic area of origin, and major field of study for 218 foreign students enrolled in one of the graduate divisions of the University of Florida, and who had attended for at least two full semesters and whose GRE scores and GPA results were accessible. It was established that both GRE scores and GPA differed significantly within the foreign student group, on the basis of geographic area of origin and the major field. It was also found that the GRE could not be used as a predictor of GPA.

1452. Dembo, Miriam. "Pre-Screening of Foreign Students to Reduce Dropouts." College and University 40 (Winter, 1965): 140-144.

1453. Dudley-Evans, A., and J. Swates. "Study Modes and Students from the Middle East." In Study Modes and Academic Development of Overseas Students, edited by G. M. Greenall, and J. E. Price, pp. 91-103. London: British Council, 1980.

1454. Elting, Robert A., and Mary Butterfield. "Academic Performance of Cuban-Teacher Students at the University of Miami." College and University 44 (Spring, 1968): 263-267.

1455. Froehlich, Dieter, and Burkhard Schade. "Zur Frage der Ruckenanpassung von Studenten Aus Entwicklungslandern." Koelner Zeitschrift fur Soziologie und Sozial-Psychologie 18 (1966): 271-299.

1456. Hamalian, Arpi. "The Learning Experience of Nigerian and Bahamian Students in Montreal." CORE 3 (No. 1, 1979).

1457. Howes, R., Macfarlane Smith, and K. Shepherd. "A Study of the Validity of a Battery of Tests for Predicting the Success of Overseas Students Attending Institutions of Further Education." Vocational Aspect 29 (December, 1977): 119-125.

1458. Huxham, G. J., A. Lipton, and R. A. Cummins. "Student Test Type Preference and Its Relation to Personality and Achievement." Medical Education 10 (No. 1, 1976): 90-96.

1459. James, Kenneth. "Overseas Students' Listening Problems: An Inquiry." Spoken English 8 (September, 1975): 97-106.

1460. Katz, F. M., and C. N. Katz. "Appraisal of Students: Evaluations by Academics Visiting the United States." Journal of Educational Research 62 (January, 1969): 231-237.

1461. Keats, Daphne. "New Study Patterns." In Overseas Students in Australia, edited by S. Bochner, and P. Wicks, pp. 105-118. Auburn: New South Wales University Press, 1972.

1462. Maehr, Martin L. "Motivating Students of Diverse Sociocultural Backgrounds to Achieve." International Journal of Intercultural Relations 2 (Spring, 1978): 38-70.

> This paper addresses a problem of major importance to educators: the motivation of students of differing sociocultural backgrounds. While the analysis builds on the earlier work of McClelland, the focus is by no means confined to that perspective. Indeed, achievement motivation is essentially redefined and a more comprehensive analysis is attempted in which personality, situation, and other factors are all concerned. The central thrust of the article, is on what one can change about personality and situations to increase the achievement motivation of students. In this regard, various intervention studies are reviewed and evaluated, and new possibilities are suggested. There is a decided emphasis on the efficiency, practicality, and general appropriateness of concentrating on situations (or contextual) change rather than attempting to change enduring personality patterns.

1463. Matteson, H. R., and J. R. Hamann. "Satisfaction and Dissonance Between Professors' and Students' Value Orientations." College Student Journal 9 (September-October, 1975): 258-268.

1464. McAdam, Ken. "The Study Methods and Academic Results of Overseas Students." In Overseas Students in Australia, edited by S. Bochner, and P. Wicks, pp. 97-104. Auburn: New South Wales University Press, 1972.

> The primary goal of the foreign student is to pass his/her examinations and thereby obtain the academic qualification and credentials which will enable him/her to

obtain rewarding professional employment upon returning home. The author of this chapter discussed obstacles in the realization of this goal, mostly with respect to the fact that in many "problem cases" not only the foreign student's training but also his/her study methods are not appropriate for higher education studies in Australia. An empirical study was carried out by the author in 1968 with the first-year overseas students at Monash University. Two standardized study questionnaires were used: the Warren Study-Habits Inventory (WSHI) and the Brown-Holtzman Survey of Study-Habits and Attitudes (SSHA). Information obtained show that the foreign students, in general, are "achieving their academic goals, but that is all they are achieving." This goal is realized with drain on foreign students' personal resources and demands on their time.

The author postulates that foreign students would benefit considerably if they modified their pattern of study behavior, and used study methods more appropriate to the Australian context and better adapted to the particular demands of Australian tertiary educational institutions.

1465. "Objectifs et Succes des Etudes des Etudiants Etrangers en Republique Federale d'Allemagne." Bildung und Wissenschaft/ Education en Allemagne (No. 9, 1974): 138-140.

1466. Paraskevopoulos, J., and R. Dremuk. "Grading Patterns for Foreign Students." International Educational and Cultural Exchange 4 (Winter, 1969): 55-60.

1467. Putman, Ivan, Jr. "The Academic Performance of Foreign Students." Annals of the American Academy of Political and Social Sciences 335 (May, 1961): 41-53.

In this article on the academic performance of foreign students, Professor Putman indicates the basic problems concerning foreign students. They are: (1) the selection of students; (2) the academic ability of students, or the ability of the receiving institution to judge their educational levels; (3) the problem of English proficiency; (4) adaptability of the student to the environment; (5) the home institution's qualifications orientation to the United States and particularly to the school; (6) the academic performance of the students citing the Koenig study of 1953 in which it was found that 13% of foreign students received "superior grades, 35% were above average," etc. Putman also outlines the need to maintain standards of educational programs listing three major responsibilities of the institution to the foreign students: (1) that foreign students should be discouraged in every possible way from dealing with or going to substandard United States educational institutions; (2) that no foreign students should be admitted without determining from a formal application and records of previous studies if he was a superior student, etc. and every effort should be made to

provide    adequate    orientation,    counseling,    English
instruction and other means to help the foreign student
adjust, etc.

1468.    Saigh, Philip A.    "The Validity of the Lorge Thorndike Nonverbal
Battery as a Predictor of the Academic Achievement of Interna-
tional Students."    Educational and Psychological Measurement 41
(Winter, 1981):    1315-1318.

1469.    Smith, Macfarlane I.    "The Use of Diagnostic Tests for Assessing
the Abilities of Overseas Students Attending Institutions of
Further Education."    Vocational Aspect of Education 22 (Spring,
1970):    1-8, and 23 (Spring, 1971):    39-48.

1470.    Watt, J. C.    "Performance of Overseas Postgraduate Students:    A
Management Teacher's View."    In Study Modes and Academic
Development of Overseas Students, edited by G. M. Greenall, and
J. E. Price, pp. 38-43.    London:    British Council, 1980.

1471.    Wayman, Sally G.    "The International Student in the Academic
Library."    Journal of Academic Librarianship 9 (No. 6, 1984):
336-341.

1472.    Weiss, James M., and David Davis.    "Predicting Success in Psychiatric Training for Foreign Medical Graduates:    II.    Patterns in
Course."    Psychological Medicine 7 (No. 2, 1977):    311-316.

1473.    White, A. J., et al.    "Academic Factors Affecting the Scholastic
Performance of International Students."    College Student
Journal 17 (Fall, 1983):    268-272.

### Reportage

1475.    "China's Students Not as Well Prepared as Americans in Sciences,
Tests Indicate."    Chronicle of Higher Education 19 (February
21, 1980):    9.

## 21.    ATTITUDINAL AND BEHAVIORAL STUDIES

1476.    Achalu, Onuegbunam Emmanuel.    "Prevalence of Drug Use Among
Nigerian Students in Selected American Universities."    Unpublished Ph.D thesis, Southern Illinois University at Carbondale,
1982.

1477.    Alivand-Farsi, Iraj.    "Leadership Personality and Political
Culture in Iranian University Students in the U.S."
Unpublished  Ph.D  thesis,  United  States  International
University, 1980.

1478.  Amaran, Donatus.  "The Influence of Selected Factors on the Choice
       of Fields of Study by Nigerian Students in the United States."
       Unpublished Ph.D thesis, Ohio State University, 1976.

1479.  Athar, A. N.  "A Study of Career Motivations of Male Graduate
       Students from Five Selected Foreign Countries."  Unpublished
       Ed.D thesis, Indiana University, 1980.

1480.  Baer, Kenneth L.  African Students in the East and West:  1959-
       1966:  An Analysis of Experiences and Attitudes.  Syracuse,
       N.Y.:  Syracuse University, Program of Eastern African Studies,
       1970.

           This study analyzes the educational experiences and
       attitudes of 33 African students from 11 countries who
       studied in Russia and Eastern European countries and then
       moved to study in American colleges and universities
       between 1963 and 1965.  The most immediate purpose of the
       study was to evaluate the success or failure of a
       scholarship program for the Office of Education and
       Cultural Affairs, and relevant data cover the years from
       1959 until 1966.  The paper discusses a time when the
       politics of independence generated large scholarship
       programs and heated debate.  This study also adds a
       dimension to the understanding of the East as well as of
       the Americans.  The students were highly critical of the
       East while their images of the U.S.A. were not necessarily
       positive.  The paper takes up four major themes:  (1)
       program evaluation; (2) an aspect of African educational
       history; (3) an aspect of the Eastern and Western world's
       relationship with African students; (4) social and
       political criticism.

1481.  Baghban-Cichani, I.  "College Student Satisfaction: A Comparative
       Study of Selected Foreign and American Students at Iowa State
       University."  Unpublished Ph.D thesis, Iowa State University,
       1981.

1482.  Barnes, Carol Ruth.  "A Study of the Processes of Attitude Forma-
       tion and Change as Applied to Foreign Students."  Unpublished
       Ph.D thesis, University of Texas at Austin, 1975.

1483.  Barry, Jean.  "The Thai Students in the United States: A Study in
       Attitude    Change."    Unpublished    Ed.D    thesis,    Columbia
       University, 1966.

           Four aspects of the attitudes of Thai students namely,
       religious beliefs, occupational values, views on education
       and attitudes on courtship and family life, were examined
       in this study.  In March 1965 structured questionnaires
       were mailed to 1,214 Thai students.  At the end of June 911
       sets of answers, that is 84% of the questionnaires, were
       received, of which 880 found usable were processed.
       Geographically speaking, the group of respondents in the

survey was not representative of the whole population of Thailand since nearly three-fourths of them came either from Bangkok or from the rich rice lands surrounding the capital. Religious beliefs of the students were found to remain stable throughout their international experience on certain issues, but generally speaking the population of Thai students had moved away from the traditional religious concerns of Thailand towards a system of values which tended to be less religious, and more naturalistic and nationalistic. On occupational values, there was a gradual trend of the Thais to view the world of work and careers according to the American way of life. In the area of educational values among the trends that developed during those years of stay were a greater valuation of the academic aspect of education and a greater desire to pursue knowledge. Even though several differences were noted with respect to dating behavior, the Thai students' attitudes on family life seemed to remain stable throughout the years spent away from Thailand.

1484. Behringer, Gerhard. Untersuchung des Zusammenhangs Zwischen Interkulturellen Erfahrungen und Einstellung zur Internationalen Zusammenab reit am Beispe il des Auslandsstudiums in den U.S.A. Regensburg: Lehrstuhl Sozial-Psychologie, Universitat Regensburg, 1983.

1485. Boateng, Felix Agyako. "The Ghanaian Student in American Universities: Selected Attitudes and Perceptions." Unpublished Ph.D thesis, University of Southern California, 1977.

1486. Bower, Thomas James. "Effects of Short-Term Study Abroad on Student Attitudes." Unpublished Ph.D thesis, University of Colorado-Boulder, 1973.

1487. Central Research Services. Evaluation Study of Japanese Returned Fulbright Grantees. Tokyo: Central Research Services, 1958.

1488. Chang, Hwa-bao. "A Study of Some Attitudes of Chinese Students in the United States." Unpublished Ph.D thesis, University of Texas at Austin, 1972.

1489. Chang, Kai Yoen. "A Comparison of the Personal Development of American and Chinese College Students Within an Eriksonian Framework." Unpublished Ed.D thesis, University of Tennessee, 1979.

1490. Chang, Shu Yuan Hsieh. "The Views and Contributions of Chinese Students and Intellectuals in the United States." Unpublished Ph.D thesis, University of Utah, 1971.

1491. Colacicco, Mary Grace. "A Comparison of Item Responses on the MMPI by Selected American and Foreign Students." Unpublished Ph.D thesis, Purdue University, 1970.

1492. Dahhan, Omaymah. "A Study of the Factors Influencing Future Plans and Career Goals of Arab Ph.D Students in the United States." Unpublished Ph.D thesis, University of Texas at Austin, 1976.

1493. Dalton, Starrette. Foreign Student Perceptions of the United States. Bloomington, Indiana: Bureau of Educational Studies and Testing, Indiana University, 1972.

1494. Da Silva, Paulo Viera. "African and Latin American Graduate Student Assessment of Situations Related to Their Academic Life in the United States." Unpublished Ph.D thesis, University of Southern California, 1974.

1495. Davies, M. W. "Investigation-Participant Perception Value Overseas Study." Unpublished Ph.D thesis, University of Toledo, 1974.

1496. Davis, James L. Foreign Students Look at International House. New York: International House, 1965.

1497. Davis, James. "A Survey of Present and Former Foreign Students Regarding the Effects of Their Residence in the International House of New York." Unpublished Ph.D thesis, Columbia University, 1964.

1498. Demoze, Fisseha. "A Preliminary Survey of the Relationships of Foreign Students' Self-Concept and Personality Characteristics to their Region of Origin." Unpublished Ph.D thesis, Marquette University, 1976.

1499. Ekpe, C. P. "The Reactions of Foreign Students to Their Training in the United States." Unpublished Ph.D thesis, University of Pittsburgh, 1980.

1500. El-Sowygh, Hamad Ibn Zeid. "Performance of a Piagetian Test by Saudi Arabian Students in Colorado Colleges and Universities in Relation to Selected Sociodemographic and Academic Data." Unpublished Ph.D thesis, University of New Mexico, 1981.

1501. Erdogan, Irfan. "Television and Newspaper Uses and Gratifications of Foreign Graduate Students at the University of Pittsburgh: Some Correlates." Unpublished Ph.D thesis, University of Pittsburgh, 1977.

1502. Erickson, Douglass Eugene. "Differential Personality, Academic, and Biographical Characteristics of International Graduate Students at the University of N. Dakota." Unpublished Ed.D thesis, University of North Dakota, 1970.

1503. Etemadi, Ahmad. "Personality Traits and Personality Change as Influenced by Cultural and College Experiences of Iranian and American Students." Unpublished Ph.D thesis, Louisiana State University, 1977.

1504. Framhein, Gerhild, and Hansgert Peisert. Abiturienten und Auslandsstudium: Eine Untersuchung uber Motive und Bedingungen fur ein Auslandsstudium. Bonn: Bundestimister fur Bildung und Wissenschaft, 1977.

1505. Galiouridis, George. "A Perceptual Study of International Students Satisfaction at the University of Alabama." Unpublished Ph.D thesis, University of Alabama, 1980.

1506. Garside, Jayne. "A Cross-Cultural Comparison of Personality." Unpublished Ph.D thesis, Brigham Young University, 1966.

1507. Gazi-Tabatabie, Jaleh. "Aspirations and Realities of Future Educational Plans for Children of Iranian and American Students Attending Utah State University and the University of Utah." Unpublished Ed.D thesis, Utah State University, 1982.

1508. Geuer, Wolfgang, D. Breitenbach and R. Dadder. Psychische Probleme Auslandischer Studenten in der Bundesrepublik Deutschland. Bonn: Deutscher Akademischer Austauschdienst, 1983.

1509. Gleason, Thomas P. "Social Adjustment Patterns and Manifestations of World-Mindedness of Overseas-Experienced American Youth." Unpublished Ph.D thesis, Michigan State University, 1969.

1510. Goodman, Norman G. "The Institutionalization of Foreign Education and the Effects of the Charter: A Study of Malaysian Student Attitudes and Adjustment to Overseas Educational Opportunity." Unpublished Ph.D thesis, Stanford University, 1981.

1511. Goodwin, Crauford and Michael Nacht. Fondness and Frustration: The Impact of American Higher Education on Foreign Students with Special Reference to the Case of Brazil. New York: Institute of International Education, 1984.

1512. Goth, Barbara. Wie Lebt Man in der Bundesrepublik? Zum Deutschlandbild Auslandischer Gastwissenschaftler. Bonn-Bad Godesberg: Verlag Dr. Josef Raabe, 1977.

1513. Haile, Tesfa. "A Survey-Analysis on Attitudes of National and International College Students Toward Older People." Unpublished Ph.D thesis, University of Southern Mississippi, 1979.

1514. Heilpen, Florence Froelich. "A Case Study of the Effects of Visiting in American Homes on the Opinions of a Selected Group of Students from Abroad." Unpublished Ed.D thesis, Columbia University, 1965.

1515. Hlsaffar, Admed Abdullah. "A Survey of International Students' Opinions and Attitudes at the University of Tennessee, Knoxville." Unpublished Ed.D thesis, University of Tennessee, 1976.

1516.  Ibrahim, Saad Eddin Mohamed.  "Political Attitudes of an Emerging
       Elite:  A Case Study of the Arab Students in the United
       States."  Unpublished Ph.D thesis, University of Washington,
       1968.

            This is an attitudinal study based upon a
       questionnaire distributed to approximately 400 students
       from Arab countries studying in the United States.  The
       author attempted to determine the attitude of students in
       the following areas:  (1) nationalism; (2) democracy; (3)
       socialism, and (4) global alignment.
            The underlying assumption was that the individual's
       attitude toward such issues form a broad and coherently
       organized pattern, sometimes termed "ideology."  The
       findings held that "the consistency principle" was
       operative in less than 65% of the cases studied.

1517.  International Public Opinion Research.  Interviews with Six
       Brazilians Who Came to the United States under the
       International Exchange Program.  New York:  International
       Public Opinion Research, 1952.

1518.  International Public Opinion and Market Research.  Impressions of
       State Department Grants from Burma.  Bielefeld, Germany:
       International Public Opinion and Market Research, 1961.

1519.  International Public Opinion Research.  German Exchanges:  A Study
       in Attitude Change.  New York:  International Public Opinion
       Research, 1953.

1520.  Ismail, Mohamed Abdul-Rahman.  "A Cross-Cultural Study of Moral
       Judgements:  The Relationship Between American and Saudi
       Arabian University Students on the Defining Issues Test."
       Unpublished Ed.D thesis, Oklahoma State University, 1976.

1521.  Jaafar, Abdullah Sher Kawi.  "An Examination of the Assertive
       Behavior of Malay Students Enrolled in American Colleges and
       Universities Using Selected Variables."  Unpublished Ed.D
       thesis, Texas Southern University, 1982.

1522.  Javadi, Yadollah.  "The Effects of Cultural Values on Decision-
       Making Style:  A Cross-Cultural Comparative Study."
       Unpublished Ph.D thesis, George Peabody College for Teachers,
       1981.

1523.  Johnston, G. W.  "Perceptual Change of Culture and Belief System
       Among Selected University Age Mexican and Japanese Foreign
       Students in the U.S."  Unpublished Ph.D thesis, University of
       Arizona, 1982.

1524.  Karkia, Parvaneh.  "A Survey of Attitudes of Selected Iranian
       College Students Concerning English as a Foreign Language."
       Unpublished Ph.D thesis, University of Illinois at Urbana-
       Champaign, 1979.

The major purposes of this study were to determine whether there was a significant difference in attitudes of science and humanities students concerning their English as a Foreign Language (EFL) study and to discover if the students accepted the rationale for English study presented by Iranian EFL educators. Information and opinions for the study were secured directly from 314 Iranian college students--enrolled in EFL courses at Tehran University Language Center. The analysis of the data showed that the difference in science and humanities students was only in the degree of their satisfaction or dissatisfaction with the objectives and format of the EFL program. A desire for more explanation of grammar, more exercises in grammar and vocabulary and more focus on reading, listening, and speaking were popular with both groups. Even though there was general interest in the use of audio-visual materials and other enrichment activities, both groups were generally dissatisfied at the TULC. They showed little interest in learning about the culture of the English-speaking people and were not happy with the teachers and textbooks. The study makes several recommendations, including the tailoring of the EFL programs to meet the perceived needs of the students; revising the EFL curriculum to enable the Iranian science students to deal with deductive/inductive learning strategies and the provision of funds for the implementation of the recommendations.

1525. Kim, Hyung Tae. "Relationships Between Personal Characteristics of Korean Students in Pennsylvania and their Attitudes Toward the Christian Churches in America." Unpublished Ph.D thesis, University of Pittsburgh, 1966.

1526. Lee, Seok Jae. "The Analysis of Foreign Students' Attitudes Toward the United States at the University of Florida." Unpublished Ph.D thesis, University of Florida, 1982.

1527. Limpanich, A. Wisessuwan. "Perceptions of Foreign Students at University of Northern Colorado of their College Experiences." Unpublished Ed.D thesis, University of Northern Colorado, 1979.

1528. Liu, Chain-Kuo. "Factors Influencing the Attitude of International Students Toward America at Southern Illinois University at Carbondale." Unpublished Ph.D thesis, Southern Illinois University at Carbondale, 1977.

1529. Loomis, Charles P., and Edgar A. Schuler. Acculturation of Foreign Students in the United States. East Lansing: Social Research Service, Michigan State College, 1948.

1530. Lozada, Rhodelia Corazon Buenaventura. "Foreign Students at Purdue University: A Study of Selected Personal and Academic Characteristics in Relation to Current Experiences and Future Expectations." Unpublished Ph.D thesis, Purdue University, 1970.

1531.  Manunpichu, Kanchana.  "A Survey of Social Attitudes Among Thai Students in American Educational Institutions."  Unpublished Ph.D thesis, Colorado State College, 1964.

1532.  Marion, Paul Blaine, Jr.  "Relationships of Student Characteristics and Experiences with Attitude and Value Changes in a Program of Study Abroad."  Unpublished Ph.D thesis, University of Colorado-Boulder, 1974.

1533.  Marquardt, William F., ed.  The Foreign Student Speaks.  Seattle: University of Washington, 1958.

1534.  Maslog, Crispin Chio.  "Filipino and Indian Students' Images: Of Themselves, of Each Other and of the United States."  Unpublished Ph.D thesis, University of Minnesota, 1967.

1535.  Mastroianni, George Anthony.  "A Study of Attitudes Toward the United States Held by Former Participants in a United States' Educational Exchange Project in Radio and Television."  Unpublished Ph.D thesis, Syracuse University, 1971.

1536.  Meyerson, Dean Winston.  "College and University Goal Preferences of Brazilian Nationals Attending Higher Educational Institutions in the United States."  Unpublished Ph.D thesis, American University, 1980.

1537.  Miller, Jake Charles.  "African Students and the Racial Attitudes and Practices of Americans."  Unpublished Ph.D thesis, University of North Carolina, Chapel Hill, 1967.

1538.  Mosalai, Tayebeh Beigom.  "Perceived Importance of Maslow Needs By Foreign Graduate Students in Education at the University of Missouri."  Unpublished Ph.D thesis, University of Missouri-Columbia, 1980.

Using Maslow's hierarchy of human need as a theoretical basis, this study attempted to identify and compare perceived need importance of the foreign graduate students in education at the University of Missouri-Columbia. The sample consisted of 85 foreign students and of this number 73 or 85.8% responded. Five independent variables: sex, nationality, degree level, level of teaching experience, and years of teaching experience and five dependent variables: security, social, esteem, autonomy, and self-actualization (levels of need) were examined. The conclusions reached were that: (1) foreign graduate students in education did not differ with regard to the "perceived need importance" when grouped by sex, degree level, teaching experience level, and years of teaching experience; however, they did differ with regard to the "autonomy need" when the students were grouped on the basis of nationality. Except for the Arab students, who ranked autonomy first in importance, the ranking of perceived need importance was consistent with Maslow-Porter models for all groups of foreign graduate students. Replication of this study with different groups of foreign students and a larger sample size and an investigation into the perceived need satisfaction and need deficiency of foreign graduate students in education are recommended for further study.

1539. M'Tukudzi, Bonet. "International Students' Perceptions of the Environment at Southern Illinois University-Carbondale." Unpublished Ph.D thesis, Southern Illinois University at Carbondale, 1979.

1540. Nelson, Donald Theodore. "The Impact of Foreign Undergraduate Students Upon American Undergraduate Students." Unpublished Ph.D thesis, Indiana University, 1966.

This study is an investigation of the impact of foreign undergraduate students upon a group of American undergraduate students who had close association with them. This group was then compared with a control group of American undergradute students whose contact with foreign undergraduate students was minimal. Data for the study were obtained from personal data records, personality inventories, interview, and foreign student questionnaire. Analysis of the data, using the chi-square test, found significant differences between the American student groups on age and involvement in college activities. The only significant variable for both men and women was the religious variable. Specific new interests, a more accepting attitude and cross-cultural academic plans for the future were found among American students whose close friends were foreign students. Foreign students from Africa, Anglo-Caribbean America and South America were found to display more interest in cross-cultural interaction than the students from Asia and Oceania, Europe, and the Middle East.

1541. Nolan, Martin Edward. "Terminal Values After Foreign Education: A Survey of Students at Utah Universities." Unpublished Ph.D thesis, University of Utah, 1973.

1542. Opara-Nadi, Bernadette Ego. "The Relationship of Authoritarianism and Dogmatism to Cognitive Style Among American and Third World Foreign Students." Unpublished Ed.D thesis, Loyola University of Chicago, 1980.

1543. Pierce, Frank Nicholson. "Foreign Student Views and Attitudes Toward Advertising in the United States." Unpublished Ph.D thesis, University of Illinois, 1969.

1544. Quinn, Walter Albert, II. "A Study of Selected Sojourn Preferences and Priorities of Stanford University Foreign Students." Unpublished Ph.D thesis, Stanford University, 1975.

The general objectives of this study were: (1) presentation of basic factual information on the large population of foreign students for utilization by the appropriate university policy-makers; (2) examination of a series of hypotheses to determine if pronounced differences were observable among different groupings of Stanford foreign students, and (3) description of certain academic, social, and attitudinal values held by foreign students at Stanford to ascertain the relationships, if any, between Stanford and the changing or nonchanging of them. A six-page questionnaire was the major information-gathering technique. Of the 900 students who were given the questionnaires, over 500 responded. The study demonstrates that background information of foreign students coupled with their academic standing and years at Stanford could be important indices for successful adjustment at Stanford. Several results in the study include the finding that Canadians and Europeans were more similar to each other than they were to Middle Easterners and all of them were different from Latin Americans. The author emphasizes that no foreign student, regardless of the general background statistical probabilities for his success at Stanford, should be admitted without a specific and individually preplanned place for him.

1545. Rasheed, Mohammed Ahmed. "Saudi Students in the United States: A Study of their Perceptions of University Goals and Functions." Unpublished Ph.D thesis, University of Oklahoma, 1972.

1546. Restivo, Sal Philip. "Visiting Foreign Students at American Universities: A Study of the Third Culture of Science." Unpublished Ph.D thesis, Michigan State University, 1971.

1547. Royeen, Abdul Matin. "A Study in Perceptions and Attitudes of the Taiwanese and Indian Students Towards the U.S. and the American People During Their First Year of Study at the University of Cincinnati." Unpublished Ph.D thesis, University of Cincinnati, 1980.

1548. Russell, J. G. "Effects of Reference Group Identifications on the Relative Importance of Ascribed Problems by Iranian and Latin American Students at the University of Oklahoma." Unpublished Ph.D thesis, University of Oklahoma, 1965.

1549. Selltiz, Claire, et al. Attitudes and Social Relations of Foreign Students in the United States. Minneapolis: University of Minnesota Press, 1963.

1550. Shandiz, Mahmood Taali. "Factors Influencing Foreign Students' Adjustments and Attitudes in the Community of Oklahoma State University." Unpublished Ph.D thesis, Oklahoma State University, 1981.

1551.  Shna's, Z. A. "A Study of Foreign Student Attitudes Toward Females in the Professions." Unpublished Ph.D thesis, University of Missouri—Columbia, 1978.

1552.  Siriboonma, Umporn. "An Analysis of Student Satisfaction as Perceived by Foreign Students at Iowa State University." Unpublished Ph.D thesis, Iowa State University, 1978.

This is a study of the relationships between foreign student satisfaction and nine demographic variables (sex, classification, age, region, source of support, curriculum, marital status, type of residence, and length of stay) as measured by the College Student Satisfaction Questionnaire (CSSQ) Form C. In the winter of 1978, 500 randomly selected foreign students enrolled at Iowa State University were asked to complete the CSSQ. Out of the 500 questionnaires, 261 or 52.20% returned were found usable and processed. Significant differences were found between foreign student satisfaction and certain demographic variables. Classification, age, marital status, and type of residence were found related to students' perceived satisfaction with working conditions, compensation, quality of education, recognition, and overall college experience. While sex differences seemed to be related only to satisfaction with compensation, and region was related only to satisfaction with social life, it was found that the combined effects of classification and age were related to students' reported levels of satisfaction with compensation, recognition, and overall college experience. It is suggested that source of support, curriculum, and length of stay be further investigated so as to determine if any or all of them influence foreign students' levels of satisfaction since the CSSQ measurement did not show any significant effect on students' levels of satisfaction of those variables.

1553.  Sofola, Johnson Adeyemi. "American-Processed Nigerians: A Study of the Adjustment and Attitudes of the Nigerian Students in the United States of America." Unpublished Ph.D thesis, American University, 1967.

1554.  Stauffer, Mildred Louise James. "The Impact of Study Abroad Experience on Prospective Teachers." Unpublished Ph.D thesis, Ohio State University, 1973.

1555.  Tajfel, Henri, and John L. Dawson. Disappointed Guests: Essays by African, Asian, and West Indian Students. New York: Oxford University Press, 1965.

1556.  Tinpangka, Banlue. "The Attitudes of American and Foreign Graduate Students at the University of Iowa Toward the Graduate Student Academic Milieu." Unpublished Ph.D thesis, University of Iowa, 1979.

The attitudes of American and foreign graduate students at the University of Iowa toward the graduate student academic milieu were compared in this study. In the Spring semester of 1979, 100 randomly selected American graduate students and 100 foreign graduate students selected in the same manner were asked to complete survey questionnaires based upon the semantic differential technique. A 70% and 71% usable return were obtained from the American and foreign students respectively. Using t-tests for computation of the data, the means for both the American students and the foreign students were found to be positive. While the study identifies several significant differences between American graduate students and foreign graduate students, the general conclusion was that both American and the foreign students were sufficiently grounded in the working of the graduate student academic milieu. Two areas for further examination are recommended: (1) In-depth studies of the eight concepts on which the American students and foreign students differed significantly, and (2) studies of foreign students' attitudes toward the graduate student academic milieu at different stages of their graduate student careers.

1557. Udeinya, Chukwunweolu Simon. "Psychological Differentiation of Nigerian Undergraduate Students in the U.S." Unpublished Ph.D thesis, University of Pittsburgh, 1980.

1558. United States Information Agency, Office of Research. U.S. Exchange Programs with Greece: Reactions of Participants. Washington, D.C.: U.S. Information Agency, 1972.

1559. Vaziri-Kashani, Nahid. "Effects of Study in the United States on the Values of Iranian Teacher Education Students." Unpublished Ph.D thesis, George Peabody College for Teachers of Vanderbilt University, 1980.

## Articles

1560. Aich, Prodosh. "Soziale Determinanten der Politischen Einstellung der Afrikanischen und Asiatischen Studenten in Deutschsprachigen Landern." Koelner Zeitschrift fur Soziologie und Social-Psychologie 18 (1966): 482-515.

The article discusses formation and changes in the political attitudes of African and Asian foreign students in Western European higher education institutions. The author points out that if in general foreign students consider study abroad to be an important factor in their professional and social advancement, for industrialized countries motives to promote enrollment of foreign students in their higher education are often of economic and political nature.

Economic motivation is based on hope that after foreign students return to their respective home-countries, they will be more open towards trade and industrial links with their host-countries.

Political motivations are less easy to formulate, especially after some negative experience (in the 1950s and 1960s) with students who, after their studies in the Western countries, turned out to be ideologically against Western societies. Another political reason is to counter-balance efforts made by socialist and communist countries to recruit and train in their universities, future favorable African and Asian intellectual and political elite.

In this context formation of political attitudes among foreign students cannot be viewed as irrelevant. The author points out that difficulties in the socialization processes especially in the first years of study abroad are the main obstacles in the formation of "sympathetic" political attitudes especially among African and Asian foreign students studying in Western European universities.

The socialization process is slowed down by social, cultural, as well as financial problems, with which many students have to cope. For example, the majority of these students come from middle- or upper-middle classes of their own societies, thus they enjoy relatively better status and material position than the rest of the society. This situation very often changes upon the student's arrival in the host-country and often results in the radicalization of the political, ethnic, cultural, and racial views of the student.

The empirical base for the author's view is a survey carried out among 709 students from 55 African and Asian countries studying in eight different academic centers in Austria, the Federal Republic of Germany, and Switzerland (Aachen, Berlin, Bonn, Gottingen, Cologne, Munich, Vienna, and Zurich).

Findings (in the form of correlation tables) are presented at the end of the article.

One of the author's finding is that at the end of the studies (lasting 4-5 years) "sympathetic attitudes" toward the "Western Bloc," increased among the surveyed students. At the same time, there was a rapid decline in such attitudes towards the "Eastern Bloc," as well as a decline in political interest regarding this group of countries and their respective ideologies.

1561. Allen, Donald E., and Ibtihaj S. Arafat. "Procreative Family Attitudes of American and Foreign Students." International Journal of Comparative Sociology 12 (June, 1971): 134-139.

1562. Amir, Yehuda, and Chana Garti. "Situational and Personal Influence on Attitude Change Following Ethnic Contact." International Journal of Intercultural Relations 1 (Summer, 1977): 58-75.

The study undertook to examine the validity in Israel of several conclusions reached by investigations in the U.S. on the effect of intergroup contact on change in ethnic attitudes, as well as to extend "contact" research to topics which heretofore have received only scant attention. There were 100 subjects: 12-year-old Israeli girls of different ethnic background, participating in a summer camp. Results indicated that: (1) as a result of contact, a positive change in attitude of the high-status towards the low-status group occurred with regard to people and activities that were both related and not related to contact situations; (2) only subjects without previous ethnic contact showed changes; (3) enjoyment of the contact situation was related to attitude change, while (4) authoritarianism was not related to attitude change.

1563. Arubayi, Eric A. "Perceptions of Problems Identified by Nigerian Students in American Higher Institutions: A Comparative Analysis." College Student Journal 15 (Summer, 1981): 116-120.

1564. Bailey, K. "Foreign Teaching Assistants at U.S. Universities: Problems in Interaction and Communication." TESOL Quarterly 17 (June, 1983): 308-310.

1565. Bailyn, Lotte, and H. C. Kelman. "The Effects of a Year's Experience in America on the Self Image of Scandinavians: A Preliminary Analysis of Reactions to a New Environment." Journal of Social Issues 8 (No. 1, 1962): 30-40.

The study on which this paper is based concerns the effects of a year's experience in America on the self-image of Scandinavian visitors. It deals particularly with the process by which a change in a person's image comes about when he is placed in a new environment, or conversely, the process by which the person's existing image maintains itself in the face of new experiences. The central purpose of the study is to identify and analyze some of these distinct patterns, and to relate them to theoretical framework for the study of change. The sample consists of three groups of Danes, Norwegians, and Swedes visiting the U.S. for the first time in 1958. Three components of self-imagery—those elements shaped by profession, nationality, and by the structure of one's personal relations—are specified for investigations of their reactions. The paper discusses patterns of reaction to the American experience by identifying change or maintenance in self-image, and classifying the adjustment process into internal structure and social anchorage of the social image.

1566. Bardis, P. D. "Attitudes Toward Dating Among Foreign Students in America." Marriage and Family Living 18 (November, 1956): 339-344.

1567. Basu, A. K., and R. G. Ames. "Cross-Cultural Contact and Attitude Formation." Sociology and Social Research 55 (October, 1970): 5-16.

This study tests the hypotheses that the formation of attitudes positive to the United States by foreign students in the United States is related: (1) positively to the degree of their contact with the United States prior to and after their arrival; (2) inversely related to the degree of their alienation, and (3) inversely related to the degree of their authoritarianism. The interview and questionnaire data for the study were obtained in 1967 from 562 students, mostly unmarried males and majoring in some branch of engineering, from India studying in universities and colleges in the Los Angeles metropolitan area. Prior contact was not found to be statistically related to the formation of positive attitudes toward the United States while after-arrival contact, alienation, and authoritarianism were. It is concluded that the formation of attitudes in a cross-cultural milieu is a complex syndrome in which reference groups, selective processes, and supportive interpersonal relations are involved.

1568. Baty, Roger M., and Eugene Gold. "Cross-Cultural Homestays: An Analysis of College Students' Responses After Living in an Unfamiliar Culture." International Journal of Intercultural Relations 1 (Spring, 1977): 61-76.

The purpose of this exploratory study was to investigate the effects of the Johnston College cross-cultural homestay program upon student attitudes and health. During the four years of the program, 59 students lived for a period of one month in unfamiliar cultures in the Southwest and Mexico. Subjects for this study were 45 undergraduate students with a median age of 19 who came from relatively affluent family backgrounds. A one-group pretest/posttest design was used, employing five instruments. Participating students resembled, in most respect, the Johnston College students. It was concluded that the experience was more unsettling for the men students than it was for the women students. Future research was recommended to determine the extent to which these are set differences in cross-cultural adaption.

1569. Beals, R. L. "Mexican Student Views the United States." Annals of the American Academy of Political and Social Science 295 (September, 1954): 108-115.

1570. Becker, Tamar. "Cultural Patterns and Nationalistic Commitment Among Foreign Students in the United States." Sociology and Social Research 55 (July, 1971): 467-481.

Observers of foreign scholars and students in the United States have found some positive effects of their

American sojourn on the individuals involved as well as on
their host- and home-societies.  The main issue in this
article concerns the changes in the foreigner's attachment
to his home country that are associated with a prolonged
study abroad.  The three patterns which the article uses
are:  (1) commitment to the home-country's cultural values;
(2) commitment to the "role of the national," and (3)
commitment to "the sacredness of the state."  Three
hypotheses are proposed, namely:  commitment to the home
country's cultural values is the least vulnerable to
erosion through prolonged sojourn; commitment to "the role
of the national" and to the "sacredness of the state" are
highly vulnerable and tend to give way to an individual-
centered ideology; the individual is pushed in the direction of general political disengagement, a state of dual
detachment from both home and host societies.  The article
is based on a random sample of foreign students representing seven nationality groups at UCLA during the 1967-68
academic year.  The initial interview on which the discussion is based included 187 students--23 Indians, 23
Iranians, 27 Israelis, 24 Japanese, 17 Mexicans, 16
Scandinavians--the 57 black Africans from various countries
south of the Sahara excluded in the discussion are dealt
with in a separate paper:  "Black Africans and Black
Americans on an American Campus:  The African View," by the
same author.

Among models of attachment to the national state it
was found that:  commitment to national cultural values is
least vulnerable to erosion during prolonged stay abroad;
commitment to the "role of national" state is highly
vulnerable, and sentimental attachment to the home-state
and instrumental attachment to the host-state tend to
produce ideological disengagement from both.  These
findings, if substantiated by further research, raise new
questions concerning political socialization from the point
of view of both the national state and the individual
long-term sojourner.

1571.  Becker, T.  "Patterns of Attitudinal Changes Among Foreign
Students."  American Journal of Sociology 73 (January, 1968):
431-442.

This is a study to verify, on the basis of a sample
from one university, UCLA, the u-curve proposition.
Basically the author studied a sample of 27 Indians, 25
Israelis, and 25 Europeans, on the assumption that they all
represented underdeveloped, semi-developed and higher
developed countries respectively.  The findings were that
the u-curve is differentially applicable, depending upon
whether the students come from underdeveloped countries or
developed countries.

The author found, for example, "extreme polarization
in the feelings of the Indian students to the United States
on the one hand, and the home country on the other."

The basic conclusion however, is that even given the relatively small sample, the u-curve proposition is not necessarily applicable to representatives of "underdeveloped countries both on theoretical and empirical grounds." That the Israelis and the Europeans are in fact, experiencing the u-curve more than do Third World students, or at least that is the case found with the Indian students in the sample.

1572. Berger, L., J. Leibly, and B. Meunier. "An Attitude Survey of College Freshmen and Seniors: Preference Toward Seven Nationalities." Psychological Reports 33 (December, 1973): 837-838.

1573. Bhatnagar, J. K. "The Values and Attitudes of Some Indian and British Students." Race 9 (July, 1967): 27-35.

1574. Bjerstedt, Ake. "Informational and Non-Informational Determinants of Nationality Stereotypes." Journal of Social Issues 8 (No. 1, 1962): 24-29.

1575. Blood, R. O., and S. O. Nicholson. "Attitudes of American Men and Women Students Toward International Dating." Marriage and Family Living 24 (February, 1962): 35-41.

1576. Bochner, S., B. M. McLeod, and A. Lin. "Friendship Patterns of Overseas Students: A Functional Model." International Journal of Psychology 12 (No. 4, 1977): 177-294.

The respondents of this study were 30 foreign students at the University of Hawaii (six each from Japan, Korea, the Philippines, Taiwan, and Thailand), and six host national (American) students, balanced for sex. The subjects identified their best friends, and the five people with whom they spend most of the time. The subjects were then presented with a list of 15 activities, and identified a preferred companion for each of the situations. The data were used to test a functional model of the academic sojourn, which predicts that foreign students will belong to three social networks, in descending order of salience: (a) a conational network whose function is to affirm and express the culture of origin; (b) a network with host nationals, whose function is the instrumental facilitation of academic and professional aspirations, and (c) a multinational network, whose main function is recreational. The results confirmed the existence, predicted differential function, and salience hierarchy of these three social networks, and reconciled previous conflicting reports regarding the social relations of foreign students.

1577. Bochner, S., and F. E. Orr. "Race and Academic Status as Determinants of Friendship Formation: A Field Study." International Journal of Psychology 14 (No. 1, 1979): 37-46.

1578.  Brady, M. W.  "African View of an American Experience."  _Interna-_
       _tional Educational and Cultural Exchange_ 12 (Fall, 1976):
       24-28.

1579.  Bulhan, Hussein A.  "Dynamics of Cultural In-betweenity:    An
       Empirical Study."  _International Journal of Psychology_ 15 (No.
       2, 1980): 105-121.

           The Dialectical Theory of Cultural In-Betweenity
       proposes three main identification patterns among the black
       intelligentsia:  (1) capitulation to the dominant culture;
       (2) revitalization of the indigenous culture, and (3)
       radicalization of both so as to arrive at a new and higher
       synthesis.  Three scales corresponding to the identifica-
       tion patterns were constructed and a comparative study was
       conducted on two college samples.  One group consisted of
       45 Somali students being trained in the U.S.  The other
       group consisted of 57 Somali students being trained in
       Somalia.  Specific hypotheses comparing the two groups were
       tested and mostly confirmed by means of various psychologi-
       cal instruments.
           Investigation into the component features of each
       identification pattern led to further refinement of the
       theory.  Factor analytic explorations suggested the
       prevalence of distinct ethos, group reference, and
       self-image within each orientation.  The Dialectic Theory
       of Cultural In-Betweenity and the empirical findings are
       then discussed within the broad historical framework of
       colonialism and racism.

1580.  Bulhan, Hussein A.  "Reactive Identification, Alienation, and
       Locus of Control Among Somali Students."  _Journal of Social_
       _Psychology_ 104 (February, 1978): 69-80.

           The author studied 45 Somali students by conducting
       in-depth interviews with the students, who were attending a
       college in the northeast United States.  All students in
       the sample are male.
           The Theory of Reactive Identification formulates three
       reactions of Western-educated Africans to the Euro-American
       world:  (a) "Moving Toward"; (b) "Moving Away"; and (c)
       "Moving Against" identifications.  Three scales corres-
       ponding to these patterns of identification were construct-
       ed and specific hypotheses tested by means of multiple
       assessments involving 45 Somali students in the United
       States.  The results generally followed the predicted
       pattern.
           "Moving Toward" was not found to be the predominant
       course of identification.  Moving Toward scores were
       significantly associated with scores on alienation and
       external control but also with activities and attitudes
       antagonistic to Somali Nationalist, Pan-Africanist, Black
       Nationalist, or Socialist ideology.  Exactly the opposite
       trend was obtained from Moving Against scores.  Moving Away

was, however, characterized only by heightened <u>racial</u> awareness.

The findings were based upon the theory of reactive identification.

1581. Brown, Cardle, et al. "Reasoning about Implication: A Comparison of Malaysian and Australian Subjects [University Students]." <u>Journal of Cross-Cultural Psychology</u> 11 (December, 1980): 395–410.

1582. Chang, Hwa-Bao. "Attitudes of Chinese Students in the United States." <u>Sociology and Social Research</u> 58 (October, 1973): 66–77.

The most significant determinants of foreign student's attitude toward the host-country include, as previous studies suggest: the national status of his home-country, the degree of his contact with Americans, the frustration he encounters during the sojourn, the length of time he has been in the United States, and his authoritarianism.

This study of Chinese students was intended to investigate the life situation of Chinese students in the United States and their attitudes toward the United States, as well as to test the hypotheses developed by earlier studies. The study involved a sample of 250 Chinese students, 40% selected from Austin, Texas; 43% from Los Angeles, California; and the remaining 17% were almost evenly distributed among New York City, Seattle, Washington, and Urbana, Illinois. The sex ratio was approximately two males to each female. The median age was 28, ranging from 18 to the 50s. A majority of the students came from middle and upper socioeconomic strata. The study found Chinese student attitudes toward the United States positively associated with contact with Americans but negatively associated with authoritarianism. A U-curve hypothesis with respect to attitude change through time was partially supported. No association was established between a Chinese student's attitude and the perceived national status of his home-country or his degree of frustration.

1583. Chunnual, N., and A. J. Marsella. "Convergent and Discriminant Validation of a Traditionalism Modernism Attitude Questionnaire for Thai Exchange Students." <u>Journal of Social Psychology</u> 96 (No. 1, 1975): 21–26.

1584. Clifton, Rodney A. "The Effects of Students' Ethnicity and Sex on the Expectations of Teachers." <u>Interchange</u> 12 (1981–1982): 31–38.

1585. Coelho, George V. "Personal Growth and Educational Development Through Working and Studying Abroad." <u>Journal of Social Issues</u> 8 (No. 1, 1962): 55–87.

This essay first attempts to define the range and salience of the valued outcomes underlying student exchange programs. Next it illustrates how certain dependent variables are selected for treatment as outcomes of the cross-cultural educational experience. The author proposes that a new approach in research is needed to clarify short-term development patterns of competence in the sojourn so that the organization of attitude and behavior changes over time in a specific direction can be related to significant preparatory experiences in individuals. The author indicates how practitioners can formulate the major goals of student exchange and how social science can contribute toward an empirical clarification of the outcomes and processes of cross-cultural education in the light of these goals.

1586. Consalvi, Conrad. "Some Cross- and Intracultural Comparisons of Expressed Values of Arab and American College Students." Journal of Cross-Cultural Psychology 2 (March, 1971): 95-107.

In this study comparisons of expressed values were made between Arab and American university students and between groups within the Arab sample. The American sample comprised 128 students between the ages of 18 and 37, with a median age of 20.5. All were Christians, primarily Protestant and there were equal numbers of males and females. The Arab sample was made up of 200 students between the ages of 17 and 37 with median age of 20.1. There were 50 each of Moslem males, Moslem females, Christian males and Christian females, the nationality composition being: Lebanese, 44%; Jordan, 16.5%; Syrian, 14.5%; Palestinian, 10%; North African and Arabian, 15%. The expressed values of the students were sampled by means of ratings of 55 statements representing situations commonly considered to involve morality. The findings reflected significant differences between the Arab and American median ratings on 21 of the 55 items. The ratings in 19 instances by the Arab students were more severe, while large differences occurred in unexpected areas such as gambling and physical punishment of children. Overall, the expressed values of the Eastern and Western students were similar, both in terms of general level of severity and the rankings of the situations presented. Few significant differences were also produced in the intra-Arab comparisons, Moslem-Christian and male-female. A systematic interpretation of the differences obtained between Moslems and Christians was not evident, while the males and females differed primarily on questions involving sexual behavior. It is suggested that even if the Arab sample is biased and does not represent Arabs in general, it probably does approximate that segment of the Arab population which is educated and has been exposed to Western culture.

1587. Desai, Arvindrai. "Aspirations and Value Preferences of Rural Urban and Overseas Students in Making Occupational Decisions." Indian Journal of Psychology (March, 1974): 39-46.

1588. Deutsch, Stephen E. "Impact of Cross-Cultural Relations on the Campus." Sociology and Social Research 53 (January, 1969): 137-146.

1589. Donahue, F. "International Student: His Sex Roles." Clearing House 45 (September, 1970): 51-55.

1590. Ekanem, E. I. "African Students and Their Attitudes Toward Black Consciousness in the United States." Journal of Afro-American Issues 2 (February, 1974): 1-10.

1591. Epstein, Helen. "Overseas Students in Israel: Problems and Possibilities." Midstream 16 (February, 1970): 3-16.

Based upon a 1970 study of the attitudes after the 1976 Arab-Israeli war, the author is concerned with the over 6,000 foreign students studying in Israel. There is a distinct difference between the attitudes and experiences compared to Israeli students. Israeli students are found to be essentially older, less committed to the university milieu, married, and having out-of-school responsibilities, such as employment and service in the military. In contrast, the foreign students, particularly students drawn from the United States, Eastern Europe, and South America, tend to cluster in their own student ghettos within the university community. The emphasis of the study is the attitudes of foreign students attending a Hebrew university primarily. A contrast is drawn between the Israeli attitude of sense of community, the concept of group allegiance which underscores the Israeli students relationships to the university.

The Israeli students move in a group through elementary school through college and military service and tend to stay within their communal grouping, whereas the foreign students tend to affect extravagances that are not typical of the Israeli experience. Israeli students tend to be much less oriented toward challenges in the academic environment.

The author found that there was a great deal of emphasis on sexual activities on the part of American and South African students and their expectation level of Israeli women was quite different than the reality. American and other students are somewhat disenchanted with the curricular offerings and the nature of the relationship between the German-dominated university concept in Israel and the more free-wheeling discussions that normally take place in an American university. In addition, the presence of foreign students, particularly Americans, has caused the Hebrew University, at least, to tighten up its administrative procedures.

Overall, apparently foreign students in Israel who are Jewish in religious preference tend not to have any difficulty in identifying with Israel and feel comfortable in the country, but do not feel comfortable with the Israeli students, and thereby the foreign students self-segregate themselves from the Israeli students, or more accurately perhaps, both groups tend to segregate themselves from each other.

1592. Farah, T. E. "Group Affiliations of University [Foreign Arab] Students in the Arab Middle East [Kuwait]." Journal of Social Psychology 106 (December, 1978): 161-165.

1593. Farrahi-Zadeh, Ali, and William F. Eichman. "The Impact of Socio-Cultural Factors on Middle Eastern Students in the U.S." International Educational and Cultural Exchange 5 (Winter, 1970): 82-94.

1594. Forston, R. F., and C. U. Larson. "Dynamics of Space: An Experimental Study in Proxemic Behavior Among Latin Americans and North Americans." Journal of Communication 18 (June, 1968): 109-116.

1595. Galtung, J. E. "The Impact of Study Abroad: A Three-by-Three Nation Study of Cross-Cultural Contact." Journal of Peace Research 3 (1965): 258-275.

The article reports some results from a UNESCO sponsored study that involved students in three countries, the UAR, India, and Iran, who had returned to their home-countries after two years or more of study in the German Federal Republic, the United Kingdom, and the USA. These students were interviewed, and they reported varying degrees of adjustments to their host-countries. In general, the Indian students reported fewer changes than the other two student groups, apparently choosing social coexistence rather than conformity to a foreign culture. This finding cannot be substantiated satisfactorily by differences between the samples, or by the Indian students' possibility of contact with fellow nationals. It is suggested that such factors as training in cultural pluralism, ideologies that regulate degrees of acculturation, cultural distance, the image of the home-country abroad, and its rank in the international system are relevant for the students in their adjustment and degrees of acceptance of the foreign culture.

1596. Gezi, Khalil. "Arab Students' Perceptions of American Students." Sociology and Social Research 45 (No. 4, 1961): 47-57.

1597. Glaser, William A., and G. Christopher Habers. "The Decision to Study Abroad." In The Brain Drain: Emigration and Return, edited by William A. Glaser, and G. Christopher Habers, pp. 175-203. Oxford: Pergamon Press, 1978.

1598.   Greenblot, Cathy.   "Foreign Students in the United States:   A
        Study of Attitudes and Orientation."   Sociological Focus 4
        (Spring, 1971):   17-35.

           This is a report of a study of students from four
        developing countries: Chile, Colombia, Greece, and Turkey,
        who were enrolled in colleges and universities in New York
        City.  Its purpose was to discover the relationship between
        their attitudes toward modernization of their own countries
        and their attitudes toward the U.S.   The students were
        classified as "Constrictors," or conservative in their
        orientation toward modernization; "Adjustors," or those who
        tended to accept the course of modernization as it is
        occurring, or "Ideologists," or those who desired changes
        that were different or more rapid in their home countries.
        Hypotheses were developed and tested concerning the differ-
        ential attitudes the three types would hold toward the
        United States.   Findings: In each national group the
        direction of difference between perception and desire is as
        expected.   Constrictors manifest the least disparity
        between what they see taking place and what they would like
        to see, and Ideologists manifest the greater disparity.
        The typology of orientation to modernization is both valid
        and useful in predicting the nature of attitudinal change
        that occurs when students from developing countries come to
        the U.S.   Presumably these attitude changes will also
        affect the adjustment of the student to his or her return
        to the home-country.

1599.   Hamid, P. N.   "Orientation of Authority Versus Independence of
        Thought in Malaya and New Zealand Students."   Journal of Social
        Psychology 108 (August, 1979):   269-270.

1600.   Helms, J. E., and T. W. Giorgis.   "A Comparison of the Locus of
        Control and Anxiety Level of African, Black American, and White
        American College Students."   Journal of College Student
        Personnel 21 (November, 1980):   503-509.

1601.   Hensley, T. R., and D. K. Sell.   "Study Abroad Program:   An
        Examination of Impacts on Student Attitudes."   Teaching
        Political Science 6 (July, 1979):   387-411.

           This is a study of the impact of the nationally
        recruited Kent State University Geneva semester program for
        undergraduate students.   Students for this program are
        selected through application to Kent State University from
        the United States.
           Specifically the study deals with attitude change on
        the part of American students going to study in Geneva.
        The study was conducted in 1977 with 52 students in Geneva,
        Switzerland.   The primary design of the questionnaire was
        to measure students' attitudes toward world-mindedness,
        student support for the United Nations, student self-
        esteem, and student tolerance for ambiguity.

In the comparison of world-mindedness attitudes before and after the semester, the students, before they went to Geneva, scored 46% on world-mindedness and after the experience it dropped by 6% to 40%. In terms of the student attitudes toward the United Nations, students' support before Geneva was 27% and after the experience it dropped 5 percentage points to 22%, and moderate or low support for the United Nations, before was 29% and afterward 32%.

As the authors indicate, "familiarity may not breed contempt but our data suggest that these interactions with the UN bureaucrats do not enhance one's view of the organization (p. 401)." The most significant finding was that the students' self-esteem was enhanced by the experience in the Geneva program. However, in terms of international impact on students' attitudes, it would "appear then, that some of the hopes of the promoters of overseas educational programs had not been realized and claims about the potentiality of these programs need to be given some careful scrutiny." (p. 409)

1602. Herr, Edwin, and Gilbert Moore. "English and American Student Expectations of College: Some Comparisons." NASPA Journal 7 (July, 1969): 35-39.

1603. Hull, W. Frank, and Walter Lemke, Jr. "The Assessment of Off-Campus Higher Education--The Effects of Study Abroad." International Review of Education 21 (1975): 195-206.

After acknowledging the general ignorance concerning the changes which occur in American undergraduates who study off campus, either domestically or internationally, the authors describe various studies which have attempted to assess off-campus educational experiences. These research efforts may be categorized in two ways: (1) those that used existing standardized instruments, and (2) those that used locally designed instruments. Yet both kinds of studies are found wanting. A new instrument, currently being tested, "The Individual Opinion Inventory." is designed to locate affective levels of perceptual change in those American undergraduates studying off campus, either in the U.S. or abroad.

1604. Ibrahim, Farah I. "A Survey of International Students' Perceptions of Male/Female Relationships in the United States." In International Women Students: Perspectives for the 80s. Report of the International Women Student Conference (Boston, Mass., August 1981), edited by Leslie Rowe, and Stephen Sjoberg, pp. 60-66. Washington, D.C.: National Association for Foreign Student Affairs, 1981.

1605. Ibrahim, S. E. M. "Interaction, Perception, and Attitudes of Arab Students Toward Americans." Sociology and Social Research 55 (October, 1970): 29-46.

This article provides an analysis of a case of cross-cultural interaction and tests the hypotheses that: (1) interaction between members of different cultures (or nationalities) results in more favorable attitudes; (2) perceiving an out-group as having a favorable attitude toward the in-group results in a favorable attitude toward this out-group by members of the in-group; (3) interaction between members of different cultures (or nationalities) results in mutually favorable perception. Data for the study were collected from Arab students in the United States during the early part of 1967. Out of 6,449 names in a master list, a random sample of 625 names was drawn and questionnaires were mailed to them. The questionnaire returns totaled 414, or 66.2% of the sample. The Likert method of scaling was used to construct the interaction, attitude and perception scales. The survey revealed that the interaction between Arab students and Americans seems to be moderate. This interaction is associated with sex, marital status, academic status, length of residence in the United States and Canada. The younger unmarried undergraduate Arab students tend to interact with Americans more. On the attitudes of Arab students toward Americans, the Arab students seem to have generally favorable attitudes toward the American people. More than one-third of the students (37%) considered Americans' attitude toward the Arabs as negative or unfavorable while less than one-third (32%) perceived Americans' attitudes as favorable.

1606.  Johnson, Dixon C. "Asian Alumni Look Back on Their American Experiences." International Educational and Cultural Exchange 6 (Summer, 1970): 77–81.

1607.  Kelman, H. C. "Changing Attitudes Through International Activities." Journal of Social Issues 18 (1962): 68–87.

1608.  Kelman, Herbert C., and Lotte Bailyn. "Effects of Cross-Cultural Experience on National Images: A Study of Scandinavian Students in America." Journal of Conflict Resolution 6 (December, 1962): 319–334.

1609.  Kinch, J. W. "Experiments on Factors Related to Self-Concept Change." Journal of Social Psychology 74 (1968): 251–258.

1610.  Kumagai, Fumie. "The Effects of Cross-Cultural Education on Attitudes and Personality of Japanese Students." Sociology of Education 50 (January, 1977): 40–47.

This is a longitudinal study of the effects of cross-cultural education on attitudes and personality in a sample of 104 Japanese male graduate students starting before their sojourn in the United States and continuing until after their return to Japan. There was a steady increase in favorability toward America and in interaction with

Americans. Cross-lagged correlations suggest that interaction with Americans influences favorability toward
America more than favorability toward America influences
interaction with Americans.

Japanese students' favorability toward Japan stayed
constant throughout the study, and measures of personality
traits (the Japanese version of the California Psychological Inventory) before and after the sojourn revealed
that the experience had no significant impact on Japanese
students' personality. Neither the basic pattern of
Japanese students' personality nor their esteem for their
own society and culture were affected by their cross-
cultural experiences in America. Their sojourn experience
served to increase their appreciation of American culture
and society, but not at the expense of a lowered appreciation of their own society and culture.

1611. Kuo, H. K., and A. J. Marsella. "Meaning and Measurement of
Machiavellianism in Chinese and American College Students."
Journal of Social Psychology 101 (April, 1977): 165-173.

1612. Kureshi, Afzal, Rahat Ali-Khan, and C. Jayanta Singh. "Fear of
Failure Among Indian and Non-Indian Students at Aligarh: A
Cross-Cultural Study." Psychological Studies 25 (No. 2, 1980):
86-89.

1613. Kurlansky, M. J. "Students and Colleges Profit from American
Study Abroad Programs in France." Change 13 (March, 1981):
48-51.

1614. Lambert, Richard D., and Marvin Bressler. "Indian Students and
the United States: Cross-Cultural Images." Annals of the
American Academy of Political and Social Science 295
(September, 1954): 62-72.

1615. Leonard E. W. "Attitude Change in College Program of Foreign
Study and Travel." Educational Record 45 (1964): 173-181.

1616. Mangalam, J. J. "Decision-making of Pakistani and Kentucky Students." International Review of Sociology 30 (No. 3-4, 1972):
51-68.

1617. Maria, Angela, and Brasil Biaggio. "Achievement Motivation of
Brazilian Students." International Journal of Intercultural
Relations 2 (Summer, 1978): 186-196.

1618. Marion, Paul B., Jr., and H. Thomas, Jr. "Residence Hall
Proximity to Foreign Students as an Influence on Selected
Attitudes and Behaviors of American College Students." Journal
of College and University Student Housing 10 (Summer, 1980):
16-19.

1619. Matross, R., R. M. Paige, and G. Hendricks. "American Student
Attitudes Toward Foreign Students Before and During an

International Crisis." Journal of College Student Personnel 23 (January, 1982): 58-65.

1620. Miller, Delbert C. "Measuring Cross-National Norms." International Journal of Comparative Sociology 13 (September-December, 1972): 201-216.

1621. Miller, Milton. "The Cross-Cultural Student: Lessons in Human Nature." Bulletin of the Menninger Clinic (March, 1971): 128-131.

1622. Mowlana, Hamid, and G. W. McLaughlin. "Some Variables Interacting with Media Exposure Among Foreign Students." Sociology and Social Research 53 (July, 1969): 511-522.

1623. Nash, Dennison. "The Personal Consequences of a Year of Study Abroad." Journal of Higher Education 47 (No. 2, 1976): 191-203.

Using a design involving experimental and control groups, this study evaluates the effect of a year of study abroad on the self-realization of a group of junior-year students in France. The kind of self-realization which is proposed by the ideologues and custodians of such programs is seen to be aimed at producing a liberal-international version of a typically modern individual. Using this model as a guide, a series of hypotheses regarding the effects on individuals of a year of overseas study were developed. The tests of these hypotheses involved the comparison of changes in the junior-year group and a group which remained at home. Some support for the hypotheses was obtained from assessments made at the end of the year abroad, but a later assessment, using less-than-adequate data, suggests that most of the personality changes derived from the overseas experience did not persist after return home.

1624. Okanes, M. M., and L. W. Murray. "Machiavellian and Achievement Orientations Among Foreign and American Master's Students in Business Administration." Psychological Reports 50 (April, 1982): 519-526.

That cultural differences exist with respect to the values, work goals, and behavior of managers and workers in various countries have been shown in a number of studies. This study examined the effect of cultural differences on two important dimensions of motivation: the motive to achieve and a manipulative form of power motivation labeled "Machiavellianism." The achievement and Machiavellian orientations were explored among 185 U.S. and foreign students enrolled in two master's (MBA) programs in business administration. Large samples from Algeria, Iran, Philippines, Taiwan, and the United States were selected for analysis. The basic assumption was that a relationship existed between the cultural background of each country and the Machiavellian and achievement motivations of its citizens. The Mach IV scale and the Mehrabian test of achievement orientation were used to design the questionnaires which were distributed and completed during regular class time. The results suggest that the hypothesis which predicted that students from the Philippines and the U.S.A. would produce significantly higher scores on both tests than those from Arab countries tends to be confirmed by the achievement scores but not by the Mach scores. The hypothesis that stated that the scores of Filipino and American students on both tests would not differ significantly was confirmed by the Mach scores but not by achievement scores. Hypothesis three predicted that the students from Algeria and Iran would differ significantly on the two tests. The results tend not to support this hypothesis. The fourth hypothesis, which stated that both the achievement and Mach scores of the Taiwanese students would fall into the midrange was not supported by either test.

1625. Pratt, Cornelius. "How Media Credibility Ratings of African and U.S. Students Compare." Journalism Quarterly 59 (No. 4, 1982): 581-587.

1626. Pratt, Dallas. "The Relation of Culture-Goals to the Mental Health of Students Abroad." International Social Science Bulletin 8 (No. 4, 1956): 597-604.

1627. Salter, Charles A. "Status Comparability and Attitudes Toward a Foreign Host Nation: A Cross-Cultural Study." Journal of Psychology 88 (November, 1974): 201-214.

Examined in this study are four models of status--the Equal Status model, Status Change model, Reference Group model and Status Outcome model--to see the effects of status inter-relationships during an overseas sojourn on the attitudes toward the nations visited. Questionnaires were given to 158 students studying in four groups. Group I was made up of 44 American students from Loyola University of Chicago studying at the Loyola Center in Rome while Group II, the American control group, consisted of 37 Loyola students still in Chicago. In Group III were 32 Italian students studying in North American universities. There were 45 Italian students in the Italian control group, Group IV, who were learning English at the Loyola Rome Center and had an interest in coming to the United States. In all groups there were roughly 70% male subjects and 30% female subjects. The results of the study indicated cross-cultural support for the hypothesis that status in a foreign country is an important element of satisfaction and attitudes toward the country. Concerning overseas Italians, superiority to the reference group in terms of prestige, intellectual, and mean status was a significant predictor of attitudes. For overseas Americans, merely present status, without a referent, was significant, but only with attractiveness status. The equal status principle and status gain models were not significant with either group. Of nonstatus variables, satisfaction with the entertainment facilities was the most significant correlate for both groups. The social exchange theory was supported by the cross-cultural similarities while the differences supported popular stereotypes of the two cultures and a field of theoretical position on insecurity reduction.

1628. Salter, C. A., and C. D. Salter. "International Contact, Social Rewards, and Attitudes Toward the Country Visited." Psychological Reports 35 (August, 1974): 49-50.

1629. Salter, C. A., and H. P. Smith. "Change in Attitudes ... Type of International Contact." Sociometry 38 (1975): 213-222.

1630. Selltiz, C., and S. W. Cook. "Factors Influencing Attitudes of Foreign Students Toward the Host Country." Journal of Social Issues 18 (No. 1, 1962): 7-23.

This paper presents a brief summary of what the most common answers seem to be when the host-country is the U.S.A., and then examines evidence about factors that make for differences among students in their views of the host-country. It draws heavily on two studies carried out by the Research Center for Human Relations of New York University. The focus of foreign students in the U.S.A. reflects the distribution of studies of cross-cultural education. The authors made the following observations: (1) the average foreign students attributed more desirable than undesirable traits to Americans; (2) the general impact of the cross-cultural experience cannot be overestimated; (3) many factors contribute to differences in attitudes of foreign students toward the U.S.A., among them are: the set of preconceptions or expectations brought by the visitors; motivations of their study in the U.S.A.; and most importantly, differences in national background; (4) foreign students typically go through a U cycle in their feelings toward the host-country.

1631. Sewell, W. H., et al. "Scandinavian Students' Images of the United States: A Study in Cross-Cultural Education." Annals of the American Academy of Political and Social Science 295 (September, 1954): 126-135.

1632. Smith, H. P. "Effects of Intercultural Experience--Follow-up Investigation." Journal of Abnormal and Social Psychology 54 (1957): 266-269.

1633. Smith, I. M., et al. "Study of the Abilities and Interests of Overseas Students." The Vocational Aspect of Education 28 (August, 1976): 55-65.

1634. Story, Kathryn E. "The Student Development Professional and the Foreign Student: A Conflict of Values?" Journal of College Student Personnel 23 (January, 1982): 66-70.

1635. Triulzi, A. "Italian View of the U.S. Campus." Overseas 3 (October, 1963): 10-13.

1636. Tuttle, H. G., et al. "Effects of Cultural Presentations on Attitudes of Foreign Language Students." Modern Language Journal 63 (No. 4, 1979): 177-182.

1637. Useem, John, and Ruth Useem. "Interfaces of Binational Third Culture ... India." Journal of Social Issues 23 (No. 1, 1967): 130-143.

1638. Uwanno, T., and J. R. Stabler. "Black and White as Perceived by Euro-Americans, Afro-Americans, and Africans." Perceptual and Motor Skills 44 (April, 1977): 507-510.

1639. Vyas, Premila. "International Student Perceptions Studied in Urban University Setting." National Association for Foreign Student Affairs Newsletter 30 (November, 1978): 36ff.

1640. Williamson, Robert C. "Modernism and Related Attitudes: An International Comparison Among University Students." International Journal of Comparative Sociology 11 (June, 1970): 130-145.

1641. Wohl, J., et al. "Some Personality Characteristics of Thai and American University Students." Psychology Reports 27 (August, 1970): 45-46.

1642. Yavas, U. "Attitudes of Turkish Students Toward International Business and Foreign Firms." Akron Business and Economic Review 11 (No. 1, 1980): 34-38.

1643. Yeh, Eng-Kung, et al. "Psychiatric Implications of Cross-Cultural Education: Chinese Students in the U.S.A." Acta Psychologica Taiwanica 21 (No. 1, 1979): 1-26.

1644. Zelleke, Kefelev. "Auslandische Studenten in der Bundesrepublik: Erwartungen Hoffnungen und die Wirklishkeit." Diakonie 8 (No. 3, 1971): 10-19.

## Reportage

1645. Kanein, W. "Zur Politischen Betatigung Auslandischer Studententen." Die Deutsche Universitatszeitung 23 (No. 8-9, 1968): 23-26.

1646. "Latin American Students in U.S. More Satisfied than Africans and Asians." Chronicle of Higher Education 22 (March 9, 1981): 17.

1647. O'Neill, Peter. "When West Is Not Necessarily the Best. Two Views of the Education which Overseas Students receive in Britain." Times Higher Education Supplement (June 9, 1978): 8.

1648. Wojtas, O. "Son of Our Very Own Cultural Revolution." Times Higher Education Supplement (July 11, 1980): 7.


## 22. CROSS-CULTURAL ISSUES AND ACTIVITIES


1649. Althen, Gary. Learning With Your Foreign Roommate. Ames, Iowa: University Press, 1982.

1650. Althen, Gary. Manual for Foreign Teaching Assistants. Ames, Iowa: University Press, 1981.

1651. Arnov, Venice Beaulieu. "Analysis of the Effects of Language on Impression Formation: Evaluation Reactions of Miami-Dade Community College Students to the Voices of Cuban-Americans Speaking in English and in Spanish." Unpublished Ed.D thesis, Florida Atlantic University, 1978.

1652. A Balance Sheet for East-West Exchanges: Working Papers [Conference on Scholarly Exchanges with the USSR and Eastern Europe: Two Decades of American Experience, Washington, D.C., 1979]. New York, International Research and Exchanges Board, 1980.

1653. Batchelder, Donald, and Elizabeth G. Warner, eds. Beyond Experience: The Experiential Approach to Cross-Cultural Education. Brattleboro, Vermont: Experiment in International Living, 1977.

1654. Beckles, Marjorie. Teaching Abroad. New York: Institute of International Education, 1973.

1655. Benne, Max Erwin. "The Influence of Foreign Visitors on the Interest of Certain Adult Members of a Hosting Community in Participating in Internationally Oriented Activities." Unpublished Ed.D thesis, Michigan State University, 1967.

1656. Bericht uber das Studium in Ausland und uber den Austausch Junger Wissenschaftler. Dusseldorf: Der Minister fur Wissenschaft und Forschung, 1980.

1657. Boewe, Charles E. The Green Book: American Scholar in Pakistan. Islamabad, Pakistan: United States Educational Foundation in Pakistan, 1977.

1658. Breitenbach, Dieter. _Auslandsausbildung als Gegenstand Sozialwissenschaftlicher Forschung_. Saarbrucken: Verlag der SSIP Schriften, 1973.

1659. Brislin, Richard W., and Paul Pedersen. _Cross-Cultural Orientation Programs_. New York: Gardner Press, 1976.

1660. Bureau of Educational and Cultural Affairs. _International Teacher Development Program_ 1961-62. Washington, D.C.: BECA, 1963.

1661. Calvert, Robert. _Your Future in International Service_. Garret Park, Maryland: Garret Park Press, 1969.

1662. Chothia, Fali. _Other Cultures, Other Ways_. Denver: Center for the Orientation of Americans Going Abroad, 1979.

1663. Committee- on International Programs. _The Future-International Programs at the University of Illinois, Urbana--A Ten-Year Glimpse_. Champaign, Illinois: University of Illinois, 1968.

1664. Cormack, Margaret. _An Evaluation of Research on Educational Exchange_. Brooklyn: Brooklyn College, 1962.

1665. Council of Europe. _The Conference on Academic Mobility in Europe (Strasbourg, 17-19 March 1981): Dossier_. Strasbourg: Council of Europe, 1981.

1666. Dissara, Wichai. "A Comparison of the Organizations and Administrations of Student Teaching Programs in the United States and Thailand." Unpublished Ph.D thesis, University of Akron, 1973.

1667. Education and World Affairs. _Coordinating International Programs and Activities at U.S. Colleges and Universities: A Directory_. New York: EWA, 1967.

1668. Education and World Affairs. _Intercultural Education_. New York: EWA, 1965.

1669. Education and World Affairs. _Inter-Institutional Cooperation and International Education_. New York: Education and World Affairs, 1969.

1670. Eicher, Carl K., ed. _An Analysis of U.S.-Iranian Cooperation in Higher Education_. Washington, D.C.: American Council on Education, 1976.

1671. European Center for Higher Education. _Interuniversity Cooperation in the European Region_. Bucharest, Rumania: CEPES, 1981.

1672. Farrell, Shirley Nalty. "The Relationship of Personality, Age, Sex, and Educational Level to Short-Term Student Travel Abroad." Unpublished Ph.D thesis, University of Southern Mississippi, 1982.

1673. Fisher, Glen. United States-India Educational and Cultural Relations: Trends, Factors, Prospects. Washington, D.C.: Bureau of Educational and Cultural Affairs, Department of State, 1977.

1674. Fisher, Glen. United States International Educational and Cultural Relations: Changing Factors in the Middle East and Africa. Washington, D.C.: Bureau of Educational and Cultural Affairs, Department of State, 1976.

1675. Flack, Michael J., ed. Five Studies in International Cultural and Educational Exchange. Pittsburgh: Graduate School of Public and International Affairs, University of Pittsburgh, 1964.

1676. Garraty, J. A., and N. Adams. Main Street to Left Bank: Students and Scholars Abroad. East Lansing: Michigan State University Press, 1959.

1677. Hartmann, Kalus-Dieter. Wirkrugen von Auslandsreisen Junger Leute. Starnberg, West Germany, 1981.

1678. Juergensmeyer, John F. "Democracy's Diplomacy: The People-to-People Program: A Study of Attempts to Focus the Effects of Private Contacts in International Politics." Unpublished Ph.D thesis, Princeton University, 1960.

1679. Klineberg, O. International Exchanges in Education, Science, and Culture: Suggestions for Research. Paris: Mouton, 1966.

     This extended essay places great emphasis on the role of evaluation in assessment of international programs.
     Originally this work grows out of the Economic and Social Council resolution, at the United Nations, in July, 1960. This resolution affirms the request for close cooperation between peoples for peace and improvement of international cooperation.
     The essay gives consideration to: (a) the racial and ethnic nature of exchanges, (b) technical cooperation, (c) the role of personal contact at the international level, (d) the role of governments.
     Although this essay was originally developed for a "Round Table on Research in the Field of International Educational Exchanges in 1964," the essential subjects reviewed are relevant in 1984. The main drawback of this work is its now dated bibliography.

1680. Mitter, Wolfgang, and Ulla Maichle. Auslandsbeziehungen von Lehrerausbildungsinstitutionen in der Bundesrepublik Deutschland. Bonn-Bad Godesberg: DAAD, 1974.

1681. Moellar, Phillip William. "Cultural Exchange: A Communication Model for Re-Entry Transition." Unpublished Ph.D thesis, American University, 1977.

1682. Morris, B. S. International Community?--Welfare of Overseas Students. London: National Union of Students, 1967.

1683. National Association for Foreign Student Affairs. International Educational Interchange: The College, the University and the Foreign Student. Washington, D.C.: NAFSA, 1974.

1684. Renwick, George W. State-of-the-Art Report: A Description and Assessment of Intercultural Education, Training and Research. La Grange Park, Illinois: Intercultural Network, Inc., 1978.

1685. Research on Exchanges. Proceedings of the German-American Conference at Wissenschaftszentrum, 24-28 November 1980. Bonn: DAAD, 1980.

1686. Spitzberg, I. J., Jr., ed. Exchange and Expertise. Boulder, Colorado: Westview Press, 1978.

1687. Taylor, Harold. The World as Teacher. New York: Doubleday, 1969.

1688. Textor, Robert, ed. Cultural Frontiers of the Peace Corps. Cambridge: M.I.T. Press, 1966.

> Textor gives an early overview of the Peace Corps from the experience of its Washington office and that of the volunteers in the field. Primary focus of this work is on the 12 countries served in the first phases of the Peace Corps effort.
> The countries explored are: Philippines, Malaya, Thailand, Afghanistan, Somalia, Tanganyika, Nigeria, Sierre Leone, Morocco, Jamaica, Peru, and Bolivia.

1689. Thomas, Alexander, ed. Erforschung Interkultureller Beziehungen: Forschungsansatze und Perspektiven. Saarbrucken: Verlag Breitenbach, 1983.

1690. Tillman, Seth. The Peace Corps: From Enthusiasm to Disciplined Idealism. Washington, D.C.: Peace Corps Office of Public Affairs, 1969.

1691. United States Advisory Commission on International, Educational and Cultural Affairs. Notes on Educational and Cultural Exchange Between the United States and Countries in the Middle East: A Special Report by Members of the U.S. Advisory Commission on International, Educational and Cultural Affairs on a Trip to Egypt, Saudi Arabia, Kuwait, the United Arab Emirates, Iran and Turkey. Washington, D.C.: Government Printing Office, 1977.

1692. U.S. Department of State, Bureau of Educational and Cultural Affairs. Teacher and Scholar Abroad. Washington, D.C.: Government Printing Office, 1964.

1693. Universitat und Dritte Welt. Giessen, West Germany: Justus-Liebig - Universitat Giessen, 1983.

## Articles

1694. Arum, S. "International Matchmaker Extraordinaire; His Approaches to U.S.-Foreign Student Relations." International Educational and Cultural Exchange 5 (Fall, 1969): 69-75.

1695. Batchelder, D. "My Phys Ed Teacher Wears a Sari; Teacher Ambassador Program." International Educational and Cultural Exchange 8 (Winter, 1972-73): 1-10.

1696. Bennet, J. W. "Innovative Potential of American Educated Japanese." Human Organization 21 (Winter, 1963): 246-251.

1697. Blackmore, John. "Summary of International Activities of U.S. Colleges of Agriculture." In Foreign Assistance Authorization: Examination of U.S. Foreign Aid Programs and Policies [Hearings Before the Subcommittee on Foreign Assistance], pp. 355-360. Washington, D.C.: Government Printing Office, 1975.

1698. Callen, Earl, and Michael Scadron. "The Physics Interviewing Project: A Tour of Interviews in Asia." Science No. 4345 (1978): 1018-1022.

1699. Carter, William D. "Estudios no Exterior e Desenvolvimento Educacional." Cadernos de Pesquisa No. 22 (1977): 87-110.

1700. Caty, G. "La Cooperation Universitaire en Europe." Problemes Politiques et Sociaux. Articles et Documents d'Actualite Mondiale No. 147 (1972): 4-30.

1701. "La Conference des Ministres Europeens de l'Education et le reforcement de la Cooperation Regionale dans le Domaine de l'Enseignement Superieur." Informations Universitaires et Professionnelles Internationales (February-March, 1974): 51-56.

1702. "La Cooperation Universitaire Internationale (Reflexions de la Conference des Presidents d'Universites)." Ministaire de l'Education. Infomations Rapides No. 38 (1974): 1-8.

1703. Dart, Francis E. "The Rub of Cultures." National Association for Foreign Student Affairs Newsletter 14 (April, 1963): 18-23.

1704. Dent, I., and L. R. Gue. "Thailand Students Study the Composite High School." ATA Magazine 47 (March, 1967): 14-19.

1705. Derham, D. T. "Mobility of Students and Staff Internationally." In Pressures and Priorities, edited by T. Craig, pp. 359-364. London: Association of Commonwealth Universities, 1979.

1706. Detweiler, Richard A. "Intercultural Interaction and the Categorization Process: A Conceptual Analysis and Behavioral Outcome." *International Journal of Intercultural Relations* 4 (No. 3/4, 1980): 275-294.

1707. Deutsch, S. E. "Impact of Cross-Cultural Relations on the Campus." *Sociology and Social Research* 53 (January, 1969): 137-146.

1708. Dube, W., and L. Desramaux. "Citizenship of Full-time Teaching Staff in Canadian Universities and Colleges by Major Field of Specialization." *Service Bulletin* (December, 1971): 3-13.

1709. Dubois, A. "Bruxelles, Centre de Scolarite Internationale." *Syntheses* No. 292-293 (1970): 11-15.

1710. Dulst, A. J. "New Developments in International Educational Co-operation in the Netherlands." *Higher Education and Research in The Netherlands* 20 (No. 2, 1976): 24-32.

1711. Earls, Gerard W. "Some Reflections on the Problems and Opportunities of International Co-operation Between Higher Educational Institutions and Systems." *Higher Education in Europe* 2 (November-December, 1977): 28-34.

1712. Eide, Ingrid. "Students as Bridges Between Cultures." *Kultura* 17 (1972): 95-110.

1713. Eisemon, Thomas. "Educational Transfer: The Implications of Foreign Educational Assistance." *Interchange* 5 (No. 4, 1974): 53-61.

This paper examines foreign educational assistance to institutions of higher education in developing countries in the perspective of educational transfer, i.e., the transmission of educational forms and practices from the donor to the recipient society. The paper is divided into two sections. The first section presents an overview of the importance of the foreign assistance as an instrument of educational change and then describes motivations for providing and seeking foreign assistance, preconditions of the transfer process, and the role of foreign reference groups. The second section considers American assistance to Indian engineering institutions as a case study of educational transfer, illustrating various concepts developed in the earlier section. In brief, the two sections propose a framework for studying the transfer process and indicate how this framework might be applied to analyzing the impact of foreign educational assistance in a developing country. The conclusion of the paper draws attention to the potential hazards of securing educational assistance from one of the developed nations.

1714. Eisemon, Thomas. "The Emerging Scientific Communities: What Role Does Counterpart Training Play?" International Development Review 19 (No. 2, 1977): 14-17.

1715. Fisher, C. E., et al. "AACRAO-AID Project." College and University 49 (Summer, 1974): 626-630.

1716. Garner, J. "A Swirl of Differing Values Enriches One Canadian." Varsity Graduate 13 (May, 1967): 30-38.

1717. Graves, H. M. "Comparative Political Experience; the Toronto Internship/Seminar." Teaching Political Science 6 (January, 1979): 222-234.

1718. Griffin, Willis H. "Cross-Cultural Problems." National Association for Foreign Student Affairs Newsletter 14 (May, 1963): 2ff.

1719. Halstead, Carol P. "Focusing the Spotlight on International Education." National Association for Foreign Student Affairs Newsletter 33 (December/January, 1982): 63ff.

1720. Hellmann, F. W. "Internationale Hochschulbeziehungen-- Gratwanderung Zwischen Euphorie und Resignation." Zeitschrift fur Kulturaustausch 28 (No. 1, 1978): 22-29.

1721. Herman, S. N. "Contexts for Study of Cross-Cultural Education." Journal of Social Psychology 52 (1960): 231-250.

1722. Hong, L. K. "Risky Shift and Cautious Shift: Some Direct Evidence on the Culture-Value Theory." Social Psychology 41 (December, 1978): 342-346.

1723. Hrudka, Karel, and Jaroslaw Kubrycht. "International Co-operation of Czechoslovak Institutions of Higher Learning." Higher Education in Europe 7 (January-March, 1982): 37-40.

1724. Hull, W. Frank, IV. "Changes in World-Mindedness After a Cross-Cultural Sensitivity Group Experience." Journal of Applied Behavioral Science 8 (January-February, 1972): 115-121.

1725. Klinger, Robert. "International Education." National Association for Foreign Student Affairs Newsletter 15 (May-June, 1964): 1ff.

1726. Klitgaard, Robert. "Why International Studies? A Prologue." National Association for Foreign Student Affairs Newsletter 32 (June, 1981): 1ff.

1727. Kuper, Adam. "The Troubles of Prospero: The Expatriate Academic." East Africa Journal 6 (December, 1969): 28-34.

1728. Kuroda, Yasumasa. "Cross-Cultural Education." National Association for Foreign Student Affairs Newsletter 14 (April, 1963): 9-12.

1729. Lunstrum, John P. "The Peace Corps as Educator: Some Critical Issues." Liberal Education 53 (March, 1967): 187-215.

1730. Maheu, Rene. "The University in Europe: From Detente to Co-operation." Perspectives 4 (1974): 3-10.

1731. Mize, D. "World Education Series Review: Algeria." College and University 52 (Summer, 1977): 532-538.

1732. Moran, R. T., J. A. Mestenhauser, and P. B. Pederson. "Dress Rehearsal for a Cross-Cultural Experience." International Educational and Cultural Exchange 10 (Summer, 1974): 23-27.

1733. Moravcsik, Michael J. "Foreign Students in the Natural Sciences: A Growing Challenge." International Educational and Cultural Exchange 9 (Summer, 1973): 45-56.

    In this article, a science professor suggests specific remedies for some of the difficulties faced by foreign students--particularly those from underdeveloped countries --who seek an education in the U.S. to prepare themselves for careers as scientists back home. The discussion was structured in terms of a chronological survey of the students' education--information gap, application fee, evaluation, transportation cost, advisers, specialty choice, development of problem-solving skills, and the return of the graduates. The author suggests ways for the foreign students to overcome fear of isolation, and arrangements to broaden bilateral exchanges between science departments in the U.S. and in less-developed countries.

1734. Norton, S. M. "Seeking the Foreign Perspective." International Educational and Cultural Exchange 12 (Spring, 1977): 26-30.

1735. Paige, R. Michael. "Cultures in Contact: On Intercultural Relations Among American and Foreign Students in the U.S. University context." In Handbook of Intercultural Training, Volume III: Area Studies in Intercultural Training, edited by Dan Landis, and Richard W. Brislin, pp. 102-132. New York: Pergamon Press, 1983.

    New cultures in contact has become a fact of contemporary American university life. The purpose of this paper is to shed theoretical and empirical light on the nature of intercultural relations between foreign and American students in the university context, especially in terms of the impact of intercultural contact on the American student population. This focus represents a deliberate shift from the past emphasis of the "sojourn literature" upon foreign students in the U.S. or U.S. students abroad as the subject of analysis. This chapter explores the challenges and opportunities posed by the foreign-student population in the U.S., and then examines the American sociocultural context within which foreign—and American—student intercultural contact is occurring. The author presents a multivariate conceptual model for analyzing U.S.-foreign student relations, along with findings from recent empirical studies testing various components of the model. In closing, conclusions are drawn regarding implications for future theory construction, empirical research, and programmatic application.

1736. Pankau, Peter. "Universitatskonferenz Berlin—Moskau." Das Hochschulwesen 18 (No. 1, 1970): 47-49.

1737. Peterson, A. D. C. "Applied Comparative Education: The International Baccalaureate." Comparative Education 13 (No. 2, 1977): 77-80.

1738. Picht, Robert. "Foreign Languages and International Studies: A Plea for Greater European Co-operation." European Journal of Education 18 (No. 2, 1983): 103-108.

1739. Powell, Judy M. "Trans-National Learning Experience." Journal of European Industrial Training 3 (No. 7, 1979): 26-28.

1740. Pratt, Alice Reynolds. "Citizen Diplomat: The Community's Role [in Educational Exchange] Today." Annals of the American Academy of Political and Social Science 424 (March, 1976): 96-106.

1741. "Principaux Renseignements sur les cours Internationaux aux Pays-Bas." Enseignement Superieur et Recherches Scientifiques aux Pays-Bas 12 (No. 4, 1968): 40-47.

1742. Quick, H. G. La Fondation des Universites Neerlandaises pour la Cooperation." Les Cahiers de l'A.U.P.E.L.F. (No. 2, 1970): 113-118.

1743. Rendosh, Ladislav. "Student International Scientific Cooperation —Factor of Integration." Sovremennaya Vysshaya Shkola 39 (No. 3, 1982): 209-213. (in Russian)

1744. Ret, R., and M. Tolnai. "The United Nations International University." Tudomanyszervezesi Tajekoztato 11 (No. 3-4, 1971): 566-574. (in Hungarian)

1745. Ritter, Ulrich Peter. "Forms of International Co-operation in Staff Development." Higher Education in Europe 7 (January-March, 1982): 30-33.

1746. Robinson, Beatrice E., and Darwin D. Hendel. "Foreign Students as Teachers: An Untapped Educational Resource." Alternative Higher Education 5 (No. 4, 1981): 256-269.

This paper examines the idea of viewing the many foreign students studying in the colleges and universities of the United States as educational resources. It is argued that foreign students have a unique educational perspective and specialized knowledge about their culture to offer to their American counterparts. An overall scheme for using foreign students in a teaching capacity is discussed. An experimental class at the University of Minnesota, which uses foreign students as teachers to illustrate the processes of development on the three countries of Nigeria, Thailand, and Turkey, is examined in some detail. The results of a formative evaluation of this class are presented. Some implications of the widespread development and implementation of similar types of courses at other colleges and universities are suggested.

1747. Robison, Olin. "Toward a Definition of International Education." National Association for Foreign Student Affairs Newsletter 29 (Summer, 1978): 1ff.

1748. Rowe, Leslie. "Managing an International Office." National Association for Foreign Student Affairs Newsletter 32 (December, 1980): 25ff.

1749. Segars, Jackie. "Defining Cultural Differences." National Association for Foreign Student Affairs Newsletter 28 (May, 1977): 22ff.

1750. Shutter, Robert. "Cross-Cultural Small Group Research: A Review, an Analysis, and a Theory." International Journal of Intercultural Relations 1 (Spring, 1977): 90-104.

The small group research reported in the literature was conducted predominantly with American subjects, and thus it was speculated that the findings may not be applicable to groups in other societies. After examining the available cross-national small group research, the investigator found that group behavior frequently varied from culture to culture, particularly with regard to leadership, conformity, and network performance. In discussing cultural differences in group behavior, a value theory of small group development was posited. Essentially, the theory maintains that cultural values determine how a small group and its members behave. Research strategies for testing the theory are also examined in the article.

1751. Smith, Alan. "EEC Scheme of Joint Study Programmes—Its Efficacy and Future Development." Higher Education in Europe 4 (April-June, 1979): 28-31.

1752. Smith, Alan. "From 'Europhobia' to Pragmatism: Towards a New Start for Higher Education Co-operation in Europe?" European Journal of Education 15 (No. 1, 1980): 77-95.

1753.   Smith, Alan.  "International Communication Through Study Abroad:
        Some Priorities and Pitfalls for Future Research."  European
        Journal of Education 18 (No. 2, 1983):  139-150.

        Despite the advent of computer-assisted language
        learning and other advanced technologies supplementing more
        traditional media and helping to broaden and widen the
        opportunities available for acquiring language proficiency,
        there is a widely held view that nothing can replace actual
        first-hand acquaintance with a foreign country when it
        comes to acquiring "foreign academic experience."  This
        article concentrates mainly on the identification of some
        reasons for and lines of research inquiry into academic
        mobility, specifically on matters dealing with student
        study abroad and research into faculty exchange whether for
        research or teaching purposes.  In arguing for the desir-
        ability of solid research on study abroad, the article
        outlines a possible framework for carrying out such re-
        search.  The author believes that the type of research
        outlined would not only make a substantial contribution to
        elucidating the principles concerned, but also give rise to
        findings which could have enormous impact on policy-making
        in international higher education.

1754.   Stamp, R. M.  "Canadian Universities and Canadian Identity."
        Canadian and International Education 3 (June, 1974):  17-33.

        The author discusses the nationalist debate that
        occurred in Canada in the late 1960s concerning the
        overabundance of American texts and faculty members at
        Canadian universities, and the perceived dominance of some
        departments of Canadian universities by Americans.
        This is in effect a discussion of neo-colonialism of
        Canada by United States scholars.  The author points out
        that the debate has turned from an issue of national
        citizenship to the course content of Canadian university
        courses with an emphasis on Canada's unique national
        concerns and role.  In effect, this debate has caused a
        heightened increase in Canadian consciousness which will
        enable Canada to make more positive contributions both to
        international higher education and to world affairs in
        general.

1755.   Stening, Bruce W.  "Problems in Cross-Cultural Contact:  A
        Literature Review."  International Journal of Intercultural
        Relations 3 (No. 3, 1979):  269-314.

        An examination is undertaken of literature bearing on
        the matter of misunderstanding between persons engaged in
        cross-cultural relationships.  The dimensions of the
        problem are outlined using the following sub-headings:
        subjective culture and social construction of reality;
        intercultural communication; stereotyping; ethnocentrism
        and prejudice; time factor; cultural distance;

personality; and contact and attitudes. Further, a description is made of various approaches which have been adopted in investigating the problems of cross-cultural contact in international organizations. A critical analysis reveals that the most significant gaps in current knowledge of the problems are at the interpersonal level. Suggestions are made as to what research questions demand urgent attention.

1756.  Stevens, J. W. "West German Police Language Program." Police Chief 50 (April, 1983): 48.

1757.  Suzuki, Eisuki. "Foreign Students and the American Dream." Yale Review 68 (Spring, 1979): 369-382.

The author presents in a very eloquent fashion the inevitable conflict between the foreign student caught between two cultures. As an international law student, he particularly finds the black law journals' report of minority group law teachers planning conference relevant to not only minority people within the context of the United States, but relevant to Asian scholars and other members of a minority group, i.e. foreign students, vis-a-vis the West.

1758.  Touscoz, Jean. "Problematik der Interuniversitaten Kooperation Zwischen Frankreich und dem Maghreb." Zeitschrift fur Kulturaustausch 25 (No. 4, 1975): 65-69.

1759.  "The United Nations University: New Program Developments." Convergence 10 (No. 1, 1977): 71-72.

1760.  Useem, John, Ruth Hill Useem, and John D. Donoghue. "Men in the Middle of the Third Culture: The Roles of American and Non-Western People in Cross-Cultural Administration." Human Organization 22 (Fall, 1963): 169-179.

Patterns generic to the intersections of societies is the focus of this study. This complex of patterns labeled the "third culture" is defined as the behavior patterns created, shared, and learned by men of different societies who are in the process of relating their societies, or sections thereof, to each other. Themes relevant to the administration of cross-cultural programs are examined and it is argued that a third culture and the community of men who carry it, has the potential for both supporting and obstructing cross-cultural programs but the third culture and the community of men who carry it are more than just the cross-cultural programs within which they are engaged. The men in the middle, those who carry the binational third cultures, the American community overseas and binational functional and locality-bound groups are discussed. Some implications (theoretical and applied) for cross-cultural administration are made. The general hypothesis suggested is that whenever there exists a viable, coordinate third culture there is a greater probability of more effective administration—and as a direct result, more successful cross-cultural programs. In terms of the evolution of human societies it is proposed that the future "civilized" nation-states will be characterized by those with high access to and creative participation in the emergent worldwide third cultures.

1761. Warmbrunn, Croson. "The Cultural Dimensions of International Education." National Association for Foreign Student Affairs Newsletter Supplement (April, 1963): 1-9.

1762. Warmbrunn, Werner. "Idealism and Hypocrisy in International Education." National Association for Foreign Student Affairs Newsletter 15 (October, 1963): 1ff.

1763. Warwick, W. Sheridan. "International Houses and Centers." In International Encyclopedia of Higher Education, edited by A. Knowles, pp. 1575-1588. San Francisco: Jossey-Bass, 1977.

1764. Weinstein, Sanford A., Patricia Barthalow, and Marian V. Hamburg. "The Effects of Study Abroad on Health Educators' Attitudes Toward International Health Efforts." Journal of School Health 46 (December, 1976): 599-601.

1765. Whyte, William F. "The Role of the U.S. Professor in Developing Countries." American Sociologist 4 (February, 1969): 19-28.

This article examines the question of whether the U.S. social scientist has a useful role to play in the developing countries of the world. Political issues such as those arising from Camelot and the CIA have pushed the American social scientists into an agonizing reappraisal of their role in international education and research. This paper is aimed at those underlying problems simply aggravated by such political disturbances. The author first deals briefly with problems of financing overseas research, and then explores in more detail the pattern of the American relations with individuals and institutions overseas. He draws particularly upon his experiences in social research in Peru since 1961, which apply equally well to many other Latin American countries. American programs of social research were referred to as "academic imperialism" by Peruvian nationals. The author considers a strategy which places primary emphasis on building a collaborative research program and recognizes the relationship between research design and the organization of the project. One of the important lessons drawn from the threats and uncertainties is that those Americans doing social research in Latin American countries give as much thought to developing more effective models of international research collaboration as they do to their own research design and data analysis.

1766. Wotiz, J. H. "Education of Foreign Chemists in America." Journal of Chemical Education 54 (No. 7, 1977): 413-416.


### Reportage

1767. "China to Spend $350-Million on Science Education (Planning to Send About 3,000 Students Abroad Each Year for the Next Five Years)." Chronicle of Higher Education 25 (January 5, 1983): 24.

1768. "Chinese Economists at Princeton." Chronicle of Higher Education 22 (March 30, 1981): 17.

1769. "Chinese Educator Rejects Foreign School Models." Chronicle of Higher Education 25 (October 20, 1982): 20.

1770. Desruisseaux, Paul. "Kidnapped Beirut Official Back in U.S." Chronicle of Higher Education 26 (August 3, 1983): 13.

1771. DeWolf, C. M. "Kyoto University Is First State Institution in Japan to Hire Foreigner as a Regular Professor." Chronicle of Higher Education 26 (March 9, 1983): 21-22.

1772. Dyne, Larry Van. "Venezuela Acts to Train Scientists, Technicians for Oil-Rich Economy (3,000 Students Attended Universities in U.S.A.)" Chronicle of Higher Education 14 (May 31, 1977): 9.

1773. "First Foreign Professor Is Hired at Tokyo U." Chronicle of Higher Education 26 (June 1, 1983): 24.

1774. Herlant, M., and G. Neave. "Communing with the Europe." Times Higher Education Supplement (March 12, 1982): 11.

1775. "Luxembourg: Relance de la Cooperation Universitaire avec la France." Newsletter (No. 4, 1975): 17.

1776. "National Autonomous University of Mexico and University of New Mexico Sign Agreement." Chronicle of Higher Education 21 (December 1, 1980): 17.

1777. Paul, Angus. "Intellectuals East and West: Short Review of Political Pilgrims: Travels of Western Intellectuals to the Soviet Union, China and Cuba." Chronicle of Higher Education 23 (November 4, 1981): 25.

1778. Roth, M. "Rules Eased for Foreign Teachers." Times Higher Education Supplement (August 15, 1980): 5.

1779. Scully, Malcolm. "Canadian-U.S. University Meeting Reveals Common Interests, Startling Differences." Chronicle of Higher Education 27 (October 6, 1983): 29.

1780. Scully, Malcolm G. "Destruction of Korean Airliner Dramatizes Need for Exchanges with Soviet Union, Educators Say." Chronicle of Higher Education 27 (October 19, 1983): 33.

1781. Scully, Malcolm G. "U.S. and Soviets to Resume Talks on Exchanges." Chronicle of Higher Education 27 (September 7, 1983): 1.

1782. Scully, Malcolm G. "U.S. Drops Plan for Soviet Talks on Exchanges." Chronicle of Higher Education 27 (September 14, 1983): 1.

1783. Scully, Malcolm G. "U.S. Scholars Call for 'Pressure' on China to Reduce Its Constraints on Research." Chronicle of Higher Education 24 (June 9, 1982): 21.

1784. "657 Scholars in U.S. Receive Fulbright Awards (to Lecture or Conduct Research Abroad)." Chronicle of Higher Education 25 (January 19, 1983): 34.

1785. Walker, David. "American Studies in Great Britain: 25 Years Old and in Need of Money." Chronicle of Higher Education 20 (May 5, 1980): 19.

1786. Watkins, Beverly T. "Japan's Junior Colleges Turn to U.S. for Guidance." Chronicle of Higher Education 10 (May 12, 1975): 7.

## 23. FOREIGN SCHOLARS

1787. Bennett, John W., Herbert Passin, and Robert K. McKnight. In Search of Identity. The Japanese Scholar in America and Japan. Minneapolis: University of Minnesota Press, 1958.

    This is an anthropological study. The subject is the student's place in history, his social role, and his personal experiences and outlook. The study is conducted in such a way that the authors are able to "grasp the whole" of their subject; different means of collecting data are used: interviews, structured tests, participant observations, etc.
    The study is conducted in two parts: (1) Twenty-three Japanese students were observed in an American university for one year; (2) At the same time in Japan, 50 subjects who had previously been educated in the United States were observed.
    The book itself is divided into three parts: Part I and II deal with the first objective of the study, which is concerned with the "American ryugakusei"--the American-

bound student—in the historical context of the modernization of Japanese society and Japan's cultural relations
with the United States. Part III of the book deals with
two objectives: the first describes and portrays the
experiences of the individual Japanese student on the
American campus and back home in Japan; the second analyzes
the adjustment process of the case of Japanese students to
differing cultural environments.

Findings:
. Many returnees from America remain substantially
alienated from their own society. There are, however,
numbers of persons in Japan who have been alienated from
the traditional order and are seeking to bring about
changes so that, in some respects, the returnee is less
isolated than before.
. The Japanese woman finds greater satisfaction in her own
society, and more outlet for her ambitions and talents,
she will come to relate to America in the context of the
graduate student or the adjuster among the male
ryugakusei.
. Japanese studying abroad have had their effect upon the
course of Japan's modernization and westernization. But
the idea of modernization did not just come from the
returnees but also from the Japanese society itself.

1788. Blair, Calvin,, R. Schaedel, and J. Street. Responsibilities of
the Foreign Scholar to the Local Scholarly Community. New
York: Education and World Affairs, 1969.

1789. Brady, Mary W. Levels of Involvement: An Impressionistic Study
of the Experiences of Sixty American Fulbrighters in Western
Europe. Oxford, Ohio: Miami University, 1974.

1790. Centre Europeen pour l'Enseignment Superieur. Interuniversity
Co-operation in the European Region. Bucharest: CEPES, 1981.

1791. Committee on Educational Interchange Policy. Foreign Professors
and Research Scholars at United States Colleges and Universities. New York: Institute of International Education, 1964.

1792. Copeland, William, et al., eds. Finnish-American Academic and
Professional Exchanges: Analyses and Reminiscences. Helsinki:
Foundation for Research in Higher Education and Science Policy,
1983.

1793. Council for International Exchange of Scholars. Annual Report.
Washington, D.C.: Council for International Exchange of
Scholars. (annual publication)

1794. Doseck, Fred P., and Roy E. Wenger. The Foreign Experiences of
Kent State University Faculty Members. Kent, Ohio: Kent State
University, 1967.

1795. Dyckman, John W., and Jack C. Fisher. International Professional Exchange: The Implications of The American-Yugoslav Project. Baltimore: Johns Hopkins University, 1977.

1796. Garfield, R. R. "An Investigation of the Teacher Exchange Program: The Case of Foreign Teachers to the United States in 1958." Unpublished Ph.D thesis, University of Utah, 1964.

1797. Gullahorn, John T., and J. E. Gullahorn. International Educational Exchange: An Assessment of Professional and Social Contributions by American Fulbright and Smith-Mundt Grantees, 1947-1957. East Lansing: Michigan State University, 1960.

1798. Gullahorn, John T., and J. E. Gullahorn. Professional and Social Consequences of Fulbright and Smith-Mundt Awards. East Lansing: Michigan State University, 1958.

1799. International Faculty Exchanges: Guidelines for Reciprocal Exchanges and Sources of Funding and Information. Amherst, Massachusetts: International Programs Office, University of Massachusetts, 1983.

1800. Macgregor, Gordon. The Experiences of American Scholars in Countries of the Near East and South Asia: Report of the Problems of Selection, Planning, and Personal Adjustment of Americans in the Fulbright Programs with Egypt, India, and Iraq. Ithaca, N.Y.: Society for Applied Anthropology, 1962.

1801. Rose, Peter I. Academic Sojourners: A Report on the Senior Fulbright Programs in East Asia and the Pacific. Northampton, Massachusetts: Smith College, 1976.

1802. Sweet, Charles. Educational Impact in the U.S. of Fulbright Professors. Washington, D.C.: Development Alternatives, Inc., 1973.

1803. Von Zur-Muehlen, Max. Foreign Academics at Canadian Universities: A Statistical Perspective on New Appointments during the Seventies. Ottawa: Statistics Canada, 1981..

## Articles

1804. Bischoff, Jean-Marc. "Structure et Mobilite des Jeunes Membres Personnel Academique." CRE-Information No. 52 (1980): 23-38.

1805. Kyle, Regina M. J. "Geographies III: Global Interdependence, the One and the Many." Trends 2000 1 (No. 4, 1979): 2-14.

1806. Mason, Hugh, and John Tunbridge. "Academic Exchange: A Practical Guide to Promise, Planning and Pitfalls." Journal of Geography of Higher Education 4 (Spring, 1980): 23-30.

1807. Masters, R. D. "Toward Improved Franco-American University Exchanges." International Educational and Cultural Exchange 7 (Winter, 1972): 7-15.

1808. McCormack, W. "Problems of American Scholars in India." Asian Survey 16 (No. 11, 1976): 1064-1080.

1809. Mendelsohn, Harold, and F. E. Orenstein. "A Study of Fulbright Award Recipients: Cross-Cultural Education and Its Impacts." Public Opinion Quarterly 19 (Winter, 1955-56): 401-407.

1810. Newell, J., and J. L. Davies. "Reflections on an International Faculty Exchange." Educational Administration 9 (Spring, 1981): 62-67.

1811. Roeloffs, Karl. "International Mobility in Higher Education: the Experiences of an Academic Exchange Agency in the Federal Republic of Germany." European Journal of Education 17 (No. 1, 1982): 37-48.

1812. Rose, Peter I. "The Senior Fulbright-Hays Program in East Asia and the Pacific." International Educational and Cultural Exchange 12 (Fall, 1976): 19-23.

1813. von Alemann, Heine. "International Contacts of University Staff Members: Some Problems of the Internationality of Science." International Social Science Journal 26 (No. 3, 1974): 445-457.

1814. Wood, B. "Scholarly Exchanges Between Latin America and the United States." Proceedings of the Academy of Political Science 30 (No. 4, 1972): 123-140.

### Reportage

1815. Coughlin, Ellen. "Turner Says the CIA Recruits Foreign Students in U.S., Defends Agency's Use of Professors." Chronicle of Higher Education 16 (June 19, 1978): 1.

## 24. CURRICULA AND PROGRAMS OF STUDY

1816. Bennett, John Makepeace. Effectiveness of Australian Tertiary Educational Training for South East Asia Over Last Quarter Century. Sydney: Basser Department of Computer Science, University of Sydney, 1976.

1817. Benson, A. G., and J. W. Kovach, eds. Guide for the Education of Foreign Students: Human Resources Development. Washington, D.C.: National Association for Foreign Student Affairs, 1974.

1818. Brimm, Paul, and Gordon Rhum. The Objective-Type Test--A Brief Manual of Instructions and Practical Suggestions for the Foreign Student. Cedar Falls, Iowa: University of Northern Iowa, 1967.

1819. Cracknell, B. E., R. Stonemann, and R. B. W. Haines. An Evaluation of the Training Received by the Bangladesh Study Fellows in the U.K. London: Ministry of Overseas Development, 1977.

1820. Danckwortt, Dieter. The Young Elite of Asia and Africa as Guests and Students and Pupils of Europe: Problems Involved in Imparting an Understanding of European Culture to Students and Trainees from Developing Countries of Asia and Africa in Europe. Amsterdam, Netherlands: Fondation Europeene de la Culture, 1959.

1821. Das, Ajit K. International Students: Untapped Resources for Psychological Education. Washington, D.C.: American Personnel and Guidance Association, 1974.

1822. Dunnett, Stephen C. Management Skills Training for Foreign Engineering Students: An Assessment of Need and Availability. Washington, D.C.: National Association for Foreign Student Affairs, 1982.

This report presents the results of a national questionnaire administered to foreign student advisers and Deans of Engineering, during the Spring of 1982. The purpose of the two surveys was to assess the impact on foreign students studying engineering in the U.S. institutions, particularly the extent of management skills given to these students.
The final results of the survey indicate that too few foreign students receive sufficient management skills training as part of their U.S. educational program.
The study includes a review of the literature and a bibliography.

1823. Hedges, Bob A. A Critique of AID/NAFSA Workshop: "Appropriate Technology in the Graduate Curriculum." Washington, D.C.: National Association for Foreign Student Affairs, 1979. (mimeo)

1824. Hoffman, Eleanor Reeves. "The Relationship of Stateside Orientation Programs and Other Experiences to Preparation for Study Abroad." Unpublished Ph.D thesis, University of Denver, 1973.

1825. Hood, Mary Ann G., and Kevin J. Schieffer, eds. Professional Integration: A Guide for Students from the Developing World.

Washington, D.C.: National Association for Foreign Student Affairs, 1984.

1826. Jenkins, Hugh M. The Relevance of U.S. Education to Students from Developing Countries. A Report of the [4th] Agency for International Development and National Association for Foreign Student Affairs Workshop. Washington, D.C.: National Association for Foreign Student Affairs, 1980.

1827. Lee, Motokoy, Moktar Abd-Ella, and Linda Burks Thomas. Needs of Foreign Students from Developing Nations at Iowa State University. Ames, Iowa: Department of Sociology and Anthropology, Iowa State University, 1979.

1828. Mestenhauser, Josef A. Learning with Foreign Students. Minneapolis, Minnesota: International Student Advisers Office, University of Minnesota, 1976.

1829. Mestenhauser, Josef A., and Dietmar Barsig. Foreign Students as Teachers: Learning with Foreign Students. Washington, D.C.: National Association for Foreign Student Affairs, 1978.

This pamphlet is based upon the original model "learning with foreign students," a program begun in 1974 at the University of Minnesota and subsequently extended to other universities in the United States. The particular thrust of this brochure enables the university interested in the development of cross-cultural perspectives to establish university-based classes involving foreign students as teaching, learning resources for university students from the United States and also to enhance our global understanding.

The document offers the following particular five-method solution to involvement of foreign students as teaching resources:

1. how to develop new courses;
2. how to bring foreign students into the class;
3. how to interview foreign students;
4. how to develop independent study programs;
5. how to initiate laboratory practicum or field work experience.

Particularly significant are the suggestions offered by the authors on the involvement and benefit of both the personal and international nature to bring foreign students who serve with pay as resource personnel in curriculum settings.

1830. Mestenhauser, Josef A., et al. Report of a Special Course for Foreign Student Teaching Assistants to Improve their Classroom Effectiveness. Minneapolis, Minnesota: International Student Adviser's Office, University of Minnesota, 1980.

1831. New York University, Research Center for Human Relations. The Effects of an Orientation Program for Foreign Students. New York: New York University, 1957.

1832. Newark, Eileen Helen. "The Evaluation of the Effectiveness of an Intercultural Orientation Training Program for a Study Abroad Project." Unpublished Ph.D thesis, State University of New York at Buffalo, 1979.

1833. Orth, John Ludwig. "University Undergraduate Evaluational Reactions to the Speech of Foreign Teaching Assistants." Unpublished Ph.D thesis, University of Texas at Austin, 1982.

1834. Owen, Wyn E., and Larry Cross, eds. Guide to Graduate Study in Economics and Agricultural Economics in the United States of America and Canada. Boulder, Colorado: Economics Institute, 1982.

1835. Simerville, Clara. The Foreign Student in Your Classroom. Corvallis, Oregon: Oregon State University, 1965.

1836. Smith, Charles Thomas. "The Relationship of Program Characteristics of the Kalamazoo College Foreign Study Programs to Changes in Participants' Attitudes, Values, or Interests." Unpublished Ph.D thesis, University of Michigan, 1970.

1837. Task Force on Business and International Education. Business and International Education. Washington, D.C.: International Education Project, American Council on Education, 1977.

1838. Van de Guchte, Marten. "The Effect of Aural and Visual Clues on the Rating of the Speech of Foreign Students." Unpublished Ph.D thesis, Michigan State University, 1969.

1839. Williamsen, Marvin, and Cynthia Morehouse. Students, Teachers and the Third World in the American College Curriculum: A Guide and Commentary on Innovative Approaches to Undergraduate Education. New York: Council for Intercultural Studies and Programs, 1979.

## Articles

1840. Adams, M. "Teaching Students from Other Cultures." Journal of Chemical Education 58 (December, 1981): 1010-1012.

1841. Boakari, Francis Musa. "Relevance of a U.S. Education to the Third World--Challenges and Satisfactions on Returning Home." National Association for Foreign Student Affairs Newsletter 33 (November, 1981): 42ff.

1842. Bowman, J. S. "Learning about American Government: Attitudes of Foreign Students." Teaching Political Science 5 (No. 2, 1978): 181-191.

This study investigates the results of a mailing distributed to foreign students at the University of Wyoming. Of the 300 students mailed a foreign student questionnaire concerning American government there was a response rate of 73.7% or 221 students.

An attempt was being made to determine whether students from other countries should be required to take a political science course as an introductory basic American government course and it was found that 46% of the students thought that taking a political science course about American government was a good idea.

Foreign students, however, tended to feel that courses in American government required of them at the University of Wyoming or elsewhere should be comparative in nature and not simply studies of the American governmental process. Over 43% preferred an emphasis on American foreign policy, 17% preferred an emphasis in the course on political attitudes and behavior and 13% on the issues of civil rights.

1843. Brew, A. "Responses of Overseas Students to Differing Teaching Styles." In Study Modes and Academic Development of Overseas Students, edited by G. M. Greenall, and J. E. Price, pp. 115-125. London: British Council, 1980.

1844. Brodkey, Dean. "Will the Real Foreign Student Please Stand?-- Remedial Classes for Foreign Students." National Association for Foreign Student Affairs Newsletter 26 (October, 1974): 7ff.

1845. Brook, T., and R. Wagner. "Teaching History to Foreign Students at Peking University." China Quarterly No. 71 (September, 1977): 598-607.

1846. Capoor, Madan. "Foreign Students and the Curriculum." National Association for Foreign Student Affairs Newsletter 22 (December, 1970): 11ff.

1847. Chiang, Shing Ho, and Hans O. Andersen. "Perception of Under-graduate Education in Physics by Chinese Physics Graduate Students Studying in Taiwan and the United States." School Science and Mathematics 82 (No. 6, 1982): 470-477.

1848. Clapper, T. H. "Teaching American Government to Foreign Students." Teaching Political Science 3 (No. 3, 1976): 311-316.

1849. Clarke, M. A. "Second Language Acquisition as a Clash of Con-sciousness." Language Learning 26 (December, 1976): 377-390.

1850. Cooper, Kenneth J. "Increasing the International Relevance of U.S. Education." In Educating Students from Other Nations, edited by Hugh Jenkins, et al., pp. 277-294. San Francisco: Jossey-Bass, 1983.

1851. "Decision Regarding Pedagogical Practice of Foreign Students." Buylleten Ministrerstva Vysshege i Srednege Spetsial'nogo Obrazovaniya SSSR No. 9 (1983): 28. (in Russian)

1852. Dennis, Lawrence. "The Relevance of American Education to International Students." International Education 8 (Spring, 1979): 7-12.

1853. Edwards, Marcia H. "Expect the Unexpected: A Foreign Student in the Writing Center." Teaching English in the Two Year College 9 (No. 2, 1983): 157-160.

1854. Fitch, R. K. "Experiences of a Postgraduate Physics Course Tutor with Overseas Students." In Study Modes and Academic Development of Overseas Students, edited by G. M. Greenall, and J. E. Price, pp. 44-49. London: British Council, 1980. (ELT Document 109)

1855. Fitterling, Dorothea. "Curricula for Foreigners?" Western European Education 13 (No. 3, 1981): 38-48.

This article is essentially a critique, by the Director of Academic Foreign Office, of the Technical University of Berlin in terms of the role of foreign students in German universities. It outlines the number of foreign students in German universities (primarily from Turkey, Indonesia, and Iran); reviews the structure of the German university vis-a-vis foreign students and equal status in terms of free tuition received by foreign students in German universities and the set-aside of 6-8% of restricted course offerings available to foreign students.

The author calls for a new curriculum that would clarify for foreign students their re-orientation to their country of origin. Particularly since foreign students in Germany spend on the average 10 years studying abroad, it is important in the long-term interest as the author states, to encourage the countries of origin to develop ultimately the capacity to offer scientific educational opportunities with German support, in the home-countries.

1856. Fouad, A. A., and E. C. Jones. "Electrical Engineering Curriculum and the Education of International Students." IEEE Transactions on Education 22 (No. 2, 1979): 95-98.

1857. Franck, M. R., and M. A. DeSousa. "Foreign TAs: A Course in Communication Skills." Improving College and University Teaching 30 (Summer, 1982): 111-114.

1858. Fuenzalida, Edmund F. "U.S. Education for the Third World: How Relevant?" World Higher Education Communique 4 (1981): 15-19.

1859. Giorgis, T. W., and J. E. Helms. "Training International Students from Developing Nations as Psychologists: A Challenge for American Psychology." American Psychologist 33 (October, 1978): 945-951.

1860. James, Ken. "Considerations Psycho-socio-linguistiques sur la Conception des Programmes de Cours pour Etudiants Etrangers." Etudes de Linguistique Appliquee 43 (July-September, 1981): 50-66.

1861. Keats, Daphne. "The Effectiveness of Education Abroad." In Overseas Students in Australia, edited by S. Bochner and P. Wicks, pp. 214-226. Auburn: New South Wales University Press, 1972.

1862. La Berge, Bernard E. "Appalachia: The Lessons of Development [Workshop for Foreign Students]." International Educational and Cultural Exchange 10 (No. 3, 1975): 4-7.

1863. Lee, Motoko Y. "NAFSA National Survey of Needs of Students from Developing Nations." National Association for Foreign Student Affairs Newsletter 32 (February, 1981): 73.

1864. Lipson, C. S. "Preparing for an Influx of Foreign-Students in Technical Writing Courses--Understanding Their Background." In Technical Communication Perspectives for the Eighties, Pt. 1, edited by J. C. Mathes, and T. E. Pinelli, pp. 173-180. Washington, D.C.: National Aeronautics and Space Administration, 1981.

1865. Magrath, C. Peter. "Education for Foreigners--and Americans." National Association for Foreign Student Affairs Newsletter 34 (Summer, 1983): 179ff.

1866. Mashiko, Ellen E. "Preparing Students for Study Outside Their Home Countries." In Educating Students From Other Nations: American Colleges and Universities in International Educational Interchange, edited by Hugh M. Jenkins, et al., pp. 31-64. San Francisco: Jossey-Bass, 1983.

1867. Mendenhall, Mark, Garry Oddou, and David Stimpson. "Enhancing Trainee Satisfaction with Cross-Cultural Training Programs via Prior Warning." International Journal of Intercultural Relations 6 (No. 4, 1982): 369-380.

1868. Mestenhauser, Josef A. "Foreign Students As Teachers: Lessons From the Program in Learning With Foreign Students." In Learning Across Cultures: Intercultural and International Educational Exchange, edited by Gary Althen, pp. 143-150. Washington, D.C.: National Association for Foreign Student Affairs, 1981.

1869. Moravcsik, Michael J. "The Physics Interviewing Project." _International Educational and Cultural Exchange_ 8 (Summer, 1972): 16–22.

1870. Moulton, W. N. "Science, Education and Students from the Underdeveloped Nations." _Science Education_ 49 (April, 1965): 220–225.

1871. Nash, D. "Academic Accomplishment and Problem of Relevance in an Overseas Study Program." _Modern Languages Journal_ 60 (No. 7, 1976): 347–352.

1872. Ngong-Nassah, E. N. "They Don't Need Ivy in the Third World: Some Thoughts on International Student Training." _Journal of Geography_ 81 (September–October, 1982): 192–194.

1873. Owen, Wyn F. "Foreign Students in Agricultural Economics from the Perspective of the Economics Institute." _American Journal of Agricultural Economics_ 65 (December, 1983): 1136–1141.

1874. Owen, Wyn F. "Higher Education in Economics: Major Trends." In _Higher Education in Economics: The International Dimensions_, edited by W. F. Owen, et al., pp. 5–26. Boulder, Colorado: Economics Institute, 1981.

1875. Paige, R. Michael. "Foreign Students as Learning Resources." In _Proceedings of the Central Region Conference on International Agricultural Training_. Urbana–Champaign, Illinois: University of Illinois, 1978.

1876. Parsons, Adelaide, and Lynette Szelagowski. "Communication Skills for the International Teaching Associate at Ohio University." _National Association for Foreign Student Affairs Newsletter_ 34 (March, 1983): 114ff.

1877. Peterson, R. D. "Some Reflections on Conducting a Foreign Student Training Course." _Journal of Developing Areas_ 2 (January, 1968): 167–186.

The author discusses the development and design changes that occurred over a five-year period, 1961–1966, in the program offered by the University of Nebraska, entitled "The Economics of Agricultural Production, Resource Use, Technical Course No. 6." Essentially, the University of Nebraska, through a U.S. Department of Agriculture Program for students from a number of different countries, designed and implemented this special training course. The course's activities were divided into both classroom experiences and field trips of varying lengths.

The primary purpose of the course was to offer students a better understanding of the multiple aspects of the American agricultural programs and the various roles of universities, vis-a-vis agricultural effort in the United States such as the role extension agents, land grant universities and an understanding of the various interest groups present in American agriculture.

The author attaches Exhibit 3, which is a detailed organizational chart of the content of the 12-week course broken up by weeks, which might be useful for replication by others interested in developing a course in the economics of agriculture.

1878. Peuse, H. Gene. "Agricultural Education in a Cross-National Context: Problem Solving Among Nigerian Students." Journal of the American Association of Teacher Educators in Agriculture 24 (No. 2, 1983): 30-33, 39.

1879. Pusch, Margaret. "Cross-Cultural Training." In Learning Across Cultures: Intercultural Communication and International Educational Exchange, edited by Gary Althen, pp. 72-103. Washington, D.C.: National Association for Foreign Student Affairs, 1981.

1880. Richter, Harold. "The Teaching of Chinese to Foreign Students at Nankai University." Journal of the Chinese Language Teachers Association 12 (No. 3, 1977): 226-238.

1881. Rose, P. I. "American Studies for International Students--Smith College." American Studies International 19 (No. 2, 1981): 76-79.

1882. Schmidt, Reiner. "Die Entwicklung von Sprechfertigkeiten bei Auslandischen Schulen in der BRD." Zielsprache Deutsch (No. 2, 1976): 26-34.

1883. Schuh, G. Edward. "The Impact of Foreign Students on U.S. Economics Curricula." In Higher Education in Economics: The International Dimensions, edited by W. F. Owen, et al., pp. 39-45. Boulder, Colorado: Economics Institute, 1981.

1884. Shana'a, Joyce. "The Foreign Student: Better Understanding for Better Teaching." Improving College and University Teaching 26 (No. 4, 1978): 243-246.

1885. Smith, I. M. "Spatial Ability, Field Independence and Climate: Some Thoughts on the Testing of Overseas Students." Vocational Aspect 26 (Autumn, 1974): 121-125.

1886. Walker, William. "The International Student as Resource Person in the Less Commonly Taught Languages." National Association for Foreign Student Affairs Newsletter 32 (January, 1981): 64ff.

1887. West, Brad. "International Student Teaching." National Association for Foreign Student Affairs Newsletter 33 (February, 1982): 81ff.

1888. Weyland, U. "Das Zertifikat'--Deutsch als Fremdsprache." Zielsprache Deutsch (No. 3, 1972): 109-112.

1889. Wiggin, G. A. "What Should be Communicated? An Experiment in International Education with Educators from Bolivia, Ecuador and Peru." School and Society 77 (June, 1953): 385-390.

1890. Will, W. Marvin. "American Politics in Comparative Perspective: Thoughts on Teaching the Basic Course to International Students." Teaching Political Science 7 (No. 4, 1980): 473-480.

1891. Young, L., and T. O'Brien. "English for Academic Purposes Through Canadian Literature and History [English as a Second Language for Venezuelan Students]." Canadian Modern Languages Review 35 (No. 4, 1979): 581-586.

## Reportage

1892. David, P. "Dons Fight to Keep Foreign Students." Times Higher Education Supplement (June 18, 1982): 6.

## 25. PRACTICAL TRAINING

1893. National Association for Foreign Student Affairs. Principles for Practical Training Experiences for Foreign Students. Washington, D.C.: National Association for Foreign Student Affairs, 1982.

1894. National Association for Foreign Student Affairs. Resources for Practical Training [of Foreign Students]. Washington, D.C.: National Association for Foreign Student Affairs, 1983.

## Articles

1895. Lee, Motoko Y. "An Unmet Need of Students from Developing Nations: The Need for Practical Training." In Resources for Practical Training [of Foreign Students], pp. 5-6. Washington, D.C.: National Association for Foreign Student Affairs, 1983.

1896. Levitov, Peter, and Suzanne Prenger. "An Abridged Report of the Practical Training Feasibility Study." In Resources for Practical Training [of Foreign Students], pp. 7-14. Washington, D.C.: National Association for Foreign Student Affairs, 1983.

1897. Nilan, Michael S. "Development of Communication Expectations in Occupational Contexts: A Comparison of U.S. and Foreign Graduate Students." International Journal of Intercultural Relations 6 (No. 3, 1982): 185-210.

1898. Smith, P. C. "[Polynesian Students in the United States]; Work as Education: A Polynesian Illustration." Journal of Coop Education 17 (Spring, 1981): 64-73.

1899. Sprinkle, Robert M. "International Work Assignments for Co-op Students: Some Issues to be Considered." Journal of Cooperative Education 17 (No. 3, 1981): 99-108.

## 26. LANGUAGE PROBLEMS

1900. Akutsu, Yoshihiro. "Commitment, Self-Evaluation and Communication Activity in a Dissonant Situation: A Study of Foreign Students with English Language Deficiency." Unpublished Ph.D thesis, Michigan State University, 1969.

1901. Ali, Sehba. "Foreign Language Acquisition in Adults in Native and Non-Native Linguistic Environments--An Experiment with English-Speaking American Students Studying French at the University of Illinois and in Paris." Unpublished Ph.D thesis, University of Illinois at Urbana-Champaign, 1982.

1902. Amiri, Parkhideh Maleki. "An Adaptation of Aristotelian Rhetoric for Teaching English Persuasive Themes to Iranian College Students." Unpublished Ph.D thesis, University of Texas at Austin, 1979.

1903. Brodkey, Dean Guy. "A Self-Instructional Program in English Article Usage for Chinese, Japanese, Korean, and Thai College Students." Unpublished Ed.D thesis, University of California, Los Angeles, 1969.

1904. Burke, Jack Dale. "The Predictive Validity of English Language Screening Instruments for Foreign Students Entering the University of Southern California." Unpublished Ph.D thesis, University of Southern California, 1968.

1905. Dunnett, Stephen Charles. A Study of the Effects of an English Language Training and Orientation Program on Foreign Student Adaptation at the State University of New York at Buffalo. Buffalo: Council on International Studies, State University of New York at Buffalo, 1977.

1906. Evans, Lewis Michael. "The Effects of Pre, Post, and Interspersed Questioning Techniques on the Reading Retention of Foreign Students Studying English." Unpublished Ph.D thesis, Ohio State University, 1979.

1907. Kempf, Margaret Kohler. "A Study of English Proficiency Level and the Composition Errors of Incoming Foreign Students at the

University of Cincinnati during 1969-1974." Unpublished Ph.D thesis, Ohio State University, 1975.

1908. Kertis, Joan, ed. English Language and Orientation Programs in the United States. New York: Institute of International Education, 1982.

1909. Koosha, Mansur. "An Investigation of Several Factors Hypothesized to Affect the Achievement of Foreign College Bound Students Learning English in the United States." Unpublished Ph.D thesis, University of Colorado at Boulder, 1978.

1910. National Association for Foreign Student Affairs. Guidelines: English Language Proficiency. Washington, D.C.: National Association for Foreign Student Affairs, 1977.

1911. Nussenbaum, Gladys S. "Bicultural Sharing Through Bilingual Pairing: A Description of the Linguistic and Attitudinal Effects of a Cross-Age Reciprocal Bilingual Exchange Program." Unpublished Ph.D thesis, New York University, 1978.

1912. Odunze, O. J. "Test of English as a Foreign Language and First Year GPA of Nigerian Students." Unpublished Ph.D thesis, University of Missouri-Columbia, 1980.

1913. Ohannessian, Sirarpi, and Allison Breiby. Academic Year Programs in English for Foreign Students. Washington, D.C.: Center for Applied Linguistics, 1967.

1914. Poosarun, Puangtip. "Cognitive and Affective Factors as Predictors of Reading Comprehension for Foreign Students Studying English as a Second Language." Unpublished Ph.D thesis, Southern Illinois University at Carbondale, 1979.

1915. Powers, Donald E. The Relationship Between Scores on the Graduate Management Admission Test and the Test of English as a Foreign Language. Princeton, New Jersey: Educational Testing Service, 1980.

1916. Shay, Helga Ruth. "Effect of Foreign Students' Language Proficiency on Academic Performance." Unpublished Ed.D thesis, West Virginia University, 1975.

1917. Study Modes and Academic Development of Overseas Students. London: British Council, 1980.

1918. Suksmai, Wattana. "An Analysis of Sentence Structure in Selected Textbooks Used to Teach Foreign Students in Programs of English as a Second Language in American Universities." Unpublished Ph.D thesis, University of Minnesota, 1978.

1919. Tafazzoli-Moghaddam, Abbas. "A Study of the Interrelations of Attitudes, Perceived English Proficiency, and Academic

Achievement of Iranian Students at Kansas State University." Unpublished Ph.D thesis, Kansas State University, 1980.

1920. Ursua, Aurora Ricardo. "The Relationship Between Adeptness in the English Language and Social Adjustment of Foreign Graduate Students." Unpublished Ph.D thesis, Catholic University of America, 1969.

1921. Willis, Frank, et al. Residence Abroad and the Student of Modern Languages: A Preliminary Survey. Bradford, England: University of Bradford Modern Languages Centre and Postgraduate School of Studies in Research in Education, 1977.

## Articles

1922. Allen, Walter P. "Correlation of First Day Cloze with Final Grade in Literature for Foreign Students." Research in the Teaching of English 14 (No. 1, 1980): 61-66.

1923. Ayers, J. B., and R. M. Peters. "Predictive Validity of the Test of English as a Foreign Language for Asian Graduate Students in Engineering, Chemistry, or Mathematics." Educational and Psychological Measurement 37 (Summer, 1977): 461-463.

1924. Briere, E. J. "Limited English Speakers and the Miranda Rights." TESOL Quarterly 12 (September, 1978): 235-245.

1925. Burke, J. D., et al. "Criterion-Related Validity of English Language Screening Instruments for Foreign Students Entering the University of Southern California." Educational and Psychological Measurement 29 (Summer, 1969): 503-506.

1926. Cooper, R. L., and F. B. Stieglitz. "English Proficiency of Foreign Students at Columbia University; Judged by Their Performance on Two Tests." Journal of Higher Education 36 (March, 1965): 131-136.

1927. Cowan, S. "English Proficiency and Bicultural Attitudes of Japanese Students." English Teachers' Magazine 17 (1968): 37-42.

1928. Dabene, Michel. "L'acquisition de la Competence de Lecture en Francais, Langue Etrangere: Courants Methodologiques Actuels." Systeme 9 (No. 3, 1981): 215-221.

1929. Dizney, H. "Concurrent Validity of the Test of English as a Foreign Language for a Group of Foreign Students at an American University." Educational and Psychological Measurement 25 (Winter, 1965): 1129-1131.

1930. Duda, R., and O. Regent. "L'Entrainement a la Comprehension Ecrit des Etudiants Etrangers de la Faculte des Sciences." Melanges Pedogogique (1977): 1-16.

1931. Gue, L. R., and E. A. Holdaway. "English Proficiency Tests as Predictors of Success in Graduate Studies in Education; TOEFL." Language Learning 23 (June, 1973): 89-103.

1932. Hay, Robert G. "'Here by Tygers...', The Language Barrier." In Overseas Students in Australia, edited by S. Bochner, and P. Wicks, pp. 129-140. Auburn: New South Wales University Press, 1972.

1933. Hendel, D. D., and K. O. Doyle, Jr. "Predicting Success for Graduate Study in Business for English-Speaking and Non-English-Speaking Students." Educational and Psychological Measurement 38 (Summer, 1978): 411-414.

1934. Hill, S. S., et al. "Teaching ESL Students to Read and Write Experimental-Research Papers." TESOL Quarterly 16 (Summer, 1982): 333-347.

1935. Hughes, A. "Conversational Cloze as a Measure of Oral Ability." English Language Teaching Journal 35 (January, 1981): 161-168.

1936. Jameson, S. C., and D. J. Malcolm. "TOEFL; the Developing Years." International Educational and Cultural Exchange 8 (Winter, 1972-73): 57-62.

1937. Jones, R. A., et al. "Predictive Validity of a Modified Battery of Tests in Language Skills for Foreign Students at an American University." Educational and Psychological Measurement 24 (Winter, 1964): 961-966.

1938. Jordan, R. R., and R. Mackay. "A Survey of the Spoken English Problems of Overseas Postgraduate Students at the Universities of Manchester and Newcastle Upon Tyne." Newcastle Institute of Education Journal 25 (November, 1973): 39-46.

1939. Jordan, R. R. "Comment Ameliorer l'Anglais Ecrit de l'Etudiant Etranger en Universite Britannique." Etudes de Linguistique Appliquee 43 (July-September, 1981): 105-117.

1940. Kaplan, Robert B. "English as a Second Language: A Guide to Sources." In Bridges to Knowledge: Foreign Students in Comparative Perspective, edited by Elinor Barber, Philip G. Altbach and Robert Myers, pp. 247-258. Chicago: University of Chicago Press, 1984.

1941. Kaplan, Robert B. "English Language Proficiency and the Foreign Student." International Educational and Cultural Exchange 4 (Winter, 1968): 43-47.

1942. Legay, F. "L'IAESTE et la Langue Francaise." Enseignement Technique No. 76 (1972): 29-36.

1943. Martin, A. V. "Teaching Academic Vocabulary to Foreign Graduate Students." TESOL Quarterly 10 (No. 1, 1976): 91-97.

1944. Monshi-Tousi, M., et al. "English Proficiency and Factors in Its Attainment: A Case Study of Iranians in the United States." TESOL Quarterly 14 (Summer, 1980): 365-372.

1945. Oller, J. W., Jr., et al. "Attitudes and Attained Proficiency in ESL: A Sociolinguistic Study of Native Speakers of Chinese in the United States." Language Learning 27 (June, 1977): 1-27.

1946. Palmer, L. A., and P. E. Woodford. "English Tests: Their Credibility in Foreign Student Admissions." College and University 53 (Summer, 1978): 500-510.

1947. Sharon, Amiel T. "English Proficiency, Verbal Aptitude, and Foreign Student Success in American Graduate Schools." Educational and Psychological Measurement 32 (Summer, 1972): 425-431.

1948. St. George, R. "Language Achievement Tests for Overseas Students-- LATOS--A Kiwi Controversy." New Zealand Journal of Education 16 (No. 2, 1981): 111-127.

1949. Thomas, Ronald E., and John W. Richardson. "Study of English Proficiency Standards for Foreign Graduate Students." College and University 53 (No. 2, 1978): 201-208.

1950. Yalden, Janice. "TOEFL and the Management of Foreign Student Enrollments." TESL Talk [Canada] 9 (No. 2, 1978): 16-21.

### Reportage

1951. Jordan, R. R., and R. Mackay. "Overseas Students Have Difficulty Writing English." Times Higher Education Supplement No. 86 (June 8, 1973): 8.

1952. "Mean Scores, by Country, on English Test (Fact-File)." Chronicle of Higher Education 23 (January 20, 1982): 8.

1953. Schmetzer, U. "Language Problems Spark Hunger Strike." Times Higher Education Supplement (July 25, 1980): 5.

1954. Wright, L. "Language Row Prompts Board Inquiry." Times Higher Education Supplement (August 1, 1980): 5.

## 27. INTERNATIONAL EDUCATIONAL EXCHANGE AND STUDY ABROAD

1955. Abrams, Irwin, and Francis H. Heller. Evaluating Academic Programs Abroad. New York: Council on International Educational Exchange, 1978.

1956. Allaway, William H., ed. International Educational Exchange in the United States: A National Profile. Los Angeles: University of California, Education Abroad Program, 1971.

1957. Althen, Gary L., ed. Learning Across Cultures: Intercultural Communication and International Educational Exchange. Washington, D.C.: National Association for Foreign Student Affairs, 1981.

This publication is for the use of anyone who works with students or scholars involved in international educational exchanges. Its purpose is to bring together ideas that the field of intercultural communication has produced and that appear to have value in the day-to-day work of people involved in educational interchange. The contributors believe that the field of inter-cultural communication offers international exchanges practitioners a useful approach to planning and conducting their training and orientation programs, and pursuing their own professional development. The book is in three parts: Part I, "Aspects of intercultural education activity," contains chapters on adjustment to new cultures, cross-cultural training, and problem-solving in new cultures. Part II, "Research on learning and implications for educational interchange," contains two complementary essays that summarize research on the topic of learning, and draw some implications for people designing and conducting exchange programs. Part III offers two case studies of the application of ideas from the intercultural communication field to work in international educational interchange. The ideas in the book stem from a U.S. cultural frame of reference.

1958. American Association of State Colleges and Universities. International and Intercultural Education in Selected State Colleges and Universities. Washington, D.C.: AASCU, 1977.

1959. Baddoo, Paul. Summary Report on 1963 Summer Program for African Students. New York: Africa Service Institute, 1964.

1960. Batoon, Irma Masa. "Residual Effects of the International Christian Youth Exchange Program." Unpublished Ed.D thesis, University of California, Los Angeles, 1968.

1961. Bennington College. An Inquiry into the Effects of European Student Exchange. Bennington, Vermont: Bennington College, 1958.

1962. Blumenthal, Peggy. American Study Programs in China: An Interim Report Card. Bethesda, Maryland: ERIC Document Reproduction Service, 1982.

1963. Board of Foreign Scholarships. Exchange Scholars—A New Dimension in International Understanding. Washington, D.C.: Board of Foreign Scholarships, 1965.

1964. Board of Foreign Scholarships. Fulbright Program Exchanges; Board of Foreign Scholarships Annual Report. Washington, D.C.: Board of Foreign Scholarships. (annual publication)

1965. Boewe, Charles. American-Egyptian Educational Exchange 1975-1980. Lexington, Kentucky: Transylvania University, 1981.

1966. Bower, T. J. "Effects of Short-Term Study Abroad on Students' Attitudes." Unpublished Ph.D thesis, Colorado State University, 1973.

1967. Boyan, Douglas, ed. Open Doors, 1981-1982: Report on International Educational Exchange. New York: Institute of International Education, 1983.

This publication is the basic source of statistical information concerning foreign students in the United States. The annual census of foreign students in the United States, now in its 28th year, is the source of data for this publication. Open Doors has been published since 1955. Among the data reported annually in this publication are: nationality of foreign students, academic characteristics, distribution by state, personal characteristics, distribution of foreign students among academic institutions, institutions with the most foreign students, expenditures for living costs for foreign students, intensive English language programs and U.S. Study Abroad programs. A variety of appendices providing detailed data for many of the categories mentioned above are also included. Tables, graphs, charts, and other means of reporting data make the presentation of this information clearer. Open Doors is the most comprehensive source of information on foreign students and it should be one of the first publications anyone concerned with foreign students turns to in order to obtain a general overview of the situation in the United States.

1968. Breen, John Peter. "A Comparison of Perceptions of Principals and Cross-Cultural Exchange Teachers Regarding Community and Professional Responsibilities." Unpublished Ph.D thesis, University of Connecticut, 1966.

1969. Bunker, Duane Forest. "An Investigation of Selected Areas of Spanish Culture and Its Application to the Design of a College or University Study Abroad Program." Unpublished Ed.D thesis, University of Georgia, 1974.

1970. Bureau of Educational and Cultural Affairs. International Educational and Cultural Exchange--A Human Contribution to the Structure of Peace. Washington, D.C.: U.S. Government Printing Office, 1975.

1971. Byers, Philip P., ed. German-American Conference on Educational Exchange, Bonn-Bad Godesberg, Germany, 1972. Conference

Report. Washington, D.C.: National Association for Foreign Student Affairs, n.d.

1972. Byrnes, Robert Francis. Soviet-American Academic Exchanges, 1958-1975. Bloomington, Indiana: Indiana University Press, 1976.

This book analyzes academic exchanges between the U.S. and the Soviet Union, as well as some of the states of Eastern Europe, from 1958 through 1975 in the framework of Soviet-American relationship. As a scholar actively involved in the main element of the exchanges, the author provides a complete, accurate, objective, and fair account of the development of academic exchanges during this period. The central themes of this volume include the following: (1) the role dedicated individuals have played in developing the relationships between the two great giants of the world; (2) the relentless American interest in increasing knowledge and understanding of Russia and Eastern Europe; (3) the changing nature of relations between the government and universities; (4) the contrast between the two societies and governments which these programs illumine, (5) the paradoxes of the academic exchange programs and the dilemmas they raise for the American people and for both of the governments.

1973. Carter, William D. Study Abroad and Educational Development. Paris: UNESCO, International Institute for Educational Planning, 1973.

1974. Clough, Ralph N. A Review of the U.S.-China Exchange Program. Washington, D.C.: U.S. International Communication Agency, 1981.

1975. Cohen, Gail. United States College-Sponsored Programs Abroad. New York: Institute of International Education, 1979.

1976. Cohen, Marjorie Adoff. Whole World Handbook, 1974-75: A Student Guide to Work, Study and Travel Abroad, 3rd Edition. New York: Arthur Frommer Publishing, 1974.

1977. Council on International Educational Exchange. Students Abroad: High School Student Programs. New York: Council on International Educational Exchange, 1972.

1978. Crespi, Leo P. The Effectiveness of the Exchange Program. Washington, D.C.: Office of Research, United States Information Agency, 1978.

1979. Davies, James L. Work Experience as a Component of Educational Exchange: A Study of Exchange Visitor Program P-III-4320. New York: Council on International Educational Exchange, 1973.

1980. Deutsch, Steven E. International Aspects of Higher Education and Exchange: A Community Study. Cleveland, Ohio: Western Reserve University, 1965.

1981. Euwema, Ben. The Role of Undergraduate Study Abroad in American Education. New York: Institute of International Education, 1966.

1982. Exchange of Persons Service, Department of Educational Affairs, Pan American Union. Annual Survey of the Inter-American Exchange of Persons. Washington, D.C.: Pan American Union, 1963.

1983. Fessler, Loren. American Student Travel in the People's Republic of China. Hanover, New Hampshire: American Universities Field Staff, 1971.

1984. German Academic Exchange Service. Research on Exchanges. (Proceedings of the German-American Conference at Wissenschaftszentrum, 24-28 November, 1980). Bonn: German Academic Exchange Service, 1980.

1985. Gerstein, Hannelore. Das Interesse Deutscher Studenten an Einem Vorubergehenden Studium in Auslands. Bonn: Bundesministerium fur Bildung und Wissenschaft, 1976.

1986. Girault, Emily. "Effects of Residency at an Overseas Campus on Some Social Attitudes of Stanford Students." Unpublished Ph.D thesis, Stanford University, 1964.

1987. Gough, H., and W. McCormack. An Exploratory Evaluation of Education Abroad. Berkeley: University of California, Berkeley, 1967.

1988. Hanna, Willard Anderson. Semester in Southeast Asia: Sixth Session [with Student Paper by Beth Goldstein]. Hanover, New Hampshire: American Universities Field Staff, 1976.

1989. Hegazy, Mohamed Ezzat. "Cross-Cultural Experience and Social Change: The Case of Foreign Study." Unpublished Ph.D thesis, University of Minnesota, 1968.

This is a cross-national study to determine the effect of "modernization" on individuals from two different cultures, (1) Near East, and (2) West. In particular, a sample of British and Egyptian students from the University of Minnesota, Ohio State, Wisconsin, and Egyptian students only at the University of Michigan and Washington University, during 1967-1968, were studied.

The findings indicate that British students had less stereotypical views of the United States than did Egyptian students. Further, it was found that attitudes toward religion, values, and morals were found to be more resistant to change than other aspects, such as dress, taste, food, and drinking habits.

1990. Hess, Gerhard. "Overseas Academic Programming on the Community College Level. The Rockland Model." Unpublished Ed.D thesis, Columbia University Teachers College, 1979.

1991. Das Hochschulwesen in der Europaischen Gemeinschaft: Ein Studentenhandbuch. Cologne, West Germany: Verlag Bundesanzieger, 1981.

1992. Hoefer, Fred Durbin. "Participant Assessment of Exchange Program P-1-0004, University of Minnesota, 1963-1974. An International Agricultural Academic and Practical Training Program in Perspective." Unpublished Ph.D thesis, University of Minnesota, 1977.

1993. Hubbs, Clayton. Transitions--A Periodical Review of Educational Travel and Study Abroad. Amherst, Massachusetts: Transitions, 1978.

1994. Hull, W. Frank, IV, W. H. Lemke, and R. T. Houang. The American Undergraduate, Off-Campus and Overseas: A Study of the Educational Validity of Such Programs. New York: Council on International Educational Exchange, 1977.

This study identifies the specific goals sought by a group of highly qualified off-campus study program directors and develops an appropriate instrument to assess whether or not the student participants perceived these goals as having been actualized within themselves. The assumption is that the ultimate goal of international exchanges is to contribute to friendly and peaceful relations, not to mention the immediate goals, which relate to technical cooperation, changes in institutions, success in academic training, increased knowledge about foreign culture, preparation for a useful career, and readiness to cooperate in international undertakings.

Individual Opinion Inventory (IOI) between May, 1974 and September, 1975 were administered to all students arriving at and/or departing from program locations in Northern Europe, East and West Africa, and the Eastern and Western United States. All students arriving at and/or departing from sample institutions in the United States were similarly administered the appropriate form of the IOI. The home campus sample data were collected at three distinct times (May, 1974, November, 1974 and May, 1975) to obtain an approximation of opinions, attitudes, and perceptions of students remaining at their home campuses. In Chapter III the results of the study are listed by percentage response of the students to the instruments with comparisons between all groups also considered. The demographic characteristics show: the median and mean age of all students in all groups to be 20 to 21 years old; there

were slightly fewer females in the home sample; a greater
percentage of social science majors was in the domestic
sample and the majority of students on off-campus programs
were on an 11- to 16-week (4-month) sojourn. Responses
prior to the sojourn which dealt with comparisons of
background variables, students' expectations and interests
in the area of their studies, students' expectations
regarding their off-campus programs and experience, students' expectations of themselves and students' views of
themselves and some students' selected opinions are dealt
with in the final section. The following characterizations
stood out. Students going off campus on programs did have
an exciting interest in the area and in the local people of
the sojourn location. The motivation for students going
overseas seemed to be for personal reasons of getting to
know other people and/or their culture. Students involved
in domestic programs felt that their off-campus program
should be actively involved in activities which would
benefit the local community. In addition, all students
believed that their off-campus program should prove beneficial in their career preparations. The overall expectation was that the personal values of students going abroad
or participating in off-campus programs in this country
would be questioned.

1995.   Institute of International Education. The Learning Traveler.
        Volume 1: U.S. College-Sponsored Programs Abroad: Academic
        Year. New York: Institute of International Education, 1982.

1996.   Institute of International Education. Open Doors: Report on
        International Educational Exchange. New York: Institute of
        International Education. (annual publication)

1997.   Institute of International Education. Summer Study Abroad. New
        York: IIE, 1979.

1998.   Institute of International Education. United States College-
        Sponsored Programs Abroad--Academic Year. New York: IIE,
        1973.

1999.   Institute of International Education. United States College-
        Sponsored Programs Abroad: Academic Year and Summer Study
        Abroad. New York: IIE, 1979.

2000.   International Association for the Exchange of Students for Techni-
        cal Experience. Annual Report. Athens, Greece: International
        Association for the Exchange of Students for Technical
        Experience. (annual publication)

2001.   International Public Opinion Research. Evaluation of
        International Exchange Experiences of Brazilian Grantees. New
        York: International Public Opinion Research, 1953.

2002. International Research Associates. The Effectiveness of the Exchange Program: A Study in Twenty Countries in All Regions of the World. New York: International Research Associates, 1962. (2 vols.)

2003. International Research Associates. Italian Exchanges: A Study in Attitude Change and Diffusion. New York: International Research Associates, 1955.

2004. International Student Service. The Report of the Second Hokkaido Youth Overseas Training Project Members. Sapporo, Japan: Hokkaido Youth Training Promotion Council, 1971.

2005. Jenkins, Hugh M., et al. Educating Students from Other Nations: American Colleges and Universities in International Educational Interchange. San Francisco: Jossey-Bass, 1983.

2006. Kadushin, L., B. Deniton, and L. Genevia. An Evaluation of the Experiences of Exchange Participants: 1969-70 through 1974-75. New York: The International Researches and Exchanges Board, 1977.

2007. Kimmel, Paul, William L. Ockey, and Herman J. Sander. Final Report: International Training Assessment Program. Washington, D.C.: Development Education and Training Research Institute, the American University, 1972.

2008. Klineberg, Otto. International Educational Exchange: An Assessment of Its Nature and Its Prospects. The Hague: International Social Science Council, 1975.

This book was the result of an investigation over a period of three years conducted into international university exchanges, both at the student and faculty level, in seven countries, in each of which one university conducted a self-survey and served as the stimulus for a description of the national profile. In each of the studies involved, there is an account of the nature and extent of such exchanges, changes with time, relative administrative arrangements, and problems encountered. This was the first truly cross-national study which compares the experience in several different countries. As such, it brings a new dimension to the analysis of an important problem.

2009. Kupferberg, Herbert. The Raised Curtain: Report of the Twentieth Century Fund Task Force on Soviet-American Scholarly and Cultural Exchanges. New York: Twentieth Century Fund, 1977.

2010. Kwochka, Vera Faith. "A Survey of United States Students Regarding the Effects of their Residence in the International House of New York." Unpublished Ed.D thesis, Columbia University, 1970.

2011. Leaves, Walter H. C. <u>Toward a National Effort in International Educational and Cultural Affairs</u>. Washington, D.C.: Advisory Commission on Educational Exchange, 1961.

2012. Littmann, Ulrich. <u>German-American Exchanges: A Report on Facts and Developments</u>. Bonn: Fulbright Commission, 1980.

2013. Livingstone, A. S. <u>The Overseas Student in Britain</u>. Manchester: Manchester University Press, 1960.

      This study was an examination of the practical and possible trends of social welfare training in Britain as it might offer constructive experience for students from overseas, particularly those from Asia and Africa. The inquiry was mainly concerned with the forms of social welfare training found in university undergraduate courses. The study, partly documentary, was developed by direct association with overseas students in Britain, and direct contributions to the field of reference were made by students from Asian and African countries. Basic issues in course planning and course content in social welfare training in Britain were examined. The author suggests that further fundamental studies be undertaken to determine what Britain's educational role might be in assisting the social welfare needs in Asian and African countries.

2014. Manly, David Earl. "The Students' Search for Self-Identity: A Study Abroad Program Proposal for State University College, Geneseo." Unpublished Ed.D thesis, Columbia University, 1970.

2015. Martin, Robert Lee, Jr. "An Investigation of Selected Student Variables and Their Associations in Participants of Summer Study Abroad Programs in Germany." Unpublished Ed.D thesis, University of Georgia, 1971.

2016. National Association for Foreign Student Affairs. <u>NAFSA Principles for International Educational Exchange</u>. Washington, D.C.: National Association for Foreign Student Affairs, 1981.

2017. National Association for Foreign Student Affairs. <u>Principles of International Educational Exchange</u>. Washington, D.C.: National Association for Foreign Student Affairs, 1983.

2018. Pegano, Jules. <u>Education in the Peace Corps—Evolving Concepts of Volunteer Training</u>. Boston: Center for the Study of Liberal Education for Adults, Boston University, 1965.

2019. Peterson, A. D. C. <u>The International Baccalaureate: An Experiment in International Education</u>. London: Harrap, 1970.

2020. Robertson, Daniel L. <u>Evaluation of 1981 Nihon University [Japan] Overseas Summer Training Program: Final Report</u>. Urbana-Champaign, Illinois: Office of the Program of Overseas

University Collaboration, University of Illinois at Urbana-Champaign, 1981.

2021. Rose, Peter. Academic Sojourners: A Report on the Senior Fulbright Programs in East Asia and the Pacific. Washington, D.C.: Office of Policy and Plans, Bureau of Educational and Cultural Affairs, Department of State, 1976. (Mimeo)

2022. Ruiz-Fornells, Enrique, and Cynthia Y. Ruiz-Fornells. Symposium on American Academic Programs in Mexico, Spain and other Spanish and Portuguese Speaking Countries, Madrid, 1978. Madrid: Sociedad General Espanola de Librerias, 1979.

2023. Sanders, Irwin, and Jennifer Ward. Bridges to Understanding--International Programs of American Colleges and Universities. New York: McGraw-Hill, 1970.

2024. Springer, George. A Report of the Fulbright-Hays Student Exchange Program Seminar. Washington, D.C.: Institute of International Education, 1969.

2025. Sprinkle, Robert M., ed. Administration of International Cooperative Education Exchanges. Columbia, Maryland: International Association for the Exchange of Students for Technical Experience/U.S., 1978.

2026. Terrell, Marion. International Educational and Cultural Exchange. Washington, D.C.: U.S. Government Printing Office, 1969.

2027. Thompson, Mary A. Unofficial Ambassadors: The Story of International Student Service. New York: International Student Service, 1982.

2028. UNESCO. Vacation Study Abroad: Vacation Courses and Scholarships. Paris: UNESCO, 1971.

2029. United Kingdom, Ministry of Overseas Development. O.D.M.'s Training Co-operation with Tanzania. London: Ministry of Overseas Development, 1979.

2030. United States Advisory Commission on International Educational and Cultural Affairs. The Effectiveness of the Educational and Cultural Exchange Program. Washington, D.C.: IECA, 1963.

2031. U.S. Board of Foreign Scholarships, Department of State. Educational Exchanges--New Approaches to International Understanding. Washington, D.C.: Department of State, 1967.

2032. United States Bureau of Educational and Cultural Affairs. Directory of Frequent Contacts for International Educational, Cultural, Scientific and Technical Exchange Programs. Washington, D.C.: BECA, 1967.

2033. United States Bureau of Educational and Cultural Affairs. International Exchange. Washington, D.C.: U.S. Government Printing Office, 1967.

2034. United States Bureau of Educational and Cultural Affairs. International Exchange--Leaders for Tomorrow. Washington, D.C.: U.S. Government Printing Office, 1971.

2035. United States Department of Education. Study and Teaching Opportunities Abroad. Pueblo, Colorado: Consumer Information Center, 1980.

2036. United States Department of State, Office of External Research. Foreign Student Exchange in Perspective. Washington, D.C.: U.S. Department of State, 1967.

2037. United States General Accounting Office. Coordination on International Exchange and Training Programs--Opportunities and Limitations: Report to the Congress. Washington, D.C.: U.S. General Accounting Office/Government Printing Office, 1978.

2038. United States, General Accounting Office. Flexibility--Key to Administering Fulbright-Hays Exchange Program: Report to Congress. Washington, D.C.: General Accounting Office/Government Printing Office, 1979.

2039. United States Information Service, and American Embassy, Paris. Guide to American Academic Programs in France. Paris: American Embassy, 1972.

2040. United States Office of External Research, Department of State. Foreign Student Exchange in Perspective--Research on Foreign Students in the United States. Washington, D.C.: U.S. Government Printing Office, 1968.

2041. United States Public Information and Report Staff, Bureau of Educational and Cultural Affairs, Department of State. A Word of Caution: Private Work Study or Travel Abroad Organizations. Washington, D.C.: Bureau of Educational and Cultural Affairs, 1969.

2042. Van de Water, John Gilbert. "The American College Student and the Foreign Host Family: A Comparative Evaluation of the Syracuse University Foreign Study Programs." Unpublished Ph.D thesis, Syracuse University, 1970.

2043. Walton, Barbara J. Educational Exchange Within the Atlantic Community. New York: Institute of International Education, 1964.

2044. Warner, Doris S. "The Brigham Young University Study Abroad Programs in Europe: A Comparison with Other College and University Programs to Determine Their Academic, Cultural,

Social, and Spiritual Advantage." Unpublished Ed.D thesis, Brigham Young University, 1981.

2045. Williamsen, Marvin, and Cynthia Morehouse. International/ Intercultural Education in the Four-Year College: A Handbook on Strategies for Change. New York: Council for Intercultural Studies and Programs, 1979.

2046. Winks, Robin W. A Report on Some Aspects of the Fulbright-Hays Program. New Haven, Connecticut: Yale University, 1977.

2047. Woodrow Wilson International Center for Scholars. The Fulbright Program in the Eighties: Summary of Conference Proceedings. Washington, D.C.: Woodrow Wilson International Center for Scholars, 1980.


## Articles

2048. Abrams, Irwin. "The Impact of Antioch Education Through Experience Abroad." Alternative Higher Education 3 (Spring, 1979): 176-187.

2049. Abrams, Irwin. "The Student Abroad." In Higher Education: Some Newer Developments, edited by Samuel Baskin, pp. 78-103. New York: McGraw-Hill, 1965.

Although this study is somewhat dated, having been published in 1965, it offers an excellent abbreviated manual for evaluation and development of undergraduate study abroad efforts. There is little question that the student abroad has already become an established part of the American landscape. This chapter presents an overview of developments in programs of study abroad. It deals with the objectives these programs seek to achieve, the kinds of programs that have evolved, problems that have to be faced and the potential these programs hold for improving the quality of the total educational experience. Particular attention is given to the problem and to the need for maintaining standards in the programs if we are to develop programs of quality and strength.

The references and sources for additional information may prove particularly useful both to university under-graduate deans in the United States and in other countries.

2050. Abrams, F., and I. Abrams. "Different Kind of Discipline: Inter-national Work-Study Program." Overseas 2 (May, 1963): 17-22.

2051. Althen, Gary. "Intercultural Communication Central to Educational Exchange." National Association for Foreign Student Affairs Newsletter 29 (May-June, 1978): 16ff.

2052. Barnes, Leslie R. "A Sociological Analysis of an Educational Exchange Programme." Durham and Newcastle Research Review 10 (Autumn, 1982): 4-8.

2053. Baron, Marvin. "From Hand-Wringing to Action." International Educational and Cultural Exchange 10 (Fall, 1974): 5-8.

2054. Barruha, R. "Study Abroad." Modern Language Journal 55 (1971): 232-234.

2055. Batchelder, Donald. "Training U.S. Students Going Abroad." In Overview of Intercultural Education, Training and Research, Volume II: Education and Training, edited by David S. Hoopes, Paul B. Pedersen, and George W. Renuick, pp. 45-63. Washington, D.C.: Society for Intercultural Education, Training and Research, Georgetown University, 1978.

2056. Bhasin, K. "Exchange Visits an Effective Way to Learning." Convergence 15 (No. 1, 1982): 38-44.

2057. Bicknese, G. "Study Abroad; Parts 1 and 2." Foreign Language Annals 7 (1974): 325-334.

2058. Bloom, W. R., and J. Webb. "Work and Study Abroad—A Personal Account [Fulbright Scholars]." Journal of College Science Teaching 12 (February, 1983): 252-254.

2059. Battsek, M. "A Practical Analysis of Some Aspects of Study Abroad." Journal of General Education 13 (1962): 225-242.

2060. Bowman, John. "The Role of the University in Student Exchange." National Association for Foreign Student Affairs Newsletter 17 (January, 1966): 2ff.

2061. Browning, K. R., et al. "Evaluating Agency-Sponsored Study Abroad Programs." College and University 51 (Summer, 1976): 457-462.

2062. Burn, B. B. "Changes and Exchanges in Higher Education: U.S.A. and Germany." International Educational and Cultural Exchange 8 (No. 3, 1972-1973): 63-68.

2063. Burn, Barbara B. "Prospects for Student Exchange and Studies Abroad in the Countries of Western Europe." Higher Education in Europe 4 (April-June, 1979): 17-20.

    The author tries to raise the issue of student exchange in Europe. Foreign students are witnessing more restrictions of different forms concerning their enrollment in the European schools. Some restrictions are Academic, e.g., foreign language proficiency; some are Financial, e.g., adequate funds are required and fees are increasing. To control the increase of foreign students, countries such as Germany, Denmark, and Sweden apply quotas. This creates a diversification between institutions. However, one cannot make comparisons between different institutions from one country to another because the recognition of the academic programs does not always exist. The author concludes that the prospects of international exchanges cannot be predicted.

2064. Burn, Barbara B. "Study Abroad and International Exchanges." Annals of the American Academy of Political and Social Science 449 (May, 1980): 129-140.

International educational exchange was a field of major concern to the President's Commission on Foreign Language and International Studies because of its contribution to research and scholarship on other countries, to foreign language learning, and to the international education of American citizens. Despite their importance, exchanges involving high school students and teachers remain distressingly limited and it is suggested that they should be expanded. Although major federal funding of study abroad by American undergraduates is not likely, the author suggests that this field should be strongly encouraged since study abroad can have a lifelong impact on students' values and understanding of other cultures. Further, suggestions are that: the more than one-quarter million foreign students in American colleges and universities should be tapped much more as a resource for intercultural learning. Teaching and especially research abroad for faculty is essential to U.S. competence in international studies; federal funding for it through the Fulbright and other programs has seriously eroded and should be significantly increased. Scholarly exchanges should in the future be more collaborative, based on reciprocity and on the principle of equality between U.S. and foreign higher education institutions.

2065. Carroll, William E. "The Experience of Ulysses and the 'Mad Flight' to Study Abroad." Liberal Education 69 (No. 3, 1983): 269-272.

2066. Carsello, Carmen, and James Greaser. "How College Students Change During Study Abroad." College Student Journal 10 (No. 3, 1976): 276-278.

2067. Carter, William D. "Study and Training Abroad in the United Nations Systems." Annals of the American Academy of Political and Social Science 424 (March, 1976): 67-77.

The United Nations and its Specialized and Associated Agencies have, since their foundation, provided fellowships, study tours, training courses, and workshops to enable specialists from their member states to obtain further training and to exchange experience on problems of mutual interest. Such programs have played a major role in the work of the United Nations system in the developing

countries. The present article describes the main features
of these programs over the past three decades, some of the
problems they have faced, and how they have developed in
response to changing perspectives and needs of the member
states of the organizations. Some notable developments in
these programs during the past five years are discussed,
for example, the increased contribution of international,
regional, and national training institutes in the organization of training programs and their researches on program
content and methodology; new departures in the field of
evaluation; the co-ordination of international training
programs situated in the developing countries and the
potential role of technical co-operation among the developing countries.

The most significant conclusions drawn by the author
are the following: Over the last decade there appears to
have been a tightening of the relationship between
consultants' activities in the member state and the needs
of the member states. Further, international training
programs are being tied more closely to the stated
development objectives of the host-country and training
programs tend to be better designed to meet the needs of
the individuals involved in these efforts.

It is particularly noteworthy that training centers,
the regional levels, have been developed within the developed regions. The United Nations programs are taking
more seriously the role of evaluations given by participants to improve the "content" of the programs. The author
stresses the important role that the United Nations
Development Program has played in strengthening
intra-regional cooperation efforts in the developing
countries by region.

2068. Chandra, Suresh. "Junior Year Abroad: An International Dimension
to Engineering Education." Engineering Education 72 (January,
1982): 280-283.

2069. Charlier, Roger, and Patricia Charlier. "How American
Universities Educate Abroad." College and University Business
46 (April, 1969): 73-75.

2070. Christensen, George C., and Thomas B. Thielen. "Cross-Cultural
Activities: Maximizing the Benefits of Educational Inter-
change." In Educating Students from Other Nations: American
Colleges and Universities in International Educational Inter-
change, edited by Hugh M. Jenkins, et al., pp. 210-236. San
Francisco: Jossey-Bass, 1983.

2071. Churchill, R. "The Student Abroad." Antioch Review 18 (1958):
447-454.

2072. Clubine, Eugene. "International Educational Exchange on a
Shoestring—How to Cope." National Association for Foreign
Student Affairs Newsletter 27 (April, 1976): 1ff.

2073. Coombs, Philip H. "International Educational Exchange: A Work for Many Hands." Higher Education 18 (September, 1961): 3-6.

2074. "Compte Rendu de leur Voyage d'Etudes par des Boursiers Originaires d'Autriche, d'Egypte et d'Indonesie." La Comprehension Internationale a l'Ecole 37 (1979): 11-16.

2075. Copeland, W. A. "Iran's Pahlavi University. A Decade of Cooperation with the University of Pennsylvania." International Educational and Cultural Exchange 7 (No. 1, 1971): 27-33.

2076. Cormack, Margaret L. "International Educational Exchange: Visas to What?" International Educational and Cultural Exchange 5 (Fall, 1969): 46-63.

   In a broad ranging discussion of the history of international exchanges since the early 1940s, the author brings out the role in terms of contributing to peace, ideology of the American Friends Service Committee and the early work of the experiment in international living.
   In encouraging students from other countries to study in the United States, it is argued that the presence of foreign students has broadened the curricular offerings in American institutions and has strengthened the American students' understanding of cross-cultural learning.
   The author discusses the study of Barbara Walton, "Foreign Student Exchange in Perspective," prepared for the United States Department of State, and throws light on the selection and admission criteria, the adjustment problems of foreign students, acculturation, assistance toward national development, brain drain problem, and the articulation of an international intellectual community. Most students, whether coming to the United States or leaving it, among other things, are found to be searching for identity and it is concluded that students as well as professors share more in common in the world today than they find differences.

2077. Dahl, O., and E. Denninger. "Un Voyage d'Etudes a Berlin." Education et Developpement No. 111 (1976): 32-41.

2078. Dahrendorf, R. "Overseas Students--Whither Now?" Political Quarterly 53 (October/December, 1982): 449-451.

2079. Dalheimer, Rolf. "FH Special--to Portsmouth for the Bachelor's Degree: Experiences with Study Abroad." Western European Education 13 (Fall, 1981): 49-56.

2080. Davis, Dorothy. "Study Abroad: A Case Study and Some Implications." International Journal of University Adult Education 17 (April, 1978): 14-23.

2081. Davis, J. M. "Some Trends in International Educational Exchange." Comparative Education Review 8 (January, 1964): 48-57.

2082.  De Witt, K.  "Cultural Ties With the Caribbean; Caribbean-American Exchange."  International Education and Cultural Exchange 13 (Fall, 1977):  14-16.

2083.  Dudden, A. P.  "Fulbright Alumni Association."  International Educational and Cultural Exchange 13 (Spring, 1978):  17-19.

2084.  Edgerton, W. B.  "Role of the Private Sector in Educational Exchange."  International Educational and Cultural Exchange 14 (Summer, 1978):  5-7.

2085.  Edgerton, W. B.  "Trends in Educational Exchange."  International Educational and Cultural Exchange 11 (No. 1, 1975):  11-16, 44.

2086.  Edgerton, W. B.  "Who Participates in Educational Exchange?"  Annals of the American Academy of Political and Social Science 424 (March, 1976):  6-15.

   Edgerton makes the point that in the future educational exchange may be conditioned and affected by the following factors, which are important considerations as he develops them.
1.  the wealth of resource in rich nations
2.  worldwide recession and inflation
3.  diminished dominance of the United States in international affairs
4.  political factors in the developing nations and in the communist nations
5.  brain drain
6.  changing attitudes towards education, including a discussion of the future role of life-long learning, and senior citizen educational exchanges
7.  changing interests of funding agencies, their leadership role
8.  interdependence

International education has been a growing field in the United States since the beginning of major exchange activity with the establishment of the Fulbright-Hays Fellowships shortly after World War II.  In its various aspects in the United States—exchange of American and foreign students, faculty, leaders, and specialists—international education assists a minimum of 250,000 individuals each year to study, teach, or perform research.  Worldwide, the number of exchanges is several times this total.  Many of the factors that have promoted the growth of large-scale exchange can be expected to continue to promote growth in the future, but there are a number of new elements that will affect the makeup of the exchange population in the future.  This article briefly examines a number of these factors and discusses reasons why they can be expected to play a significant role in determining the future of exchange.

2087. Evans, B. "China-Canada Student Exchange—1st 20." Pacific Affairs 49 (No. 1, 1976): 93-101.

2088. "Echanges Universitaires et Scolaires Franco-Canadiens." Informations Universitaires et Professionelles Internationales 26 (May-June, 1982): 17-36.

2089. Fantini, A. E. "Formula for Success: Camp Plus Young Americans Plus New Language." International Educational and Cultural Exchange 8 (Fall, 1972): 62-69.

2090. Flack, Michael J. "The International Realm as Experience: Experiential Learning in Transnational Contexts." In Research on Exchanges: Proceedings of the German-American Conference at Wissenschaftszentrum. Bonn, West Germany: German Academic Exchange Service, 1980.

2091. Flack, Michael J. "Results and Effects of Study Abroad." Annals of the American Academy of Political and Social Science 424 (March, 1976): 107-118.

    "Results" and "effects" of study abroad present major problems for research and assessment. Positing largely post-return criteria of "effect," a number of propositions seek to indicate some aspects of "results" and "impacts" relating to (1) the individual, (2) the host institution and society, (3) the home society, and (4) intersocietal and international relations.

2092. Fontaine, R. "Exchanges d'Eleves Sejours et Voyages a l'Etranger." Inrap No. 45 (1980): 29-49.

2093. Fox, Elizabeth. "The International Baccalaureate: A Mission in Progress." World Higher Education Communique 4 (Spring, 1982): 1-3.

2094. Frey, J. S. "Agency-sponsored Study Abroad Programs." International Educational and Cultural Exchange 12 (Fall, 1976): 29-33.

2095. Fulbright, William. T. "The Most Significant and Important Activity I have been Privileged to Engage in During My Years in the Senate [International Educational Exchange Activity]." Annals of the American Academy of Political and Social Science 424 (March, 1976): 1-5.

2096. Gaer, Felice D. "Scholarly Exchange Programs with Countries Abroad: Should Learning and Politics Mix?" Vital Issues 29 (No. 10, 1980): 1-6.

2097. Goodman, Norman G. "The International Institutionalization of Education." In Bridges to Knowledge: Foreign Students in a Comparative Perspective, edited by Elinor Barber, Philip G.

Altbach, and Robert Myers, pp. 7-18. Chicago: University of Chicago Press, 1984.

2098. Gullahorn, J. T., and J. E. Gullahorn. "American Objectives in Study Abroad." Journal of Higher Education 29 (1958): 369-374.

2099. Haas, G. James. "Undergraduate Transfer Credits from Abroad." College and University 57 (No. 2, 1982): 218-225.

2100. Haas, James. "Undergraduate Transfer Credits from Abroad." National Association for Foreign Student Affairs Newsletter 30 (May, 1979): 195ff.

2101. Havens, T. R. H. "American Undergraduate Study Programs in Japan and the Needs of Japan Studies in the United States." Asian Studies Professional Review 2 (No. 2, 1973): 64-69.

2102. Hayden, Rose Lee. "U.S. Government [Educational] Exchanges: The Quest for Coordination." Annals of the American Academy of Political and Social Science 449 (May, 1980): 114-128.

2103. Higbee, Homer. "International Educational Exchange." National Association for Foreign Student Affairs Newsletter 22 (May, 1970): 3ff.

2104. Hooper, Beverly. "The Australia-China Student Exchange Scheme: Could it be more Effective?" Australian Journal of Chinese Affairs 1 (January, 1979): 113-124.

2105. Hull, W. Frank, IV. "Undergraduate Studies Abroad--Evaluation in the Context of U.S. Higher Education." Higher Education in Europe 4 (April-June, 1979): 23-25.

2106. Hull, W. Frank, IV, and W. H. Lemke. "Research Findings and Administrative Implications for Off-campus Higher Education." International Review of Education 24 (No. 1, 1978): 53-64.

2107. Hull, W. Frank, IV, and Walter H. Lemke, Jr. "Retrospective Assessment of the United States Senior Fulbright-Hays Program." International Educational and Cultural Exchange 13 (No. 2, 1978): 6-9.

2108. "International Educational Relations and Exchange." College and University 52 (No. 4, 1977): 497-557.

2109. "International Exchange and the Future; Symposium." International Educational and Cultural Exchange 11 (Summer, 1975): 3-44.

2110. "The International Exchange of Student Employees." International Labor Review 69 (February, 1954): 151-169.

2111. Jenkins, Hugh M. "Part of a Complete Education." National Association for Foreign Student Affairs Newsletter 16 (June, 1965): 1ff.

2112. Joel, M., et al. "Non-sponsored Study Abroad: How to Evaluate." College and University 47 (Summer, 1972): 707-711.

2113. Joshi, Joan H. "International [Educational] Exchange in the Arts." Annals of the American Academy of Political and Social Science 424 (March, 1976): 78-84.

2114. Jova, J. J. "Latin Americanist Looks at Exchange Programs; Review of U.S.-Latin American Cultural Relations." International Educational and Cultural Exchange 13 (Fall, 1977): 3-6.

2115. Kaplan, Robert B. "NAFSA in the Mod Mod World." International Educational and Cultural Exchange 6 (Fall, 1970): 68-75.

2116. Klineberg, Otto. "The Role of International University Exchanges." In The Mediating Person: Bridges Between Cultures, edited by Stephen Bochner, pp. 113-135. Cambridge, Massachusetts: Schenckman, 1981.

      The author offers an updated review of the literature on the role of foreign students as cultural mediators and posits the need for additional research on the effect of cultural exchanges. In particular he indicates the need for a middle ground between adaptation of the foreign student of the new culture and total rejection of the new culture.
      On mental health aspects, there is a review of the problems of students from different cultures, particularly Third World students in Western cultures. The author contends the research has shown that the vast majority of non-Western or Third World students feel vulnerable and at risk during much of their time in the United States.

2117. Kruger, K. "Student Exchange Brings Them Closer to Each Other." Zellstoff und Papier 26 (No. 10, 1977): 295-297. (in German)

2118. Kurlansky, M. J. "Students and Colleges Profit From American Study Programs in France." Change 13 (March, 1981): 48-51.

2119. Lange, D. L., and H. L. Jorstad. "Unique Experience in French Culture: A Cultural Materials Workshop in Besanson." French Review 51 (February, 1978): 391-397.

2120. Lewitter, L. R. "University of Edinburgh and Poland." Slavonic and East European Review 49 (April, 1971): 278-280.

2121. "Links with Europe." Reports on Education No. 76 (1973): 1-4.

2122. Marion, Paul B. "Relationships of Student Characteristics and Experiences with Attitude Changes in a Program of Study

Abroad." _Journal of College Student Personnel_ 21 (January, 1980): 58-64.

2123. Marks, G. "Yank at Oxford." _Twentieth Century_ 179 (1971): 37-38.

2124. Marks, Leonard H., et al. "After Helsinki." _International Educational and Cultural Exchange_ 11 (No. 3, 1976): 22-29.

2125. Marks, Leonard H., et al. "Notes on U.S.-Middle East Exchanges." _International Education and Cultural Exchange_ 12 (Spring, 1977): 18-20.

2126. Martin, L., and A. Stoll. "Foreign Study Travel Program for the Urban University." _Foreign Language Annals_ 12 (No. 6, 1979): 487-490.

2127. Martin, L., and A. Stoll. "Foreign Study Travel Program for the Urban University-2." _Foreign Language Annals_ 13 (No. 4, 1980): 319-322.

2128. McCormack, William. "New Directions in Study Abroad." _Journal of Higher Education_ 37 (October, 1966): 369-376.

2129. McPherrin, Jeanette. "Opportunities for American Students to Study at British Universities." _National Association for Foreign Student Affairs Newsletter_ 25 (February, 1974): 10ff.

2130. Michel, J. M. "Le Voyage a l'Etranger: Errance ou Moyen de Formation pour les Jeunes." _Vers l'Education Nouvelle_ No. 297 (1975): 24-34.

2131. Mortensen, E. "Conducting Computer Searches in the Exchange Field." _International Educational and Cultural Exchange_ 13 (Winter, 1978): 48-51.

2132. Murray, Douglas P. "[Educational] Exchanges with the People's Republic of China: Symbols and Substance." _Annals of the American Academy of Political and Social Science_ 424 (March, 1976): 29-42.

2133. Nash, Dennison, and Rhonda Tarr. "The Stranger Group in an Overseas Study Program." _French Review_ 49 (February, 1976): 366-373.

2134. National Association for Foreign Student Affairs." NAFSA Principles for International Educational Interchange." In _Educating Students from Other Nations: American Colleges and Universities in International Educational Interchange_, edited by Hugh M. Jenkins, et al., pp. 319-333. San Francisco: Jossey-Bass, 1983.

2135. Neff, Charles B., and Jon W. Fuller. "Organizing International Programs: The Experience of Two Consortia." Liberal Education 69 (No. 3, 1983): 273–283.

2136. Nelson, D. N., et al. "We Studied Abroad." College and University 47 (Summer, 1972): 288–291.

2137. Nilsson, K. R. "Establishing a Program for Studying Abroad." American Association of University Professors Bulletin 52 (December, 1966): 428–432.

2138. Norman, C. "Year in Vientiane." French Review 42 (October, 1968): 104–109.

2139. O'Bannon, G. W. "Project Afghanistan: Undergraduates in Dynamic Cross-Cultural Experiment." International Educational and Cultural Exchange 8 (No. 4, 1973): 14–20.

2140. Ogden, M. "The American Host Program." International Educational and Cultural Exchange 6 (Spring, 1971): 44–57.

2141. "Over There! Over There! Summer Law Programs Abroad." Student Law 10 (February, 1982): 29–34.

2142. Owen, Wynx F., and T. Noel Osborn. "Proyecto Pionero Sobre Educacion Internacional Patrocinado por el CONACYT." Ciencia y Desarrollo No. 48 (1983): 1–101.

2143. Page, Benjamin, et al. "International Training Looks to the Future." College and University 53 (Summer, 1978): 477–499.

2144. Patterson, M. E., et al. "Canadian University Service Overseas: Its Experience in Education." Canadian and International Education No. 28 (1974): 17–19.

2145. Pfnister, A. O. "Evaluation of Overseas Student Programs—2 Case Studies." North-Central Association Quarterly 46 (1971): 307–313.

2146. Pfnister, A. O. "Everyone Overseas! Goshen College Pioneers; Student-Service Trimester." International Educational and Cultural Exchange 8 (Fall, 1972): 1–12.

2147. Pfnister, A. O. "Quality Control for Study Abroad Programs." International Educational and Cultural Exchange 8 (Winter, 1972–73): 19–35.

The recent proliferation of study-abroad programs has promoted widespread concern as to their quality. This article describes a pilot project to develop a pattern of systematic evaluation or accreditation to ensure the maintenance of high academic standards. The project was undertaken by an evaluation team appointed in 1972 by the Federation of Regional Accrediting Commissions of Higher

Education for 12 study-abroad programs of American colleges and universities in Europe. The author discusses such aspects as the role of the field director, admission procedures, orientation, study and travel, library resources, and cooperative endeavors. Greater emphasis is put on pointing up problems in study abroad, emphasizing the positive achievements.

2148.   Platt, James.  "Student Exchange Programs."  In International Encyclopedia of Higher Education, edited by A. Knowles, pp. 1528-1551.  San Francisco:  Jossey-Bass, 1977.

2149.   Purkaple, R. H.  "American Students Abroad."  International Educational and Cultural Exchange 7 (No. 3, 1972):  67-81.

        At this time more American students are going abroad to study than ever before.  As the director of Study Abroad at the University of Colorado, Boulder, the author discusses the motivations of the American students going to Europe, Asia, and Latin America, the attitudes of their parents, problem of differing educational systems, some inter-university programs, the typical cycle of American students' reactions to things in the host-country, and possible futures of study abroad.  The author concludes that study abroad cannot be viewed as the luxury of the more affluent.  The further development of the right programs to achieve these goals is the challenge facing higher education in the United States today.

2150.   Reichard, John F.  "Summary and Agenda for Future Interchanges."  In Educating Students from Other Nations, edited by Hugh Jenkins, pp. 295-318.  San Francisco:  Jossey-Bass, 1983.

2151.   Rhinesmith, Stephen.  "Alienation or Education?  A case for International Exchange."  National Association for Foreign Student Affairs Newsletter 30 (October, 1978):  1ff.

2152.   Richards, James M., Jr.  "Personality Type and Characteristics of Nations in International Higher Education Exchange with the United States."  Research in Higher Education 2 (September, 1974):  189-194.

        This study was based upon Holland's personality typology.  The sample consisted of approximately 175 nation-states that send or have the potential for sending exchange students to the United States in the time frame of the 1967-1968 academic year.  It should be noted that the People's Republic of China was, in fact, included in the study although no students from China were present in American universities at that point in time.
        Consideration was given to the characteristics of nation-states as developed by Sawyer; that is size, wealth and political orientation, assuming alliance with the United States, neutral or Communist, and geographic

distance from the United States. It was found that the characteristics of a nation-state have some relationship to the personality types of the students received in international exchanges and also to the students' area of academic interest.

Large nations send many students to the U.S. who tend to study realistic and artistic fields. Communist nations send few students, and these students tend to concentrate in only one type of field. Students from wealthy countries tend to study artistic fields. The results appear meaningful at a strictly empirical level, but throw little light one way or the other on Holland's underlying theory.

2153. Ritterband, Paul. "Law, Policy and Behavior. Educational Exchange Policy and Student Migration." American Journal of Sociology 76 (July, 1970): 71-82.

This paper examines the effect of legislation, administrative rules, and policy edicts upon Israelis involved in the educational exchange programs of the United States, in light of the parallel utilitarian sources of compliance and noncompliance. The data for the study were collected by a Hebrew-language questionnaire mailed out in the late spring through the early winter of 1966 with a response rate of 67%, yielding 1,934 usable cases. The analysis presented is restricted to persons who arrived in the United States with either student (F) or exchange (J) visa. The paper examines the allocation of visas, academic achievement and the labor market in Israel, and the effectiveness of the statutes and concludes that the legislation does not achieve its end, although the initial relationship between visa and migration intentions appears to show that the law really works. It is demonstrated that the initial relationship is a function of extralegal methods which work through the home-country educational system and through needs of the labor market. The official policy of the government of the United States is frustrated by the disparate interests of the several organizational role partners. Behavior would remain largely the same if there were neither law nor policy pronouncements.

2154. Rose, Peter I. "The Senior Fulbright-Hays Program in East Asia and the Pacific." International Educational and Cultural Exchange 12 (No. 2, 1976): 19-23.

2155. Ruiz-Fornells, E. "Study in Spain and the Problem of Credit Transfer." Hispania 66 (March, 1983): 69-74.

2156. Schenck, E. A., et al. "Educational Exchange: U.S./U.K. Comparison and Interpretation." College and University 46 (Summer, 1971): 372-375.

2157. Schenck, E. A., et al. "Procedures for Inaugurating Sponsored Study Abroad Programs." College and University 47 (Summer, 1972): 594-604.

2158. Shank, Donald J., et al. "Opportunities and Problems Involved in the Study Abroad of United States Students." College and University 38 (Summer, 1963): 434-460.

2159. Shirey, W. W. "Certification for the Foreign Bound." College and University 50 (Summer, 1975): 548-556.

2160. Smith, Alan. "European Developments in International Exchange Programs." In Bridges to Knowledge: Foreign Students in a Comparative Perspective, edited by Elinor Barber, Philip G. Altbach, and Robert Myers, pp. __-__. Chicago: University of Chicago Press, 1984.

2161. Smuckler, Ralph H. "Institutional Linkages: A Key to Successful International Exchanges." Annals of the American Academy of Political and Social Science 424 (March, 1976): 43-51.

2162. Strain, William H. "Problems of Educational Exchange with English-Speaking Countries of West and East Africa." College and University 41 (Winter, 1966): 145-161.

2163. Strain, William H. "Some Doubts About Educational Exchange." College and University 42 (Winter, 1967): 141-146.

2164. Sullivan, Kathy, and Nancy Searles. "Year Abroad Programs in the Middle East." World Higher Education Communique 1 (Fall, 1979): 16-18.

2165. Thiel, F. "Sights, Sounds and Scents--The Physical Side of Foreign Study." Modern Languages Journal 64 (No. 4, 1980): 434-440.

2166. Tierney, James F. "Overview: International Exchange." In International Encyclopedia of Higher Education, edited by A. Knowles, pp. 1505-1511. San Francisco: Jossey-Bass, 1977.

2167. Toscano, J. V. "Interim-Term World Campus; Study Abroad During January." International and Cultural Exchange 8 (Summer, 1972): 23-32.

2168. "Understanding on the Exchange of Students and Scholars Between the United States of America and the People's Republic of China." International Legal Materials 18 (March, 1979): 356-360.

2169. Verner, Zenobia. "Guidelines for Professors on Short-Term Assignment with International Programs." International Education 5 (Fall, 1973): 38-40.

2170. Vogel, Ralph. "Travel Abroad." In International Encyclopedia of Higher Education, edited by A. Knowles, pp. 1565-1575. San Francisco: Jossey-Bass, 1977.

2171. Wallace, J. A. "Characteristics of Programs for Study Abroad." Journal of General Education 13 (1962): 251-261.

2172. Wang, L. L. "Peiping Program for Sending Students Abroad." Issues and Studies 15 (No. 7, 1979): 10-12.

2173. Wenner, L. N. "American Youth Overseas." Adolescence 5 (1970): 427-450.

2174. Wertheim, Albert. "Changing Overseas Study Programs." International Education 8 (Spring, 1979): 17-20.

2175. Wilcox, L., et al. "Guidelines for Institutional Follow-up on International Students." College and University 45 (Summer, 1970): 439-453.

2176. Williams, Peter. "Making Tomorrow Happen Sooner: Towards a More Equal International Exchange of Students. Teachers and Research." In Education and Development, edited by Roger M. Garrett, pp. 321-343. London: Croom Helm, 1984.

2177. Wolfson, R. G. "Innovative Living Experience in Israel." Jewish Education 44 (Spring, 1976): 68-80.

2178. Woodhouse, Chase G. "The Foreign Student in the United States: What's the Program? How is it Doing?" Vital Issues 13 (January, 1964): 16-23.

## Reportage

2179. "Americans for Language Study (in China)." Chronicle of Higher Education 21 (January 26, 1981): 15.

2180. Binyon, M. "Student Exchanges; French Hope to Double Their Numbers." Times Education Supplement (November 15, 1968): 1082.

2181. Bremiller, Lawrence. "NAS Ends Its Role in Limiting Foreign Scholars' Activities." Chronicle of Higher Education 23 (January 27, 1982): 9.

2182. "British Urge Support for Fulbright Programs." Chronicle of Higher Education 23 (November 25, 1981): 22.

2183. "California-Chile Exchange Halted." Chronicle of Higher Education 9 (January 20, 1975): 2.

2184. "Canada, China Plan Exchanges in Management Studies." Chronicle of Higher Education 25 (December 1, 1982): 22.

2185. "Canada May Renew Exchanges with Soviet Union." Chronicle of Higher Education 25 (November 24, 1982): 16.

2186. "China Restricting Numbers of Students Sent Abroad." Chronicle of Higher Education 24 (July 28, 1982): 13.

2187. "China Rules out Increase in Scholarly Exchanges." Chronicle of Higher Education 14 (July 5, 1977): 9.

2188. "Chinese Get SUNY Degrees." Chronicle of Higher Education 22 (June 8, 1981): 15.

2189. "Chinese Scientists Call for Continuation of China–U.S. Exchanges." Chronicle of Higher Education 23 (September 30, 1981): 17.

2190. "Concern Over Drop in Research Visits Abroad." Chronicle of Higher Education 22 (May 4, 1981): 15.

2191. "Congressmen Favor Expansion of U.S.-Soviet Exchanges." Chronicle of Higher Education 22 (July 6, 1981): 13.

2192. Cookson, C. "U.S. Falls Back in Exchange Programs." Times Higher Education Supplement 450 (June 19, 1981): 6.

2193. David, P. "Threat to Fulbright Exchange." Times Higher Education Supplement 470 (November 6, 1981): 6.

2194. "Deterioration of U.S.-Soviet Relations Dramatizes Need of Exchanges." Chronicle of Higher Education 18 (June 22, 1981): 17.

2195. Godsmark, R. "Lessons from a Tragedy: Hotel Fire at Sappada, Italy, in 1976." Times Education Supplement (March 10, 1978): 34.

2196. "Japan Funds Ohio U. Exchange Programs." Chronicle of Higher Education 21 (September 29, 1980): 19.

2197. Kirkpatrick, A. "Meaning of China's Friendship." Far East Economic Review 98 (October 7, 1977): 61-62.

2198. Lodge, B. "Residence Abroad and the Student of Modern Languages." Times Education Supplement (October 28, 1977): 6.

2199. "As Many as 30 Students from Columbia University to Study at Oxford or Cambridge University." Chronicle of Higher Education 25 (November 3, 1982): 21.

2200. "Minnesota Seeks Exchanges with Soviet University." Chronicle of Higher Education 8 (March 4, 1974): 2.

2201. "Penn-Nigeria Exchanges." Chronicle of Higher Education 23 (November 4, 1981): 21.

2202. R. L. J. "Academy of Sciences Wants to Expand Exchanges with U.S.S.R." Chronicle of Higher Education 15 (October 17, 1977): 8.

2203. Rich, Vera. "Poland Expels American Lecturer for 'Anti-Socialist Activities'." Chronicle of Higher Education 25 (February 16, 1983): 19.

2204. "Scholarly Exchanges with China: Who Benefits?" Chronicle of Higher Education 22 (May 25, 1981): 21.

2205. Scully, M. G. "Most Academic Exchanges Go Forward Despite Chill in U.S.-Soviet Relations." Chronicle of Higher Education 19 (January 21, 1980): 9.

2206. Scully, Malcolm G. "Science Academy Suspends Exchanges; Deploring Soviet Treatment of Sakharov." Chronicle of Higher Education 20 (March 3, 1980): 1.

2207. Scully, Malcolm G. "Soviets Call 20 Exchange Scholars Home; Cutting Fears for Their Safety in U.S." Chronicle of Higher Education 27 (September 28, 1983): 25.

2208. Sexton, Bonnie. "Exchanges with China to Continue." Chronicle of Higher Education 24 (August 4, 1982): 17.

2209. Sexton, Bonnie. "China Will Continue to Let Students Study Overseas Despite Defections." Chronicle of Higher Education 25 (November 24, 1982): 15.

2210. "Stanford Denied Permission to Locate Program to Oxford." Chronicle of Higher Education 23 (October 21, 1981): 20.

2211. "SUNY, Soviet Union Set Student Exchange." Chronicle of Higher Education 8 (April 15, 1974): 2.

2212. "20 Canadian Students to Study in Peking." Chronicle of Higher Education 8 (November 19, 1973): 6.

2213. "2 Colleges to Exchange Scholars with China." Chronicle of Higher Education 20 (May 12, 1980): 17.

2214. "U.S. Exchanges with USSR, Canada, and Sweden, Set." Chronicle of Higher Education 23 (February 10, 1982): 17.

2215. "U.S. Urged to Halt Decline in Foreign Exchange Programs." Chronicle of Higher Education 22 (June 1, 1981): 1.

2216. "U. of San Francisco to Open Business School in Tokyo." Chronicle of Higher Education 9 (October 21, 1974): 2.

2217. "NAS Extends on Soviet Exchanges." Chronicle of Higher Education 21 (August 25, 1980): 16.

2218. "Weniger Europaische Wissenschaftler Wandern in die U.S.A. aus." Deutsche Universitatszeitung No. 21 (1970): 19.

2219. Whitbread, N. "Student Study Tour to Czechoslovakia." Education for Teaching No. 80 (1969): 73-74.

2220. Whittingham, Ken. "Canadian Research Council May Suspend Scientific Exchanges with the Soviet Union." Chronicle of Higher Education 19 (February 25, 1981): 17.

2221. "Yugoslavia Ends Exchanges with Albania." Chronicle of Higher Education 22 (May 18, 1981): 15.

## 28. DISCIPLINARY STUDIES (LAW, ENGINEERING, AGRICULTURE, ETC.)

2222. American Chemical Society. Guide to Chemical Education in the United States for Foreign Students. Washington, D.C.: American Chemical Society, 1981.

2223. American Council on Education, Overseas Liaison Committee. "Africa Speaks, America Responds": A Report of the African Council on Communication Education. Washington, D.C.: American Council on Education, 1979.

2224. Bailey, Kathleen, Frank Pialorsi and Jean Zukowski. Foreign Teaching Assistants in US Universities. Washington, D.C.: National Association for Foreign Student Affairs, 1984.

     The monograph deals with the problems of preparing foreign teaching assistants for their roles in American colleges and universities. Chapters deal with training programs for foreign teaching assistants and discuss language skills orientation seminars, a one-semester course, and the overall problems of providing preparation for foreign teaching assistants. Additional chapters deal with the assessment of such programs and testing for the oral English proficiency of the assistants.

2225. Basu, Arun Chandra. "A Study of Graduate Agricultural Students from India at Selected Land Grant Colleges and Universities in the United States." Unpublished Ph.D thesis, University of Missouri, 1966.

2226. Berggren, Willard. Guidebook for Engineering Newcomers to the United States of America. New York: The Engineers Joint Council, 1968.

2227. Bernardo, F. A., and F. S. Saladaga, eds. Facilitating Academic Interchange Among Graduate Schools of Agriculture in Asia:

Proceedings of the Seminar-Workshop of Graduate School Deans in Asia, Jointly Sponsored by A.A.C.U. and S.E.A.R.C.A., Bangkok, Thailand, June 25-27, 1975. Cebu City, Philippines: Asian Association of Agricultural Colleges and Universities, 1976.

2228. Carnovsky, Leon. The Foreign Student in the American Library School. Final Report. Chicago, Illinois: University of Chicago, Graduate Library School, 1971.

2229. Committee on International Activities, ACS. Guide to Chemical Education in the U.S. for Foreign Students. Washington, D.C.: American Chemical Society, 1981.

2230. Connotillo, Barbara Cahn, ed. Study of Agriculture in the U.S.: A Guide for Foreign Students. New York: Institute of International Education, 1979.

2231. Eastin, Roy Brandon. "A Comparative Analysis of United States and Foreign Participation in a Common Course of Management Instruction." Unpublished D.B.A. thesis, George Washington University, 1969.

2232. Education and World Affairs. Internationalizing the United States Professional School. New York: EWA, 1969.

2233. German Academic Exchange Service. Studies at Fachhochschulen. Bonn: DAAD, 1980.

2234. Hoefer, Fred Durbin. "Participant Assessment of Exchange Program P-1-0004, University of Minnesota, 1963-1974: An International Agricultural Academic and Practical Training Program in Perspective." Unpublished Ph.D thesis, University of Minnesota, 1977.

2235. Institute of International Education. Engineering Education in the United States. New York: IIE, 1974.

2236. Owen, Wyn. Higher Education in Economics: The International Dimensions. Boulder, Colorado: Economics Institute, 1981.

2237. Pfau, Richard H. Teaching Expectations and Related Backgrounds of Foreign Science and Engineering Students at the University of Pittsburg. Pittsburgh, Pennsylvania: University Center for International Studies, University of Pittsburgh, 1976.

2238. Putarasangthai, Nataya. "Value of Student Teaching Experiences Relating to Attitude Toward Teaching as Perceived by Student Teachers of Silpakorn University and the University of Iowa." Unpublished Ph.D thesis, University of Iowa, 1979.

2239. Ross, Sherman. International Opportunities for Advanced Training and Research in Psychology. Washington, D.C.: American Psychological Association, 1967.

2240. Sanders, Irwin T., ed. <u>The Professional Education of Students from Other Lands</u>. New York: Council on Social Work Education, 1963.

2241. Shinouda, Elia Habib. "An Appraisal of the Program Leading to the Doctor of Education Degree at Indiana University as Related to Foreign Students." Unpublished Ph.D thesis, Indiana University, 1966.

This followup study deals with 75 foreign doctoral graduates with majors in education at Indiana University from 1954-1964. The 75 doctoral graduates' views were used to appraise the effectiveness of the doctoral program of the School of Education Data identifying the background characteristics of the 75 graduates, and a designed questionnaire in five areas of cross-cultural experience was obtained for the study. The major findings of the study were that of the 75 foreign graduates, 47 were men and 28 women with about half of the students from Southeast Asia and the second largest group from the Middle East having a mean age of 36 at the time the degree was conferred. During the period under study, 3 out of 10 foreign graduates received the Ph.D degree as against one of ten Americans; 49 out of the 75 wrote their thesis about their home-countries; less than half of the respondents had adequate knowledge about the educational system in the United States prior to their arrival. Adjustment problems were insignificant and the most valuable aspects of the doctoral program identified were course work, dissertation projects, and student-professor relationships. A majority of the group reported financial gain, promotion in rank, increased professional competence and involvement in careers that involved policy and decision making. Most of them needed between three and five months to get readjusted in their home environment. The concluding remarks include reservations about certain aspects of the program and suggestions for improvement to help future candidates.

2242. Susskind, Charles, and Lynn Schell. <u>Exporting Technical Education: A Survey and Case Study of Foreign Professionals with U.S. Graduate Degrees</u>. New York: Institute of International Education, 1969.

2243. Udoh, Christopher Ofuonye. "A Comparison of Professional Preparation Programs for Health Education in Selected Nigerian and American Colleges and Universities." Unpublished Ph.D thesis, Ohio State University, 1979.

2244. United States Congress, House Committee on the Judiciary, Subcommittee on Immigration, Refugees and International Law. <u>Admission of Alien Physicians for Graduate Medical Education: Hearing, May 14, 1980, on H. R. 7118, a Bill to Amend the Immigration and Nationality Act with Respect to the Admission of Alien Physicians for Graduate Medical Education</u>. (96th

Congress, 2nd Session). Washington, D.C.: Government Printing Office, 1980.

2245. Vorapipalana, Kowit. "A Study of the Thai Graduates' Training Program in the Field of Education from the United States." Unpublished doctoral thesis, University of Utah, 1967.

2246. Wee, Joo L. "A Study of Students from Other Lands Who Received Master's Degrees in Educational Administration from Teachers College, Columbia University, 1950-1962." Unpublished Ph.D thesis, Columbia University, 1963.


## Articles

2247. Abu-Saad, H., and J. S. Kayser-Jones. "Middle-Eastern Nursing Students in the United States." Journal of Nursing Education 21 (September, 1982): 22-25.

2248. Abu-Saad, H., et al. "Asian Nursing Students in the United States." Journal of Nursing Education 21 (September, 1982): 11-15.

2249. Abu-Saad, H., et al. "Latin American Nursing Students in the United States." Journal of Nursing Education 21 (September, 1982): 16-21.

2250. Ahimaz, F. J. "Organizational Need--Institutional Triumvirate to Structure and Offer Relevant Engineering Education at United States Universities for International Students." In Proceedings: 1979 Frontiers in Education Conference, edited by L. P. Grayson, and J. M. Biedenbach, pp. 194-197. Washington, D.C.: American Society for Engineering Education, 1979.

2251. Allen, M. E. M. "Problem of Communication in a Summer Workshop for Foreign Nurses; Psychiatric Nursing." Journal of Nursing Education 19 (January, 1980): 8-12.

2252. Barnes, S. Y. "Problems Foreign Nurses Encounter in Passing Psychiatric Nursing on U.S. Exams for Licensure." Journal of Nursing Education 19 (January, 1980): 19-26.

2253. Beck, Robert H. "The Professional Training in Education of Foreign Students in the United States." Journal of Teacher Education 13 (June, September, December, 1962): 140-149, 302-318, 402-408.

This is a cross-cultural report on the professional preparation of foreign students in education. During the five-year period 1955-1960 there were some 11,500 foreign nationals enrolled in education programs at various U.S. colleges and universities. In the first part of the article, general profiles and perceptions of these students are provided, and American values the foreign students rejected and accepted are analyzed. The second part deals with foreign students' views of the American education system and the difficulties they encountered. In the third and fourth parts, the author proposes some theoretical considerations and suggestions concerning the improvement of professional training of foreign students in a cross-cultural setting.

2254. Berendt, H. "Issue of Change: Its Relationship to Teaching Foreign Nurse Students: Attitudes Toward Mental Illness and Psychiatric Patients." Journal of Nursing Education 19 (January, 1980): 4-7.

2255. Brook, P. "Training Opportunities for Overseas Psychiatrists." British Journal of Psychiatry 127 (August, 1975): 179-184.

2256. Caquelin, Howard J. "Education for an Engineering Profession." International Educational and Cultural Exchange 5 (Winter, 1970): 44-65.

2257. Carnovsky, Leon. "The Foreign Student in the American Library School." Library Quarterly 43 (April, July, 1973): 103-125, 199-214.

2258. Cornish, D. "British Councils' Role in Education and Training in the Library and Information Science Field." In Education and Training Theory and Provision, pp. 85-87. The Hague: Federation Internationale de Documentation, 1979.

2259. Damarin, S., and G. West. "Preparation of Foreign Graduate Students to Teach Mathematics: An Experimental Course." American Mathematical Monthly 86 (June-July, 1979): 494-497.

2260. Dart, E. E., et al. "Observations on an Obstacle Course; U.S. Graduate Education for the Deserving Asian Physics Student." International Educational and Cultural Exchange 11 (Fall, 1975): 29-32.

2261. Dhillon, Gita L., and Lawrence Litwock. "Study Programs for Foreign Nurses." Nursing Outlook 24 (January, 1976): 41-44.

2262. Dickinson, John C., and John E. Stump. "Transfer of Students from U.S. and Foreign Veterinary Schools—Admissions and Performance." Journal of Veterinary Medical Education 7 (No. 2, 1980): 91-93.

2263. Eisemon, Thomas. "The Effect of U.S. Training: A Study of American-Educated Indian Engineering Faculty." International Review of Education 20 (Spring, 1974): 36-53.

The purpose of this paper is to determine whether organized exposure to American academic and professional norms has had any long-term influence on attitudes and scholarly behavior of a group of Indian engineering faculty who studied in the United States between 1953 and 1963. Foreign study is presumed to change participating scholars in ways that would not have occurred had they remained at home. It is hoped that returnees will evidence greater professional commitment than their counterparts who have not been abroad, be more productive scholars, and will identify more closely with the international professional community. This study is based on a survey of engineering teachers conducted in India during 1971-72. Two groups of teachers were sampled: (1) Individuals sent abroad under US Agency for International Development. Almost all of them were faculty members in Indian institutions prior to their American sojourn. (2) Members of the Institution of Engineers in India. The results have shown that few differences existed between the two groups, and returnees were not more productive researchers, more professionally involved or more cosmopolitan than their India-trained counterparts. The author says that professional training at American universities does little long-term harm, and at the same time it appears to have a very limited long-term benefit in the context of Indian engineering education, in terms of making a "unique" contribution to the recipient's professional career.

2264. Figueroa, T. Ludwig, and Joan E. Friedenberg. "Foreign Engineering Students: Problems and Suggestions." Engineering Education 73 (November, 1982): 183-185.

2265. Goodyear, A. "International Co-operation in Engineering Education." In Proceedings: 1979 Frontiers in Education Conference, edited by L. P. Grayson, and J. M. Biedenbach, pp. 238-243. Washington, D.C.: American Society for Engineering Education, 1979.

2266. Grand Pre, D. R. "A Window on America. Informational Program for Foreign Military Trainees." International Educational and Cultural Exchange 6 (Fall, 1970): 86-93.

2267. "Guidelines for Schools Offering a Health Education Major Which Accept International Students." Journal of School Health 49 (No. 5, 1979): 267-274.

2268. Hoak, A. H. "The International Agricultural Centre (IAC) [and Foreign Students]." Higher Education and Research in the Netherlands 20 (No. 2, 1976): 19-23.

2269. Hammond, S. B., and M. A. Kanter. "Nuclear Power-Project Training for Engineers from Developing Countries." Engineering Education 72 (January, 1982): 314-316.

2270. Hogg, F. N. "Programs for Overseas Students, College of Librarianship, Wales." In Education and Training Theory and Provision, pp. 95-97. The Hague: Federation Internationale de Documentation, 1979.

2271. Hopp, J. W. "Specialized Field Work for International Health Education Students: A Survey of Need." Journal of School Health 47 (No. 8, 1977): 481-482.

2272. Iverson, S. C. "Developmental Engineering Science-Program for International Students." In Proceedings: 1979 Frontiers in Education Conference, edited by L. P. Grayson, and J. M. Biedenbach, pp. 231-234. Washington, D.C.: American Society for Engineering Education, 1979.

2273. Jenkins, Hugh M. "Engineering Education and the International Student in the United States." National Association for Foreign Student Affairs Newsletter 34 (Summer, 1983): 186ff.

2274. Johnson, David. "Engineering Studies in Britain for Students from Commonwealth Developing Countries." European Journal of Engineering Education 6 (No. 3/4, 1981): 253-262.

2275. Kay, J. M. "Veterinary Education Abroad: An Alternative for American Students--Or Exile?" Modern Veterinary Practice 61 (No. 6, 1980): 492-495.

2276. Kelly, Judith. "Latin American Business Students Learn the Harvard Hustle." Change 8 (No. 8, 1976): 13-17.

2277. Keresztesi, Michael. "Diffusion of Modern Library Thought and Practice by Means of UNESCO Fellowships for Travel and Study Abroad." Libri: International Library Review 29 (October, 1979): 193-206.

2278. Lee, J. M. "A Dilemma of Post-Imperial Obligations? Public Administration Training for Overseas Students in Britain." Philippine Journal of Public Administration 10 (October, 1966): 414-423.

2279. Leone, L. P. "Orienting Nurses from Other Countries to Graduate Education in the United States." Journal of Nursing Education 21 (September, 1982): 45-47.

2280. Levinson, R. M. "Experiential Education Abroad: Comparative Health Care Systems Program." Teaching Sociology 6 (No. 4, 1979): 415-419.

2281. Levinson, R. M. "Potentials of Cross Cultural Field Study: Emory's Comparative Health Care Systems Program in London." Journal of Nursing Education 18 (November, 1979): 46-52.

2282. Lewis, A. B. "Training Foreign Graduate Students in Agricultural Economics." Journal of Farm Economics 49 (August, 1967): 684-704.

2283. Liebesny, H. J. "Lawyers from Developing Countries in the United States: A Special Cultural Shock." Middle East Journal 34 (Spring, 1980): 205-213.

2284. Long, M. F. "Foreign Graduate Students in Economics." American Economic Review 56 (September, 1966): 848-855.

2285. Maloney, J. O. "Broader Training for Foreign Engineering Students." Technos 5 (July-September, 1976): 41-51.

The author postulates that due to the fact that many engineering graduates returning to rapidly developing countries are frequently placed in high positions, it is essential that they are better provided with a broader perspective on project development and analytical abilities. In this context, the author describes a course that has been taught to several groups of chemical engineering students (at the University of Kansas) and lists the resources of some materials which had been used.

The basic assignment of the course was to prepare a proposal for an income-generating investment in a developing country, concerned with processing operation needs in fertilizers, metals, petrochemicals, and sugar.

The article also presents a stage-development diagram of the course and a sequential outline of the learning materials needed in preparation for class and class activity.

The article concludes with some course observations concerning:
. type of project to be selected and;
. ways of developing most effective and interesting learning materials.

2286. Markson, C. J. "What Do Foreign Graduate Students Think About Their U.S. Degree Programs?" Engineering Education 66 (1976): 830-831.

2287. McDermott, J. F., and T. W. Maretzki. "Some Guidelines for the Training of Foreign Medical Graduates: Results of a Special Project." American Journal of Psychology 132 (June, 1975): 658-661.

2288. McNown, John S. "African Students of Engineering at Home and in the U.S." Technos 4 (July-September, 1975): 43-56.

2289. Moran, Robert. "Learning Cross-Culturally: The Case Study of Management." In Learning Across Cultures: Intercultural Communication and International Educational Exchange, edited by Gary Althen, pp. 138-142. Washington, D.C.: National Association for Foreign Student Affairs, 1981.

2290. Morrison, B. L. "Conflicts and Frustration Influencing Nurses from Other Countries." Journal of Nursing Education 19 (January, 1980): 12-19.

2291. Onwere, Godfrey O. "Factors Associated with Interest in Science in West African [University] Students in Washington, D.C." Journal of Negro Education 49 (No. 2, 1980): 207-214.

2292.  Peuse, H. Gene.  "Training Foreign Students--Implications for Teachers and Agricultural Programs."  National Association of College Teachers of Agriculture Journal 27 (No. 1, 1983): 31-34.

2293.  Reyesguerra, D. R.  "Quality of United States Engineering Education vs. the Needs of Less Developed Countries."  In Proceedings: 1979 Frontiers in Education Conference, edited by L. P. Grayson, and J. M. Biedenbach, p. 237. Washington, D.C.: American Society for Engineering Education, 1979.

2294.  Russo, Celia.  "The European Engineering Programme:  A Joint Venture."  European Journal of Education 17 (No. 1, 1982): 59-64.

2295.  Schuh, G. Edward.  "The Impact of Foreign Students on U.S. Economic Curricula."  In Higher Education in Economics: The International Dimensions, edited by Wyn F. Owen, et al., pp. 39-45.  Boulder, Colorado:  Economics Institute, 1981.

2296.  Shaner, W. W.  "Teaching Engineering Students from Developing Countries."  Engineering Education 69 (November, 1978): 214-215.

2297.  Shaw, Robert A.  "The Stranger in our Midst:  Liability or Asset?" Engineering Education 72 (January, 1982):  310-313.

2298.  Suzuki, N.  "Chase of the Wild Geese:  Flying Pattern of Foreign Business Students at United States Business Schools--Why it has Happened."  Management International Review 19 (No. 4, 1979): 95-110.

2299.  Turack, Daniel C.  "Access to the State Bar Examination for Foreign Trained Graduates:  The Ohio Experience."  Ohio Northern University Law Review 8 (April, 1981):  265-298.

2300.  Vojgand, V.  "International Student Competitions in Analytical Chemistry."  Fresenius Zeitschrift fur Analytische Chemie 297 (No. 4, 1979):  271-277.

2301.  Van Eerde, J.  "Foreign Language and Culture Program for Engineers."  French Review 42 (December, 1968):  272-276.

2302.  Zindler, H.  "Prufungswesen und Ausbildungsmoglichkeiten im Bereich Deutsch als Fremdsprache an West Deutschen Hochschulen."  Zielsprache Deutsche (No. 1, 1972):  6-12.

Reportage

2303.  "Foreign Medical School Found Deficient."  Chronicle of Higher Education 21 (December 1, 1980):  14.

2304. "Foreign Troops Invade America--Peacefully: Foreign Military Students in the United States." U.S. News and World Report 80 (April 19, 1976): 50.

2305. "France: Projet de Decret sur la Reforme des Etudes Medicales. Admission des Etudiants Etrangers dans les Universites." Newsletter, Council of Europe (No. 2, 1980): 11-13.

2306. Rout, Lawrence. "Degrees of Medicine: Would-be Physicians Learn What it Means to Study Abroad; Students Are Conscientious but Schools They Attend are Below U.S. Standards." Wall Street Journal 198 (December 21, 1981): 1ff.

2307. Scully, Malcolm G. "Half of U.S. Ph.D's in Engineering Go to Foreigners." Chronicle of Higher Education 25 (October 6, 1982): 8.

2308. Watzman, Herbert M. "Israelis Defend Program for U.S. Med Students." Chronicle of Higher Education 23 (October 14, 1981): 17.

2309. Whittingham, Ken. "Medical Graduates Flocking to Take U.S. Licensing Tests." Chronicle of Higher Education 20 (April 28, 1980): 15.

---

## 29. MEDICAL STUDY ABROAD

2310. Bowers, John, and Elizabeth Purcell. New Medical Schools at Home and Abroad. Port Washington, New York: Independent Publishers Group, 1979.

2311. Buhler, Robert Gordon. "American Higher Education for Foreign Students: A Framework for Evaluation and Case Study of Three American Schools of Public Health." Unpublished Ph.D thesis, Claremont Graduate School, 1979.

2312. Dube, W. F. Characteristics of U.S. Citizens Seeking Transfer from Foreign to U.S. Medical Schools in 1975 Via the Coordinated Transfer Application System (COTRANS): [Final Report]. Washington, D.C.: Association of American Medical Colleges, 1977.

2313. Educational Commission for Foreign Medical Graduates. Handbook for Foreign Medical Students. Philadelphia: ECFMG, 1978.

2314. Institute of International Education. Guide to Foreign Medical Schools. New York: IIE, 1975.

2315.   Margulies, Harold. Foreign Medical Graduates in the United States. Cambridge, Massachusetts: Harvard University Press, 1969.

2316.   Marien, Daniel. Guide to Foreign Medical Schools. New York: Queens College Press, 1973.

2317.   Mejia, Alfonso, Helena Pizurki, and Erica Royston. Foreign Medical Graduates: The Case of the United States. Lexington, Mass., Lexington, 1980.

2318.   National Institute of Health, Division of Manpower Intelligence. The Foreign Medical Graduate. Washington, D.C.: U.S. Government Printing Office, 1972.

2319.   Pestana, Carlos. The Rejected Medical School Applicant--Options and Alternatives. San Antonio, Texas: Pestana, 1978.

2320.   United States Bureau of Health Manpower. Characteristics of U.S. Citizens Seeking Transfer from Foreign to U.S. Medical Schools in 1975 Via COTRANS (Coordinated Transfer Application System). Hyattsville, Maryland: Department of Health, Education and Welfare, 1977.

2321.   United States Congress, Subcommittee on Health. Health Manpower Legislation, 1975, Part 2. [Hearings Before the Subcommittee on Health on the Role of Foreign Medical Graduates (FMG's) in U.S. Health Manpower]. Washington, D.C.: Government Printing Office, 1976.

2322.   United States Congress, House of Representatives, Subcommittee on Health and the Environment. Oversight--GAO Report on U.S. Foreign Medical Graduates: Hearing Before the Subcommittee on Health and the Environment of the Committee on Interstate and Foreign Commerce, House of Representatives, Ninety-Sixth Congress, Second Session, on Quality of Medical Education Received by U.S. Citizens Studying Abroad, November 21, 1980. Washington, D.C.: Government Printing Office, 1981.

2323.   United States, House Committee on the Judiciary, Subcommittee on Immigration, Refugees and International Law. Admission of Alien Physicians for Graduate Medical Education. Washington, D.C.: Government Printing Office, 1980.

2324.   United States, Department of Health Education and Welfare. Labor Certification for Foreign Medical Graduates. Washington, D.C.: HEW, 1978.

2325.   United States General Accounting Office. Policies on U.S. Citizens Studying Medicine Abroad Need Review and Reappraisal: Report to the Congress by the Comptroller General of the United States. Washington, D.C.: U.S. General Accounting Office/Government Printing Office, 1980.

2326. Usher, Richard E.  The Impact of Foreign Medical Personnel in the United States.  Washington, D.C.:  Foreign Service Institute, U.S. Department of State, 1969.

## Articles

2327. Antler, Lawrence.  "Correlates of Home and Host Country Acquaintanceship Among Foreign Medical Residents in the United States." Journal of Social Psychology 80 (February, 1970): 49-57.

2328. Aronson, J. E., et al.  "American in the Foreign Medical School and Vice Versa." College and University 50 (Summer, 1975): 470-473.

2329. Arthur, G. K.  "Language-Cultural Course for Foreign Psychiatric Residents." American Journal of Psychiatry 136 (August, 1979): 1064-1067.

2330. Bamford, J. C., Jr.  "Student Transfers from Foreign Medical Schools." Journal of Medical Education 46 (May, 1971): 431-435.

2331. Blase, B. A.  "International Student Exchange." Journal of Medical Education 43 (September, 1968):  1017-1019.

2332. Browder, Halbert C.  "Foreign Dental Graduates:  Admission Criteria and Predicted Success on an American Dental School." Journal of Dental Education 44 (No. 10, 1980):  580-584.

2333. Chen, R. M.  "Education and Training of Asian Foreign Medical Graduates in United States." American Journal of Psychiatry 135 (No. 4, 1978):  451-453.

2334. Dove, D. B.  "Minority Enrollment in U.S. Medical Schools, 1969-70, Compared to 1968-69." Journal of Medical Education 45 (March, 1970):  179-181.

2335. Gaviria, Moises, and Ronald Wintrob.  "Foreign Medical Graduates Who Return Home After U.S. Residency Training--Peruvian Case." Journal of Medical Education 50 (No. 2, 1975):  167-175.

2336. Grace, Eugene.  "Orientation of the Foreign Medical Graduate--A Matter of Life and Death?" National Association for Foreign Student Affairs Newsletter 27 (April, 1976):  13ff.

2337. Garraway, W. M.  "British Medical Students in the U.S.A." British Journal of Medical Education 3 (September, 1969):  215-220.

2338. Goldblat, A., S. S. Mick, and R. Stevens.  "Licensure, Competence, and Manpower Distribution of Foreign Medical Graduates." New England Journal of Medicine 292 (No. 3, 1975):  137-141.

2339. Hodari, A. A. "Graduate Education of the Foreign Physician in Obstetrics and Gynecology in the United States." Obstetrics and Gynecology 33 (March, 1969): 443-470.

2340. Jonas, S. "State Approval of Foreign Medical Schools—Ensuring the Quality of the Training of the Students and Graduates from Foreign Medical Schools Entering New York State." New England Journal of Medicine 305 (No. 1, 1981): 45-48.

2341. Knoff, W. F., D. Oken, and J. A. Prevost. "Meeting Training Needs of Foreign Psychiatric Residents in State Hospitals." Hospital and Community Psychiatry 27 (No. 1, 1976): 35-37.

2342. Luxenberg, M. N. "Present and Future Training of Foreign Ophthalmologists in the U.S.A.—Perspective of Association of University Professors of Ophthalmology." Ophthalmology 90 (No. 2, 1983): 59-63.

2343. Margulies, H., et al. "Random Survey of U.S. Hospitals with Approved Internships and Residencies: A Study of the Professional Qualities of Foreign Medical Graduates." Journal of Medical Education 43 (June, 1968): 706-716.

2344. Mason, H. R. "Transfer of Americans Attending Foreign Medical Schools to U.S. Medical Schools." American Journal of Public Health 60 (July, 1970): 1192-1193.

2345. Mason, H. R., et al. "Students Transferring from Foreign to U.S. Medical Schools in Advanced Standing, 1959-1966." Journal of Medical Education 44 (July, 1969): 561-570.

2346. Mick, S. S. "Los Medicos Graduados en el Extranjero." Universidades 16 (No. 3, 1976): 48-61.

2347. Mitchell-Bateman, Mildred. "The Foreign Medical Graduate in American Psychiatry: The Viewpoint of a Psychiatric Administrator." Psychiatric Opinion 13 (No. 4, 1976): 24-30.

2348. Mittel, Neuman S. "The Foreign Medical Graduate in American Psychiatry: Perspectives, 1976." Psychiatric Opinion 13 (No. 4, 1976): 6-13.

2349. Osorio, Migen L. "Are Foreign Medical Students Displacing Filipinos in R.P. Schools?" Sunburst 5 (No. 7, 1977): 26-30, 66-67.

2350. Posen, S. "The Examination Results of Asian Students in Australia." Medical Journal of Australia 1 (April, 1972): 806-809.

2351. Relman, A. S. "Americans Studying Medicine Abroad: We Need a New Policy." New England Journal of Medicine 299 (November, 1978): 1012-1014.

2352. Relman, A. S. "Loans for American Students in Foreign Medical Schools." New England Journal of Medicine 301 (July, 1979): 43-44.

2353. Richert, J. A., F. Schimpfh, and K. Papp. "Prescription-based Educational Training Program for United States Students Returning from Foreign Medical Schools." New York State Journal of Medicine 80 (No. 5, 1980): 811-815.

2354. Stephens, Jennifer. "Controls Lifted on Foreign Medical Graduates." National Association for Foreign Student Affairs Newsletter 29 (October, 1977): 8ff.

2355. Stillman, P. L., et al. "Students Transferring into an American Medical School." Journal of the American Medical Association 243 (January, 1980): 129-133.

2356. Stimmel, B., et al. "United States Citizens in Foreign Medical Schools and the Future Supply of Physicians." New England Journal of Medicine 300 (June, 1979): 1414-1417.

2357. Sutnick, A. I., J. F. Reichard, and A. P. Angelides. "Orientation of Foreign Medical Graduates." International Educational and Cultural Exchange 6 (Spring, 1971): 91-99.

     The authors discuss the programs begun in the late 1960s on the part of the medical associations in Philadelphia, Pennsylvania and other groups including the Experiment in International Living, the National Association for Foreign Student Affairs and the International Hospitality Programs offered in the Philadelphia metropolitan area. The authors discuss the ways this group of medical professionals attempted to be of support to foreign graduate medical students in their community, and offers an interesting guide to appropriate orientation of foreign medical graduates to American metropolitan areas, including such concerns of the foreign visitors as English-language opportunities for wives and children, the need to offer colloquial English-language instruction for the doctors and how-to-do-it and also the need to explain to foreign doctors the unique patient-doctor relationships in the United States medical establishment.

2358. Taylor, C. E. "U.S. Medical Students in Nepal." Journal of Medical Education 53 (July, 1978): 583-589.

2359. Underwood, E. A. "English-Speaking Medical Students at Leyden." Nature 221 (March 1, 1969): 810-814.

2360. Way, P. O., L. E. Jensen, and L. J. Goodman. "Foreign Medical Graduates and the Issue of Substantial Disruption of Medical Services." New England Journal of Medicine 299 (No. 14, 1978): 745-751.

2361. Weinberg, E., et al. "Performance of United States Citizens with Foreign Medical Education on Standardized Medical Examinations." New England Journal of Medicine 299 (October, 1978): 858-862.

2362. Williams, K. N., and R. H. Brook. "Foreign Medical Graduates and Their Impact on the Quality of Medical Care in the United States." Health and Society 53 (No. 4, 1975): 549-581.

2363. Zolotukh, S. I., and E. O. Borisova. "Our Experience with Teaching Pharmacology to Foreign Students." Farmakologiya i Toksikologiya 42 (No. 5, 1979): 557-559. (in Russian)

## 30. SPECIFIC NATIONAL STUDIES

2364. Al-Banyan, Abdullah Saleh. Saudi Students in the United States—A Study of Cross-Cultural Education and Attitude Change. London: Ithaca Press, 1980.

The underlying assumption of this study was that exposure to a foreign education experience in a modern society provides the visiting student with a new standard for the evaluation of his traditional cultural values. The main objectives were the delineation of specific variables involved in the Saudi Arabian students' experiences in the United States that influence his/her attitudes toward traditional cultural values; analysis of the processes through which the variables have their effect and an investigation of the effect of selected background variables upon the student's experiences in the United States. The total population of around 700 Saudi Arabian students enrolled in American institutions of higher education for the year 1971-1972 sponsored by the Saudi Arabian government and supervised by the Saudi Arabian Educational Mission in New York City were the subjects of the study. Data collection was through mailed questionnaires and the selected variables measured were (1) length of stay in the United States, (2) exposure, and (3) adjustment. Of the 132 returned questionnaires 117 were found usable and therefore processed for analysis. The hypothesis that attitude change is associated with length of stay in the United States was supported regarding the position of women but the relationship between length of study and attitude change toward traditional family relations was statistically nonsignificant. Length of stay was also not found to be significantly related to attitudes toward occupational values. Concerning attitude change by exposure, the data indicated that no relationship existed between change in attitudes due to exposure regarding the position of woman, while a slight change occurred in the pattern of relationship between exposure and attitude toward occupational values when controlling for age. Neither adjustment nor exposure seemed in themselves to have much effect on students' attitudes toward their traditional cultural values. The study concludes with a discussion of some practical implications and recommendations for further research.

2365. Althen, Gary L., ed. Students from the Arab World and Iran. Washington, D.C.: National Association for Foreign Student Affairs, 1978.

2366. Bae, Chong-Keun. "The Effect of Traditionalism on Social Adjustment and Brain Drain: A Study of Korean Students at the University of Wisconsin." Unpublished Ph.D thesis, University of Wisconsin, 1972.2345

The purpose of this study is to discover the effects of traditional Korean values and social adjustment and the role of brain drain in a sample of Korean students registered at the University of Wisconsin. There are three major hypotheses to this study:
1. The strength of Korean traditionalism does not change over time in the United States.
2. Traditionalism is negatively related to social adjustment in the United States.
3. Traditionalism is negatively related to brain drain.

A questionnaire and an interview were used to test the hypotheses. The students tested were Korean students in Madison and Korean students from Seoul.
Findings:
Traditionalism was conservative and basically stable, most students were committed to Korean values regardless of their background or place of study (Madison vs. Seoul). The hypothesis about traditionalism and its negative relationship to social adjustment was generally sustained.
Traditionalism did not predict the decision leading to becoming a factor in brain drain.

2367. Banerjee, Nipa. "Students from India in Canadian Universities." Unpublished Ph.D thesis, University of Toronto, 1977.

2368. Beals, Ralph L., and N. D. Humphrey. No Frontier to Learning: The Mexican Student in the United States. Minneapolis: University of Minnesota Press, 1957.

2369. Bennett, John W., Herbert Passin, and Robert McKnight. In Search of Identity: The Japanese Overseas Scholar in America and Japan. Minneapolis: University of Minnesota Press, 1958.

2370.  Borhanmanesh, Mohamad. "A Study of İranian Students in Southern California." Unpublished Ed.D thesis, University of California, Los Angeles, 1965.

2371.  Chu, Jennings P. <u>Chinese Students in America: Qualities Associated with Their Success.</u> New York: AMS Press, 1978.

2372.  Clark, Violet E. W. "Ghanaian Students in the United States, 1959-60." Unpublished Ph.D thesis, University of Michigan, 1963.

The problem generating the research study is that there are certain factors relative to the academic achievement and to the academic satisfaction of Ghanaian students in the United States during 1959-60. The factors selected were from the responding students' educational background in Ghana, their characteristics in the United States and of the educational institutions they attended. The two populations sampled in the study were the Ghanaian students and the educational institutions they attended in the United States. The data were collected through mail questionnaires.

On academic achievement it was found that the students who were passing were those who received secondary school education beyond the fourth form, held government grants, were in the last two phases of cultural adjustment and attended accredited universities. The students who were academically satisfied were those who possessed secondary school certificates beyond the fourth form, were 30 years or older, were married, held United States government grants or supported themselves than those who held Ghana government grants. Those who expected to stay in the United States less than three years were more satisfied than those who expected to remain much longer.

2373.  Coelho, Victor Anthony. "Students from India in the United States: An Exploratory Study of Some Cultural and Religious Attitudes." Unpublished Ph.D thesis, Loyola University of Chicago, 1972.

The author administered a questionnaire to students living in the metropolitan Chicago area who were studying at both colleges and universities in greater Chicago.

The primary purpose of the study was to explore religious and cultural attitudes of foreign students studying in the metropolitan area and to determine their adjustment problems in the United States.

The conclusions were that Indian students in the United States exhibited a desire for individual freedom and autonomy in particular in social relationships between the sexes. Religion tended to have greater value for women students than for male students and differences in religious belief systems accounted for attitudes toward value orientation. Catholics having the most absolute values, non-Christian students tended to be concerned about ethical and social issues. Protestants place less importance on absolute religious values.

The longer the stay in the United States the more varied the attitudes toward religious observance and less consistency toward religious observances.

2374.  Cohen, Robert Douglas. "The Functions of a Co-National Group of Foreign Students in New York City." Unpublished Ed.D thesis, Columbia University, 1971.

This case study is a description and analysis of the functions of a compatriot or conational group of foreign students in an urban setting. The basic assumption in the study, which involved 35 Kenyan students and former students resident in New York City in the summer of 1970, was that the compatriot or conational group was an agency which could be adapted to serve the needs of individual students in maintaining themselves within the host-society while not losing touch with their home culture. Through structured interviews held with the respondents it was found that the students were dissatisfied with academic and social life in settings where conational contact was not available. To maintain accessibility the students lived initially with one another, thus avoiding the dormitory and host-national residential situations. Much greater contact was therefore found among Kenyans than between Kenyans and Americans. Two major functions found within the conational group were the friendship function, which made it possible for helpful interaction with regard to personal problems and the instrumental function, which allowed conationals to get together and discuss residential, college admission, and employment problems. Seventy-one percent of the conational group reported having received instrumental help from a conational. The final chapter of the study explored the implications of the conational group's functions for government agencies and university administrators and advisers. It was suggested that the conational group be given due recognition and utilized by the foreign student adviser in the promotion of the welfare of foreign students.

2375.  Committee on Scholarly Communication with the People's Republic of China. Survey Summary: Students and Scholars from the People's Republic of China Currently in the United States. Washington, D.C.: U.S.-China Education Clearinghouse/National Association for Foreign Student Affairs, 1980.

2376.  Elovainio, Liisa. Finnish Fellowship Students in the United States: A Panel Study. Helsinki: Institute of Sociology, University of Helsinki, 1964.

2377.  Fingar, Thomas, and Linda A. Reed. Survey Summary: Students and Scholars from the People's Republic of China in the United

States, August 1981. Washington, D.C.: U.S.-China Education
Clearinghouse/National Association for Foreign Student Affairs,
1981.

2378. Gerstein, Hannelore. Deutsche Stipendiaten im Ausland: Ein
Programmvergleichende uber Sicht. Bonn-Bad Godesberg: DAAD,
1978.

2379. Gerstein, Hannelore. Stipendiaten aus Frankreich. Bonn-Bad
Godesberg: DAAD, 1974.

2380. Herman, S. N. American Students in Israel. Ithaca, New York:
Cornell University Press, 1970.

The author's main interest is a set of reactions,
views and their modifications as a result of studies in the
Israeli universities represented by the American Jewish
students. Data for this study were collected from a
succession of groups of American Jewish students in Israel,
mainly at the Hebrew University. The author points out "a
unique cluster of issues" linked with their decision to
study in Israel. The first stems from the fact that most
of them come to Israel with a prior emotional attachment
which is not usually found among students sojourning in a
foreign country. The second one is the temptation and
encouragement to settle in Israel.

Although Israel mainly attracts Jewish students around
the world, it also serves as a study center for Christian
scholars. A certain relatively small number of foreign
students come from the developing countries, mainly to
study medicine.

The author's findings with regard to patterns in the
reactions of the respondents show that:
. the enthusiasm evoked by the sojourn experience was
  tempered with some disappointment--in particular in the
  area of social contact with the host;
. a visiting student obtains a deeper insight into the host
  society if he does not view it just from the outside but
  becomes a participant in some of its activities; and
. although the students return to the United States with a
  broadened conception of Jewishness and recognize the fact
  of Jewish interdependence, they nonetheless still lack a
  coherent, integrated conception of life in which Israel
  and American Jewish community may be seen as interlocking
  parts of one Jewish world.

2381. Hobbs, Mary Kay. "Chinese Students and Scholars at American
Colleges, Universities, and Research Institutes in September
1981: An Inquiry Into the Relationship Between Advanced
Orientation in China and Subsequent Interaction with U.S.
Culture." Unpublished Ph.D thesis, Michigan State University,
1982.

2382. Jenkins, Hugh M., and Frederick Lockyear. Iranian Students in the United States: Status Report. Washington, D.C.: National Association for Foreign Student Affairs, 1979. (mimeo)

2383. Lambert, Richard D., and Marvin Bressler. Indian Students on an American Campus. Minneapolis: University of Minnesota Press, 1956.

2384. Liu, Sun Chia-yung. "A Study of the Chinese Ph.D Degree Recipients at Southern Illinois University at Carbondale, 1963-1975." Unpublished Ph.D thesis, Southern Illinois University at Carbondale, 1977.

Forty-seven Chinese students who received the Doctor of Philosophy degree from Southern Illinois University at Carbondale between 1963 and 1965 were studied to determine the general characteristics and role of Chinese doctoral students at SIU and to identify their post-doctoral contributions. Data were obtained from a survey questionnaire and records in various offices at the University of Southern Illinois at Carbondale. Analysis of the data showed that a majority of Chinese doctoral degree recipients were married, came from Taiwan, and majored in either political science or philosophy. It was also found that the students received their undergraduate degree at home and their masters degree from Southern Illinois University at Carbondale. They usually lived off-campus, had close ties with fellow Chinese and played some role in the Chinese Student Association. The university provided them with financial resources and they felt their own department was capable in dealing with international students. A majority of the doctoral degree recipients stayed in the United States after graduation with most of them teaching in institutions of higher learning and receiving salaries ranging from $24,000 to $28,000 per annum. The study generated several recommendations for the improvement of the total educational experience of international students at Southern Illinois University at Carbondale. They were: followup studies of other international students (non-Chinese) at all levels who have studied at Southern Illinois at Carbondale, replication of studies of Chinese students on other campuses, followup studies on international student drop-outs, studies concerning the social adjustment of international students and studies of the adjustment problems of foreign alumni working in the United States.

2385. New Zealand, Department of Education. Educating Pacific Islanders in New Zealand: A Report of a Conference at Lopdell House, 7-12 July 1974, Wellington. Wellington: Department of Education, 1975.

2386. Panama, Instituto para la Formacion y Aprovechamiento de Recursos Humanos. Estudiantes Panamenos en el Exterior, 1973. Panama

City, Panama: Instituto para la Formacion y Aprovechamiento de Recursos Humanos, 1974.

2387. Scott, Franklin D. The American Experience of Swedish Students: Retrospect and Aftermath. Minneapolis: University of Minnesota Press, 1956.

2388. Sharma, Keshav Dev. Indian Students in the United States. Bombay: Academic Journal of India, 1970.

2389. Singh, Amar Kumar. Indian Students in Britain: A Survey of Their Adjustment and Attitudes. London: Asia Publishing House, 1963.

This pioneering study of the adjustment patterns and attitudes of a group of 400 Indian students in Britain, describes their social, emotional, academic, and financial problems. It also discusses their attitudes toward the British people and society, toward certain Indian and Western institutions and values such as marriage, family, role of women, caste, religion, and materialism. The study distinguishes between the views of students from upper- and middle-class families.

Among the most important findings were the following: Indian students reported difficulty in finding accommodation, largely because of racial discrimination. The students reported discrimination in other areas as well, and indicated that this discrimination alienated them from the British people. Upper-class students reported that they had fewer problems with discrimination than middle-class students and made more British friends. An unintegrated social life caused many of the students to feel lonely, homesick and in general to report emotional strain. Fiscal problems were another major source of worry. Indian students often tended to judge the British by the standards of Indian society, causing some further problems of perception.

A number of elements caused variations in responses: duration of stay (with high adjustment being reported early in the sojourn and then late in it, but with considerable difficulties in the middle), personality, and social class.

2390. Smith, Mansfield Irving. "The East African Airlifts of 1959, 1960, and 1961." Unpublished D.S.S. thesis, Syracuse University, 1966.

2391. Thomas, Katrina, and William Tracy. Arab Students in the United States. Brooklyn, New York: Revisionist Press, 1979.

2392. United States, Senate Committee on the Judiciary, Subcommittee to Investigate the Administration of Security Laws. Ghana Students in the United States Oppose United States Aid to Nkrumah: Staff Conferences, August 29, 1963, and January 11, 1964. Washington, D.C.: Government Printing Office.

2393. Watson, Jeanne, and Ronald Lippitt. <u>Learning Across Cultures: A Study of Germans Visiting America</u>. Ann Arbor: Research Center for Group Dynamics, Institute for Social Research, University of Michigan, 1955.

2394. Wedge, Bryant. <u>Problems in Dialogue: Brazilian University Students and the United States</u>. Princeton, New Jersey: Institute for the Study of National Behavior, 1965.

## Articles

2395. Akka, R. I. "The Middle Eastern Student on the American College Campus." <u>American College Health Association Journal</u> 15 (No. 3, 1967): 251-253.

2396. Anderson, G. "American Blacks...Involvement in Educational Exchange." <u>International Educational and Cultural Exchange</u> 8 (No. 2, 1972): 25-31.

2397. Arastch, R. "Education of Iranian Leaders in Europe and America." <u>International Review of Education</u> 8 (No. 3/4, 1963): 444-450.

2398. Baldwin, George B. "The Foreign Educated Iranian: A Profile (Based on a Survey of 414 Individuals, Teheran, Summer, 1960)." <u>Middle East Journal</u> 17 (Summer, 1963): 264-278.

> Since World War II, the source of social power in Iran has shifted from land to education. A high proportion of Iranian college students are sent abroad. Today there are 15-25,000 of them enrolled in foreign universities, while there are 18,000 college students at home. Based on a sample survey of 416 Iranian students abroad, this article describes some characteristics of those studying in foreign universities, their foreign experiences, and financing problems. Among the findings are: (1) nearly 70% were from Tehran; (2) two broad occupations account for over half the group: the medical occupations (over 30%) and office employees (25%). Important also are engineers (13%) and educators (10%). (3) Both fathers and sons have similar views on the value of foreign study. Over 80% of the students had encouragement and support from their families. (4) In terms of number of Iranian students, four countries--France, U.S.A., Britain, and Germany--are host-countries, accounting for 80% of the students in the major sample. (5) A high proportion stayed abroad a long time. Over 50% stayed away five years or more. (6) Medicine and engineering are the two largest fields of study among the respondents. The author also discusses the benefits of foreign study and its impact on educational policy.

2399. Baron, Barnett, F. "Southern African Student Exiles in the United States." <u>Journal of Modern African Studies</u> 10 (No. 1, 1972): 73-91.

This study is based upon interviews with 61 students who had been political party members of the southern African student program (SASP) and a statistical analysis of the autobiographies of 310 SASP students. This program was funded by the Bureau of Education and Cultural Affairs of the State Department based upon a model developed at the Lincoln University in 1961, for students south of the Zambesi.

The study discusses the hypotheses that early political involvement in caste societies is a vehicle for improved self-esteem. On the basis of the limited sample, it is speculated that the hypothesis is true. By joining a political party, Southern African black elites overcome a loss of face from their elite family status due to caste-like discriminations. Further, they assume that they must be active in a political party in order to inherit the mantle of post-colonial leadership responsibility in their society.

However, acculturation to American society may have a disproportionate effect upon this potential leadership as Professor Baron asserts "most scholarships designed to educate Southern Africans abroad may have indirectly served to weaken the nationalist movements in spite of contrary intentions." (p. 91)

2400. Bassam, Tibi. "Die Iranischen Studenten in Ausland als ein Gelsellschaftliches Veranderungspotential und ihre Stellung im Politischen System." Orient [Hamburg] 20 (No. 3, 1979): 100-108.

2401. Bowers, R. "The Background of Students from the Indian Sub-Continent." In Study Modes and Academic Development of Overseas Students, edited by G. M. Greenall, and J. E. Price, pp. 104-113. London: British Council, 1980.

2402. Boyan, Douglas. "Countless Students: The Problems of Surveying U.S. Students Abroad." World Higher Education Communique 4 (Spring, 1982): 26-29.

2403. Brown, M. Archer. "U.S. Students Abroad." In Educating Students from Other Nations: American Colleges and Universities in International Educational Interchange, edited by Hugh M. Jenkins, et al., pp. 65-86. San Francisco: Jossey-Bass, 1983.

2404. Chen, Hsu-ching. "The Education of Returned Overseas Chinese Students." National Association for Foreign Student Affairs Newsletter 15 (April, 1964): 7ff.

2405. "Chinese Studying Abroad." Beijing Review 25 (December 6, 1982): 25-27.

2406. Cook, D. R. "Indian Students Analyzed." Overseas 3 (January, 1964): 9-13.

2407. Davis, F. J. "Perspectives of Turkish Students in the United States." Sociology and Social Research 48 (October, 1963): 47-57.

2408. Davis, F. James. "The Two-Way Mirror and the U-Curve: America As Seen By Turkish Students Returned Home." Sociology and Social Research 56 (October, 1971): 29-43.

The two-way mirror hypothesis which the study deals with implies that foreign student's conception of self is so closely identified with his country that symbolic interactionist explanations are relevant to his general acceptance of another nation. Two links with aspiration-achievement theorizing suggested are that, the level of aspiration the foreign student brings with him has been directly related to the favorability of the national image in the prior operation of the two-way mirror and that the favorability of the two-way image later on is inversely related to the amount of deprivation experienced in the host-country. The second proposition which is tested in this study is similar to the one proposed to interpret the U-shaped relationship between favorability and length of time spent in the host-country: that feelings of deprivation increase for a time and later diminish.

Data-gathering was by mailed questionnaire dealing with views of the United States and interviews of Turks on the personal value of the foreign study and on the development of Turkey. There were 222 respondents, one-third of whom were female. Over one-fourth of the total were married during most of their sojourn, and in most cases the spouse was along. Half of the 222 grew up in Istanbul, 18% in Ankara, and 6.8% in Izmir and most of the rest in smaller cities or provincial towns.

On the issue of favorability, views of the United States ranged widely, but in general they were very favorable. The proposition that deprivations and favorability to America are inversely related over time receives only rough, ambiguous support from the data, and some contradiction, too. It appears that "Difficulty" may be a better measure of goal-achievement than "Valuation" is, for the Turkish returnees as a whole. The study calls for better theorizing and more adequate research designs, longitudinal, when possible.

2409. Drettakis, Emmanuel G. "Greek Students in Foreign Universities." Journal of Educational Research in Europe 13 (No. 3, 1978): 85-106.

This paper, a part of a more detailed quantitative study, attempts to give a more complete picture, from a Greek and international point of view, of the problem of Greek students abroad. Part I discusses the sources of data and their differences. A comparison of the two sources shows that the aggregate gap between them is closing in recent years. The international comparisons made in Part II is based on the data provided by UNESCO on foreign students abroad for 1971, 1972, and 1973. The distributions by field of study show that the Greeks (and to a lesser extent, the Turks) studying abroad are mainly concentrated in the Natural Sciences, Engineering, Medical Sciences, and Agriculture while students of other countries are more evenly spread among the three broad groups of fields of study. In Part III the development over time (1961-1975) of student numbers of all categories covered by the data compiled by the Bank of Greece is presented. The data show enormous increase of all three categories and the total of Greek students abroad in the six-year period from 1969 to 1975. The total student numbers increased to reach in 1969, roughly, the 1961 level, and undergraduate students grew more than 3/4 of the total number of Greek students abroad. Examined in Parts IV, V, and VI are the countries of study, the fields of study and the fields of study in the main countries in 1975 respectively. Part VII provides an analysis of the complementary role in Greek higher education of the foreign universities in which Greek students are studying and Part VIII discusses the factors determining the number of these students.

2410. Eberhard, W. "Cultural Baggage of Chinese Emigrants: Stories and Novels Read by Chinese Students in Malaya." Asian Survey 11 (May, 1971): 445-462.

2411. Eng-Kung, Yeh, et al. "Psychiatric Implications of Cross-Cultural Education: Chinese Students in the United States." In The Mediating Person: Bridges Between Cultures, edited by Stephen Bochner, pp. 136-168. Cambridge, Massachusetts: Scheckman, 1981.

2412. Fort, Cynthia. "Americans Who Return 'Home' for College." World Higher Education Communique 4 (Winter, 1981): 13-14.

2413. Gandhi, Rajinkant S. "Some Contrasts in Foreign Student Life-Styles." International Journal of Contemporary Sociology 9 (January, 1972): 34-43.

2414. Gresky, Wolfgang. "Materialien uber Schweizer Studenten der Gottingen Universitat." Gottingen Jahrbuch 21 (1973): 243-261.

2415. Harrison, A. J. "Scandinavia as a Laboratory--American Students in Scandinavia." Scandinavian Review 63 (March, 1975): 37-39.

2416. Hawkey, R., and C. Nakomchai. "Thai Students Studying." In Study Modes and Academic Development of Overseas Students, edited by G. M. Greenall, and J. E. Price, pp. 70-78. London: British Council, 1980.

2417. Hawkins, H. "Transatlantic Discipleship: Two American Biologists and Their German Mentor." Isis 71 (June, 1980): 197-210.

This is an interesting study of the relationship between two American students who studied in Germany in the latter part of the 1880s with a lesser known German zoologist, Professor Ernst Heinrich Ehlers, and their continuing relationship over the next 40 years. Basically, the author found that as the two Americans grew and responded to differing intellectual and professional challenges, one maintained his academic relationship to his senior professor mentor, while the other continued to maintain a more personal, less academic, or professional relationship to him. Despite the interruption of World War I, they did maintain a relationship with their senior mentor.

The study also deals with the nature of the American inferiority toward science in the latter half of the 19th century and the impact of the German university upon American science and particularly how the role of the German university professor in zoology, was able to influence two distinctly different American students who sought him out as their mentor.

2418. Hawkins, John. "Chinese Exchange Scholars." In Bridges to Knowledge: Foreign Students in Comparative Perspective, edited by Elinor Barber, Philip G. Altbach, and Robert Myers, pp. 19-31. Chicago: University of Chicago Press, 1984.

2419. Heyduk, Daniel. "South American Students in the U.S.--1980-81." World Higher Education Communique 4 (Spring, 1982): 6-7.

2420. Hironaka, Kazuhiko. "Indian Students Studying Abroad." National Institute for Education Research Bulletin 18 (March, 1979): 19-22. (in Japanese)

2421. Hodgkin, Mary C. "The Cultural Background of Southeast Asian Students in Australia." In Overseas Students in Australia, edited by S. Bochner, and P. Wicks, pp. 25-30. Auburn: New South Wales University Press, 1972.

2422. Huang, Lucy Jen. "The Imported Marriage: The Case of Nigerian Student Marriage in the United States." International Journal of the Sociology of the Family 8 (No. 1, 1978): 37-51.

The term "imported marriage" refers to Nigerian student marriages overseas. Data for this paper were collected in 1974 via in-depth interviews of 30 Nigerian student couples and several single students, as well as reports and documents from Nigerian newspapers. This paper reports on changing values and attitudes toward marriage and family overseas and patterns of creative innovations and improvisations of these student couples in the face of cultural conflict and ambivalence. A brief discussion of traditional patterns of marriage and the family in Nigeria serves as a background for comparison. It was found that members of the imported marriage show unique patterns in changing mate selection and wedding rituals, attitudes toward polygamy, the use of surrogate extended family, attitude toward children and divorce. Under stress, and cultural conflicts Nigerian student couples show certain built-in security in their innovative adjustments as sojourners in the U.S.

2423.   Kagitcibasi, Cigdim. "Cross-National Encounters: Turkish Students in the United States." International Journal of Intercultural Relations 2 (No. 2, 1978): 141-160.

This study attempts to understand and assess changes in the attitudes, world views, aspirations, adjustments, and self-concepts of young Turkish students spending a year in the United States. The study examines four topical issues in the literature: namely, the type of sojourn experience, cultural differences, attitude change through time, and personality factors. The experimental group of the study consisted of all the students chosen by the American Field Service (AFS) organization from various Turkish high schools for two consecutive years. The control group was chosen from last-year high school students in the two years. The followup study was done with the AFS'ers in the third year, one year after the second AFS'ers and two years after the first-year AFS'ers returned to Turkey. Almost all the students in the study had urban middle-class characteristics. A total of 118 questions in a detailed questionnaire were used. Scales were also used to assess the pyschological concepts. It was found that there were certain attitude changes and these were attributed to the favorable nature of sojourn experience. The changes identified were mainly decreases in authoritarianism and religiosity and increases in world-mindedness and to a lesser extent in belief in internal control and perceived family control. Several of the changes were found to be of duration longer than one year. Patriotism and achievement values decreased independently of sojourn experience, an indication of an age trend. The followup study of the returnees showed general optimism and tendency to expect much from life, greater degree of achievement motive, belief in the importance of hard work for achievement and continued world-mindedness.

The subjects did not experience severe culture shock on their return and their readjustment process started from moderate levels, reaching an optimum level in about one year.

2424.   Keshav, Dev Sharma. "Indian Students in the United States." International Educational and Cultural Exchange 4 (Spring, 1969): 43-59.

2425.   Kline, C. L.  "The Young American Expatriates in Canada: Alienated or Self-Defined?"  American Journal of Orthopsychiatry 41 (January, 1971):  74-84.

2426.   Kobayashi, Fumio.  "Recent Trends in Chinese Studying Abroad." National Institute for Education Research Bulletin 18 (March, 1979):  15-18.  (in Japanese)

2427.   Lavine, Seydou.  "Des Maghrebins a Vincennes."  Jeune Afrique No. 750 (May 23, 1975):  50-51.

2428.   Lawson, A. R.  "Pacific Islands Students in Australia."  In Overseas Students in Australia, edited by S. Bochner, and P. Wicks, pp. 39-42.  Auburn: New South Wales University Press, 1972.

2429.   Li, K., and R. Elwell.  "Chatting with the Chinese [Students]." American Education 15 (May, 1979):  17-19.

2430.   McCormack, William.  "American Juniors in Japan."  Liberal Education 53 (March, 1967):  264-270.

2431.   Mellor, W. L., and Z. Begum.  "Bangladeshi Students in Australia: Some Background."  Unicorn 4 (July, 1978):  142-156.

2432.   Nalety, Y.  "Des Chinois a Aix-en-Provence."  Pedagogie (No. 5, 1974):  440-452.

2433.   Nassefat, Morteza, and Joy Madani-Wells.  "Iranian Students Abroad."  Iranian Review of International Relations (Spring, 1976):  19-47.

2434.   Ohuche, Komanus.  "Nigerian Graduate Students in American Universities."  Journal of Engineering Education 52 (January, 1969): 222-223.

2435.   Ojiaku, M. O., and G. Ulansky.  "Early Nigerian Response to American Education."  Phylon 33 (Winter, 1972):  380-388.

2436.   Ritterband, Paul.  "The Determinants of Motives of Israeli Students Studying in the United States."  Sociology of Education 42 (Fall, 1969):  330-349.

        For Israelis in American colleges and universities, there are two avenues of arrival into the U.S.  Undergraduates tend to be students who either have been unable to enter the college preparatory system in Israel or have performed poorly.  Graduate students tend to come to the U.S. because of the superior educational opportunities offered here in their areas of specialization.  The filter mechanisms in the Israeli education and social system are traced.  Occupationally differentiated motivational patterns are found to be functions of prior education in

Israel. Some noneducational sources of motives for study abroad are analyzed.

2437. Rowe, Leslie. "Vietnamese Refugees: New Students on Campus." *National Association for Foreign Student Affairs Newsletter* 33 (June, 1982): 161ff.

2438. Sabato, L. "Yank at Oxford in the Bicentennial Year." *Virginia Quarterly Review* 52 (Summer, 1976): 476-485.

2439. Sharpes, Donald. "Overseas Students from Developing Countries: A Malaysian Case Example." *International Education* 6 (Fall, 1977): 19-25.

2440. Song, Johng Doo. "Korean American College Students: Basic Characteristics." *Korea Observer* 10 (No. 4, 1979): 443-470.

2441. Starr, P. D. "October War and Arab Students' Self Conceptions." *Middle East Journal* 32 (August, 1978): 444-456.

The author attempts to determine the differences in attitude on the part of Arab students resulting from the October 1973 Arab-Israeli War and observes that most attitudinal studies of student reactions are based upon Israeli students, not Arab students. The study was administered at the American University of Beirut on three occasions in 1973-1974. The first was April, 1973, the second October, 1973, and the third May, 1974.

The questionnaire was based upon 15 self-identification questions: i.e., Who am I? The questionnaire was administered to students enrolled in the author's courses in 1973 and 1974. Only students from Arab countries were included in the sample, but 16% were ethnic Armenians, with Syrian or Lebanese passports. In all, 67% of the respondents were Lebanese, 14% Palestinian, 8% Syrian, 3% Egyptian and 9% from Jordan, Kuwait, Saudi Arabia, and other Arab states. Males represented 69% of the respondents and females 31%.

In the April administration there were 124 students; in the October administration, 163; and in the May 1974 administration 87 students responded.

The primary significant findings were that there was a decrease in the number of students who identified themselves by country of origin, but rather emphasized their "Arab heritage." The author points out and cautions that regardless of the short-term sense of jubilation that may have been experienced by the students, the data did not support the view that the Arabs experienced a substantial lasting change in self-conception as a result of the war.

2442. Thomas, Katrina, and William Tracy. "America as Alma Mater [A Study of Arab Students in the United States and Saudi Arabian Alumni of American Universities Who Have Returned Home]." *Aramco World Magazine* 30 (May-June, 1979): 1-32.

2443. Umakoshi, Toru. "Asian Students Studying Abroad: Korean Foreign Students Since the 'Liberation'." National Institute of Education Research Bulletin 18 (March, 1979): 11-14. (in Japanese)

2444. Veroff, J. "African Students in the United States." Journal of Social Issues 19 (January, 1963): 48-60.

2445. Yao, Esther Lee. "Chinese Students in American Universities." Texas Tech Journal of Education 10 (No. 1, 1983): 35-42.


Reportage

2446. "American Students in Britain: Symposium." Times Education Supplement (February 21, 1969): 575-582.

2447. "Americans to Study in China." Chronicle of Higher Education 22 (July 13, 1981): 14.

2448. "Black South Africans to Attend American Institutions." Chronicle of Higher Education 21 (February 17, 1981): 15.

2449. Breeze, R. "Chinese Puzzle for France." Far East Economic Review 111 (January 30-February 5, 1981): 14.

2450. Caute, D. "Spirit of Lusaka." New Statesman 98 (October 5, 1979): 372.

2451. "Chinese Student Receiving U.S. Ph.D Degree." Chronicle of Higher Education 24 (May 12, 1982): 17.

2452. Cookson, C. "Chinese Keep Low Profile on University Campuses." Times Higher Education Supplement (February 15, 1980): 5.

2453. Coote, A. "Zimbabwean Students: Refugees or United Kingdom Citizens?" New Statesman 95 (January 23, 1978): 834-835.

2454. "500 Germans to Study Here." Chronicle of Higher Education 8 (February 4, 1974): 2.

2455. "Immigration Boost for Iranians." Times Higher Education Supplement 541 (March 18, 1983): 6.

2456. Jebbins, D. "Iran's Lost Souls." Times Higher Education Supplement (February 19, 1982): 8.

2457. L. W. "17,000 Students from Hong Kong Studying in Canada." Chronicle of Higher Education 15 (March 13, 1978): 4.

2458. MacShane, D. "Wolves Come to Britain--Turkish Students." New Statesman 97 (March 16, 1979): 346.

2459.    Middleton, Lorenzo.  "Welcome Cools for Iranians on Many Campuses."  Chronicle of Higher Education 16 (July 24, 1978): 9.

2460.    "1,212 Iranian Students Admitted Since Crisis."  Chronicle of Higher Education 19 (January 21, 1980):  1.

2461.    Sayre, N.  "Britons at Harvard."  New Statesman 69 (February 12, 1965):  232.

2462.    Scully, Malcolm G.  "Canadian Students at U.S. Colleges:  Lack of Knowledge, Lack of Concern."  Chronicle of Higher Education 24 (August 4, 1982):  7.

2463.    Scully, Malcolm.  "Number of Chinese on American Campuses Is Beginning to Decline, Study Shows."  Chronicle of Higher Education 24 (March 24, 1982):  15.

2464.    Semas, Philip W.  "Where Are All Those Germans?"  Chronicle of Higher Education 10 (February 24, 1975):  3.

2465.    "7,800 Iranians Violating Visas."  Chronicle of Higher Education 21 (December 8, 1980):  2.

2466.    "Taiwanese Students in U.S.A. Spying Each Other."  Chronicle of Higher Education 25 (October 27, 1982):  17.

2467.    "2 Americans Sever Ties with Center in France."  Chronicle of Higher Education 25 (December 1, 1982):  18.

2468.    "Venezuela to Send Students to U.S. for Training."  Chronicle of Higher Education 9 (October 7, 1974):  8.

2469.    "Vienet, R.  "New Class of Peking 1979."  Far East Economic Review 104 (April 27, 1979):  46.

2470.    "West Germany Will Send 'Surplus' Students to U.S. Colleges If Plan Goes Through."  Chronicle of Higher Education 8 (October 9, 1973):  2.

2471.    Whittingham, Ken.  "Canadian Universities Are Swamped with Inquiries from Iranians in U.S."  Chronicle of Higher Education 19 (January 21, 1980):  1.

2472.    Whittingham, K.  "Canadian Universities Are Swamped with Inquiries from Iranians in U.S."  Times Higher Education Supplement (January 21, 1980):  1.

2473.    Whittingham, Ken.  "Iranians Stranded by Embassy Closing."  Chronicle of Higher Education 19 (February 11, 1980):  19.

## 31. SPECIFIC INSTITUTIONAL STUDIES

2474. Abu Laila, Yousef. Integration und Entfremdung: Eine Empirische Studie zur Situation Auslandischer Studenten am Beispiel Clausthalzellerfeld und Gottingen. Gottingen: Edition Herodot, 1981.

2475. Bailey, Robert L., and Frances Powell. Undergraduate Foreign Student Review. Berkeley, California: Office of Admissions and Records, University of California at Berkeley, 1978.

2476. Berte, Neal Richard. "An Analytical Study of the Foreign Student Program at the University of Cincinnati." Unpublished Ed.D thesis, University of Cincinnati, 1966.

This study (1) traces the historical development of the foreign student program at the University of Cincinnati, (2) provides an analysis of the alumni and current international student evaluation of the educational experiences for the foreign student, (3) reviews some features of educational programs for foreign students at other selected institutions of higher learning in the United States and, (4) makes recommendations for needed changes concerning the foreign student program at the University of Cincinnati. Foreign student alumni who graduated from the University of Cincinnati between 1960 and 1965 and full-time students currently enrolled at the University of Cincinnati were surveyed in the study. The survey questionnaires dealt with students' feelings on such matters as housing, financial assistance, advising and counseling, placement experiences, social and educational programming, orientation practices, use of the English Language, impressions of Americans, and future plans. Conclusions reached and recommendations made were that an International Center should be established to cater for nonacademic services; that the request made by both the current and alumni foreign students for more assistance in securing adequate housing should be met from the Foreign Student Adviser's Office or from the Housing Office. The establishment of an orientation program and a special handbook for foreign students were deemed necessary. On academic experiences it was suggested that the Committee of Advisers to Foreign Students be revived, the membership of which should include the Foreign Student Adviser and faculty members of the college departments having a sizable foreign student population.

2477. Brusick, Kathleen. Report on International Students Enrolled Fall Semester 1974, Rockville Campus. Rockville, Maryland: Office of Institutional Research, Montgomery Community College, 1975.

2478. Burroughs, Franklin. "Foreign Students at U.C.L.A.: A Case Study in Cross-Cultural Education." Unpublished Ed.D thesis, University of California, Los Angeles, 1964.

> Foreign student attendance at U.C.L.A. is documented from the academic year 1927-28 to the present. This study deals with the types of problems these students have faced; the ways in which the university and community have served the students and the efforts of the foreign students themselves to affect their own organizations. Written sources and supplementary interviews involving individuals who have knowledge of the history of foreign students indicate that foreign students who have studied at U.C.L.A. have come from every geographical area of the world, majored in 57 different fields of study, and have faced several types of problems including academic, financial, and housing problems. The Faculty Committee on Foreign Students, established in 1944, and the Foreign Student Office, set up in 1947, reflected an interest in experimentation. In the 1950s however, the activities of the office have become routine in nature. In 1948 the initial move in the community to offer services to foreign students was made. In 1950 the second community organization designed to provide assistance to foreign students was set up and in 1953 the Council on International Students, emerged. The World Student Associates merged with the Council on International Students in 1957 and in 1963 the Council merged with the International Student Center. The community aspects of U.C.L.A.'s foreign student program are presently channeled through the new center located on Hilgard Avenue. To ensure the success of the new center, it is suggested that the university should take the lead in experimentation with the center following the university's lead.

2479. Davis, Jack Douglas. "Development of International Programs at the University of Alabama in Birmingham: An Analysis of Perceptions of Key Administrators, Faculty and Staff." Unpublished Ph.D thesis, University of Alabama, 1981.

2480. Duggan, Susan, and Peter Wollitzer. The World's Students in Bay Area Universities. San Francisco: Bay Area and the World, 1983.

2481. Elze, Theodor. Die Universitat Tubingen und die Studenten. Munich: R. Trofenik, 1977.

2482. Farrar, Ronald Douglas. "The Non-Visa Foreign Student at Los Angeles City College: A Study of the Relation of Various Administrative and Academic Factors to the Immigrant Student." Unpublished Ed.D thesis, University of California, Los Angeles, 1968.

2483.   Gray, Andrey W. International and Intercultural Education in Selected State Colleges and Universities: An Overview of Five Cases. Washington, D.C.: American Association of State Colleges and Universities, 1977.

2484.   Gray, Andrey. International and Intercultural Education in Selected State Colleges and Universities. Washington, D.C.: American Association of State Colleges and Universities, 1979.

2485.   Han, Pyung Eui. "A Study of Goals and Problems of Foreign Graduate Students from the Far East at the University of Southern California." Unpublished Ed.D thesis, University of Southern California, 1975.

2486.   International Education at Michigan State University in an Interdependent World. East Lansing: Michigan State University, 1980.

2487.   International Neighbors. Living in Ann Arbor. Ann Arbor, Michigan: International Neighbors, 1964.

2488.   Kajornsin, Samnao. "A Study of Foreign Graduate Students. Their Awareness of Utilization of and Attitude Toward Selected Student Personnel Services and Other Services Available to Them at Michigan State University." Unpublished Ph.D thesis, Michigan State University, 1979.

This study has three purposes:

(a) To survey the existing services available to the foreign student at Michigan State University,
(b) To evaluate the awareness of, utilization of, and attitude toward selected student personnel and other services available to foreign students on campus (graduate),
(c) To propose possible strategies to facilitate the foreign student's utilization and improvement of these services

The sample of the study was 100 new graduate students at Michigan State University and 100 other students who have already enrolled at the same University for more than two terms.

Findings:

(1) The existing services that are available to only foreign students are: Foreign Student Office, English Language Center, and Community Volunteer for International programs. Through these services, the university provides extensive help in facilitating the academic progress and personal development for all students.

(2) In general, the foreign students did not know much about the existing services. It takes about two terms for them to be aware of these services.

(3) It was found that in most cases the foreign graduate students who had been in attendance more than two years knew and used the services more than the new students.

2489. Kotenkar, Arun. Auslandische Studenten in der Bundesrepublik am Beispiel der Universitat Frankfurt. Stuttgart: Alektor-Verlag, 1980.

2490. Laughlin, Margaret Ann. "United Nations University: From Concept to Implementation." Unpublished Ed.D thesis, University of Southern California, 1978.

2491. Leong, Frederick T. L., and William E. Sedlacek. A Survey of Incoming International Students, [University of Maryland]. College Park, Maryland: Counseling Center, University of Maryland, 1982. (Research Report No. 6-82)

2492. McMillen, Patricia. "Problems of International Students at the George Washington University." Unpublished Ed.D thesis, George Washington University, 1981.

2493. Melby, John F., and Elinor K. Wolf. Looking Glass for Americans: A Study of the Foreign Students at the University of Pennsylvania. Philadelphia: National Council on Asian Affairs, 1961.

2494. Overall, J. U. First-Time International and Domestic Freshmen [at University of Southern California]: Enrollment Trends and Characteristics. Los Angeles, California: Office of Institutional Studies, University of Southern California, 1981.

2495. Overall, J. U. International and Domestic Undergraduates: Enrollment Trends and Characteristics. Los Angeles, California: Office of Institutional Studies, University of Southern California, 1981.

2496. Porter, Robert D. "A Personnel Survey of 1105 Foreign Students at the University of Washington." Unpublished Ph.D thesis, University of Washington, 1962.

2497. Rust, Val D. The Foreign Student at the UCLA [University of California at Los Angeles] Graduate School of Education. Los Angeles, California: Graduate School of Education, University of California at Los Angeles, 1981.

2498. Thomas, Ronald Edward. "The International Student Enrollment at Southern Illinois University at Carbondale." Unpublished Ph.D thesis, Southern Illinois University, 1976.

2499. University of New South Wales. Overseas Students at the University of New South Wales. Sydney, Australia: Office of the Registrar, University of New South Wales, 1983.


## Articles

2500. Abrams, Irwin. "The Impact of Antioch Education Through Experience Abroad." Alternative Higher Education: The Journal of Nontraditional Studies 3 (Spring, 1979): 176-187.

2501. Becker, Tamar. "Black Africans and Black Americans on an American Campus: The African View." Sociology and Social Research 57 (January, 1973): 168-181.

This article examines the manifestations and courses of strained relations between Africans and black Americans on the UCLA campus. The study operates on the premises that: a spontaneous sense of kinship and mutual trust would arise between black Americans and black foreigners on a visit in the United States; the cooperation between the two groups may be neutralized if the association is seen by members of either group as having unfavorable consequences; if the participants view the association as superimposed, the probability increases that relations between the groups will be marked by strain and ambivalence. The African sample, which included 57 black African students representing 16 sub-Saharan countries, was a portion of a broad cross-cultural study of foreign students conducted at UCLA during the 1967-68 academic year. The study found that higher status and tangible benefits accorded Africans in preference to black Americans, socio-cultural differences between the two groups, and perceived rejection by blacks, strengthened the Africans' inclination to emphasize their separate identity and to minimize contact with black Americans. It is suggested that only a significant reduction of race as a socially relevant factor in the internal stratification system in the United States would appear to be able to resolve the strain in relations between the two groups.

2502. Benedict, R. C. "SUNY-Thorez Academic Exchange." International Educational and Cultural Exchange 13 (Summer, 1977): 34-39.

2503. Billigmeier, R. H., and D. Forman. "Gottingen in Retrospect--A Longitudinal Assessment of the University of California's Education Abroad Program in Gottingen by 1965-66 Participants." International Review of Education 21 (No. 2, 1975): 217-230.

Participant assessment is one of the processes which can be used to evaluate the success of overseas study programs. The study on which this article is based was conducted in 1972 with University of California students who attended the University of Gottingen, Federal Republic of Germany, during the 1965-66 academic year. They were asked (by questionnaire) to review their experiences in retrospect their studies abroad, especially their use of language, as well as their assessment of the academic, intellectual, personal, social, and cultural dimensions of the program.

The results of the survey showed that there are a number of dimensions of the experience of living and studying in a foreign country, even if it lasts only a year. Certain difficulties were observed in assessment of the academic results of such programs, mostly due to an unclear position with regard to what kind of knowledge is being sought while studying abroad for a relatively short period of time.

2504. Charoule, Akim. "Les Etudiants Africains en Roumanie." Jeune Afrique No. 584 (March 25, 1972): 76-79.

2505. Cox, J. L., I. E. Babiker, and P. M. Miller. "Psychiatric Problems and 1st Year Examinations in Overseas Students at Edinburgh University." Journal of Adolescence 4 (No. 3, 1981): 261-270.

2506. Dodge, Bayard. "The American University of Beirut." Cahiers d'Histoire Mondiale 10 (No. 4, 1967): 780-800.

2507. Gabriel, Rhodelia L. "Characteristics of Foreign Students on an American Campus." Journal of the National Association of Women Deans, Administrators, and Counselors 36 (Summer, 1973): 184.

A 52-item questionnaire was administered to all 809 foreign students attending the 1969 spring semester at Purdue University. Slightly more than one-half (54%) of the sample came from upper-middle-class families; 23.3% came from lower-middle-class backgrounds. These students were found to be achieving grades equivalent to those of the average American student. The chief dissatisfactions were with informal aspects of college life. In general the students were satisfied with their study in the U.S. About two-thirds expressed positive feelings on their professors' role in their academic studies. An item-by-item comparison of seven geographical and 21 cultural groups was made. A very clear implication is that future foreign students might be helped in their social adjustments if they could be given the opportunity to participate in an orientation program conducted in the U.S. which would focus upon the informal aspects of American life.

2508. Halasz, Sari C. "University of California, Los Angeles, Study II: Graduate Students from Indonesia, Korea, Pakistan, and Thailand: Fall 1959 Through Spring 1967." College and University 45 (Fall, 1969): 44-54.

2509. Hebron, Chris de Winter. "Third World Postgraduate Students in a European University--A Case Study From Newcastle Upon Tyne." Higher Education in Europe, 11 (January-March, 1984): 54-62.

2510. Hillman, H. V. "A Follow-up Study of the Performance of Overseas Students at Norwood Technical College." Vocational Aspect: Vocational Aspect of Education 21 (Autumn, 1969): 147-157.

2511. Hsiao, Kung-ch'uan. "Pursuit of Learning on a New Continent (1): Three Years at the University of Missouri." Chinese Studies in History 12 (No. 2, 1978-1979): 3-24.

2512. Kasprzyk, Peter. "Modell Eines Einfuhrungssemesters fur Auslandische Studenten an der Universitat Stuttgart." Die Deutsche Universitatszeitung 24 (No. 9, 1969): 6-8.

2513. Matthews, Judith, and Carolyn Quattrocki. "International Students on an American Campus: An Undergraduate Research Study." Journal of Home Economics 73 (No. 1, 1981): 37-39.

2514. Pasaskevopoulos, J. "Research on Foreign Students at the University of Illinois." College and University 43 (Summer, 1968): 513-524.

2515. Ruedisili, C. H. "Foreign Students Surveyed at the University of Wisconsin." Overseas 3 (April, 1964): 18-22.

2516. Slavin, G. M., and P. W. Carroll. "Students Act: New International Center at UNM." International Educational and Cultural Exchange 8 (Fall, 1972): 70-74.

### Reportage

2517. "Foreign Students in Community Colleges." College and University 54 (Summer, 1979): 299.

2518. "Foreign Students in the Community College." College and University 55 (Summer, 1980): 411-412.

2519. "Okia Institution (South-Western College in Oklahoma) Seeks Cutback in Foreign Students." Chronicle of Higher Education 16 (March 6, 1978): 2.

## 32. WOMEN INTERNATIONAL STUDENTS

2520. Melie, Edith Ememgene. "Returning Nigerian and American College Women: A Cross-Cultural Analysis of Their Motivational

Orientations." Unpublished Ph.D thesis, University of Wisconsin-Madison, 1980.

2521. Moore, C. T. "The Effect of Assertive Training on the Assertive Behavior of Foreign Women in a U.S. Environment." Unpublished Ed.D thesis, Temple University, 1979.

2522. UNESCO. Evaluation of UNESCO Fellowships with Particular Reference to Women. Paris: UNESCO, 1978.

2523. Walawender, Marge. "The Behavior and Role Expectations of Foreign and American Graduate Women." Unpublished Ph.D thesis, Cornell University, 1964.

    An investigation into: (1) whether there are significant differences between foreign and American graduate women in behavior and in expectations for behavior in Class, Friend, Custom, and Neighbor (Roommate) relations, (2) whether such foreign students experience concern in the four behavior areas, (3) whether such foreign students are satisfied with their overall stay in the United States, and, (4) whether relationships exist between behavior, expectations, concern, and satisfaction. Responses to survey questionnaires from 57 foreign and 57 American graduate women at Cornell University were analyzed. While foreign women were found to be more restrained than their American peers, the degree of restraint varied with the specific behavior area being considered. Foreign subjects generally showed low concern and all found Class and Neighbor relations somewhat trying, regardless of categorical classification. Age had no relationship to the degree of concern as reported by foreign women. Concerning their stay in the United States, foreign graduate women were generally satisfied. Significant relationships were found in the Inter-Scale Relationships.

## Articles

2524. Blood, R. O., and S. O. Nicholson. "International Dating Experiences of American Women Students." Marriage and Family Living 24 (May, 1962): 129-136.

2525. Boyan, Douglas. "Foreign Women in U.S. Schools: Still Only a Quarter of Foreign Student Enrollment." World Higher Education Communique 4 (Winter, 1981): 21-24.

2526. Ekou-Pondza, Hazel. "Problems of the Educated Woman on Returning Home: A Case Review of Jamaica." In International Women Students: Perspectives for the 80s. Report of the International Women Student Conference (Boston, Mass., August 1981), edited by Leslie Rowe and Steve Sjoberg, pp. 40-43. Washington, D.C.: National Association for Foreign Student Affairs, 1981.

2527. Helm, Ann. "Task Force on Women International Training Program for Regional Coordinators and Students." In International Women Students: Perspectives for the 80s. Report of the International Women Student Conference (Boston, Mass., August 1981), edited by Leslie Rowe and Steve Sjoberg, pp. 98-100. Washington, D.C.: National Association for Foreign Student Affairs, 1981.

2528. Lee, Motoko. "Needs of International Women Students: Report on Findings of the National Association for Foreign Student Affairs/United States Agency for International Development National Survey." In International Women Students: Perspectives for the 80s. Report of the International Women Student Conference (Boston, Mass., August, 1981), edited by Leslie Rowe and Steve Sjoberg, pp. 90-97. Washington, D.C.: National Association for Foreign Student Affairs, 1981.

2529. Ntiri, Daphne Williams. "Continuing Education Efforts of African Student Wives in the United States." Journal of the National Association for Women Deans, Administrators, and Counselors 42 (Summer, 1979): 16-21.

2530. Sjoberg, Steve. "A Re-Entry Workshop for International Women Students." In International Women Students: Perspectives for the 80s. Report of the International Women Student Conference (Boston, Mass., August 1981), edited by Leslie Rowe and Steve Sjoberg, pp. 81-99. Washington, D.C.: National Association for Foreign Student Affairs, 1981.

2531. Stevens, Pamela. "Reentry for U.S.-Educated Women from Developing Nations: Some Shared Problems." World Higher Education Communique 2 (Summer, 1980): 1-2.

2532. White, Merry I. "The Social and Economic Context of the Overseas-Educated Japanese Woman." In International Women Students: Perspectives for the 80s. Report of the International Women Student Conference (Boston, Mass., August 1981), edited by Leslie Rowe and Steve Sjoberg, pp. 22-26. Washington, D.C.: National Association for Foreign Student Affairs, 1981.


## 33. STUDIES OF EASTERN BLOC AND CHINESE STUDENTS


2533. Hevi, Emmanuel John. An African Student in China. London: Pall Mall, 1963.

2534. Raymond, Edward A. Foreign Students: The Soviet Education Weapon. Stanford, California: Hoover Institution Press, 1973.

A study in political communication which attempts to show the degree of success which the Soviet Union has attained in extending its influence by training future elites from noncommunist countries in the Soviet Union, and then returning them to work for the Soviet brand of communism in their native lands. The organization and methods used are examined comprehensively. Schools for espionage, insurgency, codes and ciphers, and other military specialties are not part of this inquiry, nor are the educational exchanges within the communist world.

The book deals with three major aspects of the Soviet training of foreigners in the U.S.S.R.: Party cadre training, prisoner-of-war indoctrination in each of the World Wars; and academic exchanges since World War II. The author uses tables to summarize the level of influence attained by graduates and former faculty, of the schools operated by the Communist International (Comitern) in the period 1919-1943.

2535. Sheng, Yueh. Sun Yat-Sen University in Moscow and the Chinese Revolution: A Personal Account. Lawrence: University of Kansas, University Center for East Asian Studies, 1971.

2536. Stanis, V. F. University of Friendship. Moscow: Progeess Publishers, 1980.

2537. Taubman, William. The View from Lenin Hills--An American Student's Report on Soviet Youth in Ferment. New York: Coward-McCann, 1967.

This is an American student's account of his life in Russia. The author describes his daily experience in scholarly life, personal friendships with his fellow Russian students, life in the university dorm, travel in the city and to the provinces. The author also depicts the Russian youth's political views, their taste in cultural life and their views of the Western world.

2538. U.S. Information Agency, Office of Research. Some Statistics on Exchanges in the Soviet Union and Eastern Europe. Washington, D.C.: U.S. Information Agency, 1965.


Articles

2539. Bannov, B., and T. Nikolayeva. "University Graduates [Foreign] from Moscow." Soviet Literature (No. 9, 1980): 149-153.

2540. Bernhardt, Gunter. "DDR-Absolventen Sowjetischer Universitaten Bringer Veichen Wissensschatz in Unsere Republik." Das Hochschulwesen 21 (No. 11, 1973): 325-326.

2541. Boeme, H. J. "Important Area of Fraternal Cooperation." Vestnik Vysshei Shkoly (No. 11, 1971): 90-91. (in Russian)

2542. Brumberg, Abraham. "Black, White and Red—African Students in Russia." New Leader 47 (January, 1964): 14-17.

2543. Djakova, A. P. "Together with the Soviet Students." Vestnik Vysshei Shkoly (No. 4, 1973): 53-56. (in Russian)

2544. Dolmatovsky, E. "Pupil and Teacher [Ethiopian Student in Russia]." Soviet Literature (No. 3, 1977): 163-167.

2545. Erzin, P. D. "Soviet International Institution of Higher Education Presents Its First Diplomas." Soviet Education 8 (February, 1966): 52-56.

2546. Fitzpatrick, S. "Student in Moscow, 1966." Wilson Quarterly 6 (Summer, 1982): 132-141.

2547. "Foreign Students in the U.S.S.R." School and Society 95 (January 21, 1967): 44.

2548. Halevy, Zvi. "Vietnamese and Chinese Recipients of Higher Academic Degrees in the U.S.S.R." Southeast Asia 2 (Summer, 1973): 339-346.

2549. Henry, N. "African in Peking, [Tanzanian Students in China]." Crisis 83 (December, 1976): 339-341.

2550. "How African Students' Demonstration was Reported: Concerning a Malicious Uproar in the Bourgeois Press." Current Digest of the Soviet Press 15 (January 15, 1964): 17-18.

2551. Kanet, R. E. "African Youth: The Target of Soviet African Policy." Russian Review 27 (April, 1968): 161-175.

This article examines training programs established in the Soviet Union and some of the Eastern European countries for the education of a national elite of scientists, technicians, and engineers, as well as trade union organizers from African countries.

The author points out that training programs for foreigners are not new, but there have been substantial increases both in the number and attendance rates since the 1960s. In the years 1961-1966, the number of university students in the Soviet Union from African countries increased more than six times, to about 4,000. The author points out that irrespective of the field of study, their recruitment and training are strongly colored by ideological and political considerations.

In October 1960, a special university for students from the developing countries was established—Friendship University. It offers courses in six specialized fields: (1) education, (2) agriculture, (3) medicine, (4) physics, mathematics and natural sciences, (5) economics and law, (6) history and philosophy.

In 1961 a similar institution was established in Czechoslovakia. The author analyzes the benefits which such programs bring to African students (free of cost) as well as complaints of the African students (racially-based problems and lack of freedom to choose their courses).

2552.  Komorowski, Z.  "Participation of Poland in Training of African Cadres and Scientific/Research of Above."  Africana Bulletin No. 15 (1971):  135-142.

2553.  McCarry, C.  "African Students Who Quit the Soviet Union." American Federationist 70 (January, 1963):  18-21.

2554.  Mehls, Eckart.  "20 Jahre Erfolgreiche Zusammenarbeit Moskauer Staatliche Lomonossow Universitat-Humboldt-Universitat Berlin." Das Hochschulwesen 26 (No. 12, 1978):  329-331.

2555.  Metongo, Mekoffi.  "An African Student in Kiev--Unpleasant Experiences."  Ukranian Quarterly 20 (Winter, 1964/1965): 337-348.

In an attempt to woo the peoples of awakening Africa away from the West, the Soviet Union and its East European satellites have established a chain of "Friendship Universities" in large cities. African students behind the Iron Curtain have been insulted, spat upon, beaten, tortured, raped, and even murdered. A group of 28 African students who escaped the communist racial "apartheid" in the Soviet Union arrived in Israel to continue their studies at institutions of higher learning in Jerusalem, Haifa, and Tel Aviv. A 24-year-old student of medicine from Ghana gave his personal account of his life at the University of Kiev. He described how his friend was murdered and how he was treated in the Soviet Union.

2556.  Petre, Constantin.  "The Contribution of Romania to the Training of National Specialists from the Developing Countries." Higher Education in Europe 7 (January-March, 1982):  34-36.

2557.  Rosen, Vladimir.  "They [Foreign Students] Study in the U.S.S.R." New Times (Moscow) No. 12 (March, 1978):  22-24.

2558.  Roucek, Joseph S.  "The Training of Foreign Students by Communist Countries."  Ukrainian Quarterly 23 (Winter, 1967):  314-331.

The author reviews in this article historical and ideological motivations as well as development of foreign student training in the Soviet Union and other Eastern Bloc countries after the Second World War. He points out that especially in the case of the Soviet Union, such programs are an "integral part of politics."
A substantial growth in the number of foreign students in these countries has been observed in the 1960s as the followup of the decolonization process and the assistance

of the communist and socialist countries in the "national liberation struggle" of newly independent countries. The opening of the Friendship University on October 1, 1960 is a starting point of this development.

Part of this article is devoted to the racial problems of foreign students in the Soviet Union and other Eastern European countries and the final chapter describes rivalry between the Soviet Union and China to attract African students to undertake or continue their education in these two countries.

2559. Rubinstein, Alvin Z. "Lumumba University: An Assessment." Problems of Communism 20 (November/December, 1971): 64-69.

2560. "Rules on Foreign Students and Their Organizations: Regulations on Foreign Citizens Studying in Higher and Specialized Secondary Educational Institutions of the Union of Soviet Socialist Republics." Current Digest of the Soviet Press 16 (May 13, 1964): 24.

2561. Sofinski, N. N. "Development and Forms of International Co-operation in Higher Education in the U.S.S.R." Higher Education in Europe 14 (April–June, 1979): 38-39.

2562. Sokhin, S. I. "A Solid Base of Friendship and Cooperation." Vestnik Vysshei Shkoly No. 12 (1972): 86-89. (in Russian)

2563. Stanis, V. F. "The Friendship University." Higher Education in Europe 7 (January–March, 1982): 16-18.

This article presents objectives, structure, and functioning of the Patrice Lumumba People's Friendship University in Moscow. The university was established in 1960 with the primary objective to assist developing countries in training highly qualified personnel. It was organized under the auspices of the All-Union Central Council of Trade Unions of the U.S.S.R., the Soviet Afro-Asian Solidarity Committee and the Union of Societies of Friendship and Cultural Relations with Foreign Countries.

At present, the university has 87 chairs (departments). Its faculty includes 140 full professors and 650 assistant professors. The following requirements and procedures are followed for foreign student admission:
. completed secondary education;
. recommendation of such an organization as the national branch of the Friendship Association with the U.S.S.R.; and,
. approval of the University's admission commission.

The Soviet candidates have to pass a comparative entrance examination. Accepted students receive free tuition and 90 rubles of monthly stipend.

The university has the following faculties:

. preparatory (mostly for learning Russian which is the
language in which teaching is offered);
. natural sciences and mathematics;
. history and philosophy;
. economics and law;
. medicine;
. agriculture, and
. engineering

Current conditions prevailing in the developing
countries are taken into consideration in curriculum as
well as during a teaching process. A total of 10,700
persons from 110 countries have graduated from this
university since its creation, out of it, 820 with Ph.D
degrees.

The author considers that this university successfully
fulfills its mission which includes not only training of
highly qualified specialists but also "realization of the
Leninist international policy."

2564. Stanis, V. F. "The Significance of the Patrice Lumumba People's
Friendship University in the Training of Specialists for Newly
Independent Countries." Sovremennaya Vysshaya Shkola (No. 3,
1983): 13-29. (in Russian)

2565. Stepanidyn, G. "I Bow my Head in Gratitude--How Foreign Students
Are Trained at VGIK (The All Union State Cinematography Institute)." Soviet Film (No. 1, 1981): 37-38.

2566. Stewart, G. "Africans in Russia." New Statesman 69 (May 7,
1965): 716.

2567. Toins, S. "World Under One Roof." Convergence 5 (No. 3, 1972):
37-41.


Reportage

2568. Binyon, M. "Soviet Union's Controversial University for Third-
World Students." Chronicle of Higher Education 18 (April 23,
1979): 7-8.

2569. Binyon, M. "Warm Welcome Behind the Iron Curtain." Times Higher
Education Supplement (November 23, 1979): 7.

2570. "Economists Find Soviet Visits Less Useful Than East European."
Chronicle of Higher Education 27 (March 9, 1981): 12.

2571. "80,000 Foreign Students in Soviet Union." Chronicle of Higher
Education 22 (July 27, 1981): 11.

2572. Feifer, George. "The Red and the Black--African Students in
Russia." Reporter 30 (January 2, 1964): 27-28.

2573. "Foreign Students in Russia Complain about Conditions." Chronicle of Higher Education 22 (July 27, 1982): 13.

2574. Lee, M. "Peking Springs into Action." Far East Economic Review 119 (March 24, 1983): 35-36.

2575. Lorince, G. "Mao Woos Soviet Colored Students." New Statesman 73 (November 17, 1967): 677-678.

2576. Morgan, J. "Negro in Sofia." New Statesman 65 (February, 1963): 266ff.

2577. Owen, Richard. "Russia Intensifies Third-World Recruitment." Chronicle of Higher Education 24 (July 14, 1982): 17.

2578. Owen, Richard. "Russia Presses for More Third-World Students." Chronicle of Higher Education 24 (July 14, 1982): 17.

2579. Scully, Malcolm G. "U.S. Scholars in Russia: Too Many Restrictions?" Chronicle of Higher Education 15 (October 3, 1977): 6.

2580. "Students Behind the Curtain: Photographs." Times Educational Supplement No. 2542 (February 7, 1964): 294-295.

## 34. RETURN AND RE-ENTRY ISSUES

2581. Colombia, Servicio Nacional de Empleo, and Fondo Colombiano de Investigaciones Cientificas y Proyectos Especiales Francisco Jose de Caldas. Evaluacion del Programa de Retorno de Profesionales y Tecnicos. Bogota: Servicio Nacional de Empleo, 1978.

2582. Dinello, R. Re-enculturation d'Universitaires Latino-Americains. Brussels: Universite Libre de Bruxelles, 1971.

2583. Downie, Richard D. "Re-entry Experience and Identity Formation of Third Culture Experienced Dependent American Youth: An Exploratory Study." Unpublished Ph.D thesis, Michigan State University, 1976.

2584. Gama, Elizabeth M. P., and Paul Pedersen. Readjustment Problems of Brazilian Returnees from Graduate Studies in the United States. Cambridge, Mass.: Latin American Scholarship Program of American Universities, 1976.

2585. Gerstein, Hannelore. Die Ehemaligen Jahrestipendiaten des DAAD in Indien. Beschreibung Einer Zielgruppe im Kontext ihrer Beruflichen und Personlichen Situation. Bonn: DAAD, 1981.

2586. Hentgers, Harriet Ann. "The Repatriation and Utilization of High-level Manpower: A Case Study of the Korea Institute of Science and Technology." Unpublished doctoral thesis, Johns Hopkins University, 1975.

2587. Keats, Daphne. Back in Asia: A Follow-up Study of Australian-Trained Asian Students. Canberra: The Australian National University, 1969.

2588. Marsh, H. Re-entry/Transition Seminars: Report on the Wingspread Colloqium. Washington, D.C.: National Association for Foreign Student Affairs, 1975.

2589. Orr, James Darhy, Jr. "The Foreign Scholar Returned Home: A Review of Selected Research." Unpublished Ed.D thesis, Columbia University, 1971.

This study, which reviews completed followup research on foreign students who studied in American colleges and universities, examines: (1) personal changes resulting from the exchange experience, (2) readjustment to the home-country, (3) returnees' use of American-learned skills, and (4) knowledge and the effectiveness of returnees as agents of cultural exchange to discover patterns and influencing factors in foreign students' experiences after their return home.

Published and unpublished studies were critically examined for this study. The major findings of the review were that most exchangees considered themselves changed by the exchange experience—they had become more flexible, more insightful, more sensitive to others, gained self-confidence and social responsibility, better work habits and more self-discipline. In their home-countries many exchangees experienced difficulties in readjustment. While about 80% of the returnees could obtain jobs easily, those who came from rigid or developing cultures, or without influential friends and relatives, experienced considerable difficulty in securing employment. Even though about 75% of the returnees were able to use their American training at least partially and 80% were able to convey their knowledge and skills to others in the job situation, most students felt their foreign experience had no major impact on their careers. The study calls for more predeparture planning for foreign students, closer ties by home governments to the exchange process, more relevant studies in American educational institutions and more sponsor and home government postsojourn support of exchangees.

2590. Repashy, Allen James. "The Reactions of Kenyan Returnees to Their Educational Experiences Abroad." Unpublished Ed.D thesis, University of California, Los Angeles, 1966.

2591. Returning Home: A Program for Persons Assisting International Students with the Re-entry Process. Ottawa: Canadian Bureau for International Education, 1984.

2592. Shin, Kuk Bom. "The Post Graduation Residency Plans of Korean Students Attending Selected Universities in Michigan." Unpublished Ph.D thesis, Michigan State University, 1972.

2593. Useem, John, and Ruth Hill Useem. The Western-Educated Man in India: A Study of His Social Roles and Influence. New York: Dryden Press, 1955.

## Articles

2594. Berte, Neil R. "Adjustment Problems of Current and Alumni Foreign Students." NASPA Journal 5 (July, 1967): 8-11.

2595. Boakari, Francis Musa. "Foreign Student Re-entry: The Case of the Hurrying Man." National Association for Foreign Student Affairs Newsletter 34 (November, 1982): 33ff.

2596. Bochner, S. "Anticipated Role Conflict of Returning Overseas Students." Journal of Social Psychology 110 (April, 1980): 265-272.

2597. Brislin, R. W., and H. Van Buren. "Can They Go Home Again? Seminars Help Cope with Reverse Culture Shock." International Educational and Cultural Exchange 9 (Spring, 1974): 19-24.

2598. Cajoleas, Louis P. "The American-Educated Foreign Students Return Home." Teachers College Record 60 (January, 1959): 191-197.

2599. Chiang, Shing Ho, and G. E. Klinzing. "How Would That Work Back Home?" Technos 5 (October-December, 1976): 26-31.

2600. Cussler, Margaret. "The Foreign Student--Innovator of the Future." Review of International Sociology 7 (No. 1, 1971): 651-663.

2601. Eberhard, Wolfram. "Problems of Students Returning to Asia." International Educational and Cultural Exchange 5 (Spring, 1970): 41-50.

This article is based on Wolfram Eberhard's speech made on March 7, 1969 at NAFSA Conference on "The Asian Student," which was held at the University of Washington, Seattle.

The article discusses the following issues:
. nonreturning of foreign students after graduation from U.S. universities to their native country;
. how studies and research carried out by foreign students can gain more significance within U.S. universities;
. negative consequences of existence of "student national little ghettos" within a community of foreign students.

As an eventual countermeasure to intellectually motivated foreign graduates, the author advocates a scheme which would guarantee a graduate who has taken a teaching or research position in his/her own country to come back to the U.S. after 2-3 years for refreshing his/her knowledge.

2602. Gama, Elizabeth M. P., and Paul Pedersen. "Readjustment Problems of Brazilian Returnees from Graduate Studies in the United States." International Journal of Intercultural Relations 1 (No. 4, 1977): 46-59.

This is a pilot study on the adjustment problems of Brazilians returned from graduate study in the U.S. Subjects were 31 former LASPAU (Latin American Scholarship Program of American Universities) scholars who were interviewed by the senior author after they were back in Brazil. The family and professional problems they experienced as they tried to readjust to life in their country were investigated, as well as the intensity of these problems and the adequacy of coping, as perceived by the respondent. Taped interviews were coded independently twice, over a 16-month interval. High reliability levels were obtained. Results indicated that returnees had little difficulty adjusting to life with their families except for experiencing some value conflict with them and some lack of privacy. Most of their problems were related to their professional life. In that category they reported that they found some difficulty adjusting to the system as a whole and to their roles as professors. In most cases returnees felt they were coping adequately.

2603. Harder, Barbara A. "Easing the Re-Entry Culture Shock Experience: Responsibility of Higher Education." The MSU Orient 3 (No. 8, 1973): 9-19.

2604. Kizilbash, Mehdi. "The Employment of Returning U.S. Educated Indians." Comparative Education Review 8 (December, 1964): 320-326.

2605. Klinger, Robert B. "A Survey of Practical Training and Return Home." National Association for Foreign Student Affairs Newsletter 16 (February, 1965): 5ff.

2606. LaBerge, Bernard E. "International Student--No-Return." National Association for Foreign Student Affairs Newsletter 27 (November, 1975): 1ff.

2607. Mirsky, Mark J. "Show Me the Way to Go Home." Partisan Review 36 (No. 3, 1969): 517-524.

2608. Murase, A. E. "Problems of Japanese Returning Students." International Educational and Cultural Exchange 13 (Spring, 1978): 10-14.

2609. Nelson, Donald N. "Foreign Students Do Return Home." Journal of the National Association for Women Deans, Administrators, and Counselors 42 (Spring, 1979): 19-21.

2610. Wichelmann, S. "Promoting Re-integration in Their Developing Countries of Origin of Professionals and Skilled Personnel Trained in an Industrialized Country." International Migration Review 15 (No. 2-3, 1977): 236-242.

## Reportage

2611. Gasling, M. "Scholarly Refuge for Students Who Cannot Go Home." Times Higher Education Supplement (December 23, 1977): 12.

2612. Magarrell, Jack. "More Refugee Programs: Higher Education Involvement Likely to Grow." Chronicle of Higher Education 10 (May 19, 1975): 2.

## 35. ALUMNI

2613. Alan, Theodore. "The Value to Foreign Student Alumni of Their Education in the United States of America." Unpublished Ph.D thesis, University of Northern Colorado, 1971.

2614. El-Senoussi, Veronica. "The UCLA Foreign Alumni Study 1945-1970." Unpublished Ed.D thesis, University of California at Los Angeles, 1973.

Questionnaires and a newsletter were sent to a total of 4,304 UCLA foreign alumni (1945-70) who were identified through a search of the university records for this study. A total of 1,086 alumni returned the questionnaires, of which 1,026 were found usable. Half of the respondents were found to be residing in the United States. Half of this number had already naturalized while the other half were current immigrants. Foreign students residing abroad were more positive than the citizens on questions relating to evaluation of the university. Attitudes towards Americans were generally favorable, but not towards the U.S. government. It was found from the official records of

4,304 alumni that the foreign students' overall grade point
average compared favorably with overall GPA for the UCLA
student body. A comparative study of 15 major countries,
five Canadian universities, and four geographical areas
were included in the academic analyses. The study also
examines the relationship of scholastic performance,
housing, participation in student activities, and other
factors in student life to the alumni evaluation of the
university. Three fourths of the alumni during their years
at UCLA managed to combine work, student activities,
marriage, and a satisfactory social life. Better represen-
tation of all groups, differentiated orientation, academic
advising, activity changes, student support, and continued
alumni contact are recommended.

2615.   Goetzl, Sylvia, and Jill D. Strutter, eds.  Foreign Alumni:
        Overseas Links for U.S. Institutions.  Washington,  D.C.:
        National Association of Foreign Student Affairs, 1980.

            The basis for this study grew out of the AID/NAFSA
        Liaison Committee Meeting in April of 1977.  The AID/NAFSA
        Liaison Group administered a questionnaire to 70 institu-
        tions who have, since 1921, received foreign alumni.
            The committee indicates the tremendous rate of growth
        in the number of foreign students in the United States.
        Beginning in 1921 with 6,000 foreign students and in 1960
        rising to approximately 65,000 and in the early 1980s to
        over 264,000 foreign students studying in the United States
        representing over 50,000 new foreign alumni annually
        completing their study and approximately 35,000 who return
        home to their nations.
            Over 70% of the foreign alumni indicated numerous
        individual and institutional advantages that accrued to
        them from foreign study.  This handbook extensively de-
        velops the rationale and recommendations with a checklist
        for the establishment of a foreign alumni overseas network
        program.  The manual goes into great detail on how to
        establish and evaluate the foreign student alumni overseas
        linkage.  Three appendices are attached to the work that
        will be of particular help to institutions having foreign
        alumni or wishing to establish a foreign alumni program.

2616.   Moore, Forrest, and Robert Forman.  The University and Its Foreign
        Alumni:   Maintaining   Overseas   Contacts.   Minneapolis:
        University of Minnesota Press, 1964.

2617.   Stevens, Thomas C.  "The Construction of a Questionnaire for
        International Alumni Follow-up."  Unpublished Ph.D thesis,
        Indiana University, 1963.

Articles

2618. Dolibois, J. E. "Alive and Well: International Alumni Program." International Educational and Cultural Exchange 11 (Winter, 1976): 32-34.

## 36. FOREIGN STUDENT ADVISERS AND PERSONNEL

2619. Association of International Education, Japan. Programs and Activities for Foreign Students. Tokyo: AIEJ, 1980.

2620. Australian Development Assistance Agency. Interstate Conference of Co-ordinating Committees and Welfare Officers: Welfare Work with Foreign Students: Conference Proceedings. Canberra: Australian Government Publishing Service, 1975.

2621. Benson, August Gerald. "On-the-job Behavior of College and University Foreign Student Advisers as Perceived by Knowledgeable Faculty Members." Unpublished Ph.D thesis, Michigan State University, 1969.

2622. Chow, Yu-Ching. "Factors Related to the Establishment of the Position, Foreign Student Advisor." Unpublished Ph.D thesis, University of Tennessee, 1963.

2623. Collamer, Shirley Patricia. "The Role of the Foreign Student Advisor in the California Community College: Problems of Definition." Unpublished Ph.D thesis, United States International University, 1974.

2624. Dalili, Farid. The International Student Office at the University of Akron: From People Processing to People Changing. Akron, Ohio: International Student Office, University of Akron, 1982.

2625. Davis, Ambrose Constantine. "The Functions of International Programs Offices in American Universities." Unpublished Ed.D thesis, University of Pennsylvania, 1982.

2626. Higbee, Homer. The Status of Foreign Student Advising in the United States Universities and Colleges. East Lansing, Michigan: Michigan State University, 1961.

2627. Ibanga, Joseph. "A Comparative Analysis of the Status, and Role of Foreign Student Advisers; and Services Provided to Foreign Students in the Public and Private Institutions of Higher Learning in the United States of America." Unpublished Ph.D thesis, University of Nebraska at Lincoln, 1975.

The role of foreign student advisers and the services foreign students receive in public and private institutions of higher learning are compared and analyzed in this study. Survey questionnaires were mailed to 200 foreign student advisers in both public and private institutions of higher learning throughout the United States. A total of 152 or 76% of the returns were found usable. A summary of findings on related studies is provided. On the survey study itself, the major findings were that the formal title of Foreign Student Adviser was held by over 65% of those designated for foreign student advising. While more FSA in the public than in the private institutions devoted full-time to foreign student services, the highest percentage of FSAs in public institutions specialized in professional educational fields; and the highest number in private institutions majored in psychology and/or counseling. Wide publicity given to the institutions abroad contributed to the overall increase in foreign student enrollment. FSA whose major characteristics were personal interest and interest in and respect for all kinds of people generally maintained that foreign students contributed "much" to the overall objectives of the institutions. Some services provided by foreign student advisers included counseling foreign students; providing information on immigration and naturalization services; admission and registration of foreign students and engaging in followup studies of foreign students after they had returned home. The study makes 19 recommendations to be considered for immediate action.

2628.  Kimball, Jack E. "A Proposed Graduate Program of Studies for Foreign Student Advisers." Unpublished Ph.D thesis, Florida State University, 1964.

It is argued in this study that although problems of international students have become the special province of a "foreign student adviser," there has been almost no development of a specialized curriculum to prepare foreign student advisers for their work. This study proposes a graduate program of studies for foreign student advisers. The curriculum content selection is based on three standard methods, namely: analytical procedure, consensual procedure and judgmental procedure. The curriculum, it is pointed out, should be essentially that of other student personnel work curricula, with provisions specially made to suit the candidate in the areas of internship or supervised practical experience; the exploration in depth of information about particular areas of the world; and acquaintance by means of courses or seminars, with special problems germane to advising foreign students. It is suggested that cooperation among professional associations, which could extend to sponsoring and fostering university graduate student research, should be encouraged. While professionalism in foreign student advising is enthusiastically accepted by some persons concerned with international education, it is summarily rejected by others.

2629. Knott, James E. Career Opportunities in the International Field. Garrett Park: Garrett Park Press, 1979.

2630. Laing, Alexander. International Campus--An Adviser to Overseas Students Looks at His Job. London: United Kingdom Council for Overseas Student Affairs, 1970.

2631. Lockett, Betty Alla. "A Study of the Effectiveness of Foreign Student Advisers at American Colleges and Universities as Reported by Foreign Students Sponsored by the United States Agency for International Development." Unpublished Ph.D thesis, American University, 1970.

The purpose of this study is to look into the effectiveness of foreign student advisers as they are perceived by foreign students.
The data were collected at the American University Development Education and Training Research Institute (DETRI). Aggregate data on 795 foreign students were utilized from items which pertained to evaluation of foreign student advisers in the participant evaluation of the AID International Training Questionnaire.
Findings and Conclusions:

(1) Foreign student advisers at American colleges and universities are effective in their role as they are perceived by the large majority of foreign students interviewed.
(2) The geographic origin of the foreign students did not determine whether or not they talked with their foreign adviser.
(3) A major determinant of usefulness of foreign student advisers as they are perceived by foreign students is related to their availability to the foreign students.

2632. Mehraban, Gholamreza G. "Perceptions of the Official and Ideal Duties and Responsibilities of the Director of International Student Affairs in the United States of America." Unpublished Ph.D thesis, North Texas State University, 1979.

2633. Miller, Richard Eugene. "A Study of Significant Elements in the On-the-Job Behavior of College and University Foreign Student Advisers." Unpublished Ph.D thesis, Michigan State University, 1968.

The main problem of the study is: Which of the many aspects of the foreign student adviser's on-the-job behavior do the foreign student advisers themselves perceive to be significant in facilitating the academic progress and/or personal development of the foreign students enrolled at their institutions. The Critical Incident Technique, which was the tool used in this study, served both as an instrument for collecting the data and for analyzing them. The study revealed 203 distinct critical elements or behaviors of foreign student advisers which the responding foreign student advisers perceived as having a significant (positive or negative) effect on the academic progress and/or personal development of foreign students. This indicates the complexity of the foreign student adviser's job.

2634. Morris, Rita Iona. "Qualifications, Career Preparation and Functions of Foreign Student Advisors." Unpublished Ph.D thesis, American University, 1979.

2635. National Association for Foreign Student Affairs. Guidelines: Responsibilities and Standards in Work with Foreign Students. Washington, D.C.: NAFSA, 1970. (revised edition)

2636. Sima, Gerald Clarence. "The Role of the Campus Administrator in the Foreign Study League." Unpublished Ph.D thesis, University of Michigan, 1970.

   The purpose of this study was explained by the author through some questions that he posed such as: What is the role of a Foreign Study League campus administrator in program development, in administrative logistics, in educational leadership, and in personnel relationships? Do differences in perception exist among administrators, counselors, teachers, and students regarding the administrator's role? What are the causes of the differences in the perception?
   It is suggested that the Foreign Study League campus administrator should have a role in program development; in administrative logistics, in educational leadership, and in personnel relationships.
   The major findings were:
   . Differences in perceptions existed among the administrators, teachers, counselors, and students.
   . The causes of the perceptual differences were assumed to result from differences in the participants' role on Program X920, his age, education, philosophy, expectations, and previous experience.

2637. Skinner, Maynard C. "The Foreign Student Adviser's Office: Practices, Problems, and Procedures in Selected Colleges and Universities." Unpublished Ph.D thesis, University of Colorado, 1963.

2638. Slocum, Joel. "Iran, Iranian Students, and Foreign Student Advisers." National Association for Foreign Student Affairs Newsletter 27 (April, 1976): 5ff.

2639. Steven, Walter Tapsoott, Jr. "The Identification of Competencies Appropriate for Foreign Student Advisors on American College and University Campuses." Unpublished Ph.D thesis, University of Southern California, 1975.

2640. Walker, B. R. "A Study of the Critical Requirements of Foreign Student Advisers in American Colleges and Universities." Unpublished Ph.D thesis, University of Southern Mississippi, 1966.

2641. Westcott, Nina Agarwala. "A Position-Analysis of the Foreign Student Adviser As Reflected by Foreign Student Advisers and Administrators." Unpublished Ph.D thesis, University of Arizona, 1967.

## Articles

2642. Caquelin, H. J. "Education for an Emerging Profession: Foreign Student Adviser?" International Educational and Cultural Exchange 5 (Winter, 1970): 44-65.

How can one prepare for the profession of foreign student adviser? What educational background or specialization is most useful? What kinds of experience are most valuable? The author offers his ideas of what a foreign student adviser can do to close the "knowledge gap" and enhance his professional competence. The paper discusses the nature of the FSA's work, types of knowledge needed, professional standards and norms, state of the profession (the academic preparation of FSAs and their distribution of years of experience). Among the most important single qualifications that the respondents selected were: (1) experience as a FSA; (2) experience in a foreign country; (3) type of education (liberal vs. technical); (4) experience in college/student personnel administration; (5) experience in administrative/executive positions; (6) level of education, etc. The author discusses the experience-education complex and suggests a program of formal study.

2643. Carpenter, Edward L. "Roles of the Foreign Student Advisor." International Educational and Cultural Exchange 4 (Spring, 1969): 38-43.

2644. Chalmers, Paul. "The Professionalization of the Foreign Student Adviser." National Association for Foreign Student Affairs Newsletter 27 (February, 1976): 13ff.

2645. Chandrasekharaiah, K. V. "Status of Foreign Student Advising in Canada." College and University 45 (Winter, 1970): 134-137.

2646. Childs, J. A. "Counselling and the Training of [Foreign Students'] Counsellors." Coombe Lodge Reports 10 (No. 6, 1977): 261-267.

2647. Hardee, Melvene D. "Challenge from Overseas--Student Personnel and the Foreign Student. The University Meets the Challenge." NASPA Journal 5 (July, 1967): 3-7.

2648. Heise, Jon O. "Overseas Opportunities Advising Survey." National Association for Foreign Student Affairs Newsletter 27 (January, 1976): 9ff.

2649. Horn, Phyllis V. "Foreign Students Adviser: Involved in Every Aspect of Adjustment." National Association for Foreign Student Affairs Newsletter 30 (May, 1979): 190ff.

2650. Jameson, S., et al. "Advising Offices Overseas; Closing the Information Gap." College and University 47 (Summer, 1972): 549-579.

2651. Jenkins, Hugh M. "The Foreign Student Advisor and His Institution." National Association for Foreign Student Affairs Newsletter 27 (May, 1976): 1ff.

2652. Martin, John. "Vietnamese Students and Their American Advisors." Change 8 (November, 1976): 11-14.

2653. Renwick, George W. "Toward an Understanding of Our Professional Ethics." National Association for Foreign Student Affairs Newsletter 28 (February, 1977): 1ff.

2654. Rose, Julie Kyllonen. "Realities Affecting Nigeria's Educational Future: Observations of a U.S. Foreign Student Adviser." National Association for Foreign Student Affairs Newsletter 34 (March, 1983): 104ff.

2655. Sasnett, Martena. "Updating Foreign Student Admission." College and University 39 (Fall, 1963): 13-24.

2656. Schmidt, Erin L. "Preparing the Foreign Student Adviser for a Cooperative Venture." National Association for Foreign Student Affairs Newsletter 28 (May, 1977): 1ff.

2657. Vigushin, Joan. "Helping Campus Personnel Help Foreign Students: A Counseling Simulation." Humanist Educator 20 (No. 3, 1982): 134-142.

2658. Viola, Joy W. "Campus International Offices." In International Encyclopedia of Higher Education, edited by A. Knowles, pp. 1588-1598. San Francisco: Jossey-Bass, 1977.

Reportage

2659. Kasprzyk, P. "Mentorer fur Auslandische Studenten." Deutsche Universitatszeitung (No. 4, 1970): 3-4.

## 37. MIGRATION OF TALENT (THE "BRAIN DRAIN")

2660. Adams, Walter, ed. The Brain Drain. New York: Macmillan, 1968.

This book comprises papers presented at an international conference on the "brain drain" held at Lausanne, Switzerland in August, 1967. The focus of the essays is on international migration of scientists, engineers, and professional workers. A tentative list of the factors primarily creating the attraction of the developed country, or the dissatisfaction with the developing country is provided. Part One deals with the history of early migration, the determinants, and significance of "brain drain" and multilateral aspects with regard to the United States, Europe, and the poorer nations. In search of an analytical framework, Part Two discusses the "internationalist" and "nationalist" models, the "national" importance of human capital and the differential push approach, while Part Three concentrates on education and migration. Part Four deals with some case studies, and in the summary and conclusions in Part Five, policies which commend themselves as appropriate and best calculated to achieve the twin objectives of optimum resource allocation and national economic growth and some "ideal" solutions are discussed. Raising salaries; the revision of salary structures; provision of more professional opportunities; increases in the receptivity to change; restructuring investment in education and the rationalization of manpower policies; the promotion of economic integration and resistance to political Balkanization; the elimination of discrimination and bigotry and the removal of monopolistic restrictions in "pull" countries are recommended. For the "losing" nations the brain drain phenomenon has a vital message--that the fault lies not only in their stars, but also in the people themselves.

2661. Awasthi, Shri Prakash. The "Brain Drain" Study--Phase 1: Analysis of Ordinary Passports Issued During 1960-1970. New Delhi: Institute of Applied Manpower Research, 1970.

2662. Awasthi, Prakesh. Migration of Indian Engineers, Scientists and Physicians to the United States. New Delhi: Institute of Applied Manpower Research, 1968.

2663. Bayer, Alan E. The American Brain Gain: The Inflow for Education and Work. Washington, D.C.: American Council on Education, 1968.

2664. Bhagwrati, Jadgish N., and Martin Partington, eds. Taxing the Brain Drain. Amsterdam: North-Holland, 1976.

2665. The Brain Drain from Five Developing Countries. New York: UNITAR, 1971.

2666. Carino, Ledivina Vidallon. "Structural Conditions and Professional Migration: A Study of the Movement of Scientists, Engineers, and Medical Personnel into the United States, 1965-1967." Unpublished Ph.D thesis, Indiana University, 1970.

2667. Chorofas, D. N. The Knowledge Revolution: An Analysis of the International Brain Market. New York: McGraw-Hill, 1970.

2668. Cohen, Louise. "International Migration of Scientists Awarded Doctorates in the United States in 1958." Unpublished Ph.D thesis, Purdue University, 1965.

2669. Colligan, Francis. Annual Indicator of the In-Migration into the United States of Aliens in Professional and Related Occupations, Fiscal Year, 1967. Washington, D.C.: U.S. Government Printing Office, 1969.

2670. Comay, Peter Yochanan. "International Migration of Professional Manpower: The Canada-U.S. Case." Unpublished Ph.D thesis, Princeton University, 1969.

2671. Committee on the International Migration of Talent. The International Migration of High-Level Manpower--Its Impact on the Development Process. New York: Education and World Affairs, 1971.

2672. Das, Mansingh. Brain Drain Controversy and International Students. Lucknow, India: Lucknow Publishing House, 1972.

2673. Education and World Affairs. Modernization and the Migration of Talent. New York: EWA, 1970.

2674. Fernandez, Perfecto. Brain Drain in the Philippines. New York: UNITAR, 1971.

2675. Friborg, et al. Brain Drain and Brain Gain of Sweden. Stockholm: Swedish Natural Science Research Council, 1972.

2676. Glaser, William A. Brain Drain and Study Abroad. New York: Columbia University, Bureau of Applied Social Research, 1974.

2677. Glaser, William A. The Brain Drain: Emigration and Return. Elmsford, New York: Pergamon, 1978.

2678. Gross, Bernd, Willi Stevens, and Manfred Werth. Akademiker aus Entwicklungslandern in der BRD: Zwischen Brain Drain and Ruckkehr. Saarbrucken: Verlag Breitenbach, 1982.

2679. Hekmati-Tehrani, Mehri. "Alienation, Family Ties, and Social Position as Factors Related to the Non-Return of Foreign Students." Unpublished Ph.D thesis, New York University, 1970.

Can a number of selected measurable variables be explored to differentiate the foreign students who intend to return to their home-countries from those who intend to remain in the United States after completing their academic studies? This study sought to answer this question by examining the relationships between the anticipation of nonreturn and anomie, alienation (that is, powerlessness and normlessness), social position, family ties, and favorable attitudes toward Americans. A random sample of 210 students from a base population of 521 male students from Greece, India, Iran, the Philippines, and Turkey studying at Columbia and New York Universities during the spring semester of 1969 served as subjects of the study. Of the 210 respondents, 110 stated their intention to remain in the United States while 100 planned to return to their home-countries after completion of their studies. The hypotheses that the nonreturning group experiences a significantly higher degree of normlessness than the returning group; that the nonreturning group experiences a significantly higher degree of powerlessness than the returning group; that the returning group comes from significantly higher social positions than the non-returning group; and that the returning group has significantly stronger family ties than the nonreturning group were all supported. The hypotheses that the nonreturning group experiences a significantly higher degree of anomie than the returning group and that the nonreturning group has significantly more favorable attitudes toward Americans than the returning group were not supported. The implications of the findings are discussed, recommendations based on the findings are made and suggestions are offered for further studies.

2680. Henderson, Gregory. Emigration of Highly-Skilled Manpower from the Developing Countries. New York: United Nations Institute for Training and Research, 1970.

2681. Herve, Michel E. A. International Migration of Physicians and Students: A Regressional Analysis. Washington, D.C.: Agency for International Development, U.S. Department of State, 1968.

2682. Hoek, F. J. Van. The Migration of High Level Manpower from Developed Countries. The Hague: Mouton, 1970.

2683.  Howland, Harold E.  Brain Drain--As It Affects the Philippines.
       Washington, D.C.:  Foreign Service Institute, U.S. Department
       of State, 1967.

2684.  Institute of Applied Manpower Research.  Migration of Indian
       Engineers, Scientists, and Physicians to the United States.
       New Delhi:  Institute of Applied Manpower Research, 1968.

2685.  Jenkins, Joan, and Michael J. Witkin.  Foreign Medical Graduates
       Employed in State and County Mental Hospitals.  Washington,
       D.C.:  National Institute of Mental Health, Survey and Reports
       Branch, 1976.

2686.  Johnson, George A.  "Exchange or Immigration Continued."  National
       Association for Foreign Student Affairs Newsletter 16 (June,
       1965):  2ff.

2687.  Kao, Ch. H. G.  Brain Drain:  A Case Study of China.  Taipei:  Mei
       Ya Publications, 1971.

2688.  Kidd, Charles V.  The International Migration of High-Level
       Manpower:  Its Impact on the Development Process.  New York:
       Praeger, 1970.

2689.  Kourvetaris, George A.  Brain Drain and International Migration of
       Scientists:  The Case of Greece.  DeKalb, Illinois:  Northern
       Illinois University, 1972.

2690.  Levy, Samuel.  "Some Aspects of the International Migration of
       Human Capital:  The Case of British Physicians."  Unpublished
       Ph.D thesis, Wayne State Univerity, 1969.

2691.  Lockett, Betty A., and Kathleen N. Williams.  The Foreign Medical
       Graduate and Physician Manpower in the United States.
       Washington, D.C.:  Office of International Health Manpower
       Studies, Bureau of Health Resources Development, Public Health
       Service, 1973.

2692.  Lynn, Richard.  The Irish Brain Drain.  Dublin:  The Economic and
       Social Research Institute, 1968.

2693.  McKnight, Allen S.  Scientists Abroad:  A Study of the Interna-
       tional Movement of Persons in Science and Technology.  Paris:
       UNESCO, 1971.

2694.  Merriam, Marshal F.  Brain Drain Study at I.I.T. Campus:  Opinions
       and Background of Faculty and Senior Staff.  Kanpur, India:
       Indian Institute of Technology, 1969.

2695.  Myers, Robert G.  Education and Emigration.  New York:  McKay,
       1972.

2696.  Niland, John R.  The Asian Engineering Brain Drain:  A Study of
       International Relocation into the United States from India,

China, Korea, Thailand and Japan. Lexington, Mass.: Heath Lexington Books, 1970.

2697. Odenthal, Joseph T. Policies and Pressures Affecting the Migration of Filipinos. Washington, D.C.: Foreign Service Institute, U.S. Department of State, 1969.

2698. Organization for Economic Cooperation and Development. The International Movement of Scientists and Engineers. Paris: Organization for Economic Cooperation and Development, 1969.

2699. Oh, Tai K. The Asian Brain Drain: A Factual and Causal Analysis. San Francisco: R and E Research Associates, 1977.

2700. Orton, John W. An Interview-Based Study of Pakistanis Employed in the United States. New York: Institute of International Education, 1965.

2701. Palmer, Roy Virgil. "The Problem of Talent Migration and the Role of the Small Private College in Foreign Student Education." Unpublished Ph.D thesis, University of Michigan, 1968.

2702. Pan American Health Organization. Migration of Health Personnel, Scientists and Engineers from Latin America. Washington, D.C.: Pan American Health Organization, 1966.

2703. Pirai, Louis. Immigration and Emigration of the Professional and Skilled Manpower During the Post-War Period. Ottawa: Queen's Printer, 1965.

2704. Rao, G. Lakshmana. Brain Drain and Foreign Students: A Study of the Attitudes and Intentions of Foreign Students in Australia, the U.S.A., Canada, and France. New York: St. Martin's, 1979.

2705. Razavi, Mascumeh Zinat. "Personality Correlates Relating to the Brain Drain Among Foreign Students from Far Eastern and South American Countries." Unpublished Ph.D thesis, University of Southern California, 1975.

2706. Report of the Inter Ministerial Group on the Brain Drain. New Delhi: Institute of Applied Manpower Research, 1971.

2707. Ritterband, Paul. The Non-Returning Foreign Student: The Israeli Case. New York: Bureau of Applied Social Research, Columbia University, 1968.

2708. Ritterband, Paul. "Out of Zion: The Non-Returning Israeli Student." Unpublished Ph.D thesis, Columbia University, 1968.

2709. Rodriguez, O. "Foreign Student Non-Return in the United States: Opportunities and Their Perception." Toronto: Research Committee on Migration, 1976.

2710.  Rodriguez, Orlando.  "Social Determinants of Non-Return:  A Study of Foreign Students from Developing Countries in the United States."  Unpublished Ph.D thesis, Columbia University, 1975.

2711.  Schipulle, Hans Peter.  Ausverkauf der Intelligenz aus Entwicklungslandern? Eine Kritische Untersuchung zum Brain Drain.  Munich:  Weltforum Verlag, 1973.

2712.  Scully, Grace.  "An Exploratory Study of Students from Abroad Who Do Not Wish to Return to Their Country."  Unpublished Ph.D thesis, Teachers College, Columbia University, 1956.

2713.  Sharma, Y. D.  Brain Drain in India:  An Interim Report.  New Delhi:  University Grants Commission, 1967.

2714.  Singh, Harmohinder Paul.  "A Survey of Socioeconomic Problems and Non-Return of Selected Foreign Graduate Students at the University of Tennessee."  Unpublished Ed.D thesis, University of Tennessee, 1976.

2715.  Sours, Martin Harvey.  "The Brain Drain and World Politics."  Unpublished Ph.D thesis, University of Washington, 1971.

2716.  United Nations, Instituto para la Formacion Profesional y la Investigacion.  The Brain Drain from Five Developing Countries:  Cameroon, Colombia, Lebanon, the Philippines and Trinidad and Tobago.  New York:  United Nations, Instituto para la Formacion Profesional y la Investigacion, 1971.

2717.  UNESCO.  Scientists Abroad:  A Study of the International Movement of Persons in Science and Technology.  Paris:  UNESCO, 1971.

2718.  United States Congress, Committee on Government Operations.  Scientific Brain Drain from the Developing Countries.  Washington, D.C.:  U.S. Government Printing Office, 1968.

2719.  United States Congress, House Committee on Foreign Affairs, Subcommittee on National Security Policy and Scientific Developments.  Brain Drain:  A Study of Persistent Issues of International Scientific Mobility.  Washington, D.C.:  U.S. Government Printing Office, 1974.

2720.  United States, National Science Foundation.  Immigrant Scientists and Engineers in the United States.  A Study of Characteristics and Attitudes.  Washington, D.C.:  U.S. Government Printing Office, 1973.

2721.  United States, National Science Foundation.  Foreign Participation in U.S. Science and Engineering Higher Education and Labor Markets.  Washington, D.C.:  National Science Foundation, 1981.

2722.  Valipour, Iraj.  "A Comparison of Returning and Non-Returning Iranian Students in the United States."  Unpublished Ed.D thesis, Columbia University, 1967.

2723. Van Hoek, F. J. The Migration of High Level Manpower from Developing to Developed Countries. The Hague, Mouton, 1971.

2724. Vas-Zoltan, Peter. The Brain Drain: An Abnormal Relation. Budapest: Academic Publishers, 1975.

2725. Zahlan, A. B. The Brain Drain: Lebanon and Middle Eastern Countries. New York: UNITAR, 1971.

2726. Ziaii-Bigdeli, Mohammad. "A Comparative Study of Returning and Non-Returning Students from Iran and Nigeria Studying in the United States." Unpublished Ph.D thesis, Florida State University, 1982.


## Articles


2727. Abraham, P. M. "An Outline for a Study of Brain Drain from India." Manpower Journal (New Delhi) (No. 3, 1977): 15-44.

2728. Abraham, P. M. "Regaining High Level Indian Manpower from Abroad." Manpower Journal (New Delhi) 3 (No. 4, 1968): 83-117.

2729. Asher, Robert E. "Brain Drain to Brain Gain." A.I.F.L.D. Review 2 (No. 3, 1970): 45-54.

2730. Awasthi, S. P. "Brain Drain from Developing Countries: An Exercise in Problem Formulation." Manpower Journal (New Delhi) 2 (April-June, 1966): 80-98.

2731. Awasthi, Prakash. "An Experiment in Voluntary Repatriation of High-Level Technical Manpower: The Scientists' Pool." Development Digest 4 (April, 1966): 28-35.

2732. Baldwin, George B. "Brain Drain or Overflow?" Foreign Affairs 48 (January, 1970): 358-372.

2733. Baskin, Solomon. "The Economic Costs and Benefits and Human Gains and Disadvantages of International Migration." Journal of Human Resources 2 (Fall, 1967): 495-516.

2734. Beaubrun, M. A. "Foreign Medical Training and the Brain Drain: The Viewpoint of the Developing World." Psychiatry 34 (1971): 247-251.

2735. Beijer, G. "Selective Migration for and 'Brain Drain' from Latin America." International Migration 1 (1966): 28-36.

   The whole of Latin America is engaged in a race between population and production. Development in agriculture and industry depends much on the available supply of specialized manpower. This article examines the

immigration of highly educated and trained persons on the
one hand, the growing and flow of highly qualified manpower
on the other.  During 1960-63, South America contributed
more than 500 scientists and engineers to the United
States, 5% of all immigrants by country or region of birth.
The Latin American countries are taking measures to adapt
immigration laws and procedures to encourage the
immigration of sorely needed skills.  Hundreds of ICEM
selective migration programs were sponsored to attract
skilled and trained manpower from Europe and North America
to Latin America.  The author argues that every effort to
develop the infrastructure of Latin American countries, to
contribute to their economic growth process is in the
interest of the Western world.

2736.  Bello, Walden F.  "Brain Drain in the Philippines."  In
       Modernization: Its Impact in the Philippines, IV, pp. 93-146.
       Quezon City:  Ateneo de Manila University Press, 1969.

2737.  Bernard, Thomas L.  "United States Immigration and the Brain
       Drain."  International Migration (No. 1/2, 1970).

2738.  Bhagwati, Jagdish.  "The Brain Drain."  International Social
       Science Journal 28 (No. 4, 1976):  691-729.

2739.  "The Brain Drain in the Arab World."  World Higher Education
       Communique 3 (Fall, 1981):  11-18.

2740.  Caquelin, Howard.  "Exchange or Immigration--The Phony Contro-
       versy."  National Association for Foreign Student Affairs
       Newsletter 17 (October, 1965):  2ff.

2741.  Chathaparampil, Joseph.  "The Brain Drain: A Case Study."  Asian
       Forum 2 (No. 4, 1970):  236-244.

2742.  Chesson, Eugene.  "The Future Shortage of Faculty: A Crisis in
       Engineering."  Engineering Education 70 (April, 1980):
       731-738.

2743.  Das, Man Singh.  "Asian Students and Brain Drain."  Manpower
       Journal (New Delhi) 5 (October, 1969, March, 1970):  45-62.

The study examined empirically the attitudes of 654
male students toward returning to home-country upon completion of their studies and training in the U.S. and the
effect of these attitudes on the loss of professional
skills by the country of origin.  The sample represented 11
less-developed and developing countries of Asia based on
Berry's "technological and demographic scales." The sample
was drawn from 20 American universities and colleges with a
minimum enrollment of 400 foreign students.  The investigation was needed both for the development of the scientific fund of knowledge and as some objective standard by
which to assess the frequently stated notion that

impoverished countries have been robbed of their talent and stripped of their human resources. The research evaluated the concept of "gain" or "loss," inherent in the international exchange of professionals, which is ambiguously referred to as "brain drain." It may more appropriately be treated, however, as "brain exchange."

2744. Das, Man Singh. "The 'Brain Drain' Controversy in a Comparative Perspective." Social Science 46 (January, 1971): 16-25.

2745. Das, Man Singh. "Brain Drain Controversy of African Scholars." Studies in Comparative International Development 9 (Spring, 1974): 74-83.

2746. Das, Man Singh, and Bankey Lal Sharma. "Brain Drain Controversy and Latin American Scholars." Sociologus (New Series) 24 (No. 4, 1973): 160-175.

This study examined empirically the attitudes of 374 Latin American students toward returning to their country of origin upon completion of their studies and training in the United States, and the effect of these attitudes on the loss of professional skills by the country of origin. The sample represented five less-developed and five developing countries of Latin America, based on Berry's 1960 "technological and demographic scales." Recent trends indicate that students and scholars from less-developed and developing countries may go to the more highly developed and industrialized countries with intentions to return home but change their minds and decide to stay there permanently. However, this trend does not seem to hold for the Latin American students. From the results of the study, students came with the idea to return home but they end up either staying longer periods of time or not returning at all, regardless of the home-country: 281 students--both from developing and less-developed countries--planned to return after completion of their studies. After they lived in the United States for a few months, 107 students switched in favor of staying for a short period of time after completion of their studies. The percentage of students planning to return home dropped from 75% to 47%. The percentage of students that wanted to stay for a short period of time (from 2 to 5 years) increased from 16% to 44%; the percentage of students wanting to stay permanently also increased.

2747. Dedijer, Stevan. "Migration of Scientists: A World-Wide Phenomenon and Problem." Nature 201 (March, 1964): 964-967.

2748. De Suro, Piedad. "The Brain Drain and Latin America." National Association for Foreign Student Affairs Newsletter 18 (February, 1967): 4ff.

2749. Devoretz, Don, and Dennis Maki. "The Immigration of Third World Professionals to Canada; 1968-1973." World Development 11 (No. 1, 1983): 55-64.

2750. Gish. O. "Brain Drain. Some Critical Comments." International Migration 8 (No. 4, 1970): 203-204.

2751. Glaser, William A., and G. Christopher Habers. "The Effect of Reasons on Actual Plans to Return Home or Stay Abroad." In Brain Drain: Emigration and Return, edited by William A. Glaser, and G. Christopher Habers, pp. 242-248. Oxford: Pergamon Press, 1978.

2752. Glaser, William A., and G. Christopher Habers. "Losses and Gains from Brain Drain." In The Brain Drain: Emigration and Return, edited by William A. Glaser, and G. Christopher Habers, pp. 204-224. Oxford: Pergamon Press, 1978.

2753. Glaser, William A., and G. Christopher Habers. "Variations Among Home Countries." In The Brain Drain: Emigration and Return, edited by William A. Glaser, and G. Christopher Habers, pp. 24-51. Oxford: Pergamon Press, 1978.

2754. Glaser, William A., and G. Christopher Habers. "Variations Among Countries of Study." In The Brain Drain: Emigration and Return, edited by William A. Glaser, and G. Christopher Habers, pp. 52-72. Oxford: Pergamon Press, 1978.

2755. Glaser, William A., and G. Christopher Habers. "Variations by Specialty." In The Brain Drain: Emigration and Return, edited by William A. Glaser, and G. Christopher Habers, pp. 73-87. Oxford: Pergamon Press, 1978.

2756. Glaser, William A., et al. "The Migration and Return of Professionals." International Migration Review 8 (Spring, 1974): 224-244.

2757. Gonzalez, Gustavo R. "The Migration of Latin American High-Level Manpower." International Labor Review 98 (December, 1968).

2758. Grubel, Herbert B. "The International Flow of Human Capital. Theoretical Analysis of Issues Surrounding Foreign Students Electing Not to Return to Their Native Countries." American Economic Review 56 (May, 1966): 268-274.

   This article deals with the theoretical bases of the flow of international human capital as represented by highly skilled immigrants to the United States and also of those foreign students studying in the United States who elect not to return.
   The article refutes the concept of neocolonialism by making the following assertions: that (1) immigrants raise significantly the income of their families; (2) that immigrants can influence policies in the country of "their

new residence" towards their native country; and (3) that immigrants maintain a continuing interest in their former country of birth which may prove beneficial to causing change in those countries and, lastly, that pure scientists and "engineers in foreign countries" can, through their knowledge of scientific development, make the lives of their former countrymen better.

The authors conclude that such concern with the effects on economic and military power is anachronistic and that a concern with the individual welfare of the population ought to take its place.

2759. Grubel, Herbert G. "The Reduction of the Brain Drain: Problems and Policies." Minerva 6 (Summer, 1968): 541-558.

2760. Grubel, H. G., and A. D. Scott. "Determinants of Migrations: The Highly Skilled." International Migration 5 (No. 2, 1967): 127-139.

2761. Guha, Amelendu. "Brain Drain Issue and Indicators on Brain Drain." International Migration (No. 1, 1977): 3-20.

2762. Hekwati, Mehri. "Non-Returning Foreign Students: Why Do They Not Return Home?" Die Dritte Welt 2 (No. 1, 1973): 25-43.

The rate of nonreturning foreign students in the U.S. is increasing, causing much concern of developing countries. This study is aimed at ascertaining selected socio-psychological factors—anomie, family ties, social position, favorable attitudes toward Americans—differentiating the foreign students who intend to return from those who do not intend to return to their home-countries upon completion of their academic studies in the U.S. Six hypotheses were offered for investigation and data were collected, by questionnaire, in 1969, from 210 students from five countries who were registered at Columbia and New York Universities. Among the major findings were: (1) 50% of the respondents were majoring in engineering and business, and there was no significant difference between the returning and nonreturning students as related to fields of study; (2) nearly 50% of them intended to remain in the U.S.; (3) the longer the student stays, the more likely he is to stay on. The homogeneity of the results for the five different nationalities, considered independently, adds to the validity of the theoretical and methodological considerations.

2763. Hekmati, Mehri, and William A. Glaser. "The Brain Drain and UNITAR's Multinational Research Project on the Subject." Social Science Information 12 (April, 1973): 123-138.

2764. Henderson, Gregory. "Foreign Students: Exchange or Immigration?" International Development Review (December, 1967): 19-21.

2765.   Henderson, Gregory.   "Foreign Students:   Exchange or Immigration."
        National Association for Foreign Student Affairs Newsletter 16
        (November, 1964):   1ff.

2766.   Jaafari, Lafi Ibrahim.   "The Brain Drain to the United States:
        The Migration of Jordanian and Palestinian Professionals and
        Students."   Journal of Palestine Studies 3 (Autumn, 1973):
        119-131.

                In recent years, the Middle East has suffered to a
        disturbing extent from the emigration of young, skilled
        people.  The aim of this study is to examine the reasons
        for migration and settlement in the U.S.A. of one national
        group from the area--the educated Palestinian Arabs.  A
        descriptive questionnaire was sent to 300 Palestinian Arab
        (and Jordanian) students, graduates and professionals in 27
        American states.  A total of 74.3% responded, and data
        collection was conducted in 1970.  The major reasons for
        these Arabs to choose to study in the U.S. are:  admissions
        restrictions or no degrees offered in their home-country;
        better instruction and research facilities in the U.S.;
        motivation in pursuing high status.  The major reasons for
        those remaining in the U.S. are:  political instability at
        home (32%); better career opportunities (17%); better
        education and research (13%); more satisfaction (12%).  Of
        the respondents, 27% plan to remain in the U.S. for the
        time being; 25% definitely will not remain, and another 13%
        prefer not to stay.

2767.   Jouves, J. L.   "L'exportation des Connaissances:  Du Mythe a la
        Realite."   Objectif Formation No. 20 (1978):   7-14.

2768.   Johnson, Harry G.   "Economic Aspects of Brain Drain."   Development
        Digest 7 (April, 1969):   45-54.

2769.   Johnson, Harry G.   "The Economics of the Brain Drain:   The
        Canadian Case."   Minerva 3 (Spring, 1965):   299-311.

2770.   Kannappan, Subbiah.   "The Brain Drain and Developing Countries."
        International Labor Review 98 (July, 1968):   1-26.

2771.   Kao, Charles H. C., and Jae Won Lee.   "An Empirical Analysis of
        China's Brain Drain into the United States."   Economic Develop-
        ment and Cultural Change 21 (April, 1973):   500-513.

2772.   Khoshkish, A.   "Intellectual Migration:  A Sociological Approach
        to Brain Drain."   Journal of World History 10 (No. 1, 1966):
        178-197.

2773.   Kindleberger, Charles P.   "Emigration and Economic Growth."   Banca
        Nazionale del Lavoro Quarterly Review No. 74 (September, 1965):
        235-254.

2774. Maner, Wallace. "More on Exchange or Immigration." National Association for Foreign Student Affairs Newsletter 16 (May, 1965): 8ff.

2775. Mejia, A. "International Migration of Professional Manpower." WHO Chronicle 34 (1980): 346-355.

2776. Muir, Douglas J. "Should the Brain Drain be Encouraged?" International Migration 7 (No. 1, 1969): 34-53.

2777. Myers, Robert G. "The Brain Drain and Foreign Student Non-Return." International Educational and Cultural Exchange (Spring, 1967): 63-73.

2778. Myers, Robert G. "Comments on the State of Research: 'Brain Drain' and 'Brain Gain.'" International Development Review 9 (December, 1967).

2779. Myers, Robert G. "International Education, Emigration, and National Policy." Comparative Education Review 17 (February, 1973): 71-90.

2780. Naficy, Habib. "Brain Drain: The Case of Iranian Non-Returnees." In International Development, edited by H. W. Suger. New York: Oceana Publications, 1967.

2781. Oh, Tai K. "Analysis of Motivational Patterns in the Asian Student Brain Drain to the United States." Indian Journal of Industrial Relations 9 (April, 1974): 547-562.

2782. Oh, Tai K. "A New Estimate of the Student Brain Drain from Asia." International Migration Review 7 (No. 4, 1973): 449-456.

2783. Okeidiji, O. O., and F. O. Okeidiji. "African Brain Drain to Highly Industrialized Nations." African Review (No. 1, 1971): 44-52.

2784. Okeidiji, O. O., and Francis Olu. "A Consideration of Some Factors Influencing the Loss of Nigerian Medical and Paramedical Personnel to Developed Nations." West African Journal of Education (February, 1973): 71-87.

2785. Okeidiji, O. O., and Francis Olu. "Nigeria 'Brain Drain' to the United States of America: A Sociological Perspective." Journal of Eastern African Research and Development 2 (1972): 137-163.

2786. Oteiza, Enrique. "Emigration of Engineers from Argentina: A Case of Latin American 'Brain Drain.'" International Labor Review 92 (December, 1965): 445-461.

2787. Parthasarathi, Ashok. "India's 'Brain Drain' and International Norms." International Educational and Cultural Exchange (Summer, 1967): 4-13.

2788.   Pavalko, Ronald M.   "Talent Migration:  Canadian Students in the United States."  *International Review of Education* (No. 3, 1968):  300-324.

2789.   Perkins, J. A.  "Foreign Aid and the Brain Drain."  *Foreign Affairs* 44 (1966):  608-619.

2790.   Portes, Alejandro.   "Determinants of the Brain Drain." *International Migration Review* 10 (No. 4, 1976):  489-508.

2791.   Psacharopoulos, G.  "On Some Positive Aspects of the Economics of the Brain Drain."  *Minerva* 9 (No. 2, 1971):  231-242.

2792.   Saha, Lawrence, J., and Claire M. Atkinson.  "Insiders and Out-siders:  Migrant Academics in an Australian University." *International Journal of Comparative Sociology* 19 (September-December, 1978):  203-218.

        Little is now known about the performance of immigrant intellectuals as compared with national scholars, nor of their social and intellectual contribution to their host-countries.  This paper discusses the flow of intellectuals and scholars between nations in three aspects:  (1) The extent of academic migration between nations; (2) The ideological implications of academic migration for host-countries, and (3) The social integration and professional performance of academic migrants as compared with national scholars.  The paper examines the social and behavioral correlates of migrant status in one Australian university: (1) Their background characteristics and institutional status; (2) Professional performance; (3) Political and career commitments, and (4) The determinants of academic rank.

2793.   Saha, L. J., and A. S. Klovdahl.  "International Networks and Flows of Academic Talent:  Overseas Recruitment in Australian Universities."  *Higher Education* 8 (January, 1979):  55-68.

2794.   Schmiedeck, Raoul A.  "The Foreign Medical Graduate and the Nature of Emigration."  *Psychiatric Opinion* 15 (No. 3, 1978):  38-40.

2795.   Shapira, Rina, and Eva Etzioni.  "Attitudes of Israeli Students Towards Emigration."  *Comparative Education Review* (No. 2, 1970):  162-173.

2796.   Shearer, John C.  "In Defense of Traditional Views of Brain Drain Problem."  *International Educational and Cultural Exchange* (Fall, 1966):  17-25.

2797.   Shearer, John C.  "International Talent Migration and the Foreign Student:  An Educator Suggests that 'Brain Drain' can Best be Contained by Selecting Students Whose Fields of Study are Relevant to Home Country Needs."  *Monthly Labor Review* 93 (May, 1970):  55-59.

2798. Smith, B. L. R.   "The Brain Drain Re-Emergent:   Foreign Medical Graduates in American Medical Schools."  Minerva 17 (No. 4, 1979):  483-503.

2799. Thistlethwaite, F.  "Mobility of Students and Staff Internationally."  In Pressures and Priorities, edited by T. Craig, pp.  372-386.   London:   Association   of   Commonwealth Universities, 1979.

2800. Van der Kroef, Justus M.  "Asia's 'Brain Drain.'"  Journal of Higher Education 39 (May, 1968):  241-253.

2801. Van der Kroef, Justus M.  "The United States and the World's Brain Drain."  International Journal of Comparative Sociology 11 (September, 1970):  220-239.

2802. Watanabe, S.  "The Brain Drain from Developing to Developed Countries."  International Labor Review 99 (April, 1969):  401-433.


### Reportage

2803. Charney, C.  "Reluctant Immigrants."  Times Higher Education Supplement (July 23, 1982):  7.

2804. "Exchanges to Proceed Despite Fear of Brain Drain."  Chronicle of Higher Education 21 (December 15, 1980):  13.

2805. "Flight of the Scientists:  U.S. Can Offer More."  Times Educational Supplement No. 2543 (February 14, 1964):  379.

2806. "Government Extends Visas for Foreign Physicians."  Chronicle of Higher Education 25 (October 20, 1982):  12.

2807. King, Robert.  "Taiwan Launches New Programs to Try to Cut Drain of Academic Talent to U.S. and Europe."  Chronicle of Higher Education 27 (October 6, 1983):  27.

2808. Kirkaldy, J.  "Glut of Doctors May Mean Limit on Overseas Recruits."  Times Higher Education Supplement (March 3, 1978):  3.

2809. Liu, M.  "Replacing a Lost Generation."  Far East Economic Review 101 (September 15, 1978):  10ff.

2810. Middleton, Lorenzo.  "China Sees Exchange Program Leading to Shortage of Scholars."  Chronicle of Higher Education 20 (July 14, 1980):  1.

2811. Prugh, Peter H.  "Lure of America:  More Foreigners Stay After United States Schooling."  Wall Street Journal (November 21, 1966):  168.

# ABOUT THE AUTHORS

PHILIP G. ALTBACH is Professor and Director, Comparative Education Center, Faculty of Educational Studies, State University of New York at Buffalo. He is Editor of the Comparative Education Review and North American Editor of Higher Education. He serves as advisory editor to the Praeger Comparative Education Series. He is author of Higher Education in the Third World: Themes and Variations (1982), Comparative Higher Education (1979) and is co-editor of Bridges to Knowledge: Foreign Students in Comparative Perspective (1984).

DAVID H. KELLY is Assitant Professor of History at D'Youville College, Buffalo, New York. He is co-author of American Students (1973) and Higher Education in Developing Nations (1974).

Y. G.-M. LULAT is a doctoral student in comparative education at the State University of New York at Buffalo. He holds a Masters degree from the University of Lancaster in England and is author of the Comparative Education Review's bi-annual bibliography series.